The Unanimous Champions
of College Football,
1869–2019

The Unanimous Champions of College Football, 1869–2019

ROBERT J. REID

McFarland & Company, Inc., Publishers
Jefferson, North Carolina

ISBN (print) 978-1-4766-8355-3
ISBN (ebook) 978-1-4766-4265-9

LIBRARY OF CONGRESS AND BRITISH LIBRARY
CATALOGUING DATA ARE AVAILABLE

Library of Congress Control Number 2022014247

© 2022 Robert J. Reid. All rights reserved

*No part of this book may be reproduced or transmitted in any form
or by any means, electronic or mechanical, including photocopying
or recording, or by any information storage and retrieval system,
without permission in writing from the publisher.*

On the cover: (top) Halfback Joe Guyon (left) running the ball for the 1917 Georgia Tech football team (Georgia Institute of Technology Archives); (bottom) LSU running back John Emery Jr. (right) carries the ball against Georgia Southern in 2019 (photograph by Tammy Anthony Baker)

Printed in the United States of America

*McFarland & Company, Inc., Publishers
Box 611, Jefferson, North Carolina 28640
www.mcfarlandpub.com*

To my daughter, Sarah,
who encouraged me to finish it during adverse times.
Love you … more …

Table of Contents

Preface   1

Introduction   5

1. Polling and Mathematical Selection Systems   9
2. Why Were Certain Teams Not Unanimous?   13
3. The Early Years   24
4. Yale 1900   30
5. Yale 1909   39
6. Georgia Tech 1917   47
7. Notre Dame 1943   55
8. Michigan 1948   70
9. Texas 1963   79
10. Nebraska 1971   90
11. Southern California 1972   102
12. Nebraska 1995   112
13. Tennessee 1998   122
14. Florida State 1999   134
15. Miami 2001   143
16. Southern California 2004   151
17. Texas 2005   162
18. Alabama 2009   171

19. Florida State 2013	180
20. Ohio State 2014	188
21. Alabama 2015	199
22. Clemson 2018	210
23. LSU 2019	220
24. Summary and Conclusions	229
25. Is There a "Best Ever" Team?	240
Appendix A: Walter Camp	247
Appendix B: Awards and Coaches	250
Appendix C: Francis Gordon Brown Letters	301
Appendix D: Service Teams of 1943	304
Chapter Notes	307
Bibliography	311
Index	315

Preface

This book was written over several years. It was begun in 2005, after I had finished *A Memorable Season in College Football: A Look Back at 1959*. I grew up in Central New York, followed Syracuse University football, and that book was originally going to be about the Orangemen's national championship year. However, the more I researched, the more I realized that 1959 was a pivotal year in college football for many reasons, and therefore the book became more encompassing.

Around that time, my wife's breast cancer returned and had metastasized after a five-year hiatus. Originally diagnosed in 1993, Kris and our family would endure 16 years of chemotherapy, radiation, surgeries, promising results, and setbacks until she passed away in December 2009. For a long time, what I had begun languished in a file cabinet. It was several years after Kris passed before I was finally able to complete this study with the encouragement and support from our daughter, Sarah.

In reviewing and editing, I have noticed differences: (1) in writing style; (2) in the approach taken with various teams; and (3) in the emphasis placed on various factors that appeared to contribute to a unanimous selection. I believe these differences occurred because the times of researching and writing the various chapters were often far apart. I have chosen not to change to a uniform format. Each team is different, and the style used reflects my vision of that team at the time of the research.

As a lifelong fan of college football, its roots, and its history, I wondered why so few teams were unanimously chosen as the national champion. What were the criteria or biases that influenced selectors? It didn't help that it took years for college football to establish a working championship format. During the 150 years in question, what were the major criteria necessary for a team to be a unanimous national champion?

I originally concentrated solely on the 20th century (1900–1999). In the early years (1869–1899), few schools had football, the earliest teams were concentrated in the East, and teams outside the East found few quality opponents. Similarly, at the other end, the formation of the Bowl Championship Series (BCS) in 1998 attempted to use existing post-season bowls to determine a national champion. This system was replaced in 2014 with a better, but less than perfect, College Football Playoff (CFP). These approaches produced results that were still indecisive, often with consensus, but not unanimous champions.

I started by considering several criteria (or categories), to determine what made a unanimous selection. (See Chapter 24. Conclusions and Summary.) Some were easily dismissed, others, given serious thought, were not likely candidates, and a few seemed they had merit, and therefore, would hold sway with selectors. Problems arose in subjective categories, those that could not be assessed objectively by data, as it is far more difficult to determine their influence.

Which categories, or (I hoped) which one, would produce a unanimous national champion of college football during the years 1900–1999? Was it possible to simplify to just one category that all selectors agreed made a unanimous selection? I realized that more than likely it would be a variety of factors.

Journeying through these 100 years, college football alternately evolved at a snail's crawl and a cheetah's speed. Rules changes and styles of play are briefly documented to understand the game as it was played in each varying timeframe where a unanimous selection emerged. The evolution of the selection process is also discussed. There are a surprising number of pundits using vastly different criteria to judge a team. The methods used by the various selectors of college football's annual national champion are examined in Chapter 1. These include: (1) early selectors; (2) mathematical analyses developed; and (3) polling systems.

It is said that early player, coach, and football historian Parke Davis was the only accredited selector whose choices were made from research alone. Other systems use polling of members or sophisticated mathematical analyses, and each one seems to have a slightly varying opinion about the importance of certain criteria. Many selectors have backdated their choices, often many years or even decades. Chapter 3, The Early Years, includes Davis' historical (interviews-based) re-creation of the Princeton–Rutgers game of 1869 that began collegiate football.

Also, not just the unanimous "winners" are examined. In Chapter 2, Why Were Certain Teams Not Unanimous? certain prominent and historically important teams are assessed. What had persuaded usually a single selector to settle on a less obvious or, in some cases, hard to understand choice?

Because the early years of the 1900s and their three unanimous selections, Yale 1900 and 1909, and Georgia Tech 1917, did not have the benefit of weekly polling, summarized national statistical leaders for both individual players and teams, and the myriad of individual awards (See Appendix B, Awards and Coaches) that have sprung up since the Heisman Trophy was begun in 1935, some obvious categories of importance are missing in the selection of these teams. Early game records that can be substantiated are hard to find, as are individual and team statistics.

One exception was found in the "Francis Gordon Brown Papers" in the Yale University archives. Brown was captain of the 1900 Yale team, and his correspondence provided rare insight into the season and football in that era (See Appendix C, Francis Gordon Brown Letters).

Even with these handicaps of historical research, an attempt is made to relive the magical season of each unanimous team. In an effort not to disrupt the flow of the narrative, use is made of a few appendices in order to supply additional and pertinent information. An extensive appendix (B) lists: (1) The majority of awards and trophies given each year to deserving players and coaches; (2) Highlights the careers of several notable coaches of these 150 years. The achievements of all coaches of the unanimous teams are listed. So are the coaches of teams mentioned in Chapter 2, those great teams that were denied a unanimous vote for one reason or another. A few other prominent coaches are discussed.

The years of World Wars I and II disrupted college football around the nation. Much less information is readily available for the World War I years. During World War II, however, service teams composed of college and professional players competed with university teams and were included in the weekly AP poll. Appendix

D has a complete list of service teams for 1943, the year Notre Dame was selected unanimously.

As the game evolved, changes occurred: (1) in the rules; (2) in the standards; and eventually (3) in the workings of the big business of college football. These changes have all helped shape championship teams, both consensus and unanimous. Of course, the question that always arises, Is There a Best Ever College Football Team? Chapter 25 delves into this question, states the author's opinion, and shares the musings of others.

I hope this book appeals to inquisitive fans of college football history.

Introduction

In the 150 years of college football (1869–2019) only 33 teams were unanimously voted the national champion. These teams are diverse in geographic location, in their histories, and in the rules of play for their particular time. They encompass both teams that have been successful throughout the history of American college football and those with a limited time frame in which they excelled.

What made these teams special enough to be unanimously declared the national champion? Why were these teams different from other great teams that were crowned national champion by a consensus, but not unanimous, vote? What is the common thread that connects these teams? After first following and paying homage to their achievements through the regular season, the post-season (where applicable), and the era in which they played, this book will also attempt to determine what it took to be a unanimous national champion, particularly in the last century, when post-season bowls were often aligned to conferences and not necessarily to matching the two best teams.

For statistical convenience, the entire breadth of the 1900s is examined, even though the last five years overlap with the Bowl Alliance and BCS Standings. With that in mind, the selection of teams for this book could have been approached in a different way. Spanning the 100 years from 1900 to 1999, 55 different teams have, at one time or another, been voted national champion by one or more of the respected polls or rating systems. Of these 55 teams, 14 were selected only once during those years. Another 11 teams were selected in two seasons, one during three seasons, four teams in four different seasons, etc.

It might be argued that over these 100 years, if a football program was selected as the number one team in a certain number of seasons (say 10 seasons, 10 percent of that time period), that program could be considered one of the dominant football programs. This approach would reduce the field to eight schools: Pittsburgh (11 seasons), Nebraska (12), Ohio State and Southern California (13 each), Oklahoma (14), Michigan (15), Alabama (17), and Notre Dame (21). This approach, concentrating on the most often selected football programs, has merit. However, these eight programs alone account for 116 years of being crowned national champion by at least one selector and still doesn't consider the question: why were only certain teams the unanimous national champion?

Ultimately it was decided to heed and respect the opinions of the polls and rating systems and to concentrate on their 11 unanimously selected national champions from the 1900s and ultimately through the Bowl Alliance, BCS, and CFP years.

Through the 89 seasons where the various selectors have failed to agree unanimously during the 1900s, there has been a single dissenting vote 16 times. Six of those 16 seasons have been the result of the selector not making a decision and voting for both the predominant selection and another team. Another consideration is changing a vote. In politics this is referred to as "flip-flopping" and is usually frowned upon. Having selected Ohio State as its choice in 1998, the Sagarin ratings system later changed its vote, making Tennessee a unanimous selection. After consideration, it was decided that it would not be fair to Volunteers players and fans to omit such a worthy team from inclusion in this book because of a delayed unanimous decision. The teams selected from the 1900s (with the exception of Tennessee, 1998), were based on the National Poll Championship section of the *Official NCAA Football Records, 2002*. Sagarin changed its vote after 2002.

Some selectors chose teams only during a certain window of years, whereas others retroactively made selections after several decades. Especially early selectors often relied on actually viewing games, whereas others used game summaries and statistics. There is logic and expertise to both approaches. Actually viewing teams and watching games certainly allows a "feel" that is missing from an after-the-fact review of team records, statistics, and trends. On the other hand, by employing a statistical overview of a complete season and its top contenders, a clear choice of a national champion often emerges.

The first approach, although limited by the number of games one can view, was predominant in the early years of the 20th century and was helped by having fewer top teams to watch and having them concentrated in a relatively small geographic area. From the first collegiate game in 1869 up to 1899, the national champion was almost exclusively decided from among what would eventually be Ivy League schools. Only twice was a non–Ivy team considered (and never unanimously): Colgate in 1875 and Lafayette in 1896.

The great Michigan "Point-a-Minute" teams from 1901–1905 were the first to crack the Eastern monopoly (see Chapter 2). A year later, in 1905, Chicago was selected, followed by Vanderbilt in 1906 and LSU in 1908. The next decade and a half found the West represented with Texas A&M in 1919 and California from 1920–1923. From there on, teams across the nation were equally represented.

The various polls and statistical methods have actually complemented each other fairly well throughout this period. During the 89 years when selectors disagreed during the 1900s, it was a disagreement between two teams 36 times. Three teams were involved during 28 seasons. However, the remaining 25 college football campaigns found wide differences of opinion involving as many as six teams (1981). With the advent of attempts at a more definitive method, ultimately leading to a much-needed playoff system (CFP) in 2014, the total subjectivity of the selection process was minimized. Even so, the recent (1995–2019) national championship teams were not always unanimous even with these systems in place. Why? That is a question this book will attempt to answer.

Below is a table showing the programs voted national champion by decade through the 1900s.

Teams Selected National Champion by Decade

Team	1900 to 1909	1910 to 1919	1920 to 1929	1930 to 1939	1940 to 1949	1950 to 1959	1960 to 1969	1970 to 1979	1980 to 1989	1990 to 1999
Alabama*			+	+	+		+	+		+
Arizona State								+		

Introduction

Team	1900 to 1909	1910 to 1919	1920 to 1929	1930 to 1939	1940 to 1949	1950 to 1959	1960 to 1969	1970 to 1979	1980 to 1989	1990 to 1999
Arkansas							+	+		
Army		+			+					
Auburn*		+	+	+	+		+	+		
Brigham Young									+	
California			+	+						
Chicago	+	+								
Clemson									+	
Colgate				+						
Colorado										+
Detroit			+							
Florida									+	+
Florida State									+	+
Georgia			+		+		+		+	
Georgia Tech		+	+			+				+
Harvard	+									
Illinois		+	+			+				
Iowa			+			+	+			
Kentucky						+				
LaFayette			+							
Louisiana State	+			+		+	+			
Maryland						+				
Miami (FL)									+	+
Michigan*	+	+	+	+	+		+	+	+	+
Michigan State						+	+			
Minnesota				+	+		+			
Mississippi						+	+			
Missouri							+			
Navy			+							
Nebraska		+						+	+	+
Notre Dame*		+	+	+	+	+	+	+	+	+
Ohio State*				+	+	+	+	+		+
Oklahoma*					+	+	+	+	+	
Penn	+									
Penn State		+					+		+	+
Pittsburgh*		+	+	+				+	+	
Princeton	+									
Purdue				+						
Southern California			+	+			+	+		

Team	1900 to 1909	1910 to 1919	1920 to 1929	1930 to 1939	1940 to 1949	1950 to 1959	1960 to 1969	1970 to 1979	1980 to 1989	1990 to 1999
Southern Methodist				+					+	
Stanford			+		+					
Syracuse						+				
Tennessee*				+	+	+	+			+
Texas					+		+	+	+	
Texas A&M		+		+						
Texas Christian				+						
UCLA							+			
Vanderbilt	+	+								
Washington							+		+	+
Washington & Jefferson			+							
Wisconsin					+					
Yale	+									

*Teams selected in five or more decades.

Chapter 1

Polling and Mathematical Selection Systems

This chapter lists the major polling systems, both opinion-based and mathematical systems, used to select a national champion. It will be noted that most polls cover only a limited time frame. A few selectors have retroactively chosen the national champion from seasons past.

Parke Davis was a lineman at Princeton from 1890–1892 and a coach at Wisconsin (1893), Amherst (1894), and Lafayette (1895–1897, including a shared national championship 1896). He was a football researcher and historian who relied on his research alone (without mathematical analysis) to proclaim the national champions from 1869–1933.

The first method of selecting a collegiate football national champion (besides Casper Whitney and Walter Camp) was a mathematical system devised in 1926 by Frank Dickinson, an economics professor at the University of Illinois. A mathematical system is defined as a system that rates teams by a mathematical formula.[1] The formula will use factors such as wins, losses, scores, and margin of victory. Professor Dickinson's system also attempted to consider the quality of the opponent. Beginning his system in 1926, Dickinson retroactively determined a national champion back to 1924 at the urging of Knute Rockne, whose 1924 Notre Dame team was ultimately chosen by Dickinson.[2]

In 1927, Deke Houlgate of Los Angeles established his own mathematical system, which was syndicated in newspapers until 1958. His ratings also appeared annually in the *Football Thesaurus* from 1946–1958 and in *Illustrated Football* during that same period. Houlgate retroactively applied his formula to 1885–1926.

Within the next eight years, five more mathematical systems were launched: The Dunkel Index (1929–present), The Boand System (1930–1960 and retroactive from 1919–1929), the Williamson System (1932–1963), the Litkenhous System (1934–1984), and the Poling System (1935–1984 and retroactive from 1924–1934).

Dick Dunkel, Sr., used his system to rank teams from 1929–1971. Dick Dunkel, Jr., continued the system from 1972–1995. John Duck took over ranking teams by the Dunkel system beginning in 1996. This system introduced schedule strength, performance in recent games, and upsets in its calculations.

The Boand System (also known as the Azzi Ratem System) was developed by William Boand from Tucson, Arizona. The system sought to combine the best features of three rating systems into one. The three systems were those of Professors Frank Dickinson of Illinois and Ralph Powell of Ohio State, and William T. Van de Graaf, football coach and mathematics instructor at Colorado College.[3] The Boand System was published in several newspapers across the country as well as *Illustrated Football Annual* from 1932–1942 and *Football News* from 1942–1944 and again from 1951–1960.[4]

In 1932 Paul Williamson, a geologist in New Orleans, Louisiana, developed the Williamson System, which for a time was unique in ranking teams after the bowl season.

In 1934 Edward Litkenhous, a professor of chemical engineering at Vanderbilt, and his brother Frank developed this ranking system based on "a difference by score formula."[5]

Richard Poling of Mansfield, Ohio, and a former player at Ohio Wesleyan, developed a system in 1935 (used until 1984) that appeared in several newspapers and the *Football Review Supplement*.

The first newspaper poll was started in 1936 by Alan Gould, the Sports Editor of the *Associated Press* (AP). In 1935, Gould compiled his own Top Ten and included it in his column. The next year, the AP polled a network of 44 sportswriters beginning on October 19, 1936, and proceeding weekly, finally crowning a National Champion (Minnesota) on November 30, 1936, before any bowl games were played (Minnesota did not play in a bowl that year).

The AP's competitor, the *United Press* (UP) began polling 35 college football coaches to establish their own official poll in 1950. In 1958, UP merged with *International News Service* and became the UPI poll. This changed in 1991 when it became the USA Today/CNN poll, and again in 1995 becoming the USA Today/ESPN poll. From 1952–1957, before merging with *United Press*, the *International News Service* conducted a football rankings poll among its members.

In 1965, the AP poll was taken following the bowl games. But in 1966 and 1967, the AP reverted to naming a national champion before the bowls. The following year, and continuing to the present, the AP waits until after the bowl games to take its final poll for the season. It wasn't until 1974 that the UPI waited until after the bowl games to conduct their final poll. Throughout the years, many other polling systems have begun and added their "two cents' worth."

The Helms Athletic Foundation, founded by Paul H. Helms of Los Angeles, selected a national champion from 1941–1982 (and retroactively from 1883–1940).

In 1945 Harry DeVold, originally from Minneapolis, Minnesota, a World War II marine veteran who played at Cornell, developed a mathematical ranking system.[6] The DeVold System appeared in *Football News* from 1955–1991.

From 1954 to the present, the Football Writers Association of America, an organization of nearly 1,000, polls 16 of its members weekly. The Association then gives their national champion selection the Grantland Rice Trophy in honor of the legendary sports writer.

From 1958–2002, *Football News* polled its staff and published their own rankings.

The National Football Foundation was established in 1947 and began selecting a national champion in 1959, continuing to the present. The Foundation has over 100 chapters and over 13,000 members. Each year it awards the MacArthur Bowl to its national champion.

Matthews Grid Rankings (1966 to present), was developed by mathematician Herman Matthews. The rankings appeared in several newspapers, the Scripts Howard News Service, and *Football News*.

FACT (the Foundation for the Analysis of Competitions and Tournaments) began a computer-based ranking system in 1968 and continues to the present. The system was developed by David Rothman, a statistician. The margin of victory and the strength of schedule are especially important in this system.

The Billingsley Report (1970 to present, and retroactively from 1869–1969), is a mathematical power ranking system, developed by Richard Billingsley. He publishes the poll through his own company, The College Football Research Center, and takes into account: (1) The game site; (2) Most recent performance; and (3) Defensive scoring, in addition to a team's record and strength of schedule.

Sporting News is a national publication based in St. Louis that has polled its staff to determine college football rankings from 1975 to the present.

The Sagarin Ratings (1978 to present and retroactively from 1938–1977) were developed by mathematician Jeff Sagarin of Bloomington, Indiana. The system is based primarily on strength of schedule, scoring margin, and game location.

The *New York Times* Computer Ranking System (1979–2004) considered late-season games more important, and bowl games counted as a win-and-a-half.

The National Championship Foundation has over 120 chapters and 12,000 members (similar to the National Football Foundation). It was established by Mike Riter of Hudson, New York, and selected a national champion from 1980–2001 (and retroactively from 1869–1969) based on membership voting.

The Eck Ratings System (1983 to present), developed by aerospace worker Steve Eck, is a "mathematical point system." Besides the usual considerations, Eck rates each team based on a set number of games. Therefore pre-season games or "extra" games, such as conference championships, do not slant the rating. The 1990s saw another cluster of ranking systems appear. The Berryman System (1990 to present) was developed by Clyde Berryman of Washington, D.C. It is a Quality Point Rating System that considers a team's win-loss record, points scored versus points allowed, and strength of schedule. Unlike some other more recent systems, Berryman rates early games equal to late-season games.

The Colley Matrix (1992 to present), devised by Wes Colley of Virginia, was published in the *Atlanta Journal-Constitution*. The formula is based on the team's record being the most important determining factor. The strength of a team's schedule is considered, and adjustments are made as its strength of schedule alters throughout the season.[7]

Peter Wolfe, an MD who specializes in infectious diseases, and Ross Baker developed a mathematical power-rating matrix that they describe as a "maximum likelihood estimate."[8] His rankings have run from 1992 to the present. In this system, game location is considered but not the margin of victory.

Anderson/Hester (1993 to present) is also known as the *Seattle Times* Rankings. It is a mathematical system that rewards team wins against opponents with a higher schedule strength.

Congrove Computer Rankings (1993 to present). This computer program attempts to predict winners and scores. Game results are used to alter future predictions. A Team's rating is calculated by the strength of its opponent, whether the team won or lost. Therefore running up a score does not greatly influence its rating.[9]

The Alderson System (1994–1998) was developed by Bob Alderson of Muldrow, Oklahoma, and is a mathematical "point value" system.

The Massey College Football Ratings (1995 to present) was developed by Carson-Newman College mathematics professor Ken Massey. Ratings are broken down to show a team's record: overall ranking, offensive ranking, defensive ranking, strength of schedule ranking, and home field advantage ranking.

There are other lower-profile systems. These mentioned are well established, the most popular, and have been used for decades to decide the yearly national champion of college football.

Chapter 2

Why Were Certain Teams Not Unanimous?

The question asked in this chapter is one to which I do not always have a ready answer. As seen in Chapter 1, selectors vary widely in what they look at and the importance they place on their varied criteria.

Here I select some teams for study. In only two seasons (Michigan 1901 and Oklahoma 1956) do I allow more than one other team to have been selected. Usually, I allow only one selector's vote to prevent a unanimous decision. These two exceptions were because of the historical importance of these two teams: Michigan's Point-A-Minute teams of the early 1900s represented a milestone in opening up the rest of the country to consideration beyond the eastern schools, and Oklahoma's dominance in the 1950s (a 47-game winning streak followed by a 31-game winning streak) has never been duplicated.

Here is a study and comparison of teams that shared the title in a particular season with (usually) a single "spoiling" vote preventing a unanimous selection for the consensus winner.

1901 and 1902 Michigan

Fielding "Hurry Up" Yost (See Appendix B, Awards and Coaches) played tackle at West Virginia and Lafayette from 1894 to 1896, and the next year began a coaching career that would span 30 years. He coached at Ohio Wesleyan, Nebraska, Kansas, Stanford, and San Jose State before moving to Michigan in 1901.

From 1901–1923, his Michigan teams went 165–29–10. During those 204 games, the Wolverines shut out opponents 112 times (54.9 percent) including 48 times in 57 games (84.2 percent) from 1901–1905. During that five-year period, known as Michigan's Point-A-Minute teams, the Wolverines were 55–1–1 and outscored opponents, 2772–42.

1901 Michigan

The 1901 Michigan squad featured center George Gregory, end Ev Sweeley, quarterback Boss Weeks, All-America fullback Neil Snow, and most of all Willie Heston, All-America (in 1903 and again in 1904) and one of the best backs of the era. Heston was "recruited" by Yost out of California, where he was working as a schoolteacher. Heston later stated that he felt the 1901 team was the best of those years.

Yost brought to Michigan an offensive plan of speed and "Hurry Up" that was new to the Western Conference (later the Big Ten). Heston later described how this offense worked. Quarterback Weeks would call the next play (by number) as soon as the current play was over. At the line of scrimmage, Weeks would call out numbers, but that first number was the one to "go" on. If the opposing team caught on, the system was changed. The Michigan players would not move on the signal, and the opposing team would be off-side.[1]

The 1901 Michigan team went to the very first Rose Bowl to face the Glenn "Pop" Warner-coached Stanford team. Stanford was 3-1-2 and had scored only 34 points all year while allowing eight points. The Cardinals (later the Cardinal) had played four athletic clubs before a 12-0 win over Nevada and a 2-0 loss to California.

The game wasn't close. Michigan, playing only its starting eleven, kept Stanford from crossing mid-field, compiled 503 yards rushing, and kicked for 881 yards (Yost believed in kicking on any down in order to maintain field position). Stanford requested that the game be ended with around 10 minutes remaining. Michigan won, 49-0, and it would be 14 years before the Rose Bowl resumed.

While the Wolverines claimed the most nods from selectors, Billingsley opted for 12-0 Harvard, while Parke Davis (bewilderingly) chose Yale despite the Eli being tied by Army and shut out by Harvard, 22-0. Yale and Harvard shared six opponents, but a comparison is pointless as the two met at the end of the season. Harvard and Michigan had one common opponent; Harvard beat Carlisle, 29-0, while Michigan topped the Indians, 22-0. Yale's opponents combined for a very mediocre 59-54-9 record, while Harvard's opponents managed a more respectable 71-56-8. Opponents of Michigan, of arguably lesser quality (see table below) compiled a 54-38-9 record.

As the AP poll did not begin until 1936, use is made here of the power Rating System later developed by Sorensen.

Comparison of Michigan, Harvard and Yale Opponents
1901 Based on Power Ranking by Sorensen System

	in Top 10	in Top 20	in Top 40
Michigan	0	1	6
Yale	3	6	12
Harvard	3	6	12

1902 Michigan

It could also be argued that the best of those teams was the 1902 squad that went 11-0 and outscored opponents, 644-12. Michigan shut out Notre Dame (6-2-1), 23-0, Ohio State (6-2-2) 86-0, Wisconsin (6-3) 6-0, and Chicago (11-1) 21-0. The combined win-loss record of all Michigan opponents for that year was 62-35-4. The 1902 team again featured All-America Willie Heston.

Again, enter Parke Davis, a proponent of Eastern football, who selected both Michigan and Yale (11-0-1) that year and was the only selector voting other than for Michigan. Davis, a former Princeton player, coach (Wisconsin, Amherst, LaFayette), and early football historian, selected solely by personal experience. He did have a valid argument, although I contend that selectors should make a single decision.

Once more use is made here of the power Rating System later developed by Sorensen. Based on this system, Yale played a much more difficult schedule than did Michigan (see Table below). The 1902 Yale team outscored opponents, 286–22, and defeated powerful Harvard, 23–0. However, Yale's season was blemished by a 6–6 tie with Army (6-1-1).

Comparison of Michigan and Yale Opponents 1902 Based on Power Ranking by Sorensen System Number of Opponents

	in Top 10	in Top 20	in Top 50
Michigan	2	3	6
Yale	3	8	10

1924 Notre Dame

"Outlined against a blue-grey October sky, the Four Horsemen rode again." With these dramatic words, written as the Fighting Irish defeated Army at the Polo Grounds in New York, sportswriter Grantland Rice ushered the era of the Four Horsemen of Notre Dame into football lore.[2] An article in *Collier's* magazine on November 1, 1930, noted that the 1924 Notre Dame wasn't necessarily the best, but this publicity gained them lasting renown.

This picture of the 1924 Notre Dame backfield propelled them into national prominence as the "Four Horsemen." From left to right—Don Miller, Elmer Layden, Jim Crowley, and Harry Stuhldreher (author's collection).

Knute Rockne (see Appendix B, Awards and Coaches) is probably the best-known coach of the early years of college football. He was an innovator. During his playing days as an end at Notre Dame in 1913, he and quarterback Gus Dorais showed a skeptical college football world how the forward pass could be an effective offensive weapon. After working as an assistant for four years under Notre Dame head coach Jesse Harper, Rockne took over in 1918 and remained until his tragic death in an airplane crash in 1930. His head coaching record was 105–12–5. Rockne had much talent at Notre Dame, with several players named All-America.

The 1924 Fighting Irish outscored regular season opponents, 258–44, and defeated a 7–0–1 Stanford team, coached by Glenn "Pop" Warner and featuring three All-Americas (Jim Lawson 1924, Ernie Nevers 1925, and Ted Shipkey 1926), 27–10 in the post-season Rose Bowl. Notre Dame was the only major undefeated and untied team in 1924. Relying on Sorensen's Power Rating of the major schools, Notre Dame played one team in the top 10, two in the top 20, and seven in the top 50 Power Ratings.

Even today, Knute Rockne remains a standard by which other coaches are compared. And yet he never had a unanimous national champion team. Of all Rockne's Notre Dame elevens, including five undefeated and untied teams (1919, 1920, 1924, 1929, 1930), the 1924 team was a public relations miracle. Notre Dame capitalized on Rice's exuberant description. The nation followed the football exploits of these biblical figures of ruin and mayhem. Three of the "Four Horsemen" were named First Team All-America that year (Jim Crowley, Elmer Layden, and Harry Stuhldreher). Why was this not Rockne's unanimous championship team?

Yet again, enter Parke Davis. Once again, he selected an Eastern team and not on a split vote. His choice (Penn) is particularly hard to justify. Penn posted a record of 9–1–1. The Quakers started the season 8–0, defeating, among others, Ursinus (0–2–1), Drexel Tech (1–8), Franklin & Marshall (3–5–1), and Georgetown (2–6). The last three games of the season were a scoreless tie with 6–3–1 Penn State, a 20–0 shutout of 4–4 Cornell, and finally a 14–0 loss to California (8–0–2).

Penn played one team in the top 20 (by Sorensen's Power Rating System) and only three in the top 50. Their opponents combined for an unimpressive 40–37–9 record. Parke Davis often selected more than one team as national champion; however, in few years did his selection not include a team from the Northeast.

1944 and 1945 Army

Army 1944

Army, coached by Earl Blaik (see Appendix B, Awards and Coaches), entered the first poll of 1944 (October 9) ranked third behind Notre Dame and North Carolina Pre-Flight, while Ohio State began a distant eighth. By the October 30 poll, Army was ranked number one with Notre Dame second, Ohio State third, and all three perfect at 5–0. The next week, Notre Dame fell. Army and Ohio State were at the top, although the Buckeyes later had to be content with bouncing between third and fourth until the final poll on December 4, where they ranked second.

Running backs Glen Davis and Felix "Doc" Blanchard, Mr. Outside and Mr. Inside for Army, dominated defenses:

Davis / Blanchard Rushing 1944 and 1945 Combined

	Yds.	Rushes	Avg. / Rush	TDs
Davis	2031	161	12.6	35
Blanchard	1319	169	7.8	25

In 1944, Army was the consensus national champion with one dissenting/split vote. The National Championship Foundation chose both Army and Ohio State. Below is a comparison of the teams.

	Army	Ohio State
Record	9–0	9–0
Points Scored-Allowed	504–35	287–79
Opponents' Record	42–35–2	45–37–5
Teams Played in Top 20 Poll	#5, #2	#19, #6, #6

The Sorensen Power Ranking System favors OSU: 21480 to 19495, with Randolph Field between them at 20248. The opponents' records appear fairly even, yet Sorensen ranks the Ohio State strength of schedule at tenth-most difficult and Army's at 44th. Although they defeated two of the top five opponents at the time by a combined 82–7, Army was denied a unanimous vote.

1945 Army

The 1945 Army team not being a unanimous champion is a bit puzzling and challenges my conclusion regarding the 1943 Notre Dame unanimous national champion season (in Chapter 7). In 1943, Notre Dame had one loss (one of only three unanimous choices not to be undefeated). That year, the Irish beat teams ranked, at the time, #2, #3, #3, #8, and #2. It appeared obvious that Notre Dame was chosen unanimously because they had played and defeated the top contenders.

In 1945, Army, at 9–0, played teams ranked, at the time, #9, #19, #2, #6, and #2. Alabama (beneficiary of another National Championship Foundation split vote) was 10–0 with a win over #11 Southern California in the Rose Bowl and a win over LSU, which would end the season at #14. (Alabama and LSU played before the first poll of the year.)

Sorensen ranked Army, Navy, and Alabama the top three, with 8556 points separating first and third. Army was also ranked as having the second-most difficult schedule, Navy the third-most difficult, with Alabama at 24th.

1955 and 1956 Oklahoma

From the second game of the 1953 season until the eighth game of 1957, the Oklahoma Sooners were unbeaten and untied. That 47-game winning streak has not been equaled since. And yet Oklahoma, for all their dominance during that stretch, was never a unanimous national champion.

1955 Oklahoma

In 1955, UCLA started the season atop the Associated Press poll, with Oklahoma a close second. By the Sorensen System, UCLA had nine opponents in the top 45, including three in the top 10. The Bruins also played eight teams in the AP Top 20, and their opponents posted a combined 62-37-6, the best among major contenders. But the Bruins lost early to undefeated Maryland and then to #2 Michigan State in the Rose Bowl, ending hopes of the national title. By season's end, Oklahoma was the consensus champion, yet Boand chose Rose Bowl victor Michigan State (9-1).

Michigan State didn't enter the AP poll until September 26, but suffered their only loss that year to then-#2 Michigan on October 1. The Spartans then won seven straight games, outscoring those opponents, 209-42, and worked their way steadily to the #2 ranking after impressive wins over #20 Stanford (38-14) and #4 Notre Dame (21-7).

Comparison of Oklahoma, Michigan State 1955
(Number of Opponents Based on Power Ranking by Sorensen System)

	in Top 10	in Top 20	in Top 50
Oklahoma	1	2	8
MSU	2	4	8

Overall Record

	Of All opponents	Number of Opponents in AP Top 20 Polls
Oklahoma	47-61-2	3
MSU	44-44-5	7

1956 Oklahoma

The 1956 season started with Oklahoma riding a 30-game winning streak and firmly entrenched atop the pre-season AP poll, garnering 111 of 149 first-place votes. The Sooners would record another perfect season, extending the winning streak to 40 games, but still not secure a unanimous national title. By the time all selectors had their say, Oklahoma had to share the title with three other teams: Georgia Tech (10-1, Berryman), Iowa (9-1, Football Research), and Tennessee (10-1, Sagarin split vote).

The Sooners were, again, the victims of a weak schedule. They played only two teams in the AP top 20: Notre Dame (#3 pre-season) at 8-2, and Colorado, which despite an 8-2-1 season never ascended the AP past #18.

Coach Bud Wilkinson's (see Appendix B, Awards and Coaches) teams of the early to mid-1950s were truly great. The Sooners accomplished an amazing 47-game winning streak and another 31-game winning streak. Wilkinson's record at Oklahoma was 145-29-4. But playing mostly conference games within the relatively weak (at the time) Big 8 appeared to doom their hopes for a unanimous national title.

1958 LSU

LSU was unranked in the pre-season polls to become #1 after their sixth game. To this point, the Tigers had outscored unranked opponents (29-30-3 combined record), 142-29. From thereon, LSU, coached by Paul Dietzel (see Appendix B, Awards and Coaches), would not relinquish the top spot.

At season's end, only the Football Writers Association did not acknowledge the undefeated Tigers as national champion. Their choice was the 8-1-1 Iowa Hawkeyes. Other worthy teams with no losses but with ties or with one loss are compared below.

Comparison of Possible Contenders 1958

Team	Record	Opponent Record	Points Scored-Allowed
LSU	11-0-0	57-53-3	282-53
Iowa	8-1-1	56-33-8	272-146
Air Force	9-0-2	63-47-3	247-102
Oklahoma	10-1-0	56-52-3	300-55
Army	8-0-1	43-43-2	264-49
Auburn	9-0-1	40-48-4	173-62

Number & Ranking of Opponents in AP Poll

LSU	2	#6, #12
Iowa	7*	#8, #6*, #4, #8, #16, #15, #16
Air Force	4**	#2, #19**, #9+, #10
Oklahoma	4	#13, #16, #9, #9
Army	3	#18, #4, #13
Auburn	0	

* Unranked at the time, Air Force ends season at #6
** Unranked at the time, Oklahoma State ends at #19
\+ Unranked at the time, Colorado had been #9 early

Number of Opponents
(Based on Power Ranking by Sorensen System)

	in Top 10	in Top 20	in Top 50
LSU	1	3	8
Iowa	3	7	9
Air Force	2	3	5
Oklahoma	0	3	5
Army	0	2	6
Auburn	0	1	6

As the only undefeated team, LSU certainly deserved to be the national champion. However, based on an analysis of the season, Iowa (alone among the contenders) also had a strong case based primarily on strength of schedule. The Hawkeyes allowed the most points, but that was balanced by the strength of their competition. Iowa's late-season loss to Ohio State and the early-season tie with Air Force sealed their fate with the consensus of selectors. However, the Football Writers Association's lone dissenting vote cost LSU.

Note: Ohio State was the pre-season #1 and, although undefeated, bounced around in the top five before a 7–7 tie with #13 Wisconsin in game five and a 21–0 shutout by #11 Northwestern in game six ruined any championship hopes.

1979 and 1992 Alabama

1979 Alabama

From 1958 until 1982, Alabama was coached by the legendary Paul "Bear" Bryant (see Appendix B, Awards and Coaches). In 1979, Southern California was the pre-season favorite and held that position through five games before a 21–21 tie with Stanford dropped them to #4. Alabama ascended to the #1 spot and kept it for several weeks. The AP poll of November 26 read: #1 Alabama, #2 Southern California, and #3 Ohio State. The following week, Alabama beat #14 Auburn, while Southern California and Ohio State had completed their regular seasons. The next AP poll on December 3 ranked the top three as: #1 Ohio State, #2 Alabama, #3 Southern California. Polls are sometimes hard to understand!

By Rose Bowl agreement, the Big 10 winner (#1 Ohio State) and the PAC 10 winner (#3 Southern California) would meet. Alabama at #2 would face #6 Arkansas in the Sugar Bowl. The Tide easily defeated the Razorbacks, 24–9, while Southern California upset Ohio State, 17–16.

The January 2, 1980, poll ranked Alabama #1, and all selectors agreed except Football Research. That selector factors the later games more heavily than early season games, and therefore chose Southern California.

Comparison of Alabama and Southern California

Team	Record	Opponent W-L	Pts. Scored-Pts. Allowed
Alabama	12-0-0	59-75-2	383-67
USC	11-0-1	67-65-5	389-171

Number and Ranking of Opponents in AP Poll

Alabama	3	#18, #14, #6
USC	4	#20, #9, #15, #1

Number of Opponents Based on Power Ranking by Sorensen System

	in Top 10	in Top 20	in Top 50
Alabama	1	2	6
USC	1	2	10

Southern California did beat the top-ranked team in the Rose Bowl; however, the Trojans suffered a 21-21 tie at home against mediocre (5-5-1) and unranked Stanford. The Cardinals played only Tulane (ranked #15 in final poll) and Southern California (#1 at the time) of the top 20 teams. Their opponents' record was 63-59-4, but taking out Tulane (9-3) and Southern California (11-0-1), it becomes 43-56-3.

1992 Alabama

Sagarin was the only selector to choose Florida State over consensus Alabama, another choice difficult to understand. Alabama was ranked #9 in the pre-season and slowly worked its way to #2 by the November 9 poll. The Tide then beat #1 Miami, Florida, 34-13 in the post-season Sugar Bowl and took over the #1 spot.

Sagarin's choice, Florida State, had lost to Miami, 19-16 on October 3. However, Sagarin does factor in scoring margin, and Florida State scored 80 more points in one fewer games.

Comparison of Alabama and Florida State

Team	Record	Opponent W-L	Pts. Scored-Pts. Allowed
Alabama	13-0	78-69-2	366-122
Florida State	11-1	79-60-1	446-186

Common Opponents

Team	Alabama	Florida State
Florida	28-21 W	45-24 W
Miami (Fla.)	34-13 W	16-19 L
Tulane	37-0 W	70-7 W

Number and Ranking of Opponents in AP Poll

Alabama	4	#13, #16, #12, #1
Florida State	7	#15, #16, #2(L), #16, #23, #6, #11

Number of Opponents Based on Power Ranking by Sorensen System

	in Top 10	in Top 20	in Top 50
Alabama	1	4	9
Florida State	2	5	9

Whereas Florida State had advantages in some areas, the facts remain that:

1. In game 5, they lost to Miami, the #1 team at the end of the regular season.
2. In a dream match-up between the top two-ranked teams, #2 Alabama dominated #1 Miami, 34–13, in the Sugar Bowl.

In at least one of these seasons, Alabama should have had the distinction of joining the elite programs that boast unanimous national champions. That would be fulfilled later when the Tide won unanimously in 2009 and 2015.

1988 Notre Dame

Clyde Berryman uses a mathematical system for his "Quality Point Rating System." For the 1988 season, he stood alone in selecting Miami (FL) over consensus Notre Dame, coached by Lou Holtz (see Appendix B, Awards and Coaches).

The two teams appear more even than in many disputed years. A comparison shows this apparent parity.

Comparison of Notre Dame and Miami

Team	Record	Opponent W-L	Pts. Scored-Pts. Allowed
Notre Dame	12–0	73–61–4	393–156
Miami	11–1	84–55–1	418–116

Common Opponents

Team	Notre Dame	Miami
Michigan	19–17 W	31–30 W

Number and Ranking of Opponents in AP Poll

Notre Dame	4	#9, #1, #2, #3
Miami	6	#1, #15, #4 (L), #11, #8, #6

Number and Ranking of Opponents in AP Poll
(Number of Opponents Based on Power Ranking by Sorensen System)

	in Top 10	in Top 20	in Top 50
Notre Dame	4	4	8
Miami	4	6	7

Chapter 2. Why Were Certain Teams Not Unanimous?

These comparisons are interesting except that Notre Dame and Miami played head-to-head in Miami's fifth game and Notre Dame's sixth, on October 15. At that time, Miami was ranked #1 and Notre Dame #4. The Irish won the game, 31–30, further cementing the equality of these two teams. Once again, a single vote prevented a unanimous champion.

No unanimous champion emerged during the Bowl Coalition of 1992–1994. For this study, the Bowl Coalition years were included in what is called here the "Old System," where bowl-conference alliances often hindered a playoff between the two top-ranked teams. With the short-lived Bowl Alliance (1995–1997), the Bowl Championship Series (BCS, 1998–2013), and the College Football Playoff (CFP, 2014 to present), the chances for a unanimous national champion have improved.

	Old System 1900–1994	*Bowl Alliance 1995–1997*	*BCS 1998–2013*	*CFP 2014-*
Years	95	3	16	6
# Unanimous	9	1	7	4
% unanimous	9.4	33.3	43.8	66.7

From 9.4 percent through much of the 1900s, the selectors have agreed 66.7 percent through the first years of the CFP. Hopefully, this trend will continue, and future teams will not be deprived of the exalted title of "unanimous."

Chapter 3

The Early Years

College football began on November 6, 1869. Only two schools had teams that year, Princeton and Rutgers. They met twice, with Rutgers winning, six goals to four, in the initial contest and Princeton prevailing, eight goals to none, in the rematch.

Parke Davis was an avid fan and historian of the early college game. He played football at Princeton from 1890–1892, then coached at Wisconsin in 1893 (4–2), Amherst in 1894 (7–5–1), and at Lafayette from 1895 to 1898 (29–12–2). Davis was an early selector of the college football national champion. He relied completely on his own research, and for that his method of selecting is unique, and his selections are used to this day.

We are indebted to Davis for interviewing participants of that first football game and compiling an account of the game, which was published in *Intercollegiate Football: A Complete Pictorial and Statistical Review from 1869 to 1934*. Based on Davis' description, we get an insight into how that first game was played.

There was nothing like an official uniform and no pads or other protective gear. The players simply took off their jackets and used the suspenders as a belt. Each team consisted of 25 players. Two players from each team were known as "captains of the enemy's goal" because they were placed immediately in front of the opponent's goal. The remaining players were divided into "fielders" and "bulldogs." The fielders remained in designated areas of the field, while the bulldogs followed the play over the entire field. The teams agreed that the game would be played until 10 goals were scored.

The game began when Princeton kicked, or "bucked" the ball off a "tee" composed of soil from the field. Apparently the kick was short and to one side. The Rutgers players surrounded the ball, not letting Princeton players get near, and by a series of short kicks (dribbles) advanced it to their captains of the enemy's goal. The captains, Dixon and Gano, kicked it through for a score. Wanting to prevent this type of play, Princeton captain Gummere ordered one of his largest players, J. E. Michael, or "Big Mike," to attack the Rutgers formation. Big Mike succeeded in scattering the Rutgers defense and allowing Princeton access to the ball.

Reading Davis' full account of the game, a few things stand out: (1) the players wore street clothes much like any pick-up game; (2) the number and dispersal of players as well as predominantly kicking the ball certainly indicates that the game was more soccer-style [the agreed-upon rules were modified from the London Football Association and were essentially rules for soccer]; (3) there are some elements (precursors) of the more Rugby-like style of early football, such as the mass formations and the appearance of "Big Mike," the wedge-breaker. There was also strategy involved: Princeton assigning a wedge-breaker, and Rutgers later adjusting their kicks lower to the ground as the taller Princeton players were knocking down the higher kicks. Rutgers won that match, six goals to four.

Chapter 3. The Early Years

From 1869–1899, 13 teams were acclaimed a national champion unanimously. In most cases, little is known about these teams or their players. Changes in the game and the rules governing it were ongoing during this period. All-America selections were begun in 1889.

The teams listed below are those unanimously chosen by selectors for the years 1870–1899.

1870 Princeton

During that second season, there were only three colleges with a football program. Princeton's lone game was a 6–2 win over Rutgers, while Columbia's only game was a 6–3 loss to Rutgers.

All that is known about that Princeton team is that they played one game and had no official coach. It must be assumed that the game was similar to the 1869 game described earlier and that some of the original combatants returned.

1873 Princeton

By the 1873 season, Yale had initiated a football program (in 1872), and the number of participating schools had risen to four. Princeton again played only one game, a 3–0 win over Yale. Columbia and Yale were each 2–1, while Rutgers was 1–2.

1876 Yale

With the addition of Harvard (1875) and Pennsylvania (1876), there were now six college football programs. Yale at 3–0 was the only undefeated team, beating 3–1

The undefeated 1876 Yale football team. Freshman Walter Camp (back row, 2nd from left) would later be known as the Father of American Football for his innovations and dedication to the game until his death in 1924 (courtesy of Yale Archives).

Harvard, 3-2 Princeton, and 1-3 Columbia. Walter Camp, known as the Father of American Football, was a freshman on this Yale team.

1878 Princeton

Princeton returned to the top with a perfect 6-0 season that included a 7-1 win over 4-1-1 Yale. In 1878, Brown began a football program.

1882 Yale

By 1882, the number of participating colleges had doubled to 14. Some schools fielded unofficial football clubs. At established programs, schedules were often filled with these clubs, plus athletic clubs and high schools. Yale was undefeated at 8-0, including wins over 7-1 Harvard, 7-2 Princeton, and 6-4 Rutgers.

1883 Yale

Changes in scoring (discussed earlier) were now in place. Yale continued its winning ways by outscoring opponents, 485-2. The Eli defeated 7-1 Princeton and 8-2 Harvard on their way to a perfect 8-0 season.

1885 Princeton

In 1885, Princeton was the only undefeated team. The Tigers outscored opponents, 637-25. They beat 7-1 Yale, 6-5. They also defeated 8-5 Penn three times by a combined 213-20.

1887 Yale

Over the previous two years, the number of college teams had grown to 23. California was 4-0 and Michigan 3-0 but against more makeshift competition than in the East. Yale posted a record of 9-0, including wins over 10-1 Harvard and 7-2 Princeton, while outscoring opponents, 515-12.

1888 Yale

Yale continued to win, completing a perfect 13-0 season, outscoring opponents, 694-0, and defeating 11-1 Princeton, 10-0. The Tigers had outscored their other opponents, 609-16. The Eli did not play 12-1 Harvard, but the Crimson's one defeat was an 18-6 loss to Princeton.

1889 Princeton

Princeton's team went 10–0 and outscored opponents, 484–29. Among its victims were 15–1 Yale (10–0) and 9–2 Harvard (41–15).

In 1889, the first consensus All America Team began. The Tigers placed five players on the team: backs Edgar Allen Poe, Roscoe Channing, and Knowleton "Snake" Ames, tackle Hector Cowan, and center William George. Other starters included: ends Sport Donnelly and Ralph Warren, tackle Walter "Monte" Cash, guards House Janeway and Ashbell Newel, and back Jeremiah Black.

1890 Harvard

By 1890, 45 schools had official football programs. Harvard began the new decade by hiring two full-time coaches: George Stewart and George Adams (class of 1884 and 1886, respectively). The Harvard Crimson outscored their opponents, 555–12, including a 77–0 victory over 8–4 Cornell. The last game of the season was a showdown between the 9–0 Crimson and 13–0 Yale, a team that had outscored opponents, 486–18. Harvard won 12–6 to complete a perfect 10–0 season.

Harvard placed five men on the All America Team: backs Dudley Dean and John Corbett, end Frank Hallowell, tackle Marshall Newell, and center John Cranston. Harvard back Everett Lake was openly criticized in the *Boston Globe* for leaving the game with an injury.[1] In those days, players were expected to play an entire game, even when hurt. This mentality certainly contributed to the frequent injuries and deaths that would be addressed a few years later.

1891 Yale

The Yale team of 1891 started the season with an easy schedule that included three athletic clubs and a Y. However, in the last three contests, Yale defeated 11–2 Penn, 13–1 Harvard, and 12–1 Princeton. The Eli, at 13–0, outscored opponents, 488–0.

Yale players named to the All America Team included: back Thomas McClung, ends Frank Hinkey and John Hartwell, tackle Wallace Winter, and guard William "Pudge" Heffelfinger.

Frank Hinkey was known at the time as the "disembodied spirit." Weighing between 148–155 pounds, Hinkey could get through any compact interference to make a tackle. He played end, halfback, and quarterback. He was one of only two four-time All Americas during that era. He later coached at Yale in 1914–1915. Pudge Heffelfinger was a giant for his day at 6'3" and 210 pounds. He was a three-time All America (1889, 1890, 1891) who also coached.

1892 Yale

The following year was almost a repeat for Yale. Smaller schools, four athletic clubs, and a Y opened the season. Again, the last three opponents were 15–1 Penn, 10–1

Harvard, and 13–2 Princeton. The Eli finished 13–0 and outscored opponents, 435–0. Sophomore Frank Hinkey repeated as an All America and was joined by back Vance McCormick and tackle A. Hamilton Wallis.

It is unfortunate that so little is known about these teams. Even the rules by which they played are a bit obscure, often varying between schools. However, this era provided for the rapid spread of the game across the country. Players from the Eastern schools became coaches and helped spread their accumulated knowledge and coaching techniques. Fifty-three players, just from Yale, went on to coach.

Forty-five schools across the country benefited from these early Yale players turned coaches. These included five schools that would eventually produce a unanimous national champion: Notre Dame (1943), Michigan (1948), Southern California (1972 and 2004), Ohio State (2014), and LSU (2019). Many schools hired multiple times from this pool of former Yale players:

Coaches from Yale	*School*
5 coaches	Navy
4 coaches	California
4 coaches	Minnesota
4 coaches	North Carolina
4 coaches	Stanford
3 coaches	Army
3 coaches	Fordham
3 coaches	Lehigh
3 coaches	New York University
2 coaches	Dartmouth
2 coaches	Missouri
2 coaches	Ohio State
2 coaches	Penn
2 coaches	Syracuse
2 coaches	Virginia
2 coaches	Williams

Another 29 schools hired 1 Yale grad to coach.

During that era, 17 Eli All Americas coached at schools other than Yale. In addition, Walter Camp and Howard Jones, plus All Americas Frank Hinkey, T. A. D. Jones, and Edward "Ted" Coy, coached at their alma mater.

Yale All America	*Where Coached*	*Year(s)*
Frank Butterworth	California	1895–1896
Tim Callahan	Colorado School of Mines	1922–1923
Burr Chamberlain	Stanford	1899
Burr Chamberlain	Navy	1903
John DeSaulles	Virginia	1902

Chapter 3. The Early Years

Yale All America	Where Coached	Year(s)
Robert Forbes	Oregon	1908–1909
Charles Gill	Dartmouth	1896
Charles Gill	California	1894
Charles Gill	New Hampshire	1908–1909
John Hartwell	Navy	1893
John Hartwell	New York University	1894
Bill "Pudge" Heffelfinger	California	1893
Bill "Pudge" Heffelfinger	Lehigh	1894
Bill "Pudge" Heffelfinger	Minnesota	1895
Arthur Howe	Trinity University (Texas)	1918
T. A. D. Jones	Syracuse	1909–1910
Bill Knox	Carnegie Tech	1908
Tom McClung	California	1892
Fred Murphy	Missouri	1900–1901
Fred Murphy	Northwestern	1914–1918
Herman Olcott	North Carolina	1902–1903
Herman Olcott	New York University	1907–1912
Bill Rhodes	Western Reserve	1891
Amos Alonzo Stagg	Springfield	1890–1891
Amos Alonzo Stagg	Chicago	1892–1933
Amos Alonzo Stagg	College of the Pacific	1933–1946
Wallie Winter	Minnesota	1893

Chapter 4

Yale 1900

The year 1900 was, technically, the end of the 19th century. However, it's difficult not to envision 1900 as beginning a new century. The 50 years previous had seen the development of many marvels of industrialization. Along with industry, the United States had pushed its borders from the Atlantic to the Pacific with the addition of California (1850), Oregon (1859), and Washington (1889). As the country had spread west, so was college football to follow.

The Game 1900

The first game of "football," played between Princeton and Rutgers on November 6, 1869, most resembled what today we know as soccer. There were 25 players to a side, spread across the width of the field with a front line and a back line. The ball could be advanced by kicking, punching with a fist, or dribbling as in basketball. The ball could be caught in the arms, but a player could not run with it. See Chapter 3 for an account of the game.

In 1876, the Intercollegiate Football Association was established. The first participating schools were Columbia, Harvard, Princeton, and Yale. Harvard was the first to play a modified game where running with the ball was allowed. The Crimson were introduced to this adaptation during a game against McGill University in Quebec. The first evidence of a player running with the ball during a soccer match occurred at the Rugby School, a noted secondary school in England, in 1823. During a scoreless intramural match, with the bell sounding to end the recreation period, William Webb Ellis ran with the ball through and around protesting opponents and scored a goal. This apparently was the beginning of the sport of rugby as played at McGill that day against Harvard. Eventually, the other schools adopted the more rugby style brought to the United States by Harvard.

From the rugby style developed a true "possession" game as opposed to the back-and-forth possession style of soccer. By 1880, the idea of scrimmage and downs was introduced. That same year, it was set that each team would field 11 players: seven players on the line of scrimmage, one quarterback, two halfbacks, and one fullback.

In 1882, it was established that a team was allowed three downs to pick up five yards. A year later, a point system was developed that allowed one point for a safety, two points for a touchdown, four points for the equivalent of a "point after touchdown," and five points for a field goal.

As of 1888, linemen were required to keep their arms in when blocking, and

Chapter 4. Yale 1900

tackling below the waist but above the knees was allowed. These changes along with individual innovations brought about the development of tight formations and set plays as opposed to the more spread-out play of rugby with multiple lateral passes.

Eventually this led to the basic T-formation. Different schools developed their own variations. The sport was evolving but still resembled rugby and, to a lesser extent, soccer. The forward pass would not enter the game until 1906. Teams of 1900 were restricted to rushing the ball. Scrimmage plays around end were used, but rushing the ball between tackles for two to three yards per down was the established offense.

Although rules required seven linemen, the guards and tackles were not required to remain on the line of scrimmage before the ball was snapped. This resulted in the guards-back formation in which the guards were allowed to move into the backfield to set up tight formations with locked arms and the ball carrier protected within. The wedge formations were often in motion (Flying Wedges) before the ball was snapped.

These formations (wedges) moved down the field much like a rugby scrum. Wedge-breakers would hurl themselves into these formations to disrupt the wedge and tackle the ball carrier. Brawn often prevailed over speed and skill. These team formations would advance the ball short distances, as only five yards in three downs was needed to retain possession.

There was no "neutral zone" over the ball. Players were literally nose-to-nose at the

The Yale team of 1894 demonstrates the "Wedge Formation." These deadly formations, with little protective equipment, resulted in numerous injuries and deaths. This type of "mass formation" was outlawed in 1894 (courtesy of Yale Archives).

line of scrimmage. Slugging and kneeing an opponent was common, as were injuries and even deaths. College football was often considered brutal. "Change the rules or banish the game" was a common call that soon would be addressed.

Football was still young in 1900 and much different from the game we know today. The ball was larger and rounder, without definite size specifications. The size of the field had varied over the first 30 years, at one point measuring 165 yards by 100 yards. After 1900, it measured 110 yards by 53⅓ yards, was marked at five-yard intervals and sometimes in a checkered pattern. There were uprights at each end but no end zones. (With the introduction of end zones, the regular field was reduced to the 100 yards we know today, and 120 yards total.) Safety equipment was optional, if not discouraged. However, a player could not wear any metal nor have any protruding from his shoes. Free substitutions were permitted.

Yale had a proud football tradition dating back to 1872. In the 28 years from 1872–1899 the Elis had been named unanimous national champions seven times (1876, 1882, 1883, 1887, 1888, 1891, and 1892) and shared the title another 12 times. In 1900, the Yale football team captain was an extremely prestigious office. He was responsible for scheduling games and practices, finding recruits when necessary, and appointing a coach. After the 1899 season, Francis Gordon Brown was elected Yale Captain for 1900 with much fanfare and congratulatory wishes from Eli alums all over the country. Brown persuaded Malcolm McBride, a 1900 Yale graduate and All America fullback in 1899, to coach the team. He was also privileged to have the help and advice of the Father of American Football, Yale alum Walter Camp (see Appendix A, Walter Camp).

As captain, Brown wrote letters to alumni, describing the previous game, rating

The undefeated 1900 Yale team became a unanimous national champion. Captain and four-time All America guard Francis Gordon Brown is in the center. Seven members of the 1900 Yale team were named All America (courtesy of Yale Archives).

individual and team performance, and seeking additional on-campus coaching help on a weekly basis from former players and coaches. In what appears to have been unprecedented at the time, Brown scheduled a three- or four-week "spring practice" to be held "immediately after the Easter vacation." He also warned players to keep up their academic studies or they would be banned from playing. (See Appendix C, Francis Gordon Brown Letters.)

The Yale team of 1900 boasted at least six first-team consensus All Americas: tackles George Stillman and Ralph Bloomer, center Beau Olcott, quarterback Bill Fincke, halfback George Chadwick, and fullback Perry Hale.[1]

Some sources state that team captain F. Gordon Brown, a guard, had been named first-team All America.[2] It is known that Walter Camp and others (including Casper Whitney) selected Brown an All America all four years he played. Frank Hinkey was the only other four-time All America of that era.[3] In 1900, Yale also placed guard Dick Sheldon and ends Charlie Gould and Sherman Coy on the second-team All America squad and halfback Al Sharpe on third team. With all 11 starters an All America, how could the 1900 Eli team not succeed?

The 1900 Season

Yale breezed through the first seven games of their schedule. With a combined record of 20-26-3, Trinity (Connecticut), Amherst, Tufts, Bates, Dartmouth, Bowdoin, and Wesleyan were outscored, 214–0, by the Elis.

The first true test came in game eight against Columbia. Although the Lions were an unimpressive 3-2-1 going into the Yale game, they had beaten the Elis the year before, featured a duo of dynamic halfbacks, Harold Weekes and All America Bill Morley, and were coached by a crafty Yale grad, Foster Sanford. The game was played on October 27. The week before had seen mostly clear skies with only an occasional sprinkling of rain. Game day had the appearance of ideal football weather, and the Yale team arrived to play in just such conditions. However, the shrewd Sanford had arranged for local fire companies to flood the field. At the same time, he made sure his players were prepared for the conditions. The team practiced on soggy ground and had appropriate footwear for the game.

A year earlier, Harold Weekes had eluded Elis tacklers for a 50-yard touchdown and the Lions' 5-0 victory was their first-ever win over Yale. On the sunken field, Weekes again scored on a long run through the slipping and skidding Elis. Again this year, the conversion was missed but Columbia took a 5-0 lead to halftime. Yale coach Malcolm McBride proved equally resourceful. After seeing the field conditions well before game time, the coach purchased two dozen pairs of shoes at a local store and had a carpenter adapt them with "cleats" for the soggy ground. Fortunately for the Elis, the shoes arrived by halftime. Now on equal footing, Yale scored twice in the second half. Fullback Perry Hale, who wasn't supposed to play after suffering a shoulder sprain in practice that week, scored once, and captain Gordon Brown scored to defeat Columbia, 12-5.[4]

Interestingly, Captain Brown's weekly alumni letter that week to W. C. Rhodes, among other alumni, never mentioned the field condition nor how it had come about. He simply stated that the team "played a poor game in the first half and were in fact outplayed by Columbia."[5]

This type of hijinx, which coach Sanford tried in order to get an advantage, wasn't all that unusual in the early years of college football. When Glenn "Pop" Warner coached Carlisle against Syracuse, he had patches in the shape and color of a football sewn onto the players' jerseys. This made it all but impossible for the Syracuse players to determine who actually was carrying the football. Carlisle's next opponent was Harvard, and the Crimson had assistant coach Harry von Kersburg at the Syracuse game to scout the Indians. The following week Harvard was ready with a deception of its own. Harvard coach Percy Haughton had prepared game balls dyed to perfectly match Harvard's crimson uniforms. After a heated discussion, the game was played with an un-dyed football and with the football-shaped patches removed from the Carlisle jerseys.[6]

Army and Carlisle proved little competition as Yale won handily, 18–0 and 35–0, respectively, and improved to 10–0. However, the Elis' perennial rivals, Princeton and Harvard, remained and appeared formidable. Princeton had outscored their first eight opponents, including: 6–3 Navy, 7–2–1 Syracuse, 9–2 Lafayette, and 7–3–1 Brown by 159–10. Then the Tigers suffered back-to-back loses to 10–2 Cornell (12–0) and 7–3–1 Columbia (6–5).

Princeton's George Mattis drop-kicked a five-point field goal to take the lead.[7] Early in the game, Eli quarterback James Wear committed several fumbles on handoffs and punts. Frustrated by both situations, Yale captain Brown took Wear aside, glared at him, and said something to the effect that he would not play for Yale ever again if he fumbled the ball once more.[8] The fumbling stopped, Yale's rushing attack, spearheaded by tackle Ralph Bloomer's blocking, took over, and Yale prevailed, 29–5. Samuel Clemens, better known as Mark Twain, was in the stands at that Yale-Princeton game and was heard to exclaim, "Those Yale men must be made of granite, like the rocks of Connecticut."[9]

The highly anticipated showdown between Harvard and Yale took place on the Yale campus, November 24, with several thousand Harvard students and alumni travelling to the contest.[10] Both teams were undefeated. Harvard had registered seven shutouts, had outscored their opponents, 205–16, and had handed mighty Penn (12–1) their only loss (17–5). Yale had nine shutouts en route to a 308–10 scoring edge. A comparison of six common opponents found little difference between the two titans.

Harvard and Yale Scores Against Common Opponents

	Harvard	*Yale*
Amherst (4–7–1)	18–0	27–0
Army (7–3–1)	29–0	18–0
Bates (4–3)	41–0	50–0
Bowdoin (7–2)	12–0	30–0
Columbia (7–3–1)	24–0	12–5
Wesleyan (5–4)	24–0	38–0
	148–0	175–5

Harvard was led by sensational quarterback Charles Daly. Walter Camp named Daly first-team All America in 1898 and 1899, and as second-team in 1900 (accounts vary, and Daly may well have been a first-team selection in 1900). In 1901, Daly would enter West Point and again be named first-string All America. The following year, although practicing and playing in only a few games, Daly was named third-string All America. Shortly after, a limit of four years on the All America team was established. Daly would further be remembered for coaching Army to three undefeated seasons, 9–0 in both 1914 and 1916, and 8–0–2 in 1922, and as the founder and first president of the American Football Coaches Association in 1922.

The Harvard and Yale senior players had met on the field several times. In their first meeting in 1897, the Yale freshmen lost to the Harvard freshmen, 54–0. The Harvard varsity went 11–0, defeating the Elis, 17–0, in 1898. The following year, Harvard was 10–0–1 after a 0–0 tie with Yale. In the previous two seasons, the Crimson record was 21–0–1, and the Elis were 16–4–1.

Unfortunately for college football, Charles Daly, the dynamic leader who had led Harvard to 32 consecutive wins, severely injured his knee in practice two weeks before and had sat out the game with Brown (the only game the Crimson struggled to win, 11–5). Accounts differ as to whether Daly actually played against Yale. Rex Fincke (cousin of Yale quarterback W. M. Fincke) is reported to have done a commendable job filling in for Daly, whether for all or part of the contest. It is likely that Daly did see limited play, for as the Harvard captain he would have been able to make on-field decisions only if he were in the game, and several accounts suggest that Daly was responsible for a judgment error early in the contest.

A Crimson punt was fumbled by Yale's Bill Fincke and recovered by Jack Hallowell of Harvard deep in Yale territory. On the play, a Yale end had been off-side, the ball brought back, and a five-yard penalty attached. However, by rule, Harvard could have

The 1900 Harvard-Yale game. A season-ending showdown between these two undefeated teams took place at Yale on November 24. This long-standing rivalry is still known at both schools as "The Game" (courtesy of Yale Archives).

refused the penalty and kept possession of the ball where recovered. Daly did not take advantage of this, losing possession and field position as Harvard re-punted to the Elis.[11]

Bloomer scored a touchdown (five points) to cap a seven-play drive, and Fincke returned a punt for another touchdown. Hale added the extra point to each score as Yale led 12–0 at the half. Early in the third quarter, Chadwick scored from the 16. Coy recovered a fumble and rushed 50 yards for the final Elis touchdown. Sharpe ended the scoring with a field goal (five points) from the 20 as Yale won handily, 28–0.[12]

Beating Harvard was always the highlight of a Yale football season. As the game wore on in Yale's favor, the student section began to chant some derogatory ditties focusing on Harvard's ultimate demise on the field.[13] At a press interview, Harvard coach Benjamin Dibble praised the Yale line, claiming it was one of the best he had ever seen.[14]

An anonymous article suggested that under-conditioning and under-preparedness doomed Harvard. It alleged that Harvard allowed its starters some leeway in training after the game with Penn.[15] However, archrivals Harvard and Yale had played to a scoreless tie in 1899. Considering the rivalry, it's difficult to imagine that the Crimson would take Yale lightly.

It was also suggested that the Yale "tackles back" offense apparently confused the larger and stronger Crimson. According to game records, Yale amassed 531 yards rushing and running back kicks to Harvard's 150 yards. One account stated that the Harvard line held their own but were often drawn offside and otherwise deceived.

Ever the Eastern gentlemen, several Harvard alumni wrote Captain Brown and Yale grad Walter Camp congratulatory letters on a fine season and particularly the win over their beloved Crimson. In no letter was the injury to Daly mentioned, nor excuses made.

Why was Yale Unanimous?

Football at Eastern schools was far ahead of the rest of the country (see table below). As collegiate football expanded, the influence and experience of top Eastern teams was there to meet it. Yale graduates alone accounted for 30 head football coaching jobs across the country before the year 1900. (See Chapter 3 for a list of Yale alums who coached at schools across the country.) Still, these developing programs had few chances to play established teams. With little, if any, extended travel, Eastern schools played Eastern schools, and the calculated schedule strengths reflected this. Yale was the only major undefeated and untied team. Harvard (10–1) had defeated Penn (12–1), and Yale (12–0) had easily defeated Harvard.

Among those teams with superior records, Western (Big Ten) Conference Iowa was 7–0–1, Wisconsin was 8–1, and Minnesota was 10–2. However, the schedule strength was much lower than Harvard, Penn, or Yale. Iowa had played Grinnell (3–6) and non–Division 1A teams Upper Iowa, Northern Iowa, and Simpson, outscoring them 235–2. Minnesota's schedule had five non–Division 1A teams, including two high schools. Wisconsin played against three non–Division 1A school plus Grinnell and Beloit. By contrast, Harvard and Yale each played only one non–Division 1A school, while Penn played two. Harvard's opponents posted a combined 73–31–6 record, while Penn's opponents were 78–40–5 and Yale's were 63–40–8, all against stronger Eastern competition.

Yale was far and away the best college football team in the nation. They deserved to be a unanimous National Champion.

In 1900, football, though important on college campuses, was not the all-consuming passion or big business it has since become. Prestige, big money, and recruiting potential have, at times, made regional bias a major factor in voting a National Champion. In the early 1900s, Walter Camp essentially ran college football. Camp selected the National Champion and All America teams. His word was authority. Camp had been actively engaged in Yale athletics, particularly football, for years. Yale President Arthur Hadley officially appointed Camp Athletic Advisor (a precursor to an Athletic Director) at Yale in 1900. A letter from President Hadley to Captain Brown stated, "You and [Coach] McBride, with the aid of Walter Camp and others, have, in the course of two years, brought Yale athletics back into the old tradition."[16] [Many facts in this book were derived from the Francis Gordon Brown Collection at the Yale Archives.] However, what could be perceived as Camp's conflict of interest doesn't explain the polls and statistical analysis systems that have since emerged to declare their selections retroactively. These have all agreed with the pundits of 1900.

The schools that would officially form the IVY League in 1954 began their football programs well ahead of the rest of the country. The table below lists Division 1A schools and the year they began their football programs.

Start of Division 1A Football Programs

1869	**Princeton**, Rutgers
1870	**Columbia**
1872	Yale
1874	**Harvard**
1876	**Pennsylvania**
1878	**Brown**
1879	Michigan, Navy
1881	**Dartmouth**, Kentucky, Richmond
1882	LaFayette,* Minnesota
1884	Boston University
1885	Denver
1886	California, Northwestern
1887	**Cornell**, Indiana, Notre Dame, Penn State, Purdue
1888	Cincinnati, Duke, North Carolina, Southern California, Virginia, Wake Forest
1889	Iowa, Syracuse, Washington, Wisconsin
1890	Army, Colgate, Colorado, George Washington, Illinois, Kansas, Missouri, Nebraska, Ohio State, Pittsburgh, Vanderbilt, Washington & Jefferson*
1891	Tennessee, VMI, West Virginia
1892	Alabama, Auburn, Chicago, Colorado State, Georgia Tech, Georgia, Iowa State, Maryland, North Carolina State, Stanford, Utah State, Utah, VPI

The Unanimous Champions of College Football, 1869–2019

1893	Boston College, Idaho, <u>LSU</u>, Mississippi, Oregon State, <u>Texas</u>, Tulane, Washington State, William & Mary, Wyoming
1894	Arkansas, New Mexico State, Oregon, South Carolina, Texas A&M, Villanova
1895	Mississippi State, Oklahoma, Tulsa
1896	<u>Clemson</u>, Detroit, Holy Cross, Kansas State, Michigan State, Texas Christian
1897	Arizona State, Hardin-Simmons, Montana State, Wichita
1898	San Jose State
1899	Arizona, Baylor
1900	New Mexico
1901	Furman, Oklahoma State
1902	Marquette
1905	Citadel, Dayton
1906	Florida
1910	West Texas State
1912	Rice
1913	North Texas State
1914	Texas Western
1915	Southern Methodist
1919	Pacific, UCLA
1922	Brigham Young
1925	Texas Tech
1927	<u>Miami (FL)</u>
1946	Houston
1947	<u>Florida State</u>
1956	Air Force

KEY

Date year school first established a football program
Team in Bold: *schools that would form the Ivy League in 1954*
<u>Team Boxed</u> *schools with unanimous National Champion*
*Originally a Division 1A school.

Note: LaFayette was selected co-National Champion in 1896, 1921, and 1926.

CHAPTER 5

Yale 1909

The Transition Years, 1900–1909

From 1900–1909, the game of college football changed dramatically. On October 9, 1905, President Theodore Roosevelt called a meeting of officials from Harvard, Princeton, and Yale to discuss football and, in particular, the brutality, deaths, and injuries that accompanied the game. Initially, little came of that meeting; however, in December 1905, Chancellor Henry M. MacCracken of New York University and Captain Palmer E. Pierce of West Point organized the Intercollegiate Athletic Association of the United States (IAAUS, later the Intercollegiate Athletic Association or ICAA).

The IAASU instituted changes in the rules to increase the safety of players. A neutral zone was established across the line of scrimmage, six players were required on the offensive line of scrimmage (to prevent wedge formations), and hurdling (throwing) a player across an offensive or defensive line was outlawed. To retain possession, the offense would now have to move the ball forward ten yards (instead of five) in three downs. The game was reduced to 60 minutes, more officials were added, player eligibility was tightened to avoid "tramps" and "ringers," and the forward pass was legalized.

Although now legal, the forward pass was highly restricted. It could be thrown only from five yards to either side of center (essentially from tackle to tackle) and behind the line of scrimmage. If a forward pass was not touched by a player of either team before the ball touched the ground, a change of possession would result. If the forward pass did not touch a player of either team, and the ball landed in the end zone, it was a touchback for the defensive team. Only the offensive team could throw a forward pass, and only the two ends on the offensive line were eligible to receive the forward pass. With these restrictions, most coaches considered the forward pass as a waste of a down.

The forward pass was used by various teams as soon as it was legalized. Wesleyan University claims to have completed the first pass on October 3, 1906, for an 18-yard gain against Yale.[1] However, according to a report by rules committee member and football historian Parke Davis, the Eastern schools resisted this addition to the offensive game. In 1911, after a vote outlawed the pass, Southern and Midwestern schools threatened to abandon the ICAA Rules Committee and establish their own rules of play. In a hurried re-vote, IAAUS president Edward Hall, who had opposed the forward pass, changed his vote. The forward pass was saved, and so too was the ICAA as a national organization.[2]

In 1913 it was demonstrated that the forward pass could be utilized as a potent offensive weapon. When a small Midwestern school called Notre Dame defeated powerful Army, 35–13, behind the brilliant passing of quarterback Gus Dorais to end Knute Rockne, football players and coaches took notice. But, although approved in 1906, the forward pass was still used sparingly as of 1909. Rushing the ball still dominated offensive play. The main focus of the rules changes implemented in 1906 was to open up the offense and eliminate the deadly wedge-type formations.

Another modification in 1906 involved the on-side kick (formerly called the quarterback kick). The kicking team could now retain possession if they recovered the ball after it hit the ground. Previously, the kicking team was allowed to retain possession only after the ball had touched a member of the opposing team. This was an important offensive strategy at the time. In the early years of the 1900s, the ball was larger, rounder, and more difficult to handle. Teams often kicked on first down to improve field position and not to risk a fumble deep in their own territory. In 1909, points awarded for a field goal (drop-kick) were reduced from five to three.

The 1909 Season

Following its unanimous National Championship season of 1900, Yale continued its winning tradition. From 1901–1908, the Elis produced a record of 78–4–5 while outscoring their opponents, 1801–145 (or 20.7 to 1.7 points per game).

Yale Football Summary 1901–1908

Year	Record	Loss	Tie	# Yale AAs
1901	11–1–1	Harvard	Army	1
1902	11–0–1	—	Army	7
1903	11–1–0	Princeton	—	2
1904	10–1–0	Army	—	3
1905	10–0–0	—	—	3
1906	9–0–1	—	Princeton	4
1907	9–0–1	—	Army	3
1908	7–1–1	Harvard	Brown	2
	78–4–5			

There were a few pundits at the time, but later systems, polls, and other authorities have retroactively announced their choice for national champions going back decades. However, it was deemed that the Elis' records over the years 1901 to 1908 fell short of a greatness worthy of being unanimous. Yale could boast no share of a national title (a vote by any of the pundits, polls or mathematical systems) in 1903, 1904, or 1908. In four years, 1901, 1902, 1905, and 1906, they shared the title, but only for the vote of Parke Davis (who split his vote in 1902). Again, in 1907, they were the consensus choice, with only Richard Billingsley's Power Rating System selecting Penn.

Edward "Ted" Coy was elected captain for the 1909 team. He recruited former Yale player Tad Jones, who had coached Syracuse in 1908, to coach the Elis. As was the custom at the time, Coy also asked around 70 former players to help occasionally with coaching. And, of course, the team had Walter Camp to advise them. It is said that success breeds success. Success was certainly expected of the returning players, recruits, and hopefuls who reported to Coach Jones for their first official practice on Monday,

Chapter 5. Yale 1909

September 20. Their first game against Wesleyan University of Middleton, Connecticut, would be the following Saturday. Wesleyan had officially dropped football in 1905, but still hosted a football Club that went 3–5–1 in 1909. Yale won their home opener, 11–0.

The following week, the Eli traveled to 4–5–1 Syracuse University, now coached by Howard Jones, Tad's brother. Both Joneses had played on Yale's 10–0 team of 1905, which had outscored opponents, 227–4. Syracuse had a strong team in 1908. Although 6–3–1, they had allowed only 38 points all season and ended with a 28–4 win over Michigan. But graduation had hit hard and it was a rebuilding year.[3] Tad Jones and the Elis prevailed, 15–0. Howard Jones went on to coach at Yale, Ohio State, Iowa, Duke, and Southern California, compiling a 193–63–20 record. His greatest success came at Southern California, where his teams won eight Pacific Coast Conference titles, were 5–0 in Rose Bowls, and were declared the National Champion by one or more selectors in 1928, 1932, and 1939.

Yale would next play three games within eight days. On October 9, they traveled to 2–4–2 Holy Cross College, defeating the Crusaders, 12–0. Four days later, the Elis hosted 5–1 Springfield College and handed the Maroons their only loss of the season, 36–0. The third game was played October 16, on the usually unfriendly field at West Point. From 1901–1907, Army had proven to be the thorn in Yale's side. The Cadets had beaten Yale once and tied three times. The loss in 1904 and two ties, in 1902 and 1907, had ruined otherwise perfect seasons for the Elis.

Yale captain Edward "Ted" Coy, a bruising, six-foot, 195-pound fullback and a first team All America in 1907 and 1908, underwent an appendectomy before the season and

1909 Yale Captain Edward "Ted" Coy drop-kicking. Coy was an excellent kicker in an era when the kicking game was an important strategy for maintaining field position as well as scoring. The checkerboard pattern on the field was common at the time (courtesy of Yale Archives).

missed the first four games. After Yale recovered a blocked Army punt for a touchdown and the lead, the Cadets came back strong and threatened to score. Coy pleaded to go in the game. He was allowed to play under the condition that he limit his play to kicking and passing.[4] Coy's return helped Yale win its fifth contest, 17–0, over the 3–2 Cadets.

Now halfway through the season, it was obvious that the Elis were something special. For its day, the Yale line was huge, averaging 209 pounds from tackle to tackle. Guard Hamlin Andrus (208 lbs.), Tackle Henry Hobbs (208), center Carroll Cooney (232), and end John Reed Kilpatrick were named to the All America team that year. Andrus had been an All America in 1908.

With Coy now healthy to run over defenders up the middle and fellow All America Stephen Philbin running behind this star-studded line, the Elis were again rolling easily. Yale lineman, John Reed Kilpatrick, later stated that the Yale team of 1909 was never challenged and never played up to their potential.[5]

Yale opened the second half of the season with another stretch of three games in eight days. The Eli played a pair of home games, the first against Colgate on October 30, followed by Amherst on November 3. Colgate was 2–1 and, after an initial 14–0 loss to Brown, had outscored its last two opponents, 106–0. Amherst would end the season a dismal 1–6–1. The Elis won both convincingly, 36–0 and 34–0. Three days later the squad traveled to Brown, then 5–2. The Bruins had defeated its first four opponents by 47–0. They then lost consecutive games to perennial powerhouse Penn (having an off-year at 7–1–2) and Harvard (then 4–0 with three shutouts) before rebounding with a 12–3 victory over Massachusetts. Again, Yale dominated, 23–0. Brown ended the season at 7–3.

Yale's two toughest opponents lay ahead. These final two home games would test their mettle and determine their legacy. Since 1900, Princeton had defeated the Elis only once (in 1903). But the past three years had resulted in a 0–0 tie and slim Yale victories by 12–10 and 11–6. This year the Elis juggernaut thoroughly dominated the Tigers, 17–0.

Ted Coy's brother, Sherman, had played on Yale's 1900 unanimous National Championship team. It may never be known if the similarities and parallels between the 1900 and 1909 seasons were realized by Sherman and Ted Coy. Both came down to the final game, both times against archrival Harvard. Each year, both teams were undefeated. Both teams were excellent and contained All America talent. The legacy of both these Yale teams would be decided by what came to be known each year, on both campuses, as "The Game."

Unlike the contest in 1900, this game would not to be decided by an injury to a key player or a suspected lapse in conditioning. Both teams were at their peak and played to a virtual stalemate. Harvard fielded a line equal to Yale's. Led by two-time All America tackle Hamilton Fish, the Crimson held the Elis to just two first downs. General Dan Sultan, who attended the game, praised both teams and claimed it was the best line play he had ever seen.[6]

It was, from all accounts, a great defensive struggle. The Yale line featured John Kilpatrick, Henry Hobbs, Hamlin Andrus, Carroll Cooney, William Goebel, Theodore Lilley, and Edward Savage. The Harvard front consisted of Gilbert Browne, Hamilton Fish, Robert Fisher, Lothrop Withington, Paul Withington, Robert McKay, and Lawrence Smith. Yale never penetrated beyond the Harvard 16-yard line, and the Crimson got no closer than the Eli 25-yard line.[7] During an interview in 1953, Yale All America end John Kilpatrick claimed Yale had difficulty running against Harvard. The Elis, as was common at the time, would kick on any down for field position and hoped Harvard would make a mistake.[8]

Chapter 5. Yale 1909

Ultimately Yale's strategy worked, and the contest was won by the kicking game. In the early part of the 20th century, kicking was a strategic weapon in football. In that game, Coy's high punts kept Harvard pinned in their own territory, and some were fumbled and lost, giving Yale excellent field position. Coy made two of four field goal attempts, and Yale forced a safety to win, 8–0. It should be noted that Ted Coy drop-kicked field goals using the instep instead of the toe. He therefore preceded Cornell's Pete Gogolak and the soccer style of kicking by over 50 years.

A Harvard account states that the Crimson outrushed the Elis by 225 yards to 100 yards. It further states that coach Percy Haughton's "mouse-trap" play consistently gained 15 to 20 yards for Harvard, and on five such plays, umpire Bill Edwards of Princeton claimed Harvard was holding, nullifying the gains and penalizing them 15 yards. The penalties were said to have had a disheartening effect on the Crimson.[9]

Yale was now undefeated, untied, and unscored-upon. Coy and the other seniors would leave Yale having achieved a four-year record of 35–1–3.

Of the nine opponents (Wesleyan, Syracuse, Holy Cross, Springfield, Army, Colgate, Brown, Princeton, and Harvard) whose game scores were found, Yale accounted for 37.2 percent of the points scored against these opponents. They held all these teams scoreless, teams which collectively averaged 12.8 points per game.

Yale's defense in 1909 was phenomenal. Accurate records are difficult to find, however, three different accounts agree that no team even advanced close to the Yale end zone. They differ slightly in how close any opponent came to scoring on the Elis, varying from 20 to 28 yards away.[10]

The undefeated and unscored-on 1909 Yale team did not allow any opponent within 25 yards of the Yale goal line. Captain Ted Coy is in the center. Six Yale players were named All America that year (courtesy of Yale Archives).

Of the 11 consensus All America players selected that year, only two were not from a school that would later be part of the Ivy League: back John McGovern of Minnesota and guard Albert Benbrook of Michigan. The Yale squad placed six men on the All America first team: backs Stephen Philbin and Edward "Ted" Coy, end John Kilpatrick, tackle Henry Hobbs, guard Hamlin Andrus, and center Carroll Cooney. Back Wayland Minot and tackle Hamilton Fish of Harvard, and end Adrien Regnier of Brown completed the first-team All America squad.

As football spread across the country, the domination of Eastern football declined, particularly the future Ivy League schools, which had ruled, practically unopposed, for so long. The table below traces the decline of All America selections from the Ivy League and Eastern schools to other areas of the country.

Decline in Percentage Consensus All America Players from the Ivy League and Eastern Schools

	All Eastern	*Big Four*	*All IVY*	*Expanded East*	*AAs*
1889–1894	100	100	100	0	11
1895	91	100	100	0	11
1896–1897	100	100	100	0	11
1898	73	73	87	13	15
1899	92	92	100	0	13
1900	73	87	100	0	15
1901	56	78	94	6	18
1902	77	92	100	0	13
1903	60	80	87	13	15
1904	60	67	80	20	15
1905	69	75	88	12	16
1906	69	88	94	6	16
1907	69	69	94	6	16
1908	53	71	88	12	17
1909	73	82	82	18	11
1910	64	73	73	27	11
1911	73	73	100	0	11
1912	64	82	91	9	11
1913	40	47	67	33	15
1914	37	58	68	32	19
1915	17	33	61	39	18
1916	25	31	69	31	16
1917	0	0	36	73	11
1918	13	13	62	38	16
1919	14	21	50	50	14
1920	28	28	56	44	18
1921	18	27	55	45	11

	All Eastern	Big Four	All IVY	Expanded East	AAs
1922	27	36	64	36	11
1923	27	45	64	36	11
1924	11	28	44	56	18
1925	14	36	50	50	14
1926	6	13	38	62	16
1927	31	31	46	54	13
1928	7	7	40	60	15
1929	7	7	29	71	14
1930	13	13	19	81	16
1931	7	7	21	79	14
1932	0	0	25	75	16
1933	8	8	15	85	13
1934	0	0	13	87	16
1935	7	7	7	93	15
1936	7	7	27	73	15
1921	18	27	55	45	11
1922	27	36	64	36	11
1923	27	45	64	36	11
1924	11	28	44	56	18
1925	14	36	50	50	14
1926	6	13	38	62	16
1927	31	31	46	54	13
1928	7	7	40	60	15
1929	7	7	29	71	14
1930	13	13	19	81	16
1931	7	7	21	79	14
1932	0	0	25	75	16
1933	8	8	15	85	13
1934	0	0	13	87	16
1935	7	7	7	93	15
1936	7	7	27	73	15

1. The big four schools that dominated the early years of college football: Harvard, Penn, Princeton, Yale
2. The Big Four schools plus the other schools which now form the Ivy League: Brown, Columbia, Cornell, Dartmouth
3. Eastern Schools: Schools in the New England states plus Maryland, New Jersey, New York, Pennsylvania
4. Number of consensus AA players listed for that year

In his book, *Yale's Ironmen*, William Wallace lists his reasons for the decline of Ivy League schools' football prestige. He believes the decline in attendance at games can be attributed to a change of culture and the presence of professional football. Wallace further believes that the 1954 establishing of the Ivy League was meant to emphasize education over football by its members: Brown, Columbia, Cornell, Dartmouth, Harvard, Pennsylvania, Princeton, and Yale.[11]

Arkansas and Colorado were the only other two undefeated teams of 1909. Quality football teams across the country were still few and far between. Unlike established Eastern programs, packed in a relatively tight geographic area, Western schools filled schedules however they could. This is reflected in the various mathematical methods employed, such as the Sorensen system. According to Sorensen, the strength of Yale's opponents was 3447 (11th-most difficult schedule), while Arkansas' opponents' strength was calculated at -673 and Colorado's was a dismal -4473.

Of more established teams with loss or tie blemishes on their records, Michigan's opponents registered 3585, #9 and 138 points more difficult than the Elis. Yale and Michigan were #1 and #2 when registering team strength (7043 and 6798), but the Wolverines had a loss to 6-3-1 Notre Dame.

Of other worthy contender, Yale had defeated Harvard and Princeton head-to-head. Penn at 7-1-2 had a loss (to Michigan) and two ties. Pitt at 6-2-1 had losses to Notre Dame and Penn State, and a tie to West Virginia. Texas A&M (7-0-1) suffered a tie with 5-2-1 TCU and had a much lower strength of opposition rating in the still-developing West.

The 1909 Yale eleven were 10-0, unscored-on, and had handed Springfield College, Princeton, and Harvard their only defeats of the season. All "experts" voted the Elis as National Champions for the second time in ten years.

Chapter 6

Georgia Tech 1917

Football has seen many great coaches. Often, over the years, these coaches and their triumphs become a distant memory until, at last, they are all but forgotten. However, thanks to the trophy in his name, John Heisman is remembered yearly. It should be noted that although Heisman was a successful and innovative coach, the trophy was named in his honor because of his affiliation with the Downtown Athletic Club of New York City. Heisman was named the club's first Athletic Director in 1930, after his coaching career had ended. The Downtown Athletic Club honors its selection of the outstanding player in college football and awards that player the coveted Heisman Trophy.

Heisman was a student and historian of football. As one of many contributors to the 1934 book, *Intercollegiate Football, 1869–1934*, he broke down the history of the game into the "Stone Age" and the "Steel Age." The Stone Age, from 1869 to 1906, was a dangerous time for college footballers. Mass formations such as the "Flying wedge," combined with lack of protective gear, few rules, and fewer officials, caused an alarming number of deaths and injuries.

Prompted by no fewer than 23 football deaths in 1905, the next year President Theodore Roosevelt demanded that the game be revised or outlawed. Heisman considered the years 1906–1912 to be transition years. The forward pass, first legalized with very restrictive rules in 1906, was the most important change toward opening the game from dangerous mass formations. By 1912, rule changes, as well as trial and error, had opened the passing game to where football resembled the "modern" game as played in 1934. Heisman never actually stated that 1912–1934 was the Steel Age; however, he did assert that players in the transition years (1906–1912) be linked with the Stone Age.

In his book, *Football's Greatest Coaches*, Edwin Pope maintains that a forward pass and subsequent touchdown was allowed to stand by officials in an 1895 game between North Carolina and Georgia (coached by Pop Warner). The pass was, in fact, a desperate attempt by a retreating North Carolina punter to get rid of the ball in the face of charging Bulldogs defenders. A North Carolina teammate caught the ball and ran unmolested 70 yards for a touchdown. The Tar Heels won the game (6–0) over the protests of Warner. John Heisman, a spectator and advocate for a safer game, viewed the "pass" as a way to change the dangerous, wedge-style offense.[1]

Heisman began petitioning Walter Camp and the Football Rules Committee, but the old guard resisted approving the pass until 1906. In that year, Heisman, supported by Penn's John Bell, Navy coach Paul Dashiell, Amos Alonzo Stagg, and the pressure of President Roosevelt's ultimatum, succeeded in changing the rules to allow the forward pass.

John Heisman has been described, among other adjectives, as arrogant. In a different article (one of three) he penned for *Intercollegiate Football, 1869–1934*, he detailed the evolution of the game. Below is his list of the top 10 innovative coaches up to that time:

Primary School Coach	*Coached*	*# of Innovations*
Knute Rockne	Notre Dame	1
Fielding "Hurry up" Yost	Michigan	2
Percy Haughton	Harvard	3
Robert Zuppke	Illinois	4
George Woodruff	Penn	4
Harry Williams	Minnesota	5
Glenn "Pop" Warner	Carlisle / Stanford	5
Walter Camp	Yale / Stanford	7
Amos Alonso Stagg	Chicago	7
John Heisman	Georgia Tech	11

Despite his apparent self-promotion, various sources do credit Heisman with several early football innovations, including: the center snap as opposed to rolling the ball to the quarterback, the "hike" signal to initiate the play, the "Heisman Shift" offense, the hidden ball play, placing pertinent information (the down, yardage needed for a first down, etc.) on scoreboards, and dividing the game into quarters instead of halves. Although acknowledging Heisman's contributions to football, Pope maintains that the number of innovations by Amos Alonzo Stagg, Pop Warner, and Walter Camp place them ahead of Heisman.[2]

As an attorney and Shakespearian actor, Heisman brought an eloquence to his coaching. Among his most popular phrases, a football became "an elongate sphere" and a lesson on how to tackle became "grasp them about the knees and deprive them of their means of propulsion." He also had a number of "dos" and especially "don'ts," many about handling the football, and one universal admonishment: "Better to have died as a small boy than to fumble this football."[3]

Heisman had "Basic Rules" for playing the game, and these are a good summary of football strategy at that time. Heisman believed you should:

Punt on any down to maintain field position.
Punt if close to your own end zone.
Do not wear out your punter by having him run the ball.
Do not wear out any one man, but divide the runs among them.
End runs are good on occasion, but never two in a row.
End runs are not good close to your own goal.
End runs are most effective on first or second down.
Passes are best on third down, but should be used sparingly.
Don't pass if the ball is inside your 35-yard line.
If a substitute comes in or you find a weak spot, exploit it.
If you are down by the fourth quarter and have not been able to run, pass 3 out of 4 downs.[4]

In the early years of the game, maintaining field position through punting, even on first down, was considered crucial. Michigan's Fielding "Hurry Up" Yost is considered the first to adapt this strategy.

In 1916, Heisman's 13th year as head coach at Georgia Tech, his Tornado or Golden Tornado (as the team was then known) crushed Cumberland College, 222–0, in a mercifully shortened game. [In four seasons, Cumberland was 0–10 and was outscored, 750–0.]

Two reasons for the rout have been proposed. Supposedly Heisman became envious when he thought Cumberland's coach Dan McGugin, while coaching Vanderbilt the year before, had run up some scores against weak competition and was rewarded with publicity and renown.[5] Another version claims it occurred because of a baseball game between the two schools. Heisman, who also coached baseball, was irked the previous year when Cumberland beat Georgia Tech, 22–0.[6] Heisman carefully plotted his revenge. He promised Cumberland a paid roundtrip to Georgia Tech and a $500 guarantee.

It seems logical that the reasons in both accounts could have played a role, and it certainly helps to highlight the coach's character. A fierce competitor, at halftime, leading 126–0, Heisman famously told his team, "Men, don't let up. You never know what those Cumberland players have up their sleeves."[7] Heisman was criticized for the score, and to his critics he replied that the Cumberland game showed how easy it was to run up a score in an easy game.[8]

The 1917 Season

In 1917, some schools had dropped football, including Georgia, North Carolina, George Washington, Arizona State, Virginia, Tennessee, and Princeton, as young men were needed for the war effort. A few players from Georgia Tech enlisted, but the majority of the team remained. Entering 1917, Georgia Tech was riding a 17-0-2 streak dating back to 1914. During 1915 and 1916, Tech was 15-0-2 while outscoring opponents, 654–44. Optimism was high for 1917.

The Golden Tornado opened the season with two conference shutout wins, Wake Forest (1–6–1) and Furman (3–5), by a combined 58–0. This was impressive as both games were played on the same day (September 29, 1917), with Heisman splitting his squad.

Position	Usual Starters	Furman	WF
Center	Phillips	Johnson	Phillips
Guards	Dowling	Welchel	Dowling
	Fincher	Wright	Thweatt
Tackles	Welchel	Higgins	Fincher
	Thweatt	Doyle	Rogers
Ends	Carpenter	Ulrich	Carpenter
	Guill	Concord	Bell
QB	Hill	Hill	Hill
HBs	Strupper	Smith	Strupper
	Guyon	Shaver	Guyon
FB	Harlan	Harlan	Armsley

A heavy rain marred field conditions during the first game with Furman. Hay was placed on the field to little avail. Furman was considered the weaker of the two teams, and Heisman played mostly subs. Al Hill, who quarterbacked both games, scored two touchdowns in the 25–0 win. Although considered the weaker of the two, the following week Furman defeated Wake Forest, 7–6.

In the second game of the day, with the heavy rain reduced to a sprinkle, the Tornado defeated Wake Forest, 33–0. Everett Strupper carried the ball nine times for 198 yards and three touchdowns. Joe Guyon added the other two touchdowns. Guyon had played for the Carlisle Indians in 1912 and 1913, the first year teaming with All America Jim Thorpe. Carlisle was then coached by the legendary Pop Warner.

The following week, perennial Eastern power Pennsylvania, with star quarterback and future NFL Commissioner Bert Bell, invaded Grant Field. Penn had a proud football history featuring six shared national championships (1894, 1895, 1897, 1904, 1907, and 1908). In those championship years, the Quakers went 75–1–1 with four perfect seasons. However, from 1909–1916 they had been a mediocre 50–24–8 and only 20–14–5 from 1913–1916.

Penn's notoriety as a top-notch program brought a huge crowd to Grant Field. Heisman played his normal starters. But once again it was hardly a contest. By halftime,

The Penn-Georgia Tech football game of 1917. In the early 1900s, Penn was a powerful football program, and this game was the first time an Eastern power played in the South. Georgia Tech won, 41–0 (permission of the Georgia Institute of Technology Library and Information Center, Archives and Records Management Department).

Georgia Tech had outgained the Quakers, 276 yards to 11 yards and had allowed Penn no first downs.

Tech continued their defensive dominance in the second half. After five pass completions by Penn got them to the Georgia Tech 6-yard line, the Quakers, after four plays, were backed up to the Georgia Tech 25, where Tech took over. In the fourth period, Judy Harlan intercepted a Penn pass and ran 68 yards for the last score in a 41–0 win. Penn coach Bob Folwell declared Georgia Tech the best team in the country and predicted that no team could or would beat them.[9]

Right from the season opener, the backfield of quarterback Albert Hill, halfbacks Joe Guyon and Everett Strupper, and fullback Judy Harlan ran Heisman's (then legal) "jump shift" off both "I" and "T" formations with great success. Football historian Bernie McCarty makes a strong case for rating the 1917 Georgia Tech backfield better than the famed Four Horsemen backfield of Notre Dame's 1924 squad.[10]

In their fourth outing, small Davidson College of North Carolina provided the only real challenge for Tech. Wildcats freshman Buck Flowers gave Davidson a 3–0 lead on a drop-kick field goal. Flowers would transfer to Georgia Tech and play for the Tornadoes from 1918 to 1920, earning honors on several All America and All Conference teams. Hill scored to make it 6–3 at the half. Tech then scored 13 points in each of the last two quarters for a 32–10 win. A pass reception for a touchdown by Hill, two touchdown runs by Strupper and, for the second straight week, an interception return for a touchdown by Harlan ended the Tech scoring. A Davidson touchdown pass from

The Georgia Tech power backfield of 1917 has been compared with the Four Horsemen of Notre Dame (1924). From left to right: Joe Guyon, Albert Hill, Strup Strupper, and Judy Harlan (permission of the Georgia Institute of Technology Library and Information Center, Archives and Records Management Department).

quarterback Henry Spann to end George King late in the game brought the Wildcats score to 10.

In a year when Tech defeated all opponents by an average of nearly 53 points, Davidson's 22-point loss was noteworthy and makes one wonder why their record was only 6–4. Tech made 16 first downs in the game to 13 by Davidson. Georgia Tech center Phillips was unable to play and was replaced by Bill Fincher. Fincher was a versatile lineman who managed to play at Georgia Tech for five years (1916–1920) because of the war. He was named All-Southern Conference as a guard in 1917, as an end in 1918, and as a tackle in 1920. Although the Georgia Tech team photo of 1917 includes 22 or more players, Fincher has stated that only 13 players were ever used, 11 starters and two substitutes.[11]

This statement appears unlikely. As shown previously, Heisman needed all players in the season openers when Georgia Tech played Wake Forest and Furman on the same day. Also, with many high-score shutouts, playing subs would seem logical. Heisman had said he liked to have at least 21 points before playing subs.[12] Then again, Heisman was not above running up scores.

Heisman would probably have been wary of their next opponent, Washington and Lee. From 1912–1916, the Generals had an overall record of 37–5–3, including a 7–7 tie with Georgia Tech in 1916, in the firstever meeting between the two schools. Washington and Lee averaged 25 points per game over that stretch while allowing only 4.2 points per game. Strupper only played in the first half but still managed 128 yards rushing and a touchdown. Hill scored four times and Guyon three times. Phillips intercepted a pass and returned it for a touchdown as the Tornado prevailed, 63–0.

The following week, Vanderbilt, which was 16–2 over the previous two seasons, gave up 83 points (of its season total 170 points allowed) to Tech in a shutout. The entire starting backfield had a field day. Joe Guyon was reported to have carried the ball nine times for 124 yards, completed four passes for 80 yards, and returned a pair of kickoffs for another 98 yards. Strupper gained 147 yards on 14 rushes and four touchdowns. He also returned punts for over 100 yards. Hill rushed 25 times for 169 yards and three touchdowns, and Harlan had 15 rushes for 132 yards and two touchdowns.

After a number of mediocre seasons, including a 45–0 drubbing by Georgia Tech the year before, the Tulane Green Wave began 1917 by shutting out four small schools by 130–0 before succumbing to Texas A&M, 35–0. A&M would end the season at 9–0, scoring 270 points while recording nine shutouts. The season would get no better for the Green Wave as Tech recorded another shutout, 48–0. All four of Georgia Tech's backs ran for over 100 yards. Guyon passed for 91 yards and two touchdowns while rushing for 112 yards and another score. Hill amassed 140 yards on 24 rushes and a touchdown. Strupper rushed for 118 yards and a touchdown and scored again on a pass reception. Harlan rushed for 111 yards. Fincher, who kicked extra points, had his streak of 31 PATs without a miss ended in the third quarter.

From 1903–1913, the Carlisle Indians were a powerhouse football program that went 108–26–5 over those 11 seasons. However, the program had declined, and the years 1914–1916 saw an 8–19–3 record. In 1917, after a 3–5 season, the Indians cancelled football. In game eight, Georgia Tech overpowered them, 98–0. Of the 14 touchdowns recorded by Tech, Strupper and Hill each had four or five (depending on the source).

The season finale was against Auburn, a team with a 33–5–2 record (3–2 against Georgia Tech) over the previous five seasons. Georgia Tech wasted little time or energy

Chapter 6. Georgia Tech 1917

beating the Tigers, 68–7. Auburn would give up 112 points in 1917, 99 of those coming from Tech (68 points) and little Davidson College (31 points) that gave the Golden Tornado a struggle in game four. Although Auburn scored 185 points in the season, Georgia Tech and Davidson allowed them only 13 points combined.

In 1917, game and individual statistics were inconsistent if they were even kept. Estimates of existing game stats and best guesstimates of others:

Player	Total Yards	Yards / carry
Everett Strupper	1150 yards	10+ yds. / carry
Joe Guyon	800 yards	7.4 yds. / carry
Albert Hill	760 yards	5.4 yds. / carry
Judy Harlan	480 yards	5.8 yds. / carry

As suggested by Bernie McCarty's article, a comparison is made here between Georgia Tech's 1917 backfield and that of the Four Horsemen backfield of Notre Dame's 1924 squad.

The rushing stats for Notre Dame's Four Horsemen team of 1924:

Player	Total Yards	Yards / carry
Don Miller	794 yards	6.4 yds. / carry
Jim Crowley	742 yards	5.6 yds. / carry
Elmer Layden	445 yards	3.7 yds. / carry
Harry Stuhldreher	19 yards	1.0 yds. / carry

Comparisons of teams or backfields in different years is inexact. Although these two teams were only seven seasons apart, their coaches' game strategies and offensive formations were quite different. Heisman employed his "shift" to focus on the running game and often punted to maintain field advantage. Notre Dame's Knute Rockne used a much more open offense. Quarterback Harry Stuhldreher amassed 520 yards passing, while Georgia Tech's quarterback Albert Hill was very much used in the running game. Both teams went undefeated against very respectable competition. It is safe to say that both backfields were the best of their day. Any further comparison is pointless.

Walter Camp named All America teams from 1889 until his death in 1924. Because of World War I, Camp did not name a team in 1917. Later All America teams by other sources differ slightly, but halfback Everett Strupper and tackle Walker Carpenter are usually included. In subsequent years, Camp placed end Bill Fincher and center Ashel Day on All America squads. Some sources also list halfback/tackle Joe Guyon as an All America.

There were five undefeated teams in 1917 (Denver, Georgia Tech, Mare Island Marines, Pittsburgh, and Texas A&M) and all, therefore, can lay claim to the national championship. A&M was the only unscored-on team, but their offensive production fell dramatically (only 106 of their 270 points) against six larger schools. The overall record of their opponents was 25-25-3. Denver (9-0) outscored opponents, 226- 45, but the competition was weak with a combined record of 17-34-4. Likewise, the Mare Island Marines (8-0) outscored a weak schedule (12-21-3 combined record) by 200-10. The

Ohio State (8–0–1) opponents' record was a more respectable 25–16–3. The Buckeyes outscored opponents, 292–6, but a 0–0 tie with Auburn, a team Georgia Tech beat handily, 68–7, should diminish their claim to the national title consideration.

The Sorensen System, which I respect and refer to frequently in this book, ranks Ohio State the top team and as having the 4th-most difficult schedule. In fact, Sorensen ranks Georgia Tech at #14, with 4–2–1 Wisconsin (2nd-most difficult schedule) and 3–2–1 Chicago (9th-most difficult) ahead of the Golden Tornado.

Another undefeated team was 9–0 Pittsburgh. For the season, Georgia Tech outscored the Panthers, 491–230, but other stats are similar: points allowed (Pitt 21, Georgia Tech 17), opponents' overall record (Georgia Tech 41–34–2, Pitt 42–21–2). However, against one common opponent, Penn, Georgia Tech prevailed, 41–0, while Pitt survived, 14–6.

As in so many years before a playoff system was developed and implemented, a case can be made for other teams. For 1917, all (of necessity) retroactive polls favored The Golden Tornado.

CHAPTER 7

Notre Dame 1943

A Brief History of Notre Dame Football

The Fighting Irish of Notre Dame have one of the proudest and longest-lasting traditions of football excellence. Notre Dame football began in 1887. Over the first three years and without a coach, the Fighting Irish, as they would later be called, posted a record of 2–3, with all three losses to Michigan. During the first two decades the team was known as the Catholics and after that the Ramblers; the nickname Fighting Irish was officially adopted in 1927.

No football was played there in 1890–1891. The game was resumed in 1892. Beginning in 1894, the team had an official coach, J. L. Morrison, who stayed 1 year and posted a 3–1–1 season. A series of coaches then followed:

Coach	Year(s)	Record	National Champions
H.G. Hadden	1895	3–1–0	
Frank E. Hering	1896–1898	12–6–1	
James McWeeney	1899	6–3–1	
Patrick O'Dea	1900–1901	14–4–2	
James Faragher	1902–1903	14–2–2	
Louis Salmon	1904	5–3–0	
Henry McGlew	1905	5–4–0	
Thomas Barry	1906–1907	12–1–1	
Victor M. Place	1908	8–1–0	
Frank C. Longman	1909–1910	11–1–2	
John L. Marks	1911–1912	13–0–2	
Jesse C. Harper	1913–1917	34–5–1	
Knute Rockne	1918–1930	105–12–5	1919, 1920, 1924, 1927, 1929, 1930
"Hunk" Anderson	1931–1933	16–9–2	
Elmer Layden	1934–1940	47–13–3	1938
Frank Leahy	1941–1943	24–3–3	1943 (Unanimous)
Ed McKeer	1944	8–2–0	
Hugh Devore	1945	7–2–1	
Frank Leahy	1946–1953	63–8–6	1946, 1947, 1949, 1953
Terry Brennan	1954–1958	32–18–0	

Note that to this point, no coach had a losing record

| Joe Kuharich | 1959–1962 | 17–23–0 | |
| Hugh Devore | 1963 | 2–7–0 | |

[Devore's overall record was 9–9–1]

Ara Parseghian	1964–1974	95–17–4	1964, 1966, 1967, 1970, 1973
Dan Devine	1975–1980	53–16–1	1977
Gerry Faust	1981–1985	30–26–1	
Lou Holtz	1986–1996	100–30–2	1988, 1989, 1993
Bob Davie	1997–2001	35–25–0	
Tyrone Willingham	2002–2004	21–15–0	
Charlie Weis	2005–2009	35–27–0	
Brian Kelly	2010–	71–36–0*	

The NCAA required Notre Dame to vacate 21 wins from the 2012–2013 seasons because of ineligible players.

In these "middle years" from 1900–1999, Notre Dame had one unanimous championship team and shared the title 20 more times, 10 times as the consensus champion. That is the most selections by any college team. The Irish share with Michigan the distinction of having a national champion in nine out of the 10 decades through the 1900s.

From 1887–1999, Notre Dame teams have been undefeated 11 times, and unbeaten but tied another nine times. One of each of these is dubious, as the 1889 team was undefeated playing only one game (at Northwestern), and the unbeaten team of 1892 played only two games, one a 56–0 win over South Bend High School.

In 1913, Notre Dame roommates and best friends, quarterback Charles "Gus" Dorais and end Knute Rockne, showed the football world that the forward pass could be a formidable offensive tool, changing football forever.

After serving as a Notre Dame assistant coach (as well as a chemistry teacher), Knute Rockne took over as head coach in 1918. Rockne's coaching career is full of early football lore: George Gipp and the famous "Win one for the Gipper" halftime speech in the game against Army in 1928; the 1924 "Four Horsemen" backfield of Layden, Crowley, Stuhldreher, and Miller; and the untimely death of Rockne in a plane crash, leaving the football world to wonder "what might have been?"

He established the "Rockne System" of football tactics (a single-wing offense) and scheduled Notre Dame to play the best teams across the United States. Against this competition, the Rockne System produced five undefeated teams and six national champions, three of them consensus. Rockne believed in his system, but he wasn't above implementing some changes after the Irish's 5–4–0 season of 1928. The result was back-to-back undefeated teams in 1929 and 1930. As shown above, all but two Notre Dame coaches had a winning record. The coaches who followed Rockne followed the Rockne System—and continued to win.

Frank Leahy, who coached the Irish from 1941–1943 and again from 1946–1953, changed the offense to the T-formation. Under the "new" system, Leahy's teams won

85.5 percent of their games, produced two undefeated seasons, another four unbeaten seasons, and were unbeaten in 39 straight games from September 26, 1946, until October 7, 1950. Thirty-six of his players became All America, and four won the Heisman Trophy: Angelo Bertelli, Johnny Lujack, Leon Hart, and John Lattner.

Notre Dame football struggled from the mid-1950s until the mid-1960s with a barely winning record of 51–48. In 1964, Ara Parseghian became the coach of the Irish and immediately turned things around. Notre Dame was 9–1 and shared the national championship in Parseghian's first year. They would own a share of the national title five times in Parseghian's 11 years: 1964, 1966 (consensus), 1967, 1970, and 1973 (consensus).

In the last quarter of the century, Notre Dame continued its winning ways, especially under Dan Devine (53–16–1 from 1975–1980 with a consensus title in 1977) and Lou Holtz (100–30–2 from 1986–1996 with three shared championships including a 1988 consensus).

The 1943 Season

By 1943, the country was adjusting to the demands of war. From converting American industry to the manufacture of war materials, to rationing, to the rapid re-building of the military, the "Greatest Generation" met every challenge as the United States fought on two fronts, the European Theater and the Pacific Theater.

The Game 1943

The game had changed considerably since the last unanimous champion, Georgia Tech, was crowned in 1917. Various rules changes modified the game, but the evolution of the passing game in the 1930s and further development of the T-Formation and its variations, as well as the man-in-motion in the 1940s, were the most significant factors.[1] Another important event occurred on September 30, 1939. Powerful Fordham defeated Waynesburg College of Pennsylvania, 34–7, in the first televised football game.[2] This event went virtually unnoticed at the time. Today football on television is a billion dollar business.

During the war years, college football was, of necessity, different. By 1943, college football teams had lost many players to the country's military needs, and schools selected to offer military training benefited from transferring players. Notre Dame was fortunate to be designated a V-12 officer training program for the Navy. They were also fortunate that freshman Bob Kelly's father, Ed, was a U.S. Congressman. Learning how the military was haphazardly transferring officer training candidates from one school to another to attend the same training, at great taxpayer expense, he had the practice stopped. Thanks to Congressman Kelly, his son and other student athletes, including tackle Ed White, were able to remain at Notre Dame. Previous transfers into Notre Dame included starting halfback Julie Rykovich from Illinois, starting guard John Perko from Minnesota, end Ray Kuffel from Marquette, and fullback Vic Kulbitski from Minnesota.[3]

The congressman intervened in another matter, as well. Army coach Earl Blaik, apparently angry at losing West Point appointees Bob Kelly and Johnny Lujack to Notre Dame, threatened to end the series between the two schools. A phone call from

Congressman Kelly changed his mind.[4] In 1945 Bob Kelly received an appointment to the Naval Academy and transferred.[5]

Football teams were also organized at military bases and training facilities. These teams, often composed of undergraduate and graduated players from various schools, played other military facilities and collegiate teams. Also, military facilities were not prevented from using professional players who were in training. Military teams were ranked along with colleges and universities in the weekly AP poll. In 1943, there were 39 competitive military teams: 24 Army, five Navy Pre-Flight, seven Navy, and three Coast Guard.[6] (See Appendix D, Service Teams 1943.)

Some schools, such as Boston College, Harvard, and Vanderbilt, played out their schedules with student-organized teams. Many schools cancelled the season rather than attempt to field a team. Seven schools that did not field a football team in 1943 had been in the top 20 in the final AP poll of 1942: Tennessee (#7), Alabama (#10), Stanford (#12), William &Mary (#14), Auburn (#16), Washington State (#17), and Mississippi State (#18).

SCHOOLS WITHOUT FOOTBALL THROUGH SOME OR ALL OF THE WORLD WAR II YEARS

- Alabama
- Auburn
- Baylor
- Detroit
- Florida
- Furman
- George Washington
- Hardin-Simmons
- Idaho
- Kentucky
- Michigan State
- Mississippi State
- Mississippi
- New Mexico State
- North Texas State
- Oregon State
- Oregon
- San Jose State
- Stanford
- Syracuse
- Tennessee
- Texas Western
- Utah State
- Virginia Polytechnic Institute (later Virginia Tech)
- Washington State
- West Texas State
- Wichita
- William & Mary
- Wyoming

Notre Dame finished the 1942 season ranked #6 with a 7-2-1 record. Coach Frank Leahy (See Appendix C, Coaches) could not have been too confident. The Irish had lost nine of 11 starters and 22 of 32 lettermen to graduation or military service.[7] He did have quarterback Angelo Bertelli, halfback Creighton Miller, and fullback Jim Mello returning. Miller came from a long line of Notre Dame football players: his father, Harry, was a back from 1906-1909, his uncle Wally played next to George Gipp, and his uncle Don was one of the Four Horsemen.[8] Beginning in 1943, because of the war, freshmen were eligible to play varsity ball.

The first AP poll of 1943 was taken on October 4. By then, all teams had played two or three games. Notre Dame was 2-0, having defeated Pittsburgh and Georgia Tech (9-1 and #5 in final 1942 poll) by a combined 96-13.

Pittsburgh

Leahy started freshman quarterback Johnny Lujack in the first game at Pittsburgh because of the proximity to his hometown and to give the freshman a boost in confidence. Having driven to the Pittsburgh 2-yard line, Lujack turned the wrong way twice, each time failing to hand the ball off to Miller. The third time he got it right, and Miller scored one of his two touchdowns. Some sportswriters were deceived, as well, and marveled at how Lujack faked twice to Miller to set up the touchdown run.[9] The Irish were too much for Pitt (3-5-0) and won, 41-0.

Georgia Tech

At home against Georgia Tech, the Irish overwhelmed a team that would finish the season 7-3 and ranked #13. Jim Mello led all rushers with 18 carries for 167 yards. Angelo Bertelli completed six of seven passes for three touchdowns as Notre Dame amassed 418 yards of offense. The Irish defense held Tech to 98 total yards in a 55-13 win.

#2 Michigan

The first real test for the Irish was second-ranked Michigan, another of the schools that benefited from having a military training program. Notable transfers were fullback Bill Daley from Minnesota and Elroy "Crazylegs" Hirsch from Wisconsin. Over their other eight contests, the Wolverines would average over 36 points/game and held opponents to less than five points/game. However, Notre Dame employed an aggressive strategy with the defensive line keying on the Michigan halfbacks to slow their potent single-wing offense. Creighton Miller, whose father played on the 1909 team that defeated Michigan, 11-3, scored two touchdowns as the Irish handed the Wolverines their only loss of the season, 35-12.

According to author Jack Connor, two unusual incidents occurred. Because of a timing error, the third quarter lasted 23 minutes, and by mutual agreement the teams played a seven-minute fourth quarter. The second incident occurred as the two coaches approached mid-field to shake hands after the game. Michigan's coach Fitz Crisler accused Leahy of dirty play by Notre Dame players. He not only kept the two schools from scheduling future games, but also tried to convince other Big Ten schools not to play the Irish. Michigan and Notre Dame would not play again until 1978.[10]

Wisconsin & Illinois

Notre Dame next faced a pair of weaker Western Conference (Big Ten) schools, Wisconsin and Illinois. The Irish had little trouble overwhelming them by a combined score of 97–0. Six different Irish backs scored a touchdown, and Miller added two more as the Irish battered Wisconsin, 55–0.

Against an Illinois team depleted of much of its strength by the war and military transfers, Leahy rested the starters for most of the game and played his entire roster in a 47–0 win. The reprieve allowed the Irish to rest before facing the powerful and highly-ranked service academies over the next two weeks. Navy, was 5–0 and ranked third, having beaten North Carolina Pre-Flight, Cornell, #5 Duke, Penn State, and Georgia Tech by 133–40.

#3 Navy

Creighton Miller scored two touchdowns and the Notre Dame defense did the rest, intercepting five Navy passes and holding the Midshipmen to -7 rushing yards. The

One of five consensus Notre Dame All Americas in 1943, Angelo Bertelli won the Heisman Trophy over Bob Odell of Penn. Interestingly, neither player was in the top ten in any individual offensive category. Bertelli learned of his Heisman win while at the Marine boot camp in Parris Island, South Carolina (author's collection).

Irish, having won handily over Navy, 33–6, would face Army without the services of star quarterback, Angello Bertelli, who was called up into the Marines after the Navy game. Bertelli would later receive a telegram during basic training at Parris Island, South Carolina, informing him that he had won the Heisman Trophy.

#3 Army

The Army Cadets were 6–0–1, had earlier been ranked #2, and defeated Villanova, Colgate, Temple, Columbia, and Yale by an aggregate 211–7, before a 13–13 tie with 6th-ranked Pennsylvania, then 5–0. The Cadets were ranked #3 going into the November 6 game with the Irish at Yankee Stadium.

Notre Dame started Johnny Lujack in place of Bertelli and 17-year-old Bob Kelly for right halfback Julie Rykovich. On their first possession, the Irish drove to the Army 3-yard line. On fourth down and two, the Cadet defense held. Army punter George Maxon kicked from deep in his end zone, and Kelly returned it to Army's 31-yard line. Lujack completed a pass to John Yonaker for a touchdown, but then missed the extra point, and the first quarter ended Notre Dame 6, Army 0. The second period was scoreless, but not without action. Carl Anderson of Army intercepted a Lujack pass and appeared to be in the clear. Lujack, the last Irish with a chance to prevent a touchdown, made the tackle and secured Notre Dame's 6–0 halftime lead.

In the third quarter, Jim Mello forced a Glenn Davis fumble into the arms of Creighton Miller. After a long, broken field run, Miller was finally brought down at the Army 13-yard line by none other than Davis. The Irish couldn't capitalize, but later in the period, Jim White recovered another Davis fumble and Lujack again hit Yonaker for a touchdown and a 13–0 lead entering the fourth quarter. Early in the final period, Lujack scored on a quarterback sneak. With Army on the move, the Irish intercepted a pass by Davis, and six plays later Fred Earley ran for a final touchdown. Army blocked the extra point for a final score of Notre Dame 26, Army 0.

Offensively, Notre Dame led Army in first downs (21–9), rushing yards (237–114), and passing yards (176–36). On defense, Notre Dame intercepted the Cadets three times and caused six fumbles. Although losing two fumbles and being intercepted once during that game, freshman fullback Glenn Davis, the future "Mr. Outside," would team with power runner Felix "Doc" Blanchard, "Mr. Inside," as one of the greatest backfield combinations ever in college football. Both would win the coveted Heisman Trophy.

Johnny Lujack, who had turned down a West Point appointment to play for the Irish, adequately replaced Bertelli, skillfully moving the Irish offense and accumulating 107 yards passing and one touchdown just in the first quarter. In all, Lujack would contribute two touchdown passes, both to end John Yoanaker, and burrow through on a quarterback sneak from the 1-yard line for a third. Four years later, after a stint in the Army, Lujack would return to the Irish and take home his own Heisman Trophy. Miller again led all rushers with 20 carries for 94 yards.

#8 Northwestern

The Irish next faced #8-ranked Northwestern (5–1) and their great quarterback, Otto Graham. The previous year, Graham had been the nation's second leading passer behind Ray Evans of Kansas, and in 1943 he finished third in Heisman voting. After a second-week loss to Michigan (20–7), the Northwestern Wildcats had run off four straight wins, defeating Wisconsin and the co-defending national champions, Ohio State, outscoring those opponents by 109–6 with three shutouts.

Again Johnny Lujack ably directed the offense as Notre Dame notched win number eight, 25–6.

#2 Iowa Pre-Flight

The Irish defended their number one ranking against another second-ranked team, Iowa Pre-Flight (IPF). At 8–0, IPF had defeated Illinois, Ohio State, Iowa State, Iowa, Missouri, Fort Riley, Marquette, and Camp Grant by a total of 238–84. The Seahawks' ranking may (in retrospect) have seemed unwarranted; of the eight teams they had played, only Ohio State (week 1, #18) and Camp Grant (week 3, #20) were ever in the top 20, and their opponents' combined record at season's end was 25–40–5. Still, the Seahawks featured some outstanding college and pro players, and proved to be a worthy opponent.

They were coached by Navy Lieutenant Don Faurot, who had been the head football coach at Missouri and was considered the architect of the Split-T Offense. Faurot would later resume his coaching career at Missouri. He had two assistants who became successful head coaches: Charles "Bud" Wilkinson at Oklahoma (six shared national championships, including two consensus) and Jim Tatum at Maryland (two shared national championships, including one consensus). Both won American Football Coaches Association (AFCA) Coach of the Year honors: Wilkinson in 1949 and Tatum in 1953.

The Seahawks scored first on a touchdown run by quarterback Art Guepe, who had played at Marquette in the mid–1930s. A late Notre Dame drive stalled inside the IPF 5-yard line, and the halftime score was 7–0.

In the third quarter, Notre Dame tied the score on a 3-yard run by Bob Kelly. The Seahawks came back after they recovered a Johnny Lujack fumble early in the fourth quarter. Dick Todd, who had been playing halfback for the NFL Washington Redskins, completed a touchdown throw to end Dick Burk. The extra point was missed, and the Seahawks led, 13–7, in the fourth period. Todd, who had 78 yards on 13 carries, suffered a broken jaw in the drive and was out for the remainder of the game.

Notre Dame rallied with a late touchdown by Creighton Miller and a successful extra point attempt to give them a one-point lead. Guepe hit Perry Schwartz, an end who had been playing for the NFLs Brooklyn Dodgers, with a pass to the Notre Dame 11-yard line, but a field goal attempt failed. Then, with time running out, Guepe threw four incompletions and the Irish hung on, 14–13. IPF won its final game against Minnesota (32–0), ended the season at 9–1 and retained its #2 ranking in the final poll.

Great Lakes Naval Training Center

The last game of the season found the Irish squaring off against Great Lakes Naval Training Center. Great Lakes was founded in May 1906, to train recruits before they were assigned to ships. President Theodore Roosevelt championed and oversaw the project while he was in office. Great Lakes fielded a football team (the Bluejackets) that often played against teams of major universities. During the two World Wars, college football players were often drafted into the military, decimating teams while strengthening the military Centers such as Great Lakes.

The 1918 Great Lakes team featured Paddy Driscoll of Northwestern, George Halas of Illinois, and Charlie Bachman from Notre Dame. The team posted wins over Iowa, Illinois, Purdue, and undefeated Eastern powerhouse Rutgers with its All America end, Paul Robeson. The Bluejackets also defeated Navy on a controversial call by none other than Annapolis Superintendent Captain E. W. Eberle. With less than two minutes to play, Navy fumbled near the Great Lakes goal. The ball was picked up by Great Lakes' Dizzy Eielson, who beheld a clear field in front of him and blockers behind him. Before reaching the Navy goal line, Eielson was tackled by a midshipman off the Navy bench. With typical Academy honor and fairness, Captain Eberle overruled the officials and declared a touchdown for Great Lakes.

The Bluejackets also recorded two ties that year. The first came against Northwestern, considered the best team of the Western Conference (Big Ten), the second against Knute Rockne's perennially strong Notre Dame unit. The team's sole loss was a 23–0 beating by Centre College in Kentucky, but games against Pittsburgh, Chicago, and St. Louis were cancelled because of the Spanish Influenza outbreak.

Great Lakes was invited to the Rose Bowl to face the Marines from the Mare Island Navy Yard. Mare Island had won the previous Rose Bowl over Camp Lewis, sported an 11–0 record, and outscored a (much weaker) schedule of opponents, 534–28. However, the Bluejackets dominated, 17–0 and were crowned National Service Champion.

Between the wars, Great Lakes alternately grew and was cut back. In 1919, the Navy placed all instruction in telephone and telegraph at Great Lakes. Around that time, the University of Illinois allowed Great Lakes training be applied to a university degree. In 1923, a Naval Reserve Air Base took up residence at Great Lakes. In 1933, amidst the Great Depression, Great Lakes was shut down. Political pressure re-opened the Center in 1935, but a year later the Naval Reserve Air Base was relocated. As the threat of war loomed closer, Navy preparation and training escalated.

At the time of the Japanese attack on Pearl Harbor, 6,000 sailors were in training at Great Lakes. Within a year that number grew to 100,000 recruits in training at the Center. Of the more than four million Americans who served in the Navy during World War II, one million had been trained at Great Lakes. Segregation was practiced in the military much as it was in society during the early 1940s. Great Lakes was chosen to train African Americans, both recruits and officers. Initially the training was segregated, but the ability of the black recruits at Great Lakes convinced the Navy to integrate.

World War II again found college stars on the roster at Great Lakes, and the team aligned with the Eastern Independents Conference. In 1943, Steve Lach of Duke, Steve Jurwik and Emil Sitko of Notre Dame, Dewey Proctor of Furman, Buist Warren of Tennessee, Ken Roskie of South Carolina, and Rag Jones of Texas all played for Great Lakes. During the war years of 1942–1945, Great Lakes had a 33–11–3 record, with seven of the losses and one tie coming against teams ranked in the top ten. So strong were the teams from military bases, camps, pre-flight schools, and training centers that in 1944 they made up ten of the top 20-ranked teams in the final AP poll.

Great Lakes was unranked despite being 9–2 with wins over Fort Riley, Iowa, Pittsburgh, Ohio State, Western Michigan, Camp Grant, Indiana, and twice over Marquette.

The Bluejackets endured two losses: one to Purdue, ranked 5th in the final poll, and then to Northwestern, ranked #9 in the final poll.

The opening kickoff was taken by Johnny Lujack, and after a sustained drive, the quarterback scored on a one-yard run for a 7–0 Irish edge. A fumbled lateral pass was recovered by Bob Kelly to thwart a Great Lakes drive into Notre Dame territory, and the score remained 7–0 at the half.

To open the third quarter, Great Lakes punched in two touchdowns, one on a 24-yard run by Emil Sitko (a former Notre Dame player and future Irish All America), the other a 51-yard scamper by fullback Dewey Proctor, who had starred at Furman. Both PATs missed, however, and the Bluejackets were up, 12–7. In the fourth period, the Irish engineered a 75-yard drive capped by a Creighton Miller touchdown run that put Notre Dame up, 14–12, with a little over a minute to play. With only seconds on the clock, former Duke star Steve Lach hit Paul Anderson of Western Reserve University on a long touchdown pass, and Great Lakes came away with an incredible 19–14 upset. Notre Dame rushers were held to a season-low 181 yards. Creighton Miller gained only 63 yards in 27 carries, and Lujack's completions totaled only 64 yards. Great Lakes rushers gained 284 yards, including 155 by Proctor and 114 by Sitko, each on 17 carries. So the questions arises—how did Notre Dame become a unanimous national champion with a loss in their last game? To suggest an answer, it becomes necessary to compare the top teams in several ways.

1943 Comparison of Top Ten Teams in Final AP Poll

No.	*Team*	*Record*	*PF-PA*	*Opponents' W-L*
1.	Notre Dame	9–1–0	340–69	62–33–1
2.	Iowa Pre-Flight	9–1–0	287–98	39–45–5
3.	Michigan	8–1–0	302–73	37–41–6
4.	Navy	8–1–0	237–80	50–28–4
5.	Purdue	9–0–0	214–55	30–48–6
6.	Great Lakes	8–2–0	257–108	49–42–8
7.	Duke	8–1–0	335–34	42–26–3
8.	Del Monte Pre-Flight	7–1–0	252–65	22–39–2
9.	Northwestern	6–2–0	189–64	42–36–2
10.	March Field	9–1–0	292–65	25–24–1

1943 Top Contenders Opponents Winning Percentage

Notre Dame	65%
Navy	63%
Duke	61%
Great Lakes	54%
Northwestern	54%
March Field	51%

Navy was closest, with opponents' winning percentage at 63 percent, and Notre Dame had beaten the Midshipmen, 33–6. Duke, Great Lakes, Northwestern, and March Field also had opponents' winning percentages over 50 percent. The other four in the Top 10 had opponents' winning percentages below 50 percent. A similar comparison can be made by the number of opponents a team played from the Top 20 and the number of weeks those teams were in the top 20.

1943 Strength of Schedule

Team	Number of Opponents in Top 20	Opponents' Total Weeks in Top 20
Notre Dame	7	51
Georgia Tech	6	36
Navy	5	39
Great Lakes	5	28
Northwestern	5	26
Michigan	5	22
March Field	4	23
Iowa Pre-Flight	4	14
Purdue	4	9
Army	3	27
Penn	2	18
Duke	2	12
Del Monte Pre-Flight	1	8
Washington*	1	7

Washington played only four games and the Rose Bowl.

Once again, the Irish are on top and by a wide margin when comparing the number of total weeks that its opponents were ranked in the Top 20.

1943 All America Selections

The Irish placed five players on the consensus All America team in 1943: End John Yonakor, tackle Jim White, guard Pat Filley, and backs Angelo Bertelli and Creighton Miller. The only two unanimous All America selections that year were center Casamir Myslinski of Army and back Bill Daly of Michigan.

The Consensus All America Team 1943

Ends	Ralph Heywood	Southern Cal	(AP, AA, UP, INS)
Ends	John Yonkor	Notre Dame	(AA, UP, INS)
Tackles	Don Whitmire	Navy	(AA, UP, INS, L)

Tackles	Jim White	Notre Dame	(AP, AA, UP, INS, COL)
Guards	Alex Agase	Purdue	(AA, UP, INS, L)
Guards	John Steber	Georgia Tech	(AP, AA, INS)
Guards	Pat Filley	Notre Dame	(UP, COL)
Center	Casimir Myslinski	Army	(AP, AA, UP, INS, COL, L)
Backs	Bill Daly	Michigan	(AP, AA, UP, INS, COL, L)
Backs	Angelo Bertelli	Notre Dame	(AA, UP, INS, COL, L)
Backs	Creighton Miller	Notre Dame	(AP, AA, UP, INS, COL)
Backs	Bob Odell	Pennsylvania	(AP, INS, COL, L)

AA—All America Board
AP—Associated Press
COL—Grantland Rice selections in *Collier's* magazine
INS—International News Service
L—*Look* magazine
UP—United Press

Individual statistical leaders Notre Dame played against:

#3 passer: Eddie Prokop of Georgia Tech
#3 receiver: James Dorough of Georgia Tech
#4 rusher (yards total): Bill Daley of Michigan
#6 rusher (yards total): Eddie Bray of Illinois
#1 rusher (yards/carry): Bill Daley of Michigan
#3 rusher (yards/carry): Eddie Bray of Illinois
#6 punter: George Maxon of Army
#9 scorer: Elroy Hirsch of Michigan
#10 scorer: Eddie Prokop of Georgia Tech

Notre Dame's Creighton Miller was the national rushing leader with 911 yards. As a team, Notre Dame led the nation in total offense and rushing offense with 418 yards per game and 313.7 yards per game respectively. The table below shows team offense and defense leaders for 1943.

Team Statistical Leaders of 1943

Total Offense	Notre Dame	418.0 yards per game
Rushing Offense	Notre Dame	313.7 yards per game
Passing Offense	Brown	133.1 yards per game
Scoring Offense	Duke	37.2 points per game
Total Defense	Duke	121.7 yards per game
Rushing Defense	Duke	39.4 yards per game
Passing Defense	North Carolina	36.5 yards per game
Scoring Defense	Duke	3.8 points per game

Team Statistical Leaders Notre Dame Played

#1 rushing offense	Iowa Pre-Flight	324.4 yards/game
#4 rushing offense	Michigan	294.2 yards/game
#6 rushing offense	Army	256.8 yards/game
#9 rushing offense	Navy	240.6 yards/game
#8 passing offense	Georgia Tech	112.3 yards/game
#2 total offense	Iowa Pre-Flight	392.9 yards/game
#5 total offense	Michigan	363.2 yards/game
#6 total offense	Army	354.5 yards/game
#7 rushing defense	Navy	74.1 yards/game
#8 rushing defense	Army	76.5 yards/game
#5 passing defense	Northwestern	51.9 yards/game
#8 passing defense	Wisconsin	58.1 yards/game
#7 total defense	Army	152.5 yards/game
#8 total defense	Navy	161.2 yards/game
#10 total defense	Michigan	164.1 yards/game

To determine if another Top 10 team was more deserving of the national championship, a comparison is made of the four teams Notre Dame did not play.

Purdue at #5 was the only Top 10 unbeaten and untied team (9–0), outscored opponents 214–55, and beat three common opponents with the Irish, including Great Lakes (a 23–13 Boilermakers win), Notre Dame's only loss. Comparing scores of other common opponents: (1) The Irish beat Illinois, 47–0, while Purdue won, 40–21; (2) The Boilermakers topped Wisconsin, 32–0, with Notre Dame winning, 50–0.

Purdue defeated Great Lakes in their first game on September 18. Emil Sitko and Dewey Proctor, who riddled the Irish defense, were only substitutes in that game.[11] This suggests that Great Lakes was definitely at full strength at the time. However, Purdue's strength of schedule cannot be overlooked. The Boilermakers' opponents' combined record was a dismal 30–48–6 (39 percent winning percentage). Except for Great Lakes, they did not play any team in the Top 20 final poll.

Who the Irish played is also important when considering #7 Duke. The Blue Devils had a record of 8–1, outscored opponents 335–28 with six shutouts, had an opponents' winning percentage of 61 percent, and were in the top 10 team leaders in six statistical categories, including #1 in four categories. They certainly appeared to be a contender and yet they were ranked #7 in the final poll. Duke played two opponents in common with Notre Dame: losing to Navy, 14–13 (Notre Dame won, 33–6) and beating Georgia Tech, 14–7 (Notre Dame won, 55–13). Besides those two opponents, Duke did not play another team in the final Top 20 poll, and its only opponent with national individual or team leaders was North Carolina (played twice). The Tar Heels led in team passing defense, allowing only 36.5 yards/game.

The final two teams in the Top 10 that Notre Dame did not play were #8 Del Monte Pre-Flight (7–1) and #10 March Field (8–1). The Del Monte Pre-Flight roster had a few players from the NFL, including Parker Hall, a non-consensus All America from Mississippi in 1938. They were ranked throughout the polling season, rising as high as #11 before losing to #10 Pacific (#19 in the final poll). Del Monte rose to #8 in the final poll after wins over UCLA, California, and other West Coast military teams. As they were limited to the West Coast and lost to the only Top 20 team on their schedule, they were not a contender.

March Field, ranked #10 at 8–1, was also located in California and featured a West Coast schedule. The high point of their season was a 35–0 win over #9 Southern California (unranked in the final poll). They suffered a 27-7 loss to unranked Washington (#12 in the final poll) and did not play any other ranked team.

1943 Other Individual Awards

Heisman Trophy

Awarded by the Downtown Athletic Club of New York
"To the Outstanding College Football Player of the United States"
Angello Bertelli, Notre Dame

Walter Camp Memorial Trophy

Awarded by the Downtown Athletic Club of Washington, D.C.
To the Outstanding College Back
Angello Bertelli, Notre Dame

Robert W. Maxwell Memorial Football Award

Nation's Outstanding Collegiate Football Player
Robert Odell, Pennsylvania

Knute Rockne Memorial Trophy

Awarded by the Downtown Athletic Club of Washington, D.C.
To the Outstanding College Lineman
Casimir Myslinski, Army

Touchdown Club of New York Award

Meritorious Service for a Period of Years
Lou Little, Pennsylvania

Coach of the Year

AMOS ALONZO STAGG, PACIFIC

Of the 11 unanimously chosen National Champions during the 1900s, Notre Dame in 1943 was the only team with a loss. So why was Notre Dame a unanimous choice? The question might better be asked, If not Notre Dame, then who? The Irish defeated the second-, third-, fourth-, ninth-, 11th-, and 14th-ranked teams. They outscored the teams ranked second, third, and fourth by 96–31. The loss at the end of the year to then-unranked Great Lakes must have been considered a fluke by all selectors.

Notre Dame has a proud tradition of football greatness. It is a tradition of innovation with Knute Rockne and Gus Darais first incorporating the forward pass into the offense while playing for the Irish. On November 1, 1913, with Dorais completing 13 of 17 passes for 243 yards in downing the Cadets of Army, 35–13, the forward pass came into its own. That same day, Notre Dame signaled a wake-up call to the football world that the Irish, too, had arrived. It became a tradition of excellence and victories as, now, Coach Rockne won 88 percent of his games for the Irish. And his successors carried on the winning tradition.

It was, also, a tradition marked by symbolism. The Four Horsemen of Notre Dame (Miller, Layden, Studeher, and Crowley) were portrayed as wreaking apocalyptic destruction on the opposition. And the Notre Dame fight song stating, "What though the odds be great or small, old Notre Dame will win over all." The country could relate to that symbolism in time of war. The President and military leaders were asking the United States to overcome great adversity, to dig deep and "win one for freedom," much as Rockne had exhorted Notre Dame to "win one for the Gipper."

In short, Notre Dame was the perfect team for the war year of 1943. They were resilient enough to win against two tough teams after the loss of their star, Angello Bertelli. They played against many top players and even some professionals who donned uniforms at Iowa Pre-Flight and Great Lakes. The spirit associated with Notre Dame football symbolized the United States during 1943. The polls must have sensed that. Beyond the game scores, beyond the wealth of talent playing for the Irish, even beyond the last-minute "Hail Mary" pass by Great Lakes to tarnish the Irish halo, the polls got it right. Notre Dame was declared the unanimous National Champion of 1943.

CHAPTER 8

Michigan 1948

A Short History of Michigan Football

As stated in the Introduction, Michigan and Notre Dame have been recognized as national champion, by at least one selector, in more decades during the 1900s than any other team. Notre Dame failed to be selected during the years 1900–1909, and Michigan from 1950–1959. In nine out of the 10 decades, these two programs have boasted at least one national champion.

During the 22 seasons from 1879–1900, Michigan football teams were a very respectable 98–31–4. In 1901, Fielding "Hurry Up" Yost took over as coach. From 1901–1905 Michigan's "Point-A-Minute" offense averaged 49.5 points per game while holding the opposition to 0.7 points per game, en route to a remarkable 55–1–1 record, including a 49–0 drubbing of Stanford in the first Rose Bowl. Yost coached the Wolverines from 1901–1923 and again in 1925 and 1926. His overall coaching record was 165–29–10. The Western Conference (later the Big Ten) officially formed in 1917. Yost's teams won one Western title and tied for first place four times.

Yost was succeeded as the Wolverines' coach by Elton Wieman (9–6–1 in 1927–1928) and Harry Kipke (46–26–4 from 1929–1937). From 1930–1933, under Kipke, Michigan was 31–1–3, tied for first in the Big Ten all four years, shared a national title in 1932, and were the consensus champions in 1933, sharing that title with Ohio State, Princeton, and Southern California.

Fritz Crisler took over from 1938–1947. Although managing only one outright Big Ten title and one shared title, Crisler led the Wolverines to a 71–16–3 record, one shared National Championship (1947), and one Rose Bowl (a 49–0 win over Southern California in January 1948). A Crisler led team never had a losing season, never lost more than three games in any year, and never finished lower than fourth in the Big Ten. Bennie Oosterbaan succeeded Crisler from 1948–1958 and had a record of 63–33–4, including the Wolverines' unanimous championship season of 1948.

From 1959–1968, Michigan was coached by Chalmers "Bump" Elliott, a star running back in the 1947 Michigan backfield that has been compared to the Four Horsemen backfield of Notre Dame's 1924 team. Elliott posted a record of 51–42–2. In general, the Wolverines struggled during Elliott's reign with five losing seasons in 11 years. In 1964, Michigan ended the season at 8–1 and ranked #4, having defeated #6 Navy, #10 Michigan State, and #10 Ohio State. They defeated #8 Oregon State in the post-season Rose Bowl. They shared the national championship that year, but only for the vote of the Dunkel System. A 21–20 loss to Purdue in game 4 hurt their title hopes as Arkansas and Alabama were undefeated. In Elliott's final year, the Wolverines were 8–2 and ranked #12.

Chapter 8. Michigan 1948

The fortunes of Michigan football turned around in 1969, when Glenn Edward "Bo" Schembechler was brought in to coach. Schembechler had been an assistant coach at five schools, including twice at Big Ten archrival Ohio State and once at Northwestern of the Big Ten. In Schembechler's 21-year reign (1969–1989), the Wolverines were 194–48–5 and shared the national championship in 1973 and 1985. Gary O. Moeller took over from 1990–1994, after being an assistant under Schembechler since 1980. Moeller posted a record of 44–13–3 and four post-season bowl victories in five seasons. His teams always ended the season in the top 25: 1990 #7, 1991 #6, 1992 #5, 1990 #21, and 1994 #12.

Lloyd Carr coached from 1995–2007 and produced a record of 122–40. In 1997, Michigan (12–0) shared a national championship with 13–0 Nebraska. Under Rich Rodriquez (2008–2010, 15–22), Brady Hoke (2011–2014, 31–20), and Jim Harbaugh (2015–present, 47–18), Michigan has not achieved a national championship.

1948

By 1948, the country was settling in to the post-war world. Veterans were flocking to colleges under the GI Bill, and young couples were lining up to purchase homes in the newly developed "suburbs." Although the United States was beginning to feel the birth pains of the Cold War with the Congressional inquests of Senator Joe McCarthy, the blacklisting in Hollywood, and the perceived threat of Communism, the nation could again enjoy an autumn afternoon of football undistracted by a cloud of war elsewhere in the world.

In the aftermath of World War II, football players at the college level were older and more experienced. Players who had left college for the military service were now returning. Both returning and new players had often participated in service ball, competing against college and pro players. There was an abundance of talent, and schools around the country vied to get the best.[1] After 26 years of not selecting a unanimous National Champion, the polls would crown their second unanimous choice in six years.

The Game 1948

A forward pass could now be thrown from anywhere behind the line of scrimmage, and handing the ball forward no longer was viewed as a forward pass. Rules permitted a kicking tee one inch high to be used on kickoffs. As of 1946, numbers were required on uniforms, and the following year a numbering system coinciding to a player's position was put in place: ends to wear numbers in the 80s, tackles in the 70s, guards 60s, centers 50s, and backs from 1 to 49.

The liberal substitution rule of 1941 was taken a step further. Unlimited substitution was permitted while the clock was stopped, as during a change of possession. The new substitution rules allowed for platoon football, the fielding of distinct offensive and defensive teams. The rule was embraced by some schools (such as Michigan) while resisted by others (Notre Dame). Similarly, the press took sides on platooning. Some felt a true football player should be equally skilled on offense and defense. There has even been speculation that Michigan's Bob Chappuis may have lost the Heisman Trophy to Notre Dame's Johnny Lujack in 1947 as a result of this bias.[2]

The 1948 college football season was unusual in that no less than four teams went undefeated and untied, and another two were undefeated with one tie by the final weekly AP poll on November 29. With some degree of bias and regional voting to be expected, a unanimous selection amid six undefeated squads would require a truly outstanding team.

Pre-season 1948

The Wolverines finished the 1947 season at 9–0, ranked #2 in the final AP poll, led the nation in total offense (412.7 yards per game), passing offense (173.9 yards per game), and scoring offense (38.3 points per game), and shut out ninth-ranked Southern California, 49–0, while setting nine records in the Rose Bowl. After Michigan's lopsided victory in Pasadena, a special AP poll was taken, and Michigan was declared the National Champion, dropping Notre Dame to #2. However, at the time, it was unprecedented to conduct a poll after the post-season bowl games. The special poll did not count, and Notre Dame remained the National Champion of 1947.

Michigan boasted one of the premier football programs in the nation. The Wolverines had a proud football tradition. Of the Division 1A teams active today, only six Ivy League schools and Rutgers began their programs before Michigan and Navy in 1879.

Michigan was expected to be good in 1948. The Wolverines appeared even more solid on defense than the 1947 squad that yielded only 53 points all season. However, the magical 1947 backfield of Bob Chappuis, Chalmers "Bump" Elliott, Howard Yerges, and Jack Weisenberger that sportswriter Francis Powers of the *Chicago Tribune* compared to Notre Dame's Four Horsemen backfield of 1924 were, mostly, graduated. Elliott, while still at Michigan, was ruled ineligible to play in 1948 by a committee of faculty from the (then) Big 9. Because Elliott had played as a marine trainee while at Purdue in 1943 and then on the Purdue team in 1944, it was decided he had used up his eligibility. Elliott remained at Michigan as an assistant coach

How to re-establish a nation-leading offense was the key to success for first-year coach Bennie Oosterbaan, a three-time consensus All America end for the Wolverines from 1925–1927. Oosterban had been a Michigan assistant for 20 years under three head coaches. He was handed the reigns to one of the top football programs in the nation, one where success was expected. He inherited a 14-game winning streak and the shoes of last season's Coach of the Year, Fritz Crisler, to fill.

The 1948 Season

Michigan State

The Wolverines, playing away, found themselves tested by a good Michigan State Spartans team in the season opener. The previous year, the Wolverines had shut out the Spartans, 55–0, and fans expected another easy victory. At this point, Michigan State was not a member of the Big 9. Their entry in 1953 would then make the Big 10 Conference.

In the first quarter, Michigan fullback Tom Peterson passed 40 yards to end Dick Rifenberg for a touchdown and a 7–0 Wolverine lead. A Peterson pass was intercepted in the third period, and with good field position Michigan State tied the game on a pass from halfback Lynn Chandnois to end Hank Minarik.

In the fourth quarter, Peterson scored on a 5-yard touchdown run, but the extra point was missed. Late in the game, Michigan State was inside the Michigan 5-yard line. Halfback/defensive back Wally Teninga intercepted a Spartans pass, and Michigan escaped with a 13–7 win. Under first-year coach Clarence "Biggie" Munn, the Spartans outgained Michigan on the ground, 158–106, causing concern on both offense and defense for the Wolverines.

Oregon

The second game found Michigan, in its home opener, playing a tough Oregon team led by quarterback Norm Van Brocklin, who would be the nation's sixth-leading passer that year. Throughout the first half of the 1900s, the Oregon team was referred to as the Webfoots. After the 1940s, the nickname was gradually changed to the Ducks.

The Wolverines completed two touchdown passes in shutting out the Webfoots, 14–0. In the second quarter, halfback Chuck Ortmann's 60-yard completion to end Dick Rifenburg made the score 7–0. The second touchdown was a short pass from reserve halfback Chuck Lentz to fullback Tom Peterson. As in the week before, the Michigan goal line defense held and averted a touchdown late in the game. The statistics for the game were surprisingly equal: the Wolverines passed for 217 yards, the Webfoots for 194 yards, Oregon led in first downs, 16 to 14, and in rushing yards, 137 to 132. Oregon would end the season at 9–1 and ranked #9 in the AP poll before losing to Southern Methodist in the Cotton Bowl, 21–13.

#15 Purdue

The first AP poll came out October 4. By that time, teams had played as many as three games. Michigan was ranked #7. The descending order of the six teams ranked above the Wolverines was: #1 Notre Dame, #2 North Carolina, #3 Northwestern, #4 Southern Methodist, #5 Army, and #6 Georgia Tech.

Michigan expected a tough game from Purdue. The Boilermakers, although 0–2, were ranked #15. Their schedule found them playing at #1 Notre Dame and #3 Northwestern before facing the Wolverines at home. Purdue had played the Irish well, losing 28–27, and then suffered a 21–0 shutout by the Northwestern Wildcats.

Michigan's Tom Peterson scored two touchdowns on short runs. Halfbacks Leo Koceski, Walt Teninga, and Chuck Lentz each ran for a score, and Chuck Ortmann connected with Dick Rifenburg for another touchdown to shut out the Boilermakers, 40–0. Michigan's defense was back in form, allowing Purdue only 36 yards rushing. After the win, Michigan climbed to #4 in the poll, replacing Southern Methodist after the Mustangs lost to Missouri 20–14. Although #1 Notre Dame and #2 North Carolina won by nearly identical scores, the Tar Heels took over #1 while the Irish dropped to #2.

#3 Northwestern

In their fourth game, Michigan faced the team many considered would be their biggest challenge of the season, the #3 Wildcats of Northwestern.

The Wolverines registered a surprisingly easy win, 28–0,, but the game remained close at 7–0 until late in the third period. Sophomore halfback Leo Koceski had scored on a run in the first quarter. With seconds remaining in the third period, Walt Teninga passed to Koceski for the Wolverines' second touchdown and a 14–0 lead. Northwestern fumbled the kickoff, Michigan recovered, and two plays later Chuck Ortmann threw to Koceski for another touchdown. Late in the game, Koceski fumbled near the Northwestern goal line, and the ball was recovered in the end zone by Michigan's center, Bob Erben, for a touchdown. Koceski, born in Canonsburg, Pennsylvania, and known as the Canonsburg Comet, was highly recruited out of high school, but always dreamed of being a Wolverine.[3]

The Michigan offense rushed for 166 yards, but again the defense was dominant, allowing the Wildcats only 47 yards on the ground, recovering a fumble, intercepting three passes, and recording 13 consecutive quarters unscored-upon. After the impressive win over Northwestern, Michigan took over the #1 spot in the weekly AP poll. They became the third team to hold the top ranking in three weeks, replacing North Carolina, the team that had replaced Notre Dame a week earlier. Next up, another good Western Conference (Big 9) team, #13 Minnesota.

#13 Minnesota

At 3–1, the #13 Golden Gophers had defeated Washington and Nebraska by a combined 49–13, before a heartbreaking 19–16 loss at Northwestern and a 6–0 scare at home against Illinois.

Minnesota scored first to take a 7–0 lead over the #1 team. In the second quarter, the Golden Gophers' unanimous All America tackle, Leo Nomellini, recovered a fumbled punt return in the Michigan end zone. The Wolverines bounced back for two scores before the half: a seven-yard Walt Teninga to Tom Peterson touchdown pass, and a one-yard Peterson rushing touchdown following senior end Ed McNeill's block of a Minnesota punt. The extra point attempt failed, but Michigan took a 13–7 lead into the half.

In the third quarter, halfback Everett Faunce scored the Golden Gophers' second touchdown to regain the lead, 14–13. Michigan produced another score in the third period on a Dick Rifenburg 37-yard touchdown reception to regain the lead, 20–14. A Chuck Ortmann to Leo Koceski 62-yard touchdown pass ended the scoring as the Wolverines defeated the Golden Gophers, 27–14, for their 19th consecutive win and the program's 400th victory.

Michigan, Notre Dame, North Carolina, California, Army, Georgia Tech, and Penn, the top seven teams all won and remained undefeated.

Illinois

The Illini were the last team to defeat the Wolverines, on October 26, 1946. Michigan's unbeaten streak now stood at 19. Coming into Ann Arbor for Michigan's Homecoming, Illinois posted a 2–3 record. But once again the Wolverines would be tested.

In the first quarter, Illinois had a first-and-goal at the Michigan 5-yard line. The Wolverines held on three plays, and a fourth-down field goal attempt failed. The first period was scoreless. In the second quarter, Michigan completed a 98-yard drive with a touchdown pass from Pete Elliott to Ed McNeill. Illinois halfback Paul Patterson scored before the half to tie the score at 7–7.

To start the third quarter, Illinois halfback Dwight Eddleman had an apparent

94-yard kickoff return for a touchdown called back on a penalty. Later in the period, Michigan scored on a 14-yard touchdown pass from Tom Peterson to Dick Rifenburg. Wally Teninga then scored on a two-yard run to put the Wolverines up, 21–7, midway through the third. After recovering a Michigan fumble, the Illini scored to cut the lead to 21–13 to end the quarter. Early in the fourth period, the Illini's Bernard Krueger followed his offensive line on a quarterback sneak. With that touchdown, Michigan held a tenuous 21–20 lead. A pair of Wolverines sophomores ended the scoring with a 38-yard touchdown pass. Chuck Ortmann's completion to Harry Allis sealed the hard-fought Michigan win, 28–20. The Wolverines' rushing defense held Illinois to 40 yards on the ground. But the Illini amassed 256 yards through the air. That was over a quarter of the 1,059 passing yards Michigan would allow all season.

That same week, Notre Dame defeated Navy, 41–7, and took over #1 while Michigan fell to #2. The top seven teams from the previous week all won and remained undefeated.

Navy

Under first-year head coach George Sauer, Navy played one of the most difficult schedules that year. All but one of the nine opponents were in the top 20 AP poll at one time, with five teams ranked at the end of the season. A 21–21 tie with #3 Army in their final game was the only bright spot in an 0–8–1 year.

Chuck Ortmann scored on a 1-yard run in the first quarter, and Tom Peterson ran for another in the second period to put the Wolverines up, 14–0 at the half. The Wolverines scored twice in the third period, a rushing touchdown by Wally Teninga and an 18-yard touchdown pass from junior halfback Bob Van Summern to Dick Rifenburg. An Ortmann to Rifenburg 60-yard touchdown pass in the fourth quarter ended the scoring in a 35–0 shutout.

Once again, the Michigan defense dominated. Navy was held to 73 yards rushing and 46 yards passing. The Wolverines intercepted two Navy passes and recovered three Midshipmen fumbles.

Michigan beat Navy by nearly the same margin as had Notre Dame the week before, but it was enough to return the Wolverines to the #1 ranking with the Irish at #2. In other games, #3 North Carolina was tied, 7–7, by Southern Conference rival William and Mary. The William and Mary Indians would finish at 6–2–2 and rank sixth nationally in scoring defense, allowing 6.7 points per game. The loss would drop the Tar Heels to #6.

Two undefeated teams lost that week: #6 Georgia Tech lost to Tennessee, 13–6, and #7 Penn was shut out, 14–0 by #14 Penn State. Georgia Tech dropped to #11 and Penn to #17. In the next polling, the ranking was: Michigan, Notre Dame, Army, and California (all undefeated) followed by Penn State and North Carolina (each with a tie), and then Southern Methodist, Northwestern, and Oklahoma (each with a loss). The #10 ranked team was Clemson at 6–0.

Indiana

Indiana featured George Taliaferro, a (non-consensus) All America halfback who ranked seventh nationally in punting with a 40.6 yard average. Taliaferro would later become the first African American drafted by a professional football franchise.

After a promising 2–0 start with wins over Wisconsin and Iowa and a #17 ranking, the Indiana Hoosiers had lost five games in a row, including a 42–6 blowout by Notre Dame the week before. This week would be no better for the Hoosiers. Eight Michigan players scored touchdowns as the offense gained 435 total yards, including 285 rushing. The Michigan defense held Indiana to 96 rushing yards and 63 yards through the air in a 54–0 shutout.

In the top 10, only #8 Northwestern lost, 12–7 to #2 Notre Dame. However, the close loss moved Northwestern up a notch to #7.

#18 Ohio State

The final game was at Ohio State, coached by Wes Fesler. Coach Fesler had been a consensus All America end from 1928–1930 for the Buckeyes, just as Oosterbaan was for the Wolverines from 1925–1927. The Buckeyes, #18, were 6–2, having lost only to Iowa and Northwestern. The Michigan-Ohio State contest had become an annual rivalry, and the game in 1948 was the 45th in the series. The Wolverines had won 29 times, Ohio State 12 times, and there had been three ties.

Ohio State scored on a first quarter, 16-yard field goal following a recovered Michigan fumbled lateral pass from Tom Peterson to Chuck Ortmann. The first quarter ended with the Buckeyes leading Michigan, 3–0. Through most of the second quarter, Ohio State played in Michigan territory, but the Wolverines' defense held, and Michigan had the ball at its own 10-yard line. Five plays later, Ortmann completed a 44-yard pass to Harry Allis, and the first half ended: Michigan 7, Ohio State 3.

After a scoreless third quarter, Michigan had the ball at their own 38-yard line following an Ohio State punt. Three passes put the ball at the Buckeyes' 11-yard line, and on their third rushing play, Peterson scored from two yards out. The extra point try failed, but the Wolverines had a hard-won victory, 13–3. They had now won 23 straight games.

The Buckeyes ran more plays (71–52), picked up more first downs (11–9), and out-rushed Michigan (130–54). The Wolverines had the edge in passing yards (116–73). Both teams committed three fumbles, Michigan losing two and Ohio State one. Michigan's season was now over. Of the other remaining undefeated teams:

#2 Notre Dame beat Washington, 46–0, and tied Southern California, 14–14, to complete their season at 9–0–1.
#3 Army tied Navy, 21–21, dropped to #6, and completed their season at 8–0–1.
#4 California beat Stanford, 7–6, and then lost, 20–14, to #7 Northwestern in the Rose Bowl to complete their season at 10–1.
#11 Clemson beat the Citadel, 20–0, beat Auburn, 7–6, and beat Missouri, 24–23, in the Gator Bowl to complete their season at 11–0.

Post–Regular Season

Michigan placed end Dick Rifenburg and tackle Alvin Wistert on the consensus All America team. Wistert, at 32, was older than any of his teammates by at least eight years. He had spent four years overseas with the Marines during World War II and was back in school through the GI Bill. Wistert's two brothers had each played tackle for the Wolverines, and both had been consensus All Americas: Francis in 1933 and Albert in 1942.[4]

Pete Elliott, younger brother of 1947 Michigan back Chalmers "Bump" Elliott, was voted All America, but not consensus.

No Michigan player was in the top 10 among the national individual leaders. As a team, the Wolverines finished sixth in passing offense (150.6 yards per game), fourth in rushing defense (87.7 yards per game), and led the nation in scoring defense (4.9 points per game). With the Big Ten "no repeat" rule, Michigan could not play in the Rose Bowl consecutive years and, therefore, their season was ended. As in the previous year, the polls would decide the national champion, and as in the previous year, it came down to #1 Michigan, 9-0, and #2 Notre Dame, 9-0 at the time of the final poll. Notre Dame played Southern California to a 14-14 tie after the last polling and ended the season at 9-0-1. Neither the Irish nor the Wolverines would play in a post-season bowl. Among other possible claimants, #3 North Carolina at 9-0-1 and #4 California, 10-0-0, lost in bowl games.

A comparison of common opponents in the first table below shows Michigan superior to Notre Dame. Likewise, a comparison of Strength of Schedule, the second table below, finds the Wolverines at the top in both the number of opponents in the Top 20 during the season and the number of weeks in the Top 20 by all opponents.

Michigan-Notre Dame Comparison of Scores vs. Common Opponents

	Michigan	*Notre Dame*
Indiana	54-0	42-6
Michigan State	13-7	26-7
Navy	35-0	41-7
Northwestern	28-0	12-7
Purdue	40-0	28-27
	170-7	149-54

1948 Strength of Schedule

Team	# of Opponents in Top 20	Weeks in Top 20
Michigan	7	36
North Carolina	6	16
Northwestern	5	31
Notre Dame	4	18
Army	3	13
SMU	3	9
Oklahoma	2	6
Georgia	2	16
Oregon	1	9
Clemson	1	3
California	0	0

1948 Regular Season Results at Final AP Poll

Rank	Team	Record	Points for–Points Against	Opponents W-L
1	Michigan	9–0	252–44	44–38–3
2	Notre Dame*	9–0	320–93	39–51–4
3	North Carolina**	9–0–1	256–80	54–39–9
4	California**	10–0	277–80	37–55–8
5	Oklahoma+	9–1	336–115	46–52–4
6	Army	8–0–1	294–89	32–38–3
7	Northwestern+	7–2	171–77	43–39–1
8	Georgia**	9–1	278–100	46–48–6
9	Oregon**	9–1	194–82	40–44–6
10	SMU+	8–1–1	229–92	55–40–7
13	Clemson+	10–0	250–53	28–49–6

regular season tie
**post-season loss*
+ *post-season win*

The strength of schedule tables explain why Clemson, a team with only one opponent in the top 20, but still the only other undefeated team, never advanced higher than #9. However, they don't explain how California, a team that played no top 20 team, advanced to #4.

The AP selected Michigan as the National Champion based on the regular season results as of the final poll on November 29. The following week, number two Notre Dame was tied by Southern California, 14–14, and ended the season at 9–0–1. In the post-season, third-ranked North Carolina (9–0–1) lost to Oklahoma, 14–6 in the Sugar Bowl, and fourth-ranked California (10–0) lost to Northwestern, 20–14, in the Rose Bowl.

The AP voters had gotten it right, and the other polls and statistical analyses would all follow suit.

Chapter 9

Texas 1963

Fifteen years had passed since the last unanimous national champion was selected. The newest national enemy, communism, had been confronted by congressional witch-hunts at home and a containment war in Korea. The country looked for security and elected World War II Supreme Allied Commander Dwight Eisenhower its 34th President in 1952, and Pacific Theater war hero and Massachusetts Senator John Kennedy its 35th President in 1960. The perceived threat of a surprise nuclear attack prompted an expanded radar network, home fallout shelters, and air raid drills in classrooms. Technological advances also brought expanded television and the ability to bring college football into homes.

The Game 1963

Significant changes had taken place in college football since Michigan's unanimous National Championship season of 1948. Substitution rules that allowed for platooning of offensive and defensive teams were abolished in 1953. Then the rules regarding substitutions got more relaxed beginning in 1959, and by 1963 unlimited substitution was allowed when the clock was stopped except on fourth down or a change of possession, when teams would be limited to two substitutions. To enhance the kicking game, uprights were widened to 23'4" (from 18'6") in 1959. That same year, a rule was added limiting a penalty to half the distance to the goal if the penalty normally would have moved the line of scrimmage back further. The two-point conversion following a touchdown was installed in 1958. Intentionally grounding the ball became illegal in 1949, and a quarterback could be a forward pass receiver as of 1963. In 1949, a blocker was now required to have his hands on his chest. A facemask was added to the helmet in 1951, and grabbing the facemask became a penalty in 1957.

The Texas Longhorns had high aspirations the year before (1962). They began that season ranked #2 in the pre-season AP poll. Texas held the #1 spot for two weeks in October before a 14-14 tie with Rice (2-6-2). Finishing the regular season at #4, they were shut out by #7 LSU, 13-0 in the post-season Cotton Bowl. Senior Johnny Treadwell was a unanimous All America selection at guard. No Longhorn was among the national leaders in any statistical category, although as a team they ranked seventh in Scoring Defense, allowing just 5.9 points per game.

In *The Official NCAA Collegiate Football Guide 1963*, Bill Van Fleet, Sports Editor of the *Ft. Worth Star-Telegram*, saw the Longhorns as a strong team that had many returning linemen and backs plus a promising group of sophomores to replace the nine lettermen lost to graduation.[1] Hopes and expectations were again high. In 1963, head coach Darrell Royal (see Appendix C, Coaches) was entering his seventh season at Texas.

The 1963 Season

As it turned out, few college football seasons would so intertwine with national events of that year. Texas began 1963 at #5 in the AP pre-season poll, and the Longhorns' first three wins came against unranked opponents.

Week 1: September 21 #5 Texas at Tulane

In its first outing of the season, Texas travelled to Tulane and overpowered the Green Wave, 21–0. Tony Crosby opened the scoring with a 27-yard field goal in the second quarter and added a 31-yarder in the third period. The Longhorns added two touchdowns in the fourth quarter on Phillip Harris runs of 13 and two yards. After the first touchdown, "Duke" Carlisle passed to Harris for a two-point conversion.

Texas outgained Tulane in total offense, 368 yards (282 rushing) to 138 yards, and in first downs 22 to 8. The game showed the balance in the Texas rushing offense as 11 players contributed positive yardage and a 4.7 yards per carry average. The Longhorns' rushing attack would sustain them throughout the year, and so would their pass defense. Texas held the Green Wave to four completions in 14 attempts for just 35 yards. Joe Dixon and Jim Hudson each had an interception.

The Texas quarterback was Emmett Augustus "Duke" Carlisle, III. With a father and grandfather both named Emmett, the nickname "Duke" was established at an early age and stuck. There were parallels between Carlisle and his coach, Darrell Royal. Both had played exclusively on defense until their collegiate senior years. In 1949, Royal was switched to quarterback, became an All America, and led Bud Wilkinson's Oklahoma team to an undefeated (10–0–0) season, a 35–0 Sugar Bowl win over #9 LSU, and a #2 ranking behind Notre Dame. Duke Carlisle was to make his own football history.[2]

Week 2: September 28 Texas Tech at #4 Texas

Texas Tech (5–5–0) gave up 49 points in the most one-sided game the Longhorns had that year. A review of the game statistics reveals the discrepancy:

	Texas	Texas Tech
First downs	23	7
Rushing yards	269	59
Avg. yards / rush	4.4	1.8
Passing yards	121	83

Tommy Ford scored on an 18-yard run in the first quarter. Ernie Koy scored twice on a pair of one-yard runs, and Duke Carlisle hit Charlie Talbert for 25 yards and another score as the Longhorns tallied 21 points in the second period. That would be the most points Texas scored in a quarter all season. Ford scored his second touchdown of the day on a one-yard run with less than a minute gone in the third quarter, and Tom Stockton added another on a 12-yard run five minutes later for a 42–0 Texas lead. Tech's lone score came with 3:50 remaining on a one-yard run by Leo Lowery. Tommy Wade ended the scoring with a four-yard touchdown in the fourth period for a 49–7 Texas win.

Week 3: October 5 Oklahoma State at #3 Texas

Oklahoma State, under first year head coach Phil Cutchin, would end the season at 1–8–0 and allow an average of 26 points/game.

Texas kicker Tony Crosby connected on a 32-yard field goal less than two minutes into the game. Oklahoma State responded with a Walt Garrison 48-yard touchdown run to take the lead. Tommy Ford ended the first quarter scoring with a four-yard touchdown, and Texas had the lead back, 10–7. The Cowboys were never a serious threat after the first quarter. Texas scored ten points in the second period: a Phillip Harris 6-yard run and a Tony Crosby 33-yard field goal to take a 20–7 lead into the second half.

The third quarter saw two more Longhorns touchdowns within a span of five minutes. Duke Carlisle ran it in from the 11, and Hix Green capped a nine-play, 70-yard drive with a 3-yard touchdown run and a 34–7 Texas victory. Texas rushed for 266 yards, bringing their three-game total to 817 yards (272 yards/game). The Longhorns had amassed 66 first downs to their opponents' 23 during that span. Oklahoma State fumbled three times and lost possession each time. The Longhorns fumbled twice and lost both.

Punter Ernie Koy, Jr., who averaged 42.4 and 43 yards/punt the first two games, was injured and out for the season. The Longhorns' average yards/punt slumped significantly over the remaining games, dipping into the 20s the last three contests. Koy was the son of Ernie Koy, Sr., who was an All-SWC back for the Longhorns in 1930, 1931, and 1932.

In week 2, top-rated Southern California had lost to #3 Oklahoma (17–12). The Sooners took over the top spot, and Texas advanced to #3, with Alabama at #2. A week later, the Tide and Longhorns reversed rankings, setting up a #1 vs. #2 "Game of the Century."

Week 4: October 12 #2 Texas vs. #1 Oklahoma in the Cotton Bowl

The Longhorns scored on their first possession, eating up almost seven minutes and covering 68 yards in 13 plays as Duke Carlisle scored from one yard out. Carlisle would make the cover of *Sports Illustrated* that week (October 21, 1963). In the second period, one of three Texas interceptions gave the Longhorns the ball at the Sooners' 22-yard line. Tommy Ford ran in another score from 12 yards out to end the half at 14–0.

Another interception gave Texas the ball on the Oklahoma 18-yard line. Phillip Harris took it in for a three-yard touchdown, and the Longhorns were up, 21–0. Oklahoma got its lone score late in the third quarter on a three-yard run by John Hammond. With less than a minute to play, the Longhorns' George Sauer scored on a 14-yard pass from backup quarterback Marv Kristynik as Texas proved they were for real with an impressive 28–7 win over the Sooners.

The Texas defense completely shut down the Oklahoma offense. Unanimous All America Scott Appleton led the way with 18 tackles (three solo tackles) and a fumble recovery. Timmy Doerr contributed 12 tackles, including three solos. Tommy Nobis, Jim Hudson, and Pete Lammons each had an interception.

The Longhorns had now defeated their first four opponents, including #1 Oklahoma, by a combined 132–21 (or 33 to 5.3 points/game). Over the next six games, Texas would struggle against unranked Southwest Conference teams.

Week 5: October 19 #1 Texas at Arkansas

The Longhorns next travelled to Little Rock to meet the Arkansas Razorbacks. The Longhorns drew first blood halfway through the first quarter when tailback Tommy Ford scored on a one-yard touchdown run. The second period saw Ford scoring again, this time on a three-yard run, and a 29-yard field goal by kicker Tony Crosby. After Texas lost a fumble at their own 12-yard line, Arkansas quarterback Jon Brittenum connected with Stan Sparks for a Razorbacks touchdown with 26 seconds remaining in the half, which ended at Texas 17, Arkansas 7.

The third quarter was scoreless. With 9:20 remaining in the game, Arkansas capped a 20-play, 90-yard drive when Brittenum took it in from the 1-yard line. A two-point conversion try failed, and the game ended, 17–13.

Texas outgained Arkansas in rushing, 247–71, and 301–162 in total yardage. Harold Phillip led all rushers with 135 yards (6.8 yards per carry), Duke Carlisle added 65 yards, and Ford 48 yards with two touchdowns. Even in winning, coach Darrell Royal had to be concerned that the Longhorns were held scoreless in the second half.

Week 6: October 26 Rice at #1 Texas

Six minutes into the first quarter, Texas fullback Tommy Ford scored on a 33-yard touchdown run, and Tony Crosby added the extra point. Six minutes later, Rice scored on a 9-yard pass from Walt McReynolds to Jerry Kelley, but the extra point attempt was blocked. Crosby added a 22-yard field goal in the second quarter. For the second straight week, Texas was shut out in the second half. Rice was also unable to score, and the 10–6 halftime score remained as the game ended.

Yardage gained was almost identical (Texas 258 yards, Rice 255 yards), but gained in a reverse manner. Texas outrushed Rice, 213 yards to 39 yards, while Rice gained 216 yards passing to 45 for the Longhorns. In the fourth quarter, Crosby missed a field goal and had another blocked.

Week 7: November 2 #1 Texas at Southern Methodist

Phillip Harris scored the first Texas touchdown on a three-yard run four minutes into the game. The Longhorns recovered three of four Southern Methodist fumbles in the game. One fumble recovery led to a two-yard Tommy Ford touchdown two minutes into the second period. Eleven minutes later, the Mustangs countered with a 22-yard touchdown pass from Dan Thomas to Billy Gannon. Tony Crosby kicked a 34-yard field goal with only one second remaining in the half to put Texas up, 17–6.

After a scoreless third quarter, Gannon scored on another 22-yard pass, this time from Mac White with six minutes left in the game. A two-point attempt failed, and the game ended with a 17–12 Longhorns win. Tommy Ford led all rushers with 13 carries for

113 yards. Tommy Wade passed for 48 of the Longhorns' 71 yards, while starter Duke Carlisle was only 1 of 6 for 13 yards and had one intercepted. SMU accumulated 291 yards of offense to 265 for Texas. The Mustangs also led in first downs, 16 to 10. More penalty yards and especially four fumbles (three lost) doomed an SMU upset.

The last three games Texas had won by a total of only 13 points. More troubling was the fact that they had been held scoreless in the second half in each of the games.

Week 8: November 9 Baylor at #1 Texas

Entering game eight against Baylor and the nation's leading passer, Don Trull, the Longhorns had managed to score only 44 points over the previous three games and had not scored in the second half. The Bears were 5–1, averaged 23.8 points/game, and allowed 11.5 per game. It wasn't until two minutes remaining in the third period that Tom Stockton capped a 45-yard drive to score on a one-yard run for a 7–0 Texas lead. Baylor had a shot to tie or take the lead. A Texas fumble near the Baylor goal was recovered by the Bears, who then marched down the field. With only 29 seconds remaining in the game, Baylor was on the Texas 19-yard line. Trull passed to his All America end, Lawrence Elkins, who had beaten Joe Dixon and appeared to be alone in the end zone. Duke Carlisle seemed to appear out of nowhere, intercepted the pass, and saved the 7–0 Longhorns win.

Carlisle had played safety the previous two years, but as he explained at the Longhorns 50th reunion, he always went out of the game when Texas was on defense. After the fumble, he started to leave the field but they motioned him to stay on defense. That was the only defense he played that year.[3]

Texas rushed for 242 yards, with Tommy Ford leading the way (27 carries for 101 yards). Duke Carlisle was back in form after an off-week, rushing 18 times for 93 yards and completing 5 of 6 passes for 60 yards (the Longhorns' total yards passing). Scott Appleton and the rest of the defense shut down the Bears' rushing attack (18 carries for 6 yards) and intercepted two Baylor passes. Trull, who would lead the nation with 2,157 passing yards, gained 204 yards and was intercepted twice.

The Texas pass defense was excellent all year. During the regular season, opponents completed only 44 percent of their passes and averaged 93.6 yards/game through the air. Longhorns defenders intercepted at least one pass each game for a total of 19. But worries continued. It had been nearly six quarters between scores for the nation's number one team, and now four straight games that the Longhorns could not score a point in the fourth period.

Week 9: November 16 #1 Texas vs. TCU

Phillip Harris, who carried only two times for five yards in the game, scored on a three-yard run early in the second quarter, and six minutes later Tony Crosby added a 42-yard field goal for a 10–0 Texas lead at the half. With a minute to go in the third period, third-string sophomore fullback Tom Stockton, starting for the first time, scored from three yards out, giving the Longhorns a 17–0 win and their second straight shutout. Stockton led all rushers with 89 yards. and TCU coach Abe Martin mused, "We knew Carlisle was a good runner, and Ford, and Harris. But with Koy and Philipp out, we thought maybe their fullback wouldn't be. He was."[4] Texas rushed for a season-low 150 yards but held the Horned Owls to 34 yards on 36 rushes. Duke Carlisle again accounted for the Longhorns' total passing attack of 91 yards with one interception.

The Longhorns had a scheduled bye for the week of November 23. Navy (#2), Mississippi (#3), and Alabama (#7) also had scheduled byes. On the day before the scheduled games, November 22, President John Kennedy was assassinated in Dallas, Texas.

As the country mourned the assassination of the President, teams ranked 4th, 5th, and 8th (Michigan State, Pitt, and Illinois) postponed their games to a later date. On November 28, #4 Michigan State lost to #8 Illinois, and on December 7, #5 Pittsburgh beat Penn State. Two games featuring AP Top Ten teams were played as scheduled on November 23: #6 Oklahoma lost to #10 Nebraska, and #9 Auburn beat Florida State.

Week 10: November 30 #1 Texas at Texas A&M

The football rivalry between Texas and Texas A&M dates back to the 1890s. Entering the 1963 season, Texas led the series, 47–17–5, and had won 10 of the past 11 games, losing only in 1956. There was often hi-jinx surrounding the game. This year, A&M students kidnapped Bevo, the Longhorns mascot, and Texas students burned a large "UT" in the center of A&M's Kyle field, where the game would be played.

Reliable kicker Tony Crosby connected on a 27-yard field goal with five minutes remaining in the first quarter. The lead was short-lived as A&M's Jim Keller threw a 54-yard touchdown pass to Travis Reagan early in the second period and then hit George Hargett for a 29-yard score half-way through the third. Starting the fourth quarter, the Longhorns were down, 13–3. In the previous nine games, Texas scoring by quarter showed:

Quarter	Points Scored
1	45
2	74
3	52
4	29 [shut out in last five games]

Texas relied primarily on its deliberate, wear-them-down rushing offense. That style of offense often takes longer, and time was running out. Passing more than usual, Texas gained 101 yards through the air, but was intercepted three times. They also committed four fumbles, losing three. Finally, with 12:23 remaining in the game, Tommy Ford ran for a two-yard touchdown. The two-point conversion failed, and Texas now trailed, 13–9. Capping an 80-yard, 15-play drive, Duke Carlisle scored from two yards out with 1:19 to play. Another two-point conversion attempt was no good, but the Longhorns hung on, 15–13, as A&M was unable to play the spoiler.

Although they remained undefeated, the Longhorns outscored their last six opponents, 83–44 (13.8–7.3 points per game), a drop in point differential by nearly 20 per game from their first four contests, 132–21 (33–5.3 points per game). In maintaining their #1 ranking, Texas was aided over the weeks by teams ascending the polls only to lose or tie:

OCTOBER 12:
- #1 Oklahoma loses to Texas, 28–7
- #3 Alabama loses to Florida, 10–6
- #4 Navy loses to SMU, 32–28

OCTOBER 26:
- #2 Wisconsin loses to Ohio State, 13–10
- #3 Pitt loses to #10 Navy, 24–12

NOVEMBER 9:
- #2 Illinois loses to Michigan, 14–8
- #5 Auburn loses to Mississippi St., 13–10

NOVEMBER 30:
- #3 Mississippi ties Mississippi St., 10–10
- #4 Michigan St. loses to #8 Illinois, 13–0

When Auburn lost on November 9, Texas became the only undefeated and untied team remaining.

The Army-Navy game, to decide the Longhorns' opponent in the Cotton Bowl, was held on December 7, but it almost wasn't played. After the assassination of President Kennedy, it was decided, at first, to cancel the game. The Kennedy family, and especially First Lady Jacqueline Kennedy, urged that the game be played as scheduled.

That game almost prevented another matchup between teams ranked #s1 and 2. Navy had been invited to play Texas in the Cotton Bowl, contingent on winning the game with Army. By agreement, had unranked Army won, they would have gone to the Cotton Bowl despite a 7-3 record that included a 28-0 loss to #4 Pittsburgh.[5] Pitt, with only a loss to Navy, was the only team in the top eight not invited to a bowl.

Tied 7-7 at the half, Navy took a 21-7 lead over the Cadets with 11 minutes to play. Army quarterback Rollie Stichweh ran for both a touchdown and a two-point conversion, then recovered an on-side kick to give the Cadets the ball with six minutes left and down, 21-15. Army, with no time-outs remaining, was at the Navy 2-yard line and had just 20 seconds left on the clock. Over the last minute, Stichweh had backed away from center several times to appeal for less noise, and referee Barney Finn had obligingly stopped the clock. However, at the 20-second mark, apparently thinking the clock would not start until the ball was snapped, Army re-huddled. The game ended at the Navy 2-yard line without another play run. Texas would play in its second #s 1-2 match-up of the season.[6]

Stichweh's last touchdown run was significant for another reason. The game was seen by millions of fans nationwide on CBS television. The director, Tony Verna, had brought a videotape machine to the game. By the fourth quarter, the "bugs" had been worked out and the television audience saw a "replay" of Stichweh's touchdown. As this was the first time it had been used, the TV announcer, Lindsey Nelson, assured viewers they were seeing a replay and that Army had not scored another touchdown.[7]

At the end of the regular season, should Navy have been ranked 2nd? Should the Midshipmen have been given a title shot against Texas in the Cotton Bowl? Or was a more deserving team overlooked? On October 12, #4 Navy lost to SMU (32–28), but finished the remainder of the season undefeated. Of the top teams, only Nebraska, which also suffered a loss on October 12, completed the remainder of the regular season unblemished. The Cornhuskers had been in and out of the polls all season, never ascending higher than 10th. In the regular season finale, Nebraska defeated #6 Oklahoma, 29–20, and by the final poll on December 9, the Cornhuskers were 9–1 and ranked 6th.

Of the other one-loss teams, Pitt had already lost to the Midshipmen, 24–12, and Auburn, which entered the Top 10 on October 21 after defeating #8 Georgia Tech, lost to Mississippi State two weeks later. Illinois jumped into the Top 10 on October 14 following a tie with #8 Ohio State, advanced steadily to #2, and four weeks later fell to Michigan, 14–8. By the end of the regular season, the Midshipmen were 9–1, had outscored opponents by an average 31.4 to 13.7 (second nationally), and ascended to #2 behind their elusive junior quarterback, Roger "The Dodger" Staubach. When the Heisman Trophy voting was announced, Staubach had won the award handily, 1,860 to 504, over second-place finisher Billy Lothridge of Georgia Tech. He would also be named a unanimous All America and picked up the Maxwell Award that year.

In hindsight, except for the Longhorns, 1963 was a year of parity. Very probably any of the above-mentioned teams could have been ranked #2 and played Texas for the national title. More than likely the outcome would have been the same. Roger Staubach later said the Navy team was anxious to play #1 Texas in Dallas. The team suffered their only loss, to SMU, in Dallas, and President Kennedy, a decorated Navy World War II veteran, was assassinated there only 40 days before.

The Cotton Bowl January 1, 1964

The Cotton Bowl stadium in Dallas had helped set the stage for the season's finale. Navy suffered an upset against SMU on October 11 in that stadium. Upon review, the officiating crew of that game was suspended. There were several suspect calls, including disallowing what would have been a winning touchdown pass for Navy late in the game.[8] The following day, #2 Texas beat #1 Oklahoma in the same stadium to take the top spot in the polls.

The oddsmakers favored Navy and Roger Staubach to win. Prior to the Longhorns' 50th reunion in 2013, Tommy Ford shared some memories of the season with the University of Texas Athletics department. He felt the Longhorns were not appreciated and that sportswriters, especially in the East, thought Navy was superior and would beat Texas easily. He said the team was very motivated to prove itself.[9] Myron Cope, an Eastern sports writer and sportscaster with the Pittsburgh Steeler's had been especially harsh, calling the Texas team a fraud.[10]

The Texas rushing offense averaged 231.6 yards/game and was ranked seventh in the nation. To counter the Longhorns' potent rushing attack, Navy started the game with its linebackers stacked up close, essentially making a tight, nine-man front, and daring Texas to pass. Duke Carlisle, who had not thrown a touchdown pass all season, took advantage of the depleted secondary to loft 56-yard and 63-yard scores, both to Phillip Harris. The first came three minutes into the game, the second five minutes into the second quarter. With two and a half minutes to play before the half, Carlisle scored his third touchdown on a nine-yard run following a Navy fumble. Texas now had a 21–0 halftime lead.

With less than three minutes remaining in the third period, Harold Philipp scored on a two-yard run for a 28–0 lead for the Longhorns. Primarily against Texas reserves, Navy finally got its offense moving. Staubach passed for 228 yards (then a Cotton Bowl record) with one interception and ran in a touchdown from the Texas 2-yard line early in the fourth quarter. The two-point conversion failed, and the final score was Texas 28, Navy 6.

Even with Navy stacked to stop the run, Texas netted 168 yards on the ground. The Longhorns kept the Midshipmen to -14 net rushing yards. Navy accumulated 213 yards of offense to 402 for Texas. Heisman and Maxwell winner Staubach had played well, but Carlisle, who amassed 267 of the Longhorns' 402 yards of offense and scored three touchdowns, was named Outstanding Back in the game. His teammate, Scott Appleton, recorded 12 tackles (three solo) and was named Outstanding Lineman. Navy coach Wayne Hardin stated after the game that Texas deserved its #1 ranking.

Of the other top teams, their post-season results are shown below:

Team	AP Ranking	Bowl	Opponent	Result
Texas	1	Cotton	Navy	W 28–6
Navy	2	Cotton	Texas	L 28–6
Illinois	3	Rose	Washington	W 17–7
Pitt	4	—		
Auburn	5	Orange	Nebraska	L 13–7
Nebraska	6	Orange	Auburn	W 13–7
Mississippi	7	Sugar	Alabama	L 12–7
Alabama	8	Sugar	Mississippi	W 12–7

The Sorensen System, one of the mathematical systems that evaluates team strength and strength of opponents, placed Texas at a strength of 4773. That was 721 ahead of second-place Illinois. In fact, Sorensen calculated that teams ranked third through eighth (AP), plus Michigan State and Mississippi State, were stronger than Navy.

Team Strength based on Sorensen

Team	Sorensen Rank	Strength Rating	Difference	% Diff.
Texas	1	4773		
Illinois	2	4052	721	15.1
Pitt	3	3742	310	6.5
Michigan St.	4	3628	114	2.4
Alabama	5	3606	22	0.5
Auburn	6	3586	20	0.4
Nebraska	7	3473	113	2.4
Mississippi	8	3440	33	0.7
Mississippi St.	9	3234	206	4.3
Navy	10	3164	70	1.5

Based on the Sorensen System, the degree of parity among those rated #2–10, and especially #s 3–10, is apparent.

Longhorns tackle Scott Appleton was a unanimous All America, fifth in the Heisman voting, and winner of the Outland Trophy as the top interior lineman of the year. Back Tommy Ford was voted to some All America teams, and Darrell Royal received Coach of the Year honors from both the American Football Coaches Association (AFCA) and the Eddie Robinson Award.

Among the nation's individual leaders, Tony Crosby was second in kick scoring with 24 of 24 PATs (point after touchdown) and nine field goals for 51 points. James Hudson recorded five interceptions to tie for sixth in that category. As a team, Texas ranked seventh in rushing offense (231.6 yards per game), second in rushing defense (allowing 80.2 yards per game), tied for ninth in total defense (194.2 yards per game), and was third in scoring defense (6.5 points per game allowed).

The Longhorns' SWC and Cotton Bowl opponents were well represented among the national individual and team leaders:

Player	*School*	*Category*	*Rank*
Don Trull*	Baylor	Passing	1
Roger Staubach+	Navy	Passing	6
Larry Elkins**	Baylor	Pass Receiving	1
Jim Ingram	Baylor	Pass Receiving	8
Jim Grisham**	Oklahoma	Rushing Yards	5
Pat Donnelly	Navy	Rushing Yards/Carry	10
Dan Thomas	SMU	Punting	1
Jim Keller	Texas A&M	Punting	4
Ken Hatfield	Arkansas	Punt Returns	1
Larry Elliott	Oklahoma St.	Punt Returns	2
Larry Elliott	Oklahoma St.	Kickoff Returns	5
Gene Fleming	Rice	Punt Returns	3
Donny Anderson	Texas Tech	Kickoff Returns	4
Fred Martin	Navy	Kick Scoring	1
H. L. Daniels	Texas Tech	Kick Scoring	6
George Jarman	Oklahoma	Kick Scoring	7
Larry Shields	Oklahoma	Interceptions	2 (tie)

All America
** *Consensus All America*
+ *Unanimous All America*

Texas Opponents National Team Leaders

School	Category	Rank
Oklahoma	Rushing Offense	4
Baylor	Passing Offense	3
Navy	Passing Offense	8
	Total Offense	6
	Scoring Offense	2

It would appear that the Texas Longhorns unanimously won college football's National Championship primarily for four reasons:

1. They were the only undefeated and untied team.
2. They benefited from losses to highly ranked teams at opportune times.
3. The second and third rankings changed six times involving five teams.
4. They defeated (then) #1 Oklahoma and top challenger (#2) Navy decisively.

As with once-defeated Notre Dame in 1943, it might be asked—if not Texas, then who?

CHAPTER 10

Nebraska 1971

Football for the University of Nebraska Cornhuskers had a varied history. They were 2-0 and unscored-on against Omaha and Doane their first season in 1890. By 1915, the Cornhuskers had achieved five undefeated seasons (1890, 1902, 1903, 1913, and 1915) and were selected as National Champion in 1915 by Billingsley (retroactive). They had intermittent periods of success, but by the 1940s and 1950s, they languished with one of the worst records, celebrating victory less than 40 percent of the time. In 1962, Bob Devaney was hired, and almost immediately the program was turned around (see Appendix C, Coaches).

From a record of 15-34-1 over its previous five years, in the first five years (1962-1966) under Devaney, Nebraska was 47-8-0. The following two years, the Cornhuskers returned to mediocrity with back-to-back 6-4 seasons, culminating in a 47-0 loss to Oklahoma. Assistant coach Tom Osborne suggested to Devaney a change in the offensive formation to provide more diversity.[1] The offensive change was from an unbalanced line, T-formation backfield to a balanced line with an I-formation backfield and a wingback.[2] Devaney agreed, and from 1969 to 1972 Nebraska's record was an astounding 42-4-2.

In 1969, Osborne was instrumental in bringing weight training and conditioning into college football. He noticed that injured players were returning to practice stronger, faster, and in better condition. The injured players had been weight training under the informal direction of Boyd Epley, a pole-vaulter. Years later, Epley explained that in pole-vaulting, he used the same kind of strength needed in football, and his training worked toward that goal. The general wisdom among college coaches at the time was that lifting weights made players slower and, therefore, was contrary to player development. Osborne and Epley convinced Devaney to try a weight-training program. Regarding the enormous success of Nebraska football following the 1967-1968 seasons, Devaney would later admit that it was Tom Osborne who should get the credit.[3]

The Cornhuskers won the National Championship in 1970. Returning in 1971 were two-year starters Jerry Tagge at quarterback and running back Jeff Kinney. Junior Johnny Rodgers was returning at end where, in 1970, he had led Nebraska with 35 receptions, averaging 19 yards per catch. The 1970 team had featured no stars. Offensive tackle Bob Newton was the sole Cornhusker named a consensus All America that year. Linebacker Jerry Murtaugh was a sporadic first-team selection but was not a consensus choice. No Husker received a major individual award, and none were among the top ten Heisman Trophy candidates. Only field goal and PAT specialist Paul Rogers finished in the top 10 of individual statistical leaders nationally (he was eighth in kick scoring with 63 points). Coach Devaney liked the "no stars" approach to a team sport. As a team,

Nebraska finished in the top ten only in scoring offense, where they were second with 37.2 points per game.

Nebraska was the consensus national champions in 1970 thanks to bowl defeats by #1 Texas (24–11 to #6 Notre Dame) and #2 Ohio State (27–17 to #12 Stanford). The #3 Cornhuskers took over #1 after beating #5 LSU in the Orange Bowl (17–12). However, 1970 was a weak consensus as Texas, Ohio State, Notre Dame, and #6 Arizona State each drew a share of the selectors. Notre Dame coach Ara Parsegian lobbied for the Irish to be national champions, as they had defeated #1 Texas. To this, Devaney replied that not even the Pope would vote for Notre Dame to be champions.[4]

On the night of May 20, 1970, 19-year-old football sensation Johnny Rodgers was involved with two other men in the armed robbery of a service station. Rodgers appeared in court and pled guilty to the felony exactly one year later. Ultimately, all three were given a sentence of two years probation. One of the three men had turned himself in, and the prosecution's case rested primarily on his testimony. It was never definitely determined what role Rodgers played, as one account had him holding the gun on the store attendant while another had him outside. The case against the three was weak. It had also been a time of racial tension in Lincoln, and fears of a potential riot over prosecuting a black celebrity athlete may ultimately have influenced the sentencing. Now it was up to Bob Devaney to decide if Rodgers would still play football for Nebraska.

Following an inquest by the Nebraska student tribunal and the Dean of Student Development, it was decided that Rodgers could remain in school but under the same conditions as his probation—namely that he stay out of trouble. Armed with the school's decision and after consulting with his assistants, Devaney announced on July 6, 1971, that Rodgers could play. Rodgers admitted years later that it had been difficult to stay out of trouble and that if he could do it over, he would take his education more seriously.[5]

1971 Season

Although they were the defending National Champions, the Cornhuskers found themselves ranked second behind Notre Dame in the AP pre-season poll in 1971. Beginning a week ahead of the Irish, Nebraska defeated Oregon, 34–7, and became the #1 ranked team to start the official polling.

As the defending champions, the pressure was on to repeat, and Nebraska's opponents needed no "psyching" to bring their best game to the Cornhuskers. Realizing the difficulty in repeating as champions and not wanting success to go to their heads, Devaney gathered the team and told them how he used to take dog crap in newspaper, put it on someone's porch, set it on fire, and ring the doorbell. Of course, the homeowner would stomp on the paper to put out the fire, getting dog crap on their feet. The moral of the story, according to Devaney, was to not believe the crap they write in the newspapers.

Oregon

Nebraska senior running back Jeff Kinney provided the only score in the first quarter on a one-yard run to end a 10-play drive. Substitute running back Gary Dixon scored three of his season total seven touchdowns, one in each of the next three quarters. Sophomore third-string runner Randy Butts scored the final touchdown in Nebraska's 34–7 win. A fumbled punt recovered by Oregon on the Cornhuskers' 11-yard line led to the Ducks' lone score on a Bobby Moore touchdown run with 3:21 remaining in the game.

Senior quarterback Jerry Tagge completed 8 of 10 passes for 98 yards and became Nebraska's top career passer with 2,989 yards. Kinney accounted for 124 of the Cornhuskers' 298 rushing yards. Oregon was held to 86 rushing yards, and Ducks quarterback Dan Fouts was intercepted three times while completing 13 of 25 passes for 118 yards. Moore, who would finish the season as the eighth-leading rusher in the nation with 1,211 yards, was held to only 53 yards by Nebraska's defense.

Minnesota

Under Murray Warmath, the AFCA and Eddie Robinson Award Coach of the Year in 1960, the Golden Gophers had struggled with a 13–15–2 record and no All America talent the past 3 years. Minnesota would fare no better in 1971, finishing at 4–7.

On their second possession, the Cornhuskers marched 50 yards in four plays and scored on a Jerry Tagge to Johnny Rodgers 28-yard touchdown pass. A recovered Minnesota fumble gave Nebraska the ball back at the Golden Gophers' 20-yard line. Running back Jeff Kinney took it in from the 1-yard line for a 14–0 lead to end the first quarter. With 9:08 remaining in the half, Minnesota capped a 79-yard drive when fullback Ernie Cook scored on a six-yard run. A recovered fumble at the Nebraska 30-yard line gave the Gophers the ball, but a 20-yard field goal attempt was missed. The Cornhuskers methodically advanced the ball 80 yards. Kinney scored from the 2-yard line, and Nebraska had a 21–7 halftime lead.

Nebraska scored twice more in the third period on Tagge to Rodgers touchdown passes of 20 and 37 yards for a 35–7 Cornhuskers win. Tagge completed 15 of 21 pass attempts for 218 yards and three touchdowns, all to Rodgers. Kinney scored two touchdowns while piling up 79 rushing yards.

Texas A&M

The Aggies were another team enduring a rough stretch with their football program. Over the previous three years they were 8–23–0. They would finish the 1971 season at 5–6–0. The Nebraska defense held the Aggies to 100 total offensive yards, 83 rushing and 17 through the air. Sophomore reserve quarterback Mark Green accounted for 60 of the A&M yards, including all 17 passing yards.

The Cornhuskers were less than impressive in the first half. Tagge suffered his first interception of the year, two fumbles were lost, a PAT was blocked, and placekicker Rich Sanger's first field goal attempt of the year failed. They managed a 13–0 halftime lead on a long touchdown run by fullback Bill Olds and a short run by Tagge ending an 89-yard drive.

Johnny Rodgers returned the second half kickoff 98 yards for a touchdown. Tagge hit Rodgers for a 32-yard touchdown, and safety Bill Kosch returned an intercepted pass 95 yards for another score. The Aggies' lone touchdown came on a 94-yard kickoff return by Hugh McElroy late in the fourth period. The Cornhuskers amassed 413 yards of offense in a 34–7 win.

Utah State

For the second week in a row, the Cornhuskers' opposition were Aggies. Nebraska used a balanced attack against the Utah State Aggies with 230 yards on the ground and 239 passing. Quarterback Jeff Tagge accounted for four touchdowns: two on short runs, a 14-yard strike to fullback Bill Olds, and a 36-yard completion to Johnny Rodgers. The defensive provided a touchdown when Dave Mason intercepted Aggies quarterback Tony Adams and ran it back 54 yards for a score. Mason would finish the season with six interceptions, returning three for touchdowns. Midway through the third quarter, Adams completed a 34-yard touchdown pass to Bob Wicks to avert a shutout. The PAT failed, and the final score read Nebraska 42, Utah State 6.

Also that week, #7 Alabama topped Mississippi, 40–6, and #8 Oklahoma beat #17 Southern California, 33–20.

Missouri

Playing in only three quarters, Jeff Tagge accounted for 319 of Nebraska's 603 yards of offense. Tagge ran for 85 yards and a touchdown, and he passed for 234 yards and another score, a 28-yarder to Johnny Rodgers. In the first half, Nebraska had amassed 214 yards rushing and 116 passing. Missouri had 24 passing yards and -2 yards rushing during the same 30 minutes. Once again, the Cornhuskers got points from the defense, this time a safety following a blocked Missouri quick-kick. Nebraska ran 108 plays to Missouri's 48 in the 36–0 shutout.

In other games, #6 Alabama shut out Vanderbilt, 42–0, while #8 Oklahoma beat #3 Texas, 48–27. As a result of those scores, Oklahoma jumped to #2 in the rankings, and Alabama advanced two spots to #4.

Kansas

Once again, Nebraska showed itself a well-oiled team with few flaws on offense or defense. The offense accrued 538 yards. Jeff Kinney accounted for 104 of 411 rushing yards, 21 of the Cornhuskers' 127 passing yards, and scored twice. Jerry Tagge, once again played less than three quarters, scored touchdowns both running and passing. Johnny Rodgers contributed two touchdowns, one running and one on a pass reception. Kansas lost five fumbles, was intercepted three times, and was held to -42 rushing yards as Nebraska won easily, 55–0.

Oklahoma, ranked #2, defeated #6 Colorado, 45–17, and #4 Alabama bested #14 Tennessee, 32–15. Other teams remaining undefeated were: #3 Michigan, #5 Auburn, #7 Notre Dame, #8 Georgia, #9 Penn State, and #17 Toledo.

Oklahoma State

The Nebraska defense had now allowed a score in only four of 24 quarters during its first six games and no points in the past nine quarters. That streak would run to 12 quarters against the Oklahoma State Cowboys. The starting Nebraska defensive unit, the Blackshirts, left the game after three quarters having allowed no points and only 68 total yards. The reserves allowed 138 yards and 13 points in the final period to skew the true dominance of the Cornhuskers' defense.

Johnny Rodgers again dazzled with a 92-yard punt return for a touchdown while returning seven punts for 170 total yards. Rodgers also scored on a six-yard pass from Jerry Tagge. Kinney scored twice on runs of 25 and 12 yards. The PAT failed after his second touchdown. Tagge connected with Jerry List on a 42-yard touchdown pass, and Dave Mason returned an intercepted pass 27 yards for a score.

Against Cornhuskers reserves, the Cowboys scored two touchdowns in the final 1:52 of the game. Running backs Bill Heilman and Steve Elliott each scored within 33 seconds. One PAT was blocked, and the final score was Nebraska 41, Oklahoma State 13.

The Nebraska Blackshirts defense was led by Bob Terrio, Rich Glover, Willie Harper, Larry Jacobsen, and Dave Mason. By season's end, those five would account for 386 tackles, four fumble recoveries, and 15 interceptions. Minnesota rushed for 124 yards against the Cornhuskers. The other six teams' rushing yards totals against Nebraska were:

Oregon	87 yards
Texas A&M	83 yards
Utah State	89 yards
Missouri	9 yards
Kansas	42 yards
Oklahoma State	100 yards

Those six games produced an average of 68.3 yards per game. The Cornhuskers' defense was equally stingy in allowing an average of 105.8 yards passing per game.

Other teams remaining undefeated were: #2 Oklahoma, #3 Michigan, #4 Alabama, #5 Auburn, #7 Penn State, #8 Georgia, and #15 Toledo.

In the first seven games, the Huskers had faced unranked teams with a combined record of 31–45–1 by season's end. The Huskers won each contest handily by an average score of 39.6 to 5.7. It was assumed that the first real test would come on October 30, against #9 Colorado. The Buffaloes, at 6–1, had lost only to #2 Oklahoma (45–17) two weeks previous. At season's end, only defensive end Herb Orvis would get any votes (not consensus) to an All America team for Colorado, but the Buffaloes did feature Charlie Davis (seventh in rushing with 126 yards per game and sixth in yards per carry, 6.3) and Cliff Branch, a dangerous punt returner (16.3 yards per return, sixth in the nation).

#9 Colorado

Nebraska's highly anticipated game with the Buffaloes turned out to be business as usual for the Cornhuskers.

Jerry Tagge scored a touchdown passing (five yards to Maury Damkroger) and rushing (a 1-yard run) while amassing 150 total yards.

Jeff Kinney scored on touchdown runs of 11 and three yards, giving him 29 touchdowns to become Nebraska's career leader.

Dave Mason intercepted a Colorado pass, his fifth of the season.

The defense held the Buffaloes to 108 yards rushing in 55 carries, two completions in nine pass attempts for 52 yards, and caused three fumbles.

Although still four weeks away, comparisons of Nebraska and Oklahoma were already being made based on their one common opponent to date, Colorado. But while eager fans and oddsmakers pondered the showdown, the Cornhuskers and Sooners were concentrating on their next opponents, Iowa State and Kansas State respectively.

The top seven ranked teams (Nebraska, Oklahoma, Michigan, Alabama, Auburn, Penn State, and Georgia), along with #15 Toledo, all won and remained undefeated.

Iowa State

If the Cornhuskers were distractedly looking ahead to Oklahoma, it was not evident. The 5-2 Iowa State Cyclones had lost only to Colorado (24-14) and Oklahoma (43-12). In their other five games, all wins, they averaged 29.8 points per game while allowing 13.

Johnny Rodgers, who had not scored the week before against Colorado, had a touchdown run of 10 yards and returned a punt 62 yards for another score. Jerry Tagge and reserve quarterback Van Brownson added touchdowns. Rich Sanger completed field goals of 26, 27, and 39 yards as Nebraska recorded its third shutout of the season, 37-0. The Cornhuskers' offense generated 304 rushing yards and 97 yards passing. The defense was again dominant, holding the Cyclones to 66 yards on the ground and 40 through the air, allowing only four completions in 15 attempts and notching three interceptions.

All teams #s 1–7 and #14 Toledo won. The following week, Penn State moved up one spot to #5, replacing Auburn, now #6.

Kansas State

The Wildcats scored 17 points against Nebraska's starting defensive unit, and quarterback Dennis Morrison completed 23 passes (in 46 attempts) for 179 yards against the Big 8 Conference's top pass defense. Jerry Tagge completed 20 of 28 passes for 285 yards and three touchdowns. That was his third game over 200 yards and his highest passing total all season. Johnny Rodgers grabbed two of Tagge's touchdown throws, giving him a team record 10 in a season. Woody Cox hauled in the second of Tagge's three scoring passes. Jeff Kinney scored on a short run in the second quarter. The Cornhuskers' offense racked up 488 yards. Nebraska's defense, while giving up a season-high 17 points, caused a fumble that led to a safety, blocked a PAT, recorded an interception, and held the Wildcats to 57 yards rushing on 34 attempts in a 44-17 win.

Now two weeks before their big showdown, Nebraska and Oklahoma both had byes the following week to rest and prepare. This week they had combined to beat up on the state of Kansas football teams, as the Sooners defeated Kansas 56-10.

Of the other unbeaten teams: #3 Michigan defeated Purdue, 20-17, #4 Alabama downed Miami (Florida), 31-3, #5 Penn State topped North Carolina State, 35-3, and #6 Auburn defeated #7 Georgia, 35-20, knocking the Bulldogs from the unbeaten. The following week, Penn State and Auburn would switch positions in the rankings once again, Alabama and Auburn enjoyed byes while #3 Michigan got by Ohio State, 10-7, #6 Penn State beat Pittsburgh, 55-18, and #13 Toledo topped Kent State, 41-6 to stay perfect at 10-0.

#2 Oklahoma

Although certainly the game of the year, many consider this to be the game of the decade if not of the century. Fourteen times since the AP poll began in 1936, teams ranked

#1 and 2 in the polls had met. Seldom had the game lived up, so well, to the hype and anticipation. It was Thanksgiving Day, November 25, 1971, in Norman, Oklahoma. Memorial Stadium housed Owen Field, named after Sooners coach Bennie Owen (1905–1926), whose record was 122–54–16, including undefeated teams in 1911, 1915, 1918, and 1920.

Oklahoma had worked its way up the polls, starting the pre-season at #10. Using a potent Wish-Bone Offense directed by senior quarterback Jack Mildren, power fullback Leon Crosswhite, and the halfback tandem of Greg Pruitt and Joe Wylie, the Sooners defeated SMU, 30–0, and Pitt, 55–29. Then on consecutive weeks, they disposed of #17 Southern California (33–20), #3 Texas (48–27), and #6 Colorado (45–17). Over the next four weeks, the Sooners defeated four unranked opponents by a combined 194–60. And, as did Nebraska, the Sooners had a bye week before the big game.

1971 Nebraska and Oklahoma Team Stats Before Showdown

	Nebraska	*Oklahoma*
Record	10–0	9–0
Points per game avg.	38.9	45
Points allowed avg.	6.4	16.2
Offense yards/game avg.	441	563
Defense ypg. allowed avg.	171.7	337.6

1971 Common Opponents

	Nebraska	*Oklahoma*
Colorado	31–7	45–17
Iowa State	37–0	43–12
Kansas	55–0	56–10
Kansas State	44–17	75–28
Missouri	36–0	20–3
Oklahoma State	41–13	58–14

The showdown for what could ultimately be the national championship was finally under way. Oklahoma received the opening kickoff and was unable to move the ball. On fourth down, Joe Wylie punted to Nebraska's Johnny Rodgers (aka The Rocket). With six Sooners around him, Rodgers fielded the ball rather than calling for a fair catch. His 72-yard return for a Cornhuskers touchdown remains one of the most memorable moments in college football history.

At the time, Greg Pruitt and Jonny Rodgers had been long-time friends. On that punt return, Pruitt was the first down the field on coverage and got a hold of Rodgers. Hoping to get bragging rights for tackling his friend, Pruitt tried to bring him down rather than hold on and wait for help to arrive. The slippery returner got loose and scored.[6] Years later, Oklahoma sophomore starting defensive tackle and 1973 unanimous All America Lucious Selmon remembered seeing Johnny Rodgers in warm-ups before the game and was unable to believe how fast he was.[7]

Down 7–0, Oklahoma moved to the Cornhuskers' 13-yard line before settling for a

30-yard field goal by John Carroll. The key play on the drive was a 32-yard completion from Mildren to split end Jon Harrison.

Oklahoma's offense, the Wishbone or Triple Option, was developed by Texas assistant coach Emory Bellard. The Wishbone challenged a team to stop: (1) a dive up the middle by the fullback; (2) the quarterback option; and (3) a pitchout to the trailing halfback, with the lead halfback as blocker. If the Wishbone had a flaw, it was that with so many options in handling the ball, teams were prone to fumble. Nebraska had made subtle changes on defense to stop the running game and especially the outside pitch to Pruitt or Wylie. First, the fullback, Leon Crosswhite, was to be hit on every play to prevent him from downfield blocking; second, the ends and tackles were moved further to the outside to contain the pitch; and third, Joe Blahak was to shadow Pruitt on every play. The thinking was that whereas Oklahoma quarterback Jack Mildren was the best in the country at running the Wishbone, he was not a particularly good passer and averaged only about half a dozen passes a game. The Cornhuskers made another change in the defensive secondary, essentially leaving safety Bill Kosch to guard Sooners split end Jon Harrison one-on-one throughout the game. The completion to Harrison exposed a possible weakness in the mighty Nebraska defense. This defensive strategy often worked as planned at stopping the Sooners' ground game. Unanimous All America Greg Pruitt, who averaged 151.4 yards/game and led the nation with 9.4 yards/rush, was held to 53 yards on 10 carries.

On Oklahoma's next possession, Pruitt fumbled at the Nebraska 46-yard line. Jeff Kinney, who would lead all rushers with 174 yards, scored from the 3-yard line, the first of his four touchdowns, and the Cornhuskers were up, 14–3. Oklahoma ground out 80 yards for a touchdown. Utilizing the quarterback option, Mildren accounted for over half the yardage and scored himself from the 2-yard line. The score read Nebraska 14, Oklahoma 10. With less than a minute before halftime, Oklahoma had the ball once more, this time at its own 22-yard line. Catching Nebraska by surprise, Mildren drove down the field by the pass, finally connecting with Harrison to take the lead, 17–14. The halftime statistics heavily favored the Sooners: first downs, 14 to 5, total offense, 311 to 91, and time of possession, 18:51 to 11:09.

Early in the third quarter, Mildren fumbled and Nebraska's monsterback, Dave Mason, recovered the ball at Nebraska's 47-yard line. It took the Cornhuskers only four plays to move the ball 53 yards as Kinney scored his second touchdown of the game. Nebraska had retaken the lead, 21–17, with 8:54 left in the period. Following an Oklahoma punt, the Cornhuskers increased their lead to 28–17 on a 61-yard drive. After a Tagge to Rodgers completion to the 1-yard line, Kinney took it over for his third score of the game. On their next possession, the Sooners tried a "reverse pass" with Jon Harrison throwing to tight end Albert Chandler. The 51-yard completion placed the ball at the Nebraska 16-yard line. From there, Mildren ran on four consecutive plays and scored with 28 seconds to go in the third period. Nebraska 28, Oklahoma 24.

Oklahoma quarterback Jack Mildren played football at Cooper high School in Abilene, Texas. His senior season, 1967, Mildren was the most highly recruited player in the country. Sportswriter Dan Jenkins wrote about Mildren's recruitment in *Sports Illustrated*'s 1968 football preview.[8] The star quarterback had almost single-handedly compensated for Nebraska shutting down the Wishbone. Mildren accounted for 267 of the Sooners' 467 total yards and all four of their touchdowns. With the fourth quarter just beginning, he wasn't finished.

A Tagge fumble and a Lucious Selmon recovery gave Oklahoma the ball at their own 31-yard line. The Sooners efficiently moved the ball to Nebraska's 21-yard line and then faced a 4th-and-2. Mildren kept the ball and picked up the first down. The Cornhuskers held and again Oklahoma faced a fourth down, but this time needing seven yards. Again Mildren answered, this time with a 16-yard touchdown pass to Jon Harrison. With a little over seven minutes remaining, Oklahoma led, 31–28.

Tagge was a calm field general, and that was what was needed now. The Cornhuskers knew they had to score, and they had to eat up some of the clock while doing it. Jeff Kinney got the ball on almost every play, consistently picking up chunks of yardage. Faced with 3rd-and-8, Tagge sent out four receivers on hook patterns. With the Sooners dropping back all but the linemen to cover a pass, Tagge had started to run the ball, then spotted Rodgers. Between two defenders, the wide receiver scooped up a low pass to make the first down. Now the offense went back to Kinney. The big I-back picked up tough yards and finally plowed into the end zone from the 2-yard line with 1:38 remaining. The Cornhuskers had managed to use five and a half minutes on the clock to take a 35–31 lead. Jack Mildren and the Sooners had one last shot, hoping to capitalize again on Harrison being covered one-on-one. Mildren overthrew his wide-open split end, bringing up fourth down and long. The Oklahoma quarterback, dropping back for one last desperate attempt, was harassed by the Nebraska defensive line, and nose tackle Rich Glover knocked the pass down. Running out the remaining few seconds of the clock, Nebraska won, 35–31.

One of the most anticipated matchups of the game was Oklahoma center Tom Brahaney and Nebraska nose guard Rich Glover. Both were All Americas in 1971 and 1972. Glover won the Outland and Lombardi Awards in 1972. Views of this matchup are varied. Greg Pruitt recalled that the offense had to give Brahaney help against Glover. Glover was a dominant force in that game and accounted for 22 tackles. But Brahaney later said that although Glover lined up over him, his pursuit allowed him to make a lot of tackles on the outside.[9]

Many involved, at all levels, recognized then or years later the scale of what they had been involved in. After the game, Oklahoma head coach Chuck Fairbanks told his players that most teams do not get the chance to play in a game of such importance. Even before it was played, the game had taken on a life of its own, especially on the two campuses. Players recalled being treated like celebrities, being asked to sign autographs, and feeling on top of the world. The surreal atmosphere affected players differently, but some, like Sooners linebacker Steve Aycock, would later feel as though this had been the summit, and it was all downhill from that point on.[10]

Hawaii

The game of the year against Oklahoma may have been over and an Orange Bowl date with Alabama all but assured, but Coach Devaney was not about to take the University of Hawaii lightly. This was a prime time for an upset, and the Nebraska players had to focus. Hawaii was 7–3 and averaged 25.2 points/game, but had also given up 18 points/game against a much weaker schedule.

Early in the game, on third down and nine at the Hawaii 15-yard line, Jerry Tagge threw to Johnny Rodgers, who, according to Coach Devaney, was illegally hit while the ball was still in the air. No flag was thrown, and the Cornhuskers settled for a Rich Sanger 33-yard field goal. After that, the Cornhuskers got serious against the Rainbows

(Hawaii's nickname changed to "Warriors" in 2000). Monster/Rover back Dave Mason intercepted quarterback Elroy Chung and returned it 20 yards for a touchdown.

Hawaii drove to the Nebraska 20 and attempted a field goal. The kick failed, and Nebraska took over. Tagge threw to Jerry List for an 80-yard touchdown. The first quarter ended, 17–0. Nebraska was forced to punt on its next possession, and the Rainbows got to the Cornhuskers' 8-yard line. Three tries netted nothing, and Henry Sovio kicked a 29-yard field goal to put Hawaii on the board. Tagge then engineered a 54-yard drive, scoring on a 12-yard run with less than four minutes to the half for a 24–3 Nebraska lead. The Cornhuskers added three more touchdowns in the second half and won, 45–3.

Of the other top teams, #2 Alabama had finished its regular season and awaited Nebraska. Oklahoma, now at #3, defeated Oklahoma State, 58–14, #4 Michigan's season had ended, and #5 Penn State lost to #12 Tennessee, 31–11. The other undefeated team, #13 Toledo, had ended its regular season.

#2 Alabama Orange Bowl

All that stood between Nebraska and a national championship was #2 Alabama, 11–0. The Crimson Tide had won the strong Southeastern Conference (SEC). The SEC was the only conference that had four teams with 10 or more wins and five teams with nine or more wins. Only the Big 8 with Nebraska, Oklahoma, and Colorado came close. Alabama averaged 32.9 points per game and allowed 7.6 points per game. They began the pre-season poll ranked #16 before defeating #5 Southern California, 17–10, and moving up to #9 to begin the regular season poll. The Crimson Tide defeated several ranked teams: #14 Tennessee, 32–15, #18 LSU, 14–7, and #5 Auburn, 31–7, to secure its place in the championship game after Oklahoma lost. They featured consensus All America running back Johnny Musso, who had scored 16 rushing touchdowns out of the Wishbone. Offensive tackle John Hannah was named to some All America teams, but was not consensus.

Alabama's head coach, Paul "Bear" Bryant, was a thorn in the side of Nebraska's Bob Devaney. Bryant's teams had defeated the Cornhuskers in the 1966 Orange Bowl, 39–28 and the 1967 Sugar Bowl, 34–7. Bryant would also receive the American Football Coaches Association (AFCA) Coach of the Year Award in 1971, although Devaney would take home the Eddie Robinson Award that year. Of the remaining teams that had hoped to contend for the title, Alabama's resume' was by far the most impressive. Nebraska had already defeated Colorado and Oklahoma. The win-loss record of the other top teams' opponents was less than impressive.

Win-Loss Record of Title Contenders Opponents

Alabama	86–50–2
Nebraska	83–63–1
Colorado	81–54–1
Oklahoma	75–59–2
Georgia	66–68–1
Arizona State	65–66–3
Penn State	60–69–2
Michigan	43–74–1

Jeff Kinney opened the scoring on a short run with 2:01 remaining in the first quarter. The PAT was missed, and the Cornhuskers held a 6–0 edge. With only eight seconds remaining in the quarter, Johnny Rodgers fielded a punt, surrounded by the opposition, and raced 77 yards for a touchdown. Jerry Tagge passed to fullback Maury Damkroger for a two-point conversion and a 14–0 lead. Alabama fumbled the kickoff return, giving Nebraska the ball on the Tide's 27-yard line. With 12:43 remaining in the half, Tagge leaped into the end zone from the 1-yard line on fourth down. Gary Dixon scored on a two-yard run following another recovered Alabama fumble, and Nebraska went to the half up 28–0.

Alabama prevented a shutout with a short touchdown run by quarterback Terry Davis in the third period. The Cornhuskers added a Sanger field goal in the third quarter and a touchdown by backup quarterback Van Brownson in the fourth period. The last score was set up by an interception by cornerback Jim Anderson. The final score was Nebraska 38, Alabama 6.

Alabama had moved the ball well, rushing for 241 yards, 58 yards more than the Cornhuskers. All America Johnny Musso accounted for 79 yards on 15 rushes. But it was the Nebraska defense that caused Alabama to turn the ball over twice on interceptions and twice on fumbles that consistently set up the offense with good field position. Coach Bryant praised the Cornhuskers as the better team and one of the greatest he had seen.

The 1971 Nebraska Cornhuskers so dominated the best teams of that year that there could be no doubt they deserved the title unanimously. In their wake they left Oklahoma, Colorado, and Alabama, undeniably the best contenders for the crown. Nebraska's schedule had them competing against some of the top nationally ranked players in the nation.

Nebraska opponents National Individual Statistical Leaders

Dennis Morrison	Kansas State	#9 Passing
Greg Pruitt	Oklahoma	#1 Rushing yards / carry
Greg Pruitt	Oklahoma	#3 Rushing yards / game
Greg Pruitt	Oklahoma	#5 All-Purpose yards
Greg Pruitt	Oklahoma	#7 Scoring
Charlie Davis	Colorado	#7 Rushing yards / game
Charlie Davis	Colorado	#6 Rushing yards / carry
Jack Mildren	Oklahoma	#8 Rushing yards / carry
Jack Mildren	Oklahoma	#6 Scoring
Bobby Moore	Oregon	#8 Rushing yards / game
Leland Glass	Oregon	#7 Receiving
Bob Wicks	Utah State	#6 Receiving
Jim Benien	Oklahoma State	#2 Punting
Cliff Branch	Colorado	#6 Punt returns
Bobby McKinney	Alabama	#10 Punt returns
Mike Fink	Missouri	#5 Kickoff returns
Johnny Musso	Alabama	#3 (tie) Scoring

Bill Butler	Kansas State	#8 Scoring
John Carroll	Oklahoma	#1 Kick scoring
Bill Davis	Alabama	#3 (tie) Kick scoring

Individually, Johnny Rodgers was third in the nation in punt returns, eighth in All-Purpose yards, 10th in scoring, and a consensus All America, joining defensive tackle (and Outland Trophy winner) Larry Jacobsen and defensive end Willie Harper. Rich Glover, the 1972 Outland Trophy winner, was named to a few All America teams (not a consensus), while quarterback Jerry Tagge made no one's All America list, yet finished seventh in the Heisman Trophy balloting. Rich Sanger was ninth in Kick Scoring with 75 points.

The national team statistics for the top four teams are shown below.

National Team Ranking 1971

	Alabama	Colorado	Nebraska	Oklahoma
Rushing Offense (ypg)	324.1 (4th)	—	—	472.1 (1st)
Total Offense (ypg)	—	412.5 (9th)	437.7 (8th)	566.5 (1st)
Scoring Offense (ppg)	32.9 (7th)	—	39.1 (3rd)	44.9 (1st)
Rush Def (ypg allowed)	116.5 (8th)	—	85.9 (2nd)	—
Total Def (ypg allowed)	219.7 (7th)	—	202.9 (5th)	—
Scoring Def (ppg allowed)	7.6 (2nd)	8.2 (3rd)	—	

KEY

ypg: yards per game
ppg: points per game

Chapter 11

Southern California 1972

The 1971 season had been difficult for head coach John McKay (see Appendix B, Awards and Coaches). The Trojans were 6–4–1 for the second year in a row. There had been some racial tension dividing the team as two quarterbacks, one white (Mike Rae) and one black (Jimmy Jones), vied for the starting job. Also, there appeared to be no strong leadership from the seniors, with speculation that some players were more concerned with their own stats and chances for an NFL future than in winning as a team.[1]

During the 1971 campaign, McKay decided to give the two quarterbacks equal playing time. He also allowed a request by some players to organize the Fellowship of Christian Athletes (FCA) on the team. These two changes helped turn the tide. The unranked Trojans, at 2–4, beat #5 Notre Dame, 28–14, and entered the AP poll at #20 the following week. They won their next three games and ascended to #15 before a 7–7 tie with unranked UCLA dropped them out of the polls.

The University of Southern California 1972 football team. The 12–0 unanimous national champions had a wealth of talent and outscored opponents, 467–134. John McKay (1st row, center) was the AFCA and Eddie Robinson Coach of the Year in 1972 (courtesy USC Athletics).

Entering the 1972 season, McKay felt he had a strong offense. The line was experienced and had been together for three years, hard-running Sam "Bam" Cunningham, who had been playing tailback, would be switched to fullback, and a pair of sophomores, Allen Carter and Anthony Davis, would bring tremendous speed at tailback. Other returning veterans included quarterback and kicker Mike Rae, Rod McNeill at running back, wide receiver Lynn Swann, and an all-senior line that included tackle Pete Adams and tight end Charles Young. Pat Haden, a quarterback, was a promising sophomore. McKay was cautiously optimistic about his defense. Although less than a handful of starters returned, the unit showed promise with great speed at all positions.

A somewhat surprising change going into the 1972 season was the ruling that freshman could play varsity football for the first time in 20 years. Not surprisingly, Nebraska, the unanimous national champion in 1971, was ranked #1 in the pre-season polls. The Trojans were ranked #8.

The Season 1972

#4 Arkansas

The season started slowly for the visiting Trojans as they were tied at the half with #4 Arkansas, 3–3. The second half showed the promise of what was to come as Southern California scored four touchdowns and the defense held the Razorbacks to one late-game score for a 31–10 win.

Quarterback Mike Rae broke the tie in the third quarter on a five-yard touchdown run. Following an interception by Trojans linebacker Richard Wood, running back Rod McNeill scored the first of his two touchdowns on a three-yard run. Rae completed 18 of 24 passes for all of the Trojans' 269 passing yards. McNeil carried 28 times for 117 of USC's 208 total rushing yards. The defense effectively shut down Arkansas' highly touted quarterback, Joe Ferguson, who completed only 10 of 36 passes and was intercepted twice. In addition to his interception, Wood recorded 18 tackles, including two sacks. Arkansas would fade from the polls, finishing the season at 6–5.

That same week, unranked UCLA dethroned the #1 Nebraska Cornhuskers, 20–17. USC was ranked #8, but after topping #4 Arkansas while #3 Ohio State, #5 Penn State, and #6 Oklahoma had byes and #2 Colorado and #7 Alabama defeated unranked California and Duke respectively, the Trojans replaced Nebraska at #1.

Oregon State

The Oregon State football team's record was 43–28–1 under head coach Dee Andros since his arrival in 1965. The 1972 season would begin a downward slide for the Beavers, as the next four years would produce a record of 8–36 under Andros and then 52–197–6 under five successive coaches through 1998.

Southern California's home opener showcased their offense, which amassed 354 yards rushing and 316 passing, 248 yards coming from Mike Rae, who completed on 12 out of 19 attempts. The Trojans' defense continued the dominance it showed the week before, allowing Oregon State only 92 yards total offense and forcing six turnovers. The final score was USC 51, Oregon State 6.

In other games, all top 10 teams won except #6 Penn State, which was beaten by #7 Tennessee, 28–21, and #5 Alabama enjoyed a bye week.

Illinois

Southern California traveled to Memorial Stadium to take on the Fighting Illini, and a battle they got through the first half. Illinois scored first to go ahead 7–0. Mike Rae tied the score, but the Illini again led, 14–7, on a short run by halfback Bob Hayes. Rae connected on his second touchdown pass to tie the score at 14–14. Leading 20–14 at the half and 35–20 after three periods, the Trojans then put the game out of reach, eventually winning, 55–20. Rae threw 13 times, completing nine for 178 yards and two first-half touchdowns. Anthony Davis scored two touchdowns, and the defense scored a touchdown on a blocked punt.

Other games found #4 Ohio State on a bye week and #6 UCLA losing to #12 Michigan, 26–9. All others in the top 10 won.

Michigan State

In spite of the final score, defense definitely ruled this game. The Southern California defense forced seven Spartans fumbles, recovering five, and intercepted three passes.[2] Six of the turnovers resulted in Trojans touchdowns, including a 25-yard interception return by linebacker Richard Wood. The Michigan State defense forced two fumbles and intercepted Mike Rae four times, but failed to convert the turnovers into points. Final score: Southern California 51, Michigan State 6.

Wide receiver Lynn Swann returned a Spartans punt 92 yards for the first score. Swann also caught a 30-yard touchdown pass to end the Trojans' 27-point, fourth quarter barrage. Michigan State did hold USC's rushing attack in check as Rae led all Trojans rushers with only 53 yards. Spartans defensive back Brad Van Pelt would be a unanimous All America and take home the Maxwell Award.

There were two upsets in the top 10: #3 Colorado lost to Oklahoma State, 31–6, and #4 Tennessee was defeated by Auburn, 10–6.

#15 Stanford

The Trojans now faced an away game against their heated/hated rival, #15 Stanford (3–0). The previous two years, the Cardinals had enjoyed two 9–3–0 seasons, two Rose Bowl victories, and two wins over Southern California. Stanford would finish this season with the nation's number five passing attack and number four passer, Mike Boryla.

With the score tied 13–13, Boryla completed a pass to the Trojans' 7-yard line, but it was called back on a penalty. On the same play, Stanford center Bill Reid injured his hand. The rules at the time allowed for only two substitutions between plays and, as the Cardinals had already substituted, Reid had to remain in the game. His bad hand caused the snap to fly over the head of punter Dave Ottmar, and it was recovered by the Trojans on Stanford's 5-yard line. Anthony Davis scored on a one-yard run, and USC took the lead for good, 20–13. This was the turning point of a hard-fought game.

The Trojans' offense gained 407 total yards, but had a pass intercepted and lost five fumbles. Stanford defensive back James Ferguson recovered one of the fumbles in the end zone for a touchdown. Boryla completed 20 of 36 passes for 199 yards and one touchdown, and he was intercepted once. Ahead 30–21 with four seconds remaining in the game and Southern California on the Stanford 19-yard line, John McKay signaled for a time-out and called for a pass into the end zone, hoping for another touchdown. The Pat Haden to J. K. McKay pass fell incomplete, but it was clear that McKay was willing to run up the score. Stanford head coach Jack Christiansen felt the Trojans had no class and, worse, were poor winners.[3]

In other games that week, all of the top 10 teams won with the exceptions that #2 Oklahoma and #6 Nebraska had byes.

California

The California Golden Bears were 1–4 when they traveled to meet the Trojans. California would end the season with the nation's seventh-leading passing attack, averaging 222.2 yards per game. They managed this with three quarterbacks sharing the duties: senior Jay Cruze (829 yards, eight touchdowns), sophomore Steve Bartkowski (944 yards, four touchdowns), and freshman Vince Ferragamo (640 yards, six touchdowns).

The Trojans enjoyed a 21–0 lead at the half and finished with a 42–14 win. The Golden Bears' passing trio would manage 260 yards of their 301 yards of total offense. Southern California's balanced offense recorded 411 total yards. Mike Rae and Sam Cunningham each scored two touchdowns rushing. The remaining two scores resulted from Pat Haden to Charles Young completions of 40 and nine yards.

The AP's top eight teams all won their games, while #9 Auburn lost to #8 LSU and #10 Texas lost to #2 Oklahoma. A total of eight teams remained undefeated.

#18 Washington

The Washington Huskies were ranked #9 in the AP pre-season poll and were co-favorites with Southern California to win the PAC 10. After winning their first five games, they had been shut out, 24–0 by Stanford the previous week. Early in that game, Huskies senior quarterback Sonny Sixkiller (4,371 yards and 28 touchdown passes in his first two years) was injured and had to sit out the game with the Trojans, as did his backup, Greg Collins. In addition, Washington's offensive line was riddled with injuries. The visiting Huskies, relying on two rookie signal-callers, fielded a different team from the one expected to compete for the PAC 10 title and a trip to the Rose Bowl.

In the first half, Sam Cunningham scored on a short run and Anthony Davis added another score on a 44-yard run. Mike Rae field goals of 22 and 26 yards put the Trojans up, 20–0 at the half. Washington's pasted-together offense had a total of -7 yards in the first half. In the third quarter, Cunningham and Davis each scored a second touchdown. Washington's third-string quarterback, Denny Fitzpatrick, put the Huskies on the board in the fourth period with a 10-yard run. Washington managed only 120 yards of total offense to Southern California's 406 yards. The Trojans won, 34–7.

Three top ten teams fell that week: #2 Oklahoma lost to #9 Colorado 14 to 20 and #8 Notre Dame and #10 Tennessee both lost. The field had begun to shrink. Only five teams remained undefeated.

Oregon

By the week of their game with Southern California, the Oregon Ducks had been blasted on successive weeks by #2 Oklahoma, 68–3, and #15 UCLA, 65–20. They lost their next two games before finding some redemption in squeaking past #13 Stanford, 15–13. The Ducks featured quarterback Dan Fouts, the nation's seventh-leading passer.

Oregon was 2–5 when they hosted the Trojans. The artificial turf at year-old Autzen Stadium was extremely slippery on game day, with cold temperatures and heavy rain. Weather conditions prevented either team from scoring in the first half. Anthony Davis found his footing in the third quarter and scored a pair of touchdowns on runs of 48 and 55 yards. Davis carried 25 times and gained 206 yards. Sam Cunningham banged in another score late in the fourth period. All three PATs were missed. The Trojans committed nine fumbles and lost six of them but still went home with a hard-fought 18–0 win.

With the exception of LSU (bye week), all the undefeated teams won.

Washington State

The Washington State Cougars gave up 376 rushing yards to the visiting Trojans. Anthony Davis, starting at tailback for the first time, accounted for 195 of the yards and scored three touchdowns. Davis returned the opening kickoff 69 yards, but Southern California had to settle for a Mike Rae field goal. Cougars placekicker Joe Danelo evened the score with 0:47 remaining in the first period. That was the extent of the Washington State scoring, and Southern California prevailed 44–3. The Trojans' defense held the Cougars to 85 yards passing and 220 total yards. Referring to Southern California, Washington State head coach Jim Sweeney quipped that only the Miami Dolphins [Super Bowl Champions and the only undefeated NFL team] were better than the Trojans.[4]

Once again, all undefeated teams continued to win. Southern California would now have a bye week before their annual cross-town rivalry game with UCLA. During the Trojans' bye week, two previously undefeated teams fell: #5 Ohio State lost to Big Ten rival Michigan State, 19–12, and #6 LSU lost to SEC rival #2 Alabama, 35–21. Nebraska, at #3 despite one loss, tied Iowa State, 23–23. Southern California at #1, #2 Alabama, and #3 Michigan were the only remaining undefeated teams.

#14 UCLA

The UCLA Bruins were unranked in the pre-season. Their first game was a 20–17 upset win over highly favored Nebraska, the defending national champion of the past two years. That win catapulted the Bruins to #8. Their next game, a 38–28 win over Pittsburgh, advanced them to #6, but the following week the Bruins lost to Michigan, 26–9. Six more wins took them to 8–1 and a #8 ranking before losing to unranked Washington.

The previous year, the 2–7–1 Bruins tied Southern California, 7–7, and the year before had beaten the Trojans, 45–20. The Trojans-Bruins game for Los Angeles bragging rights often takes on a special intensity. This year the game would decide the PAC 8 Championship and which team would play in the Rose Bowl. As always, the two schools were wary of each other. UCLA's "Wishbone" offense was led by quarterback Mark

Harmon, the son of Michigan running back and 1940 Heisman Trophy winner Tom Harmon. The Bruins' rushing offense was led by James McAllister and Kermit Johnson, who would be a consensus All America and finish tenth in the Heisman Trophy voting the following year.

The matchup pitted UCLA's rushing offense, ranked second nationally with 346.4 yards/game, against USC's third-ranked rushing defense, which allowed only 94.2 yards/game. The Trojans' defense allowed 10.6 points/game (seventh nationally), while the Bruins' offense averaged 31.9 points/game (tenth). The Bruins also boasted the nation's second-best punter, Bruce Barnes (43.3 yards/punt).

UCLA–Southern California Common Opponents

	UCLA	USC
California	W 49–13	W 42–14
Oregon	W 65–20	W 18–0
Oregon State	W 37–7	W 51–6
Stanford	W 28–23	W 30–21
Washington	L 30–21	W 34–7
Washington State	W 35–20	W 44–3

Mike Rae opened the scoring with a 32-yard field goal and then Anthony Davis raced 23 yards for a touchdown and a 10–0 Trojans lead. James McAllister closed the gap to 10–7 on a two-yard touchdown run. The first quarter ended looking as though it would be a close game. The Southern California defense then shut down the edges of the Bruins' Wishbone, essentially taking away the outside option. UCLA managed only 198 yards rushing. In the second period, Rod McNeill scored on a one-yard run for a 17–7 Southern California halftime lead. Mike Rae ended the scoring on a seven-yard run to seal the Trojans' win, 24–7.

Anthony Davis amassed 178 rushing yards and one touchdown. Mike Rae was 7 of 12 passing for 95 yards and rushed for a touchdown. On defense, linebacker Richard Wood accounted for 18 tackles. UCLA head coach Pepper Rodgers said he had never seen a better team.

The remaining undefeated teams all won: #1 Southern California, #2 Alabama (52–13 over Virginia Tech), and #3 Michigan (9–6 over Purdue). The following week, Southern California and Alabama had byes, while #3 Michigan lost to #9 Ohio State, 14–11. Oklahoma at 9–1 moved to #3, followed by Ohio State, Penn State, Texas, and Michigan, all one-loss teams.

#10 Notre Dame

The Southern California–Notre Dame football rivalry began in 1926. Going into the 1972 season, except for the war years of 1943–1945, the series was uninterrupted, with Notre Dame winning 25 games, Southern California 14, and four ties. With the win against UCLA, the Trojans won the PAC 8 and secured a place in the Rose Bowl regardless of the outcome of their game with the Irish.

From a pre-season ranking at #13, Notre Dame had risen as high as #6 before a

30–26 loss to unranked Missouri. They rebounded with four straight wins, an 8–1 record, and a #10 ranking in the polls. Once again, the Trojans faced a high-powered offense averaging 28.9 points/game. Notre Dame was fifth in rushing offense with an average of 304.3 yards/game and seventh in total offense at 423.8 yards/game. The Irish offense was led by quarterback Tom Clements (1,163 yards passing/341 rushing). Including Clements, they had five rushers with season totals over 300 yards, led by Eric Penick's 727 yards. On defense, the Irish allowed 11.9 points/game. Their defensive tackle, Greg Marx, was a unanimous All America. Somewhat of a surprise, Notre Dame's Mike Townsend, the nation's leader in interceptions (10), made no All America team.

"Davis, Davis, Davis, Davis, Davis, Davis" was the *L.A. Times* headline on December 3, 1972, the day after the game.[5] Sophomore Anthony Davis scored six touchdowns against the Irish. Davis returned the opening kickoff 97 yards for a touchdown. After a Notre Dame field goal, Davis scored twice more on touchdown runs of one and five yards. Two of the three PATs were missed, and the first quarter ended with the Trojans up, 19–3. The only scoring in the second quarter was an Irish five-yard touchdown pass from Tom Clements to Willie Townsend that closed the gap to 19–10 at the half.

Davis scored his fourth touchdown early in the third period on a four-yard run. A two-point conversion failed, but the Trojans enjoyed a 25–10 lead. Still in the third quarter, Notre Dame rallied with Clements throwing two touchdown passes, an 11-yard strike to Gary Diminick and a 10-yarder to Mike Creaney. After the second touchdown, a two-point conversion pass attempt that would have tied the game failed, but late in the third quarter,

University of Southern California players and fans celebrate a 45–23 win over Notre Dame to end the regular season at a perfect 11–0 in 1972. Tailback Anthony Davis scored six touchdowns in the game (courtesy USC Athletics).

the Irish had narrowed the margin to 25–23. Both third-period touchdowns for the Irish came after pass interceptions by Mike Townsend. Davis' fifth touchdown, a 96-yard kick-off return following the Notre Dame touchdown, was the catalyst needed for the Trojans to break the game open. Davis scored his sixth touchdown on an 8-yard run, and Sam Cunningham finished the scoring on a one-yard run for a final score of 45–23. Davis finished the game with 368 all-purpose yards (rushing, receiving, and return).

Of the top 20 teams, only eight had games scheduled that week. Alabama, at #2 and the only other previously undefeated team, lost to #9 Auburn, 17–16. Oklahoma, 9–1, defeated #20 Oklahoma State, 38–15 and moved up a spot to #2. Going into the bowl season, Southern California was the only major undefeated team. Teams ranked #2–8 all had one loss. Ever since the 1946 season, the Rose Bowl had traditionally paired the winners of the (then) PAC 8 and the Big Ten. When #9 Ohio State defeated #3 Michigan in the last regular season game for both, the Buckeyes earned the right to play in the Rose Bowl.

#3 Ohio State—The Rose Bowl

The Ohio State Buckeyes were ranked #3 in the pre-season polls. They vacillated between #3–5 until an upset loss at unranked Michigan State in their eighth game dropped them to #9. Their end of season win, at home against #3 Michigan, coupled with #2 Alabama's loss to Auburn the following week, moved them up to a #3 ranking, a berth in the Rose Bowl, and a shot at claiming the national championship.

Ohio State scored an average of 26.3 points per game and allowed 12.9. As a team, the Buckeyes were not in the top 10 in any category. Sophomore running back Harold "Champ" Henson led the nation in scoring with 20 rushing touchdowns. The team also featured future two-time Heisman Trophy winner, freshman running back Archie Griffin. The Buckeyes' offense was led by junior quarterback Greg Hare. Offensive tackle John Hicks made some All America teams, but was not a consensus. Linebacker Randy Gradishar would be a consensus All America.

The two teams had three common opponents:

	Ohio State	*USC*
California	W 35–18	W 42–14
Illinois	W 26–7	W 55–20
Michigan State	L 19–12	W 51–6

Ohio State coach Woody Hayes was 3–1 in the Rose Bowl and 2–0 against Southern California, with wins in 1955 and 1968. His last trip to Pasadena three years before was a 27–17 defeat by #12 Stanford that cost his team a shot at the national championship. Hayes was determined that his team would be ready. Using all 21 of his practice days, he kept the Buckeyes isolated, held contact drills and scrimmages, and enforced an early curfew. Southern California's John McKay, on the other hand, utilized only 17 practice days, held no scrimmages, and allowed his players more freedom.

Game day arrived. Although heavily favored, the Trojans were unimpressive as the first half ended in a 7–7 tie. A Mike Rae to Lynn Swann 20-yard touchdown pass late in the first quarter put Southern California ahead, 7–0. The second period had barely begun when the Buckeyes tied the score on a one-yard run by junior running back Randy Keith.

Ohio State tried to keep the kickoffs out of Anthony Davis' hands by kicking short, and as a result the Trojans often started with good field position. Less than three minutes into the third quarter, Southern California's Sam Cunningham scored from two yards out. Four minutes later, a Blair Conway 21-yard field goal brought Ohio State to within four points at 14–10. Again taking advantage of a short field, two and a half minutes later Davis ran for a 20-yard touchdown. Near the end of the quarter, Cunningham took the ball in from the 1-yard line. After three periods Southern California led, 28–10. The Trojans scored on each of their first five second-half possessions to put the game out of reach. Cunningham scored two more touchdowns, each on one-yard runs. Ohio State managed another late touchdown as John Bledsoe ran it in from the 5-yard line. The final score read: USC 42, OSU 17.

Davis led all rushers with 157 yards on 23 carries. Rae connected on 18 of 25 passes for 229 yards, and Swann caught six passes for 108 yards. The Trojans exhibited a balanced attack with 207 yards rushing and 244 passing. Ohio State rushed for 285 yards, with Archie Griffin contributing 95. The Buckeyes passed 11 times, completing only five for 81 yards, and were intercepted twice.

The Post Season

Results of Bowl Games

AP Rank	Team	Record	AP Rank of Opp. In Bowl	Result
1	USC	11–0	#3	W 42–17
2	Oklahoma	10–1	#5	W 14–0
3	Ohio State	9–1	#1	L 42–17
4	Alabama	10–1	#7	L 17–13
5	Penn State	10–1	#2	L 14–0
6	Auburn	9–1	#13	W 24–3
7	Texas	9–1	#4	W 17–13

With #3 Ohio State, #4 Alabama, and #5 Penn State each suffering losses in bowl games, any championship hopes they may have clung to were dashed.

Oklahoma, at #2, beat #5 Penn State in the Sugar Bowl. The Nittany Lions' outstanding junior running back, John Cappelletti (1973 Heisman Trophy and Maxwell, and Camp Awards winner) was sidelined with the flu, and the Sooners capitalized in a 14–0 shutout.

Did the Sooners have a legitimate claim to #1? In national team rankings, Oklahoma cracked the top 10 in six of the eight major categories, one more than did the Trojans.

National Team Rankings

	Oklahoma	USC
Rushing Offense	1 (368.8 ypg)	—
Total Offense	2 (477.7 ypg)	6 (430.1 ypg)

Scoring Offense	6 (35 ppg)	3 (38.6 ppg)
Rushing Defense	6 (102.2 ypg)	3 (94.2 ypg)
Total Defense	5 (226.7 ypg)	7 (230.4 ypg)
Scoring Defense	2 (6.7 ppg)	7 (10.6 ppg)

Sooners running back Greg Pruitt was a unanimous All America and runner-up for the Heisman Trophy (he had finished third in 1971). Center Tom Brahaney was a consensus All America, and defensive lineman Derland Moore was named to some teams, but was not a consensus.

Southern California's tight end Charles Young was voted a unanimous All America. Other Trojans receiving votes, but not enough to be consensus, were:

Running back: Sam Cunningham
Offensive tackle: Pete Adams
Defensive lineman: John Grant
Linebacker: Richard Wood

Anthony Davis was fourth in scoring, fifth in rushing yards, and 10th in all-purpose yards nationally. Lynn Swann was sixth in punt returns, while Mike Rae finished sixth in kick scoring. The only Oklahoma player who finished in the top 10 nationally in an individual category was Rick Fulcher, #10 in kick scoring. The Trojans' John McKay was voted Coach of the Year.

These individual and team achievements are not, of themselves, a reason to proclaim a team a national champion. They are one piece of a collage that selectors use in making their choice. Oklahoma had a mid-season loss to Colorado, a team that would record a regular season record of 8–3 and a 24–3 Gator Bowl game loss to #5 Auburn. If the Colorado loss had not occurred, the Sooners would have a stronger case, especially as bowl obligations prevented them from playing Southern California. The selectors may very well have been divided.

As it was, only a year after Nebraska's unanimous National Championship, college football again found itself with a team too powerful not to rate a unanimous choice.

Chapter 12

Nebraska 1995

The University of Nebraska began its football program in 1890. In 1971, the Cornhuskers recorded a unanimous National Championship under coach Bob Devaney. Tom Osborne took over from Devaney in 1972 and coached through 1997. He had an overall record of 255–49–3 and a second unanimous National Championship in 1995. Under Osborne's leadership, Nebraska had an impressive number of All America selections and national award winners (see Appendix C, Coaches). The field at Nebraska's Memorial Stadium was named Tom Osborne Field in his honor shortly after his retirement.

The Game in 1995

In the 23 years (1972–1995) between unanimous selections, the game was changed in subtle ways—more like a gradual fine-tuning. Rules changes to open the passing attack and then to better protect the passer were enacted:

1976	pass blockers can extend arms.
1977	offensive lineman can block downfield in certain passing situations.
1985	pass blocking rules are further eased to protect the passer.

Tougher penalties were mandated for unnecessary roughness in 1979, while a distinction was made and different penalties assessed for incidental and deliberate grabbing of a facemask in 1982. To further protect players, a teammate could no longer stand on or jump on another player in an attempt to block a field goal or a point-after-touchdown as of 1981. Other changes included:

1982	a player may ground (spike) the ball to stop the clock.
1982	pass interference only called if the pass is catchable.
1984	kickoffs that sail out of the end zone are placed at the 30-yard line instead of the 20.
1986	kickoffs are from the 35-yard line instead of the 40.
1991	distance between goalposts reduced to 18'6" from 23'4".
1992	defense can now advance a recovered fumble.
1993	hash marks are moved in toward center of field.

Addressing non-playing situations, Proposition 48 was passed in an attempt to standardize eligibility in 1983, and drug testing was begun in 1986.

The 1995 Season

In 1994, Nebraska (13–0) was the consensus National Champion but shared the title with Penn State (12–0) and Florida State (10–1–1), much like the 1970 season before their first unanimous title in 1971. Starting 1995, Florida State was ranked #1, with Nebraska #2. Texas A&M, Penn State, and Florida completed the top five.

Florida State and Nebraska sailed through the easiest part of their schedules. For the first seven games, while the Seminoles held the number one position, they averaged 56.1 points/game and gave up an average of 17.6 points against teams that would finish with a combined record of 35–43. The Cornhuskers' first six opponents would finish a dismal 25–42–1 while being outscored by Nebraska by an average of 55.3–14.5.

Game 1 Oklahoma State

Nebraska and Oklahoma State moved their game to the start of the season in order to have ESPN cover the game. Nebraska coach Tom Osborne said he hoped the Cornhuskers looked good on TV. Osborne had nothing to worry about as the Cornhuskers rocked the Cowboys, 64–21.

Nebraska I-back Lawrence Phillips fumbled the ball three minutes into the game. Phillips soon began the scoring onslaught by capping a 72-yard drive with a three-yard touchdown run five minutes later. The extra point was missed, and the first quarter ended 6–0. The Cornhuskers' Kris Brown kicked a field goal less than two minutes into the second period. Seventy-five seconds later, linebacker Terrell Farley intercepted a Cowboys pass and returned it 29 yards for a touchdown. Oklahoma State tailback David Thompson's 79-yard run set up a two-yard touchdown by Andre Richardson, and the scoreboard now read Nebraska 16, Oklahoma State 7. It took the Cornhuskers only 12 seconds to respond. Phillips ran 80 yards for a score, but the two-point conversion failed and Nebraska was up, 22–7. Later in the quarter, Phillips scored his third touchdown on a 27-yard scamper, and with under a minute left in the half, Nebraska quarterback Tommie Frazier ran the ball in for a one-yard touchdown to finish a 30-point quarter and end the half at 36–7.

Two minutes into the third quarter, Frazier hit Reggie Baul for a 76-yard touchdown. Frazier connected with Jon Vedral for a five-yard touchdown three minutes after that. Oklahoma State got their second touchdown on an 8-yard run by Thompson, but by the end of the third period, Nebraska had a 50–14 lead. Eleven seconds into the final quarter, Ahman Green added to the Cornhuskers' lead on a 14-yard touchdown run. The Cowboys' Tone Jones hit Geoff Grenier on an eight-yard touchdown for their last score of the game. Nebraska finished the scoring when sophomore reserve James Sims ran five yards to the end zone. Nebraska had won their opener (on TV), 64–21.

Phillips ended the game with 153 yards on 12 carries as Nebraska rolled up 513 rushing yards and 673 total yards. Oklahoma State gained 282 yards, equally divided rushing and passing. The Cornhuskers doubled the Cowboys in first downs (28 to 14) although their time of possession was ten seconds less.

Among the top 5, #1 Florida State topped Duke, 70–26, #3 Texas A&M beat LSU, 33–17, #4 Penn State had a bye week, and #5 Florida beat Houston, 45–21.

Game 2 Michigan State

Before the game was even played, Michigan State coach Nick Saban stated that Nebraska was a "program that's hitting on every cylinder."[1] For the second week in a row, the Nebraska offense churned out over 500 yards rushing. Cornhuskers kicker Kris Brown opened the scoring with a 22-yard field goal less than three minutes into the game. Two minutes later, Lawrence Phillips scored on a two-yard run, the first of his four touchdowns in the game. Michigan State got on the board when quarterback Tony Banks hit Muhsin Muhammad for a 16-yard touchdown. The second quarter was another 10-point performance by Nebraska. Phillips scored his second touchdown from one yard out, and Brown connected on his second field goal from 47 yards away for a 20–7 halftime lead.

Brown made his third field goal (a 20-yarder) five minutes into the third quarter. Spartans kicker Chris Gardner added a 24-yard field goal to end the Michigan State scoring. Phillips added touchdowns three and four on a one-yard run (two-point attempt failed) and a 50-yard run to close out the third period with Nebraska up, 36–10. Nebraska dominated the fourth quarter, scoring on a 57-yard touchdown run by Ahman Green, and five minutes later James Sims' only carry in the game resulted in an 80-yard score. In all, the Cornhuskers rushed for 552 yards, 206 of them by Phillips. The Nebraska defense caused Michigan State to fumble six times (losing two) and intercepted a pass.

The night following the game, star running back Lawrence Phillips was accused of assaulting a former girlfriend and was arrested. Another running back, Damon Benning, was also accused of assaulting a former girlfriend. Phillips was dismissed from the team; Benning was not dismissed, as witnesses discredited the accuser's story and the charges were thrown out. After only two games, Phillips had gained 359 yards on 34 rushes, an average of 10.55 yards/carry. He also had seven touchdowns and was a serious Heisman Trophy contender, having placed eighth in the voting the year before. Phillips would plead "no contest," but the issue would keep him off the team for six weeks. Coach Tom Osborne was severely criticized for allowing Phillips to return. Osborne replied to the criticism, saying, "I felt the only thing I could put in place that would keep him on track was football, because that was probably the only consistent organizing factor in his life."[2]

Of the other top five, #1 Florida State defeated Clemson, 45–26, #3 Texas A&M had a bye week, #4 Penn State slipped by Texas Tech, 24–23, and #5 Florida beat Kentucky, 42–7.

Game 3 Arizona State

Tom Osborne wondered aloud how his team would play after the difficult week following the Michigan State game. The team answered 11 seconds into the game when I-back Clinton Childs ran for a 65-yard touchdown. Five minutes later, Ahman Green scored from three yards out, and Tommie Frazier ran in a 15-yard score two minutes after that. Another two minutes and Jon Vedral caught a 27-yard touchdown pass from

Frazier. With less than ten minutes gone, the Cornhuskers had scored 28 points. Arizona State scored on a two-yard pass from Jake Plummer to Keith Poole. With no time remaining in the first quarter, Nebraska senior fullback Jeff Makovicka went 13 yards for a touchdown and a 35–7 Cornhuskers lead.

Only 17 seconds into the second period, Plummer again hit Poole, this time an 80-yard touchdown. On Nebraska's next two possessions, Childs ran 38 yards for his second touchdown of the game and Frazier hit Clester Johnson on a 28-yard touchdown. Plummer and Poole connected on their third touchdown, a 38-yarder, for the Sun Devils. Nebraska scored the last two touchdowns of a wild second quarter on a 26-yard run by Green and a three-yard run by Frazier with only 39 seconds remaining. At halftime, the score read Nebraska 63, Arizona State 21.

After an 84-point first half, only 21 were scored in the second half. Terry Battle scored for Arizona State on a one-yard run with two minutes remaining in the third quarter. Nebraska scored twice in the fourth period. Terrell Farley returned an intercepted pass 21 yards for a touchdown, and Lance Brown scored on a 39-yard throw from Matt Turman.

Although the Cornhuskers' rushing yards were under 400, they passed for 292 yards. Arizona State receiver Keith Poole, who caught six passes for 200 yards and three touchdowns, described the Cornhuskers as being unstoppable.

The top three all won as #1 Florida State routed North Carolina, 77–17 and #3 Texas A&M downed Tulsa, 52–9. Florida had moved up to #4 and beat #8 Tennessee, 62–37. Auburn at #5 lost to LSU, 12–6.

Game 4 University of Pacific

Pacific was outmatched and everyone knew it. Los Vegas did not have a betting line. Tom Osborne played all 102 available players and ran more conservative plays. I-back Damon Benning scored three touchdowns in the first quarter on runs of 26, 17, and 43 yards. He would carry only 10 times, amassing 173 yards in the game. In the second period, Ahman Green and James Sims both scored on short runs. By halftime, Nebraska had 446 yards of offense to 73 for Pacific.

All second-half scoring occurred in the third quarter. Tommie Frazier ran in a 5-yard touchdown, and Green scored his second of the game on a 13-yard run. Pacific averted a shutout when Nick Sellers threw a 12-yard touchdown to Tyrone Watley. Nebraska rushed for 569 yards and gained 731 total yards in a 49–7 win. The Cornhuskers dominated in first downs, 36 to 7, and in time of possession, 39:44 to 20:16. They held Pacific to 197 total yards.

While #1 Florida State defeated Central Florida, 46–14, #3 Texas A&M lost to #7 Colorado, 29–21. The #4 Florida Gators had a bye week, while new #5 Southern California beat #25 Arizona, 31–10.

Game 5 Washington State

Pesky Washington State would end the season at 3-8-0, but they gave the #2 Cornhuskers their closest game of the season. The Cougars' defense caused five Nebraska fumbles and recovered three for turnovers. They also held Tommie Frazier to 9 completions in 20 attempts for 99 yards and the Cornhuskers to a season-low 35 points.

The first Nebraska fumble, recovered at the Cougars' 10-yard line, resulted two plays later in Frank Medu racing 87 yards for a Washington State touchdown. Unable to score, Nebraska trailed at the end of one quarter. 7–0. The deficit lasted only 17 seconds into the second period as Tommie Frazier ran for a 4-yard touchdown. Frazier added a second score six minutes later, and the Cornhuskers had the lead for good. Kris Brown connected on two field goals, a 33-yarder with five minutes remaining in the period and a 22-yarder just six seconds from halftime.

The only score in the third quarter came with a half-minute remaining. Ahman Green ran for a three-yard touchdown. Brown threw a two-point conversion pass to fullback Brian Schuster, and Nebraska held a 28–7 lead going into the fourth quarter. A 33-yard touchdown pass from Chad Davis to Shawn Tims cut the Cornhuskers' lead to 28–14. Frazier answered with his third touchdown of the game, a 35-yard pass to tight end Mark Gilman. The Cougars scored once more as Davis and Tims again teamed up for a 35-yard touchdown. Nebraska had won what would be its closest game, 35–21 over the Washington State Cougars. Even with Medu's 87-yard touchdown run, the Cougars' total rushing yardage was only 72. Davis completed 20 of 37 throws for 278 yards and two touchdowns, both to Tims.

Florida State, still holding the #1 slot, had a bye week. Florida slid into #3 following Texas A&M's loss the week before and beat Mississippi, 28–10. Colorado had moved up to #4 after its win over #3 Texas A&M and beat #10 Oklahoma, 38–17. Southern California remained at #5 and beat Arizona State, 31–0. The top three of Florida State, Nebraska, and Florida would remain for the next five weeks. The Cornhuskers now had a bye week before their game with Missouri.

Game 6 Missouri

Despite being stopped at the Missouri 3-yard line in its first possession, scoring only one touchdown in the first quarter, and committing six fumbles, Nebraska overpowered the Tigers, 57–0. Tommie Frazier ran for three touchdowns and threw for another in the first half. He left the game in the third quarter with 71 rushing yards on eight carries and seven completions in 14 attempts for 133 yards and two touchdowns. A Frazier to Brendan Holbein 29-yard touchdown came with no time remaining in the second quarter. Frazier's second touchdown pass was a six-yard strike to tight end Sheldon Jackson with less than five minutes to play in the third period. Ahman Green, backup quarterback Matt Turman, and Damon Benning each scored touchdowns on runs. Linebacker Terrell Farley blocked a punt out of the end zone for a safety. In all, the Nebraska defense held Missouri to 39 rushing yards and 83 yards passing. The Tigers were intercepted twice and fumbled five times, losing two.

The other top five teams all won and held their positions in the polls. It had been a relatively easy ride for the Cornhuskers, but the next week they would face their first real challenge in #8 Kansas State.

Game 7 #8 Kansas State

Following the game, Kansas State head coach Bill Snyder noted that if a team made mistakes against Nebraska, they could only expect bad things to happen. The Nebraska defense intercepted Wildcats quarterback Matt Miller twice and held the Kansas State rushing game to -19 yards on 26 rushes. On offense, Cornhuskers quarterback Tommie Frazier threw for four touchdowns.

Nebraska scored first on a 79-yard punt return by Mike Fullman. Three minutes later, Miller connected with wide receiver Kevin Lockett for an 18-yard touchdown. The extra point attempt failed, and Nebraska led, 7–6. Just before the first quarter ended, Jon Vedral recovered a Wildcats fumble in the end zone for a 14–6 Cornhuskers advantage. Nebraska blew the game open in the second quarter. Frazier lofted an 11-yard touchdown pass to Vershan Jackson and then shovel-passed to Ahman Green for a 10-yard score. Senior linebacker Luther Hardin intercepted a Kansas State attempted shovel-pass for a three-yard touchdown return, and the first half ended Nebraska 35, Kansas State 6.

Frazier passed 32 yards to Vedral for the only score in the third period. Kansas State scored three times in the fourth quarter. Mitch Running scored on a seven-yard pass from Brian Kavanagh, and five minutes later Kavanagh connected with Kevin Lockett for a 10-yard touchdown. Jason Johnson picked up a blocked Nebraska punt and returned it six yards for a score. The Wildcats attempted a two-point pass play that failed and were one of two on extra point tries for 19 points in the quarter. With under four minutes to play, the Cornhuskers added a final touchdown on a Frazier to Green pass. The final score read Cornhuskers 49, Wildcats 25.

The Kansas State defense was ranked #1 nationally in total defense and scoring defense. They would retain that ranking in total defense and be #2 in scoring defense at the end of the season. Their defense held Nebraska to season lows of 190 yards rushing and 4.1 yards/rush.

Of the top five ranked teams, #1 Florida State beat Georgia Tech, 42–10, the #3 Florida Gators had a bye week, #4 Ohio State shut out Purdue, 28–0, but #5 Southern California lost to #17 Notre Dame, 38–10 to be replaced by #6 Tennessee on a bye week. Next up for the Cornhuskers was #7 Colorado. The Buffaloes had advanced from #13 in pre-season by defeating #21 Wisconsin, Colorado State, Louisiana at Monroe, #3 Texas A&M, and #10 Oklahoma. After a loss to #24 Kansas, they rebounded by beating Iowa State.

Game 8 #7 Colorado

Freshman I-back Ahman Green took Nebraska's first offensive play of the game 57 yards for a touchdown. Colorado countered five minutes later with a John Hessler to Phil Savoy 18-yard touchdown pass. The Cornhuskers scored two more touchdowns in the first quarter on a one-yard run by Green following a Terrell Farley interception and a Tommie Frazier to Clester Johnson 52-yard pass. The Buffaloes cut the margin to 21–14 when offensive lineman Heath Irwin recovered a Colorado fumble in the Nebraska end zone. Nebraska placekicker Kris Brown added a 25-yard field goal with 5:15 remaining in the half. The Buffaloes were forced to punt, and with only 10 seconds on the clock, Frazier hit Jon Vedral for a seven-yard touchdown. Nebraska ended the half up, 31–14.

Midway through the third quarter, Colorado scored on a Hessler to James Kidd 49-yard touchdown pass, and the Cornhuskers' lead was cut to 10 points. Brown connected from 36 yards out for his second field goal, and the third quarter ended, 34–21. In the fourth period, Brown added another field goal, this one from 37 yards. With under three minutes remaining, Frazier ran for a two-yard touchdown to seal a 44–21 Nebraska win.

The Buffaloes' defense concentrated on stopping the Nebraska rushing game. The Cornhuskers were held to 226 rushing yards, their second-lowest of the season. In a postgame press conference, Colorado linebacker Matt Russell said they had hoped to force the Cornhuskers to pass, but not as well as they did. Frazier completed 14 of 23 pass attempts for 241 yards, no interceptions, and two touchdowns, and was now to be considered a serious Heisman contender.

Florida State had a bye week. The Seminoles had not played a ranked team all season and, after beating #7 Colorado, Nebraska took over the #1 spot while Florida State dropped to #2. The teams ranked #3 to #5 all won and retained their positions in the polls.

Game 9 Iowa State

The Iowa State Cyclones would post a record of 3–8–0 for the season, scoring a respectable 24 points per game but allowing over 37 points per game. They featured sophomore sensation Troy Davis, who would lead the nation in rushing with 2010 yards (182.7/game) and finish fifth in the Heisman Tropny voting. After missing six games because of his legal issues, I-back Lawrence Phillips returned to the Nebraska lineup. Phillips was used sparingly and gained just 68 yards on 12 carries for a 5.7 yards/rush average, well below his previous average of 10.6.

In the first quarter, Tommie Frazier scored on a four-yard run and a six-yard pass to Ahman Green, who also scored on a 17-yard run. Kris Brown's third extra point attempt failed, but Nebraska was up, 20–0. Iowa State got on the board early in the second period on a Todd Bandhauer 15-yard touchdown pass to wide receiver Ed Williams. The Cornhuskers scored three times in the final half of the period. Green scored his third touchdown on a 26-yard run, and Frazier ran for a two-point conversion. Frazier then passed 36 yards to Reggie Baul for another touchdown, and with 27 seconds until the half, Brown hit a 38-yard field goal. Nebraska led, 38–7.

The second half was much like the first. The third quarter saw four Nebraska touchdowns: a one-yard run by Frazier, a 64-yard run by Green, a 13-yard run by Lawrence Phillips, and a 13-yard run by Clinton Childs. Early in the final period, the Cyclones' Graston Norris scored on a six-yard run. The Cornhuskers' Jeff Makovicka ran 18 yards for the final Nebraska score and a 73–14 win.

Nebraska dominated time of possession with nearly 12 more minutes and in first downs, 37–15. Ahman Green carried the ball 12 times for 176 yards as 15 different Cornhuskers combined for 624 rushing yards and a 9.2 yards/carry average. Nebraska had 776 yards of total offense. Iowa State managed 264 total yards, with nearly half (121 yards) coming from Troy Davis.

In other games, #2 Florida State lost to #24 Virginia, 33–28, #3 Florida topped Northern Illinois, 58–20, #4 Ohio State beat Minnesota, 49–21, and #5 Tennessee shut out Southern Mississippi, 42–0. The Cornhuskers retained their #1 ranking, followed by Ohio State at #2, Florida remained at #3, Tennessee moved to #4, and Northwestern rounded out the top five.

Game 10 #10 Kansas

The Kansas Jayhawks didn't enter the AP top 25 poll until September 25. Two weeks later, the #24 Jayhawks topped #4 Colorado, 40–24 and climbed to #10. After beating

Iowa State and #15 Oklahoma, they continued to ascend to #6 before a loss to #14 Kansas State dropped them back to #11. The week before the game with the Cornhuskers, Kansas beat Missouri and moved up one slot in the rankings.

From the game statistics alone, it would appear the contest was close. Kansas led in time of possession (31:24 to 28:36), passing yards (273–86), and first downs (25–20). Total yardage was similar (Nebraska 375, Kansas 345), and both teams fumbled three times and lost two. The Cornhuskers led in rushing yards (289–72) and return yards (108–4). The difference was that the Nebraska defense kept the Jayhawks to 2.3 yards/rush and intercepted Kansas quarterback Mark Williams three times.

Nebraska scored twice in the first quarter. Kansas fumbled a punt return, and Jon Vedral recovered the ball in the end zone for the first touchdown. Eight minutes later, another Jayhawk fumble was recovered at the Kansas 30-yard line. Tommie Frazier scored on a one-yard run to put Nebraska ahead, 14–0. The only points scored in the second period were on a 19-yard field goal by Kansas placekicker John McCord. The Jayhawks had played Nebraska tough in the first half and were down by only 14–3.

The Cornhuskers scored twice in both the third and fourth quarters. A Frazier to Vershan Jackson one-yard touchdown pass was followed by a Lawrence Phillips one-yard run to end the third period at 28–3. Early in the fourth quarter, Frazier ran for a five-yard touchdown, and cornerback Mike Fullman returned an intercepted Williams pass 86 yards for the Cornhuskers' final score to cap a 41–3 win. *Sports Illustrated* contended that the Heisman race, once wide open, was down to Tommy Frazier and Ohio State's Eddie George.[3]

The top five did not change, as all teams won with the exception of Tennessee, which had a bye week. In beating South Carolina, Florida advanced to 9–0. Along the way, the Gators had defeated teams ranked # 8, 21, and 7. In similar fashion, the Ohio State Buckeyes had moved up from 12th in the pre-season by beating #s 22, 18, 15, 12, 21, and 25 teams to reach 9–0 as well. The following week, Nebraska enjoyed a bye, and all others in the top five won, leaving the order of ranking unchanged.

Game 11 Oklahoma

The Sooners were struggling under coach Howard Schnellenberger, in his only year at Oklahoma. The team was 5–4–1 at game time, losing to #4 Colorado, #7 Kansas, and #9 Kansas State, and being tied by #18 Texas. They boasted running back Jerald Moore, who had a 6.1 rushing yards/carry average, fourth-best nationally. The Sooners would finish the season with the ninth-best rushing defense, allowing only 109.1 yards/game on the ground.

The Sooners' offense had stalled the last half of the season, and Nebraska's defense stopped it cold. Unlike the "Game of the Century" between the two teams in 1971, Nebraska recorded its first shutout of Oklahoma in over five decades. Kris Brown opened the scoring with a 31-yard field goal, and Jamel Williams returned an intercepted Sooners pass 36 yards for a touchdown in the first quarter. Brown added another field goal with one second before the half, and the Cornhuskers took a 13–0 lead.

Free safety Tony Veland returned an Oklahoma fumble 57 yards for a touchdown midway through the third period, and Brown hit a 35-yard field goal to end the quarter. To open the fourth quarter, Tommie Frazier hit Jon Vedral for a 38-yard score, and power fullback Jeff Makovicka rumbled 17 yards with under a minute remaining to finish the scoring and secure a 37–0 win. The Cornhuskers held the Sooners to 12 first downs, 51 yards rushing in 30 attempts, and 16 return yards. By contrast, Nebraska made 26 first downs, with 271 rushing yards and 215 return yards.

While the Cornhuskers shut out Oklahoma, #2 Ohio State lost to #18 Michigan, 31–23, #3 Florida beat #6 Florida State, 35–24, #4 Northwestern had completed its regular season, and #5 Tennessee slipped by Vanderbilt, 12–7.

There was one week remaining, and the only top five team in action was #2 Florida. The Gators defeated #23 Arkansas for the SEC Championship, 34–3. With that win, the national championship game was finally decided. The only two major undefeated teams, #1 Nebraska (11–0) and #2 Florida (12–0), would play for the title. This was the first year of the College Football Bowl Alliance, an attempt to establish a national championship game by inviting the two top teams. The Alliance lasted only three seasons as disputes arose over which teams and conferences were eligible for consideration.

Game 12 Florida—The Fiesta Bowl

The Fiesta Bowl was to feature the two All America quarterbacks: Tommie Frazier was the consensus, and Florida's Danny Wuerffel, the national passing leader with 3,266 yards, 35 touchdowns, and a 64.6 percent completion percentage, also received nods from some selectors. Frazier was second in Heisman voting, Wuerffel was third, but would win the Heisman Trophy the following year. As a team, both Nebraska and Florida were among the national leaders in several categories.

	Nebraska	*Florida*
Rushing Offense	1 (399.8 ypg)	—
Passing Offense	—	2 (360.8 ypg)
Total Offense	2 (556.3 ypg)	4 (534.4 ypg)
Scoring Offense	1 (52.4 ppg)	3 (44.5 ppg)
Rushing Defense	2 (78.4 ypg)	—
Scoring Defense	4 (13.6 ppg)	—

The game itself lived up to the hype for only the first quarter. Florida marched down the field on its first possession, but after two incompletions in the end zone had to settle for a 23-yard field goal by Bart Edmiston. Nebraska's first possession ended with a Tommie Frazier to Lawrence Phillips 16-yard touchdown pass, but the extra point was missed. Late in the quarter, Danny Wuerffel ran in a one-yard touchdown, and the Gators were ahead, 10–6. Phillips ran for a 42-yard touchdown early in the second period. On Florida's next possession, Wuerffel was sacked in the end zone for a safety by linebacker Jamel Williams. Ahman Green scored a touchdown on a one-yard run on Nebraska's next possession. Kris Brown added 26- and 24-yard field goals, and defensive back Michael Booker returned an intercepted pass 42 yards for another touchdown. Nebraska shut out the Gators in the second period while scoring 29 points to take a 35–10 lead into the half.

In the third quarter, Frazier opened the scoring with a 35-yard touchdown run. Wuerffel countered with a 35-yard touchdown pass to Ike Hilliard and then completed a two-point conversion pass to Reidel Anthony. Frazier scored his second touchdown of

Chapter 12. Nebraska 1995

the period on a 75-yard run. Going into the fourth quarter, Nebraska had a commanding 49–18 advantage. Phillips ran for a 15-yard touchdown early in the final period, but the extra point was missed. Reserve quarterback Brook Berringer added another Nebraska touchdown on a one-yard run. On the ensuing kickoff, Florida's Anthony returned it 93 yards for a touchdown. The pass for a two-point conversion fell incomplete, and the final score read Nebraska 62, Florida 24.

The Cornhuskers amassed 524 yards rushing in 66 attempts for a 7.9 average. Frazier led the way with 199 yards in 16 carries. Phillips rushed 25 times for 165 yards. The nation's #2 rushing defense held the Gators, who averaged 173.6 yards per game rushing, to -28 yards on the ground. Wuerffel, the nation's top passer, completed 20 of 38 attempts for 297 yards, but was intercepted three times. Frazier completed only 6 of 14 passes for 105 yards and had two interceptions.

Tommie Frazier, the Davy O'Brien Award winner and runner-up in the Heisman Trophy voting, was a consensus All America and the only Cornhusker selected. Ohio State placed three players on the All America team: Running back Eddie George, a unanimous selection, collected the Heisman Trophy and the Camp and Maxwell awards, offensive tackle Orlando Pace was another unanimous selection and took home the Lombardi Award, while wide receiver Terry Glenn was a consensus selection and Biletnikoff Award winner.

Nebraska led the nation in scoring offense (52.4 points/game) and rushing offense (399.8 yards/game) and was second in total offense (556.3 yards/game). The Cornhuskers placed fourth in scoring defense (13.6 points/game) and second in rushing defense (78.4 yards/game). Mike Fullman, tenth in punt returns (13.6 yards/return), was the only Nebraska player in the top ten in individual stats.

Viewing the top five teams in the final pre-bowl poll and the results of the bowl games, it is easy to see why Nebraska was selected unanimously.

Poll of Dec 4	Team		Result of Bowl	
1	Nebraska	(11–0)	defeated #2	62–24
2	Florida	(12–0)	lost to #1	62–24
3	Northwestern	(10–1)	lost to #17	41–32
4 tie	Ohio State	(11–1)	lost to #4	20–14
4 tie	Tennessee	(10–1)	defeated #4	20–14

The two unanimous national championship teams from Nebraska have been considered among the best teams ever. (See Chapter 25: Is There a "Best Ever" Team?)

Chapter 13

Tennessee 1998

The 1998 Tennessee Volunteers were almost not included in this book. According to the *Official 2002 NCAA Football Records*, the Sagarin System initially selected Ohio State as national champion. Sagarin later went with the majority and selected Tennessee. This is discussed at the end of the chapter.

The previous year (1997), #3 Tennessee had ended an 11–1 regular season by losing to #2 Nebraska in the Orange Bowl, 42–17. Peyton Manning, their consensus All America quarterback, who took home the Maxwell, O'Brien, and Unitas Awards and was second in the Heisman Trophy voting, was now graduated. An uncertain future awaited the Volunteers.

Game 1 #10 Tennessee at #17 Syracuse

The Volunteers opened their season at #17 Syracuse with a wild, down-to-the-wire finish and the first of three close games they would have before being crowned national champions. Coach Phillip Fulmer had said that he knew this would be a major game and thought the winner would be in a good position.

The Volunteers drew first blood with 6:38 left in the first quarter. Following a Syracuse punt, Tennessee drove 80 yards in six plays with junior quarterback Tee Martin throwing a 12-yard touchdown to Peerless Price. With just over five minutes gone in the second period, Syracuse tied the score with a 10-yard touchdown from Donovan McNabb to Step Brominski. Martin ran in a touchdown from the 1-yard line for a 14–7 Tennessee lead. Syracuse kicker Nate Trout missed a 49-yard field goal attempt and then made a 38-yard field goal as the first half ended, Tennessee 14, Syracuse 10.

At 8:29 in the third quarter, Trout booted a 20-yard field goal, making the Volunteers' lead 14–13. Three minutes later, Tennessee finished a six-play 72-yard drive with a one-yard Jamal Lewis touchdown. Volunteers kicker and co-captain Jeff Hall added an 18-yard field goal, and after three quarters Tennessee appeared to be in control, 24–13. Three minutes into the fourth period, Syracuse drove 70 yards in 12 plays, and McNabb hit Kevin Johnson for a 17-yard touchdown that cut the Tennessee lead to 24–20. Two and a half minutes later, McNabb scored on a six-yard run and Syracuse had the lead, 27–24. But it took the Volunteers only 1:20 and six plays to cover 80 yards and retake the lead, 31–27, with Martin again hitting Price for eight yards and a touchdown. On the ensuing kickoff, it appeared that Syracuse's Kyle McIntosh had open field in front of him with only Hall to beat. The kicker brought him down and likely saved a touchdown.

The Tennessee defense then held the Orangemen to only one yard in three plays

Chapter 13. Tennessee 1998

Tennessee head coach Phillip Fulmer, here celebrating another outstanding play by the Volunteers, was the AFCA and Eddie Robinson Coach of the Year in 1998. The unanimous national champions went 13–0 while outscoring opponents, 431–189 (courtesy Tennessee Athletics).

before Trout connected on a 41-yard field goal to cut the Volunteers' lead to one point. With 2:38 remaining, Trout made a 19-yard field goal, capping a seven-play 57-yard drive, and Syracuse again had the lead, 33–31. Tennessee took all of the remaining time to drive 72 yards in nine plays. Hall connected on his second field goal of the game, this one a 27-yarder as the clock ran out. Tennessee had won its opener, 34–33.

Syracuse senior Donovan McNabb, who would finish fifth in the Heisman Trophy voting, completed 22 of 28 passes for 300 yards and two touchdowns, and he ran for 53 yards (17 net after 36 yards in sacks) and another score. Syracuse's Kevin Johnson led all receivers with 92 yards and a touchdown, while Jamal Lewis carried 20 times for 141 yards (7.1 yards/carry) to lead all rushers. Tennessee's Tee Martin completed just 9 of 26 passes for 143 yards and two touchdowns, both going to Peerless Price, who led Volunteers receivers with 87 yards. Referring to Martin, Tennessee coach Phillip Fulmer said, in essence, that fans should no longer mourn the graduation of Peyton Manning.[1]

On defense, the Volunteers' consensus All America linebacker, Al Wilson, accounted for 13 tackles, including nine solo tackles. His Syracuse counterpart, linebacker Keith Bullock, made eight solo tackles and a total of 14. Syracuse led in first downs (23–18), time of possession (35:31 to 24:29), and yardage gained (445–390). But, the scoreboard was all that mattered and it read Tennessee 34, Syracuse 33.

Tennessee QB Tee Martin, shown here against Alabama, proved himself a worthy successor to graduated star Peyton Manning. Martin accounted for 26 touchdowns in leading the Volunteers to a unanimous national championship in 1998 (courtesy Tennessee Athletics).

Game 2 #2 Florida at #6 Tennessee

A crowd of 107,653 packed Neyland Stadium to see if Tennessee could break its five-game losing streak against head coach Steve Spurrier's Florida Gators. During those years, Florida had averaged 40.5 points/game against the Volunteers.

Florida scored first on a 21-yard field goal by Collins Cooper nine minutes into the game. Shawn Bryson ran for a 57-yard touchdown a minute later, and Tennessee took the lead, 7–3. In the second quarter, Jeff Hall added a 39-yard field goal to increase the lead to 10–3. Spurrier alternated his two quarterbacks, Jess Palmer and Doug Johnson, on every play. Palmer passed to Travis Taylor for an eight-yard touchdown. Tennessee avoided another Florida threat when Al Wilson caused the Gators' Terry Jackson to fumble at the Tennessee goal line. Linebacker Raynoch Thompson recovered the ball in the end zone for a touchback. The score was tied at the half, 10–10.

Halfway through the third period, Tee Martin passed 29 yards to Peerless Price for a touchdown and a 17–10 Tennessee lead. Palmer answered with an eight-yard touchdown throw to Travis McGriff and another tie score, 17–17. The fourth quarter was scoreless, and the game went into overtime. Florida won the coin toss and elected to defend first. After a holding penalty, Tennessee was faced with third down and 23 yards to go at the Gators' 38-yard line. Martin knew they needed at least 10 yards to give Hall a chance at a field goal. The quarterback scrambled for 14 yards, and Hall connected from 41 yards out and a three-point Volunteers lead.

Florida still had a chance to win with a touchdown or tie with a field goal to send the game into a second overtime. Starting at the Volunteers' 25-yard line, the Gators managed a first down to the 15. After three incomplete passes, Cooper's 32-yard attempt sailed wide left. Tennessee fans flooded the field and tore down both goal posts. The goals were cut up, and Hall still has an 18-inch piece of the south goal in his office.

After the Florida game, Tom Ogle, a friend of coach Fulmer, gave him a walking stick he had carved. Players thought Fulmer looked like Moses with the stick. Fulmer saw the similarities and possibilities. He told the team that just as Moses led the Israelites to the Promised Land, he and the other coaches would lead the Volunteers to the national championship.[2] That became the team's "synergy stick," the "center of our energy." The stick was always with the team, and everyone kept it a secret until after the season.[3]

Game 3 Houston at #4 Tennessee

After two incredibly tense games, Tennessee finally got a breather. The Volunteers took a 21–0 halftime lead on three touchdown passes from Tee Martin: a 33-yarder to Cedrick Wilson, a 16-yarder to Jamal Lewis, and a 63-yard strike to Shawn Bryson.

Houston got their only points to open the third quarter on an 80-yard drive that resulted in a 19-yard touchdown pass from Jason McKinley to Scott Regimbauld. Lewis then ran 59 yards for another Volunteers touchdown. The fourth quarter saw two more Tennessee touchdown passes: 22 yards from Martin to Peerless Price and 21 yards from freshman backup Burney Veazey to tight end John Finlayson. Tennessee won easily, 42–7. There was bad news as All America middle linebacker Al Wilson suffered a shoulder separation and would miss the next game.

Game 4 #3 Tennessee at Auburn

Auburn would end the season at 3–8, but the Volunteers had to be concerned as they had not won on the Tigers' home field since 1980. Auburn took the opening kickoff and, looking to exploit Wilson's absence, ran three option plays that moved the ball to the Tennessee 10-yard line. Defensive end Shaun Ellis intercepted a pass and ran it back 90 yards for a touchdown and a Tennessee 7–0 lead. Two minutes later, on the Volunteers' first offensive play, Jamal Lewis raced 67 yards for another score and a 14–0 Tennessee lead. Kicker Jeff Hall added a 46-yard field goal with 2:51 remaining in the first quarter to extend the lead to 17–0. In spite of Jamal Lewis' 18 carries for 140 yards, the Tennessee offense stalled, and the defense took over. Lewis left the game in the second period with a knee injury that ended his season.

In the second quarter, Auburn kicker Robert Bironas made a 40-yard field goal to make the score 17–3. On the next possession, quarterback Tee Martin fumbled, and Auburn recovered less than a foot from the Tennessee goal line. In an incredible goal line stand, the Volunteers held four downs and took possession back at the 2-yard line after linebacker Raynoch Thompson dropped Auburn fullback Tellie Embery for a loss. The defense continued to excel and held the Tigers to a pair of Bironas field goals (44 and 45 yards) in the second half. The final score read Tennessee 19, Auburn 9. Coach Fulmer praised his defense, saying they carried the day. He also predicted that the day would come when the offense would save a game.[4]

Game 5 #4 Tennessee at #7 Georgia

Al Wilson had returned to lead the defense, but with Jamal Lewis out, the offense had to rely on a pair of sophomores, Travis Henry and Travis Stephens, to handle the rushing attack.

Georgia was 4–0, outscoring their opponents, 117–42. They were ranked #12 the week before, then won a squeaker at #6 LSU, 28–27, and ascended to #7 going into the game with Tennessee.

Initially a substitute running back, Travis Henry became a workhorse following an injury that ended the season for Jamal Lewis. At 230 pounds, Henry was a powerful rusher, gaining 970 yards and scoring seven touchdowns in 1998 (courtesy Tennessee Athletics).

The two teams exchanged field goals in the first quarter. Jeff Hall kicked a 27-yarder with 8:43 on the clock, and the Bulldogs' Hap Hines connected from the 48-yard line with 1:55 remaining. Tennessee had a chance for more points when a Georgia fumble gave them the ball at Georgia's 18-yard line. Two plays later, a Tee Martin pass was intercepted by Champ Bailey at the Bulldogs' 3-yard line. The second quarter featured a pair of Hall field goals from 39 and 43 yards to end the half at 9–3. After the Bulldogs' first quarter field goal, they were unable to score against the Tennessee defense.

Martin threw for two touchdowns in the third quarter, a three-yarder to Cedrick Wilson and then another three-yard score, this time to Peerless Price. The fourth quarter yielded no scoring, and the Volunteers won, 22–3. Lewis' replacements did well: Stephens carried the ball 20 times for 107 yards, while Henry added 53 yards on 16 rushes. The defense shut down the Bulldogs' rushing game, allowing only 59 yards in 19 carries. The defense was well rested as Tennessee controlled the clock with 37:47 time of possession to 22:13 for Georgia.

Game 6 Alabama at #3 Tennessee

Going into the Alabama game, the Tennessee defense had not allowed a touchdown in nine quarters. They would extend that streak to 11. Tennessee took the opening kickoff and needed only seven plays to cover 76 yards and top it off with a one-yard touchdown run by Tee Martin. Alabama countered with a Ryan Pflugner 41-yard field goal and a 7–3 first quarter score. The second quarter saw a Martin five-yard touchdown run, and the half ended with the Volunteers up, 14–3.

With a little over five minutes remaining in the third period, Alabama's Shaun Alexander broke free on a 44-yard touchdown run. Quarterback Andrew Zow hit wide receiver Quincy Jackson for a two-point conversion, and the Crimson Tide was down by only 14–11. The Volunteers could sense the momentum changing and knew a good kickoff return was needed. Peerless Price had not returned a kickoff all season (or last season), but for some reason, the coaches put him in to handle the kick. Price ripped off a 100-yard return for a touchdown. After the run, Price saw that a flag had been thrown, but it was against Alabama.

Two minutes into the fourth period, Travis Henry scored on a one-yard run. Now down 28–11, Alabama scored their final touchdown on a two-yard run by Zow. Henry finished the scoring on a five-yard run with under a minute to play to solidify a 35–18 win. Tennessee had now beaten the Tide for the fourth straight year. Henry rushed 22 times for 113 yards and two touchdowns. Martin's game was improving as he completed 10 of 14 passes for 117 yards and rushed 13 times for 41 yards and two touchdowns. But few could foresee what he would do next.

Game 7 #3 Tennessee at South Carolina

After beating Ball State, South Carolina lost its next seven games before hosting the Volunteers. They probably wished that Tennessee, and especially Tee Martin, had stayed home.

Martin completed a record 23 passes in a row, ending up with 315 yards on 23 of 24 attempts and four touchdowns. He also rushed for 37 yards, 30 on the play following his only incompletion. Peerless Price caught two of Martin's touchdown throws. Wide receivers Jeremaine Copeland and Cedrick Wilson scored on Martin's other two touchdown passes. Shaun Bryson, Phillip Crosby, and Travis Henry each rushed for a touchdown in Tennessee's 49–14 win. The Gamecocks' two touchdowns came in a seven-and-a-half-minute span in the fourth quarter against Volunteers reserves and the game well out of reach.

At this point in the season, the top four teams remained undefeated: #1 Ohio State (8–0), #2 UCLA (7–0), #3 Tennessee (7–0), and #4 Kansas State (8–0). After the big win at South Carolina, Tennessee jumped ahead of UCLA (28–24 winners over Stanford) to take the #2 position.

Game 8 Alabama-Birmingham at #2 Tennessee

It was Homecoming at Tennessee, and the Volunteers fans were looking for a big win against the University of Alabama at Birmingham. The 2-6 Blazers had allowed 54 points against Louisiana Tech and 41 against Virginia Tech within their past three games. Tennessee fans got a big win, but not what they had expected. The Volunteers fumbled three times, losing all three, and sloppy tackling (mostly by reserves) allowed the Blazers to gain 211 yards rushing. That was more than double what the defense had previously allowed (91.4 yards/game).

Less than two minutes into the game, Jeff Hall opened the scoring with a 39-yard field goal. Later in the quarter, Travis Henry scored on an 18-yard run, and the Volunteers led, 10–0. UAB's Rhett Gallego kicked a 20-yard field goal in the second quarter, but Tennessee scored two more touchdowns, on a Travis Stephens 11-yard run and a Tee Martin one-yard run, to end the half at 24–3.

Three minutes into the third quarter, a 28-yard Martin to Cedrick Wilson completion resulted in a touchdown. Four minutes later, the Blazers got their second field goal from Gallego, a 36-yarder. Then Hall answered with a 20-yard field goal, and the Volunteers ended the quarter leading 34–6. Hall got his third field goal early in the fourth period, this one from 37 yards. UAB quarterback Lee Jolly ran in a 32-yard touchdown, making the final score Tennessee 37, UAB 13.

Coach Fulmer had been concerned about distractions: the BCS rankings, his team not taking the 2-6 Blazers seriously enough, and even the expectations for the team for Homecoming. The Volunteers had not played up to their potential, but they had survived. And more good news was on the way. About 7 p.m., with only a couple thousand fans remaining in the stadium, an announcement was made that unranked Michigan State had upset #1 Ohio State.

The Ohio State loss moved Tennessee to #1. Kansas State, unbeaten at 9–0, advanced to #2 following a 49–6 win over Baylor. UCLA (8–0) remained at #3 after beating Oregon State, 41–34. Three other undefeated teams, #8 Wisconsin, #11 Arkansas, and #16 Tulane, all won.

Game 9 #10 Arkansas at #1 Tennessee

Arkansas, 8–0, came in with a game plan to: (1) stack the defensive line to impede Tennessee's rushing game; and (2) use a passing attack against the Volunteers' shorter defenders.

A first quarter fumble by Travis Stephens led to a Razorbacks touchdown. Arkansas quarterback Clint Stoerner hit Emmanuel Smith with a 14-yard pass, and the Razorbacks were up, 7–0. Arkansas lost another scoring opportunity in the first period when a Stoerner pass into the end zone was intercepted by sophomore defensive back Deon Grant. Ten seconds into the second quarter, Volunteers defensive back Steve Johnson fell, allowing Stoerner to hit Anthony Lucas for a 62-yard touchdown. Jeff Hall connected on a 41-yard field goal with 6:23 remaining for Tennessee's first points of the game. But three minutes later, Stoerner found Lucas for an eight-yard touchdown, and the Razorbacks now had a 21–3 lead over the #1 Volunteers.

The Tennessee offense got moving late in the second quarter. Martin completed a pass to Jeremaine Copeland, and a late hit penalty moved the ball into Arkansas territory. From the 36-yard line, with 2:03 left in the half, Martin connected with Peerless Price for a touchdown that narrowed the Razorbacks' lead to 21–10.

Arkansas received the second half kickoff but was forced to punt. Copeland fumbled the punt, and the Razorbacks recovered, leading to a 33-yard field goal by Todd Latourette and a 24–10 advantage. The Tennessee offense was finally coming alive, mostly on the rushing of Travis Henry. Martin scored on a four-yard run with 8:14 remaining in the third period. Then Hall hit a 21-yard field goal with less than a minute remaining, and after three quarters it was Arkansas 24, Tennessee 20.

With eight minutes remaining, the Razorbacks had the ball on the Tennessee 13-yard line. Al Wilson sacked Stoerner for a loss, and the resulting field goal attempt was blocked by Deon Grant. Wilson picked up the loose ball and returned it to the Arkansas 36-yard line, but the Volunteers could not move the chains and had to punt it back to the Razorbacks.

With three minutes remaining, Arkansas was forced to punt the ball from its own 41-yard line. The snap went over the head of punter Chris Akin, who wisely kicked the ball out of the back of the end zone, giving up a safety but avoiding a possible touchdown. Arkansas was assessed a penalty for illegal kicking on top of the safety and having to punt to the Volunteers. Price returned the kick to midfield, but on fourth down and nine yards to go, Martin's pass fell incomplete and Arkansas took over on downs, holding a two-point lead with 1:54 on the clock.

Ten seconds later, Stoerner dropped back to pass and his feet got entangled with an offensive lineman. As he stumbled, the ball came free, and defensive tackle Billy Ratliff recovered for the Volunteers. On the ensuing Tennessee drive, Henry carried the ball five straight times, the last for a one-yard touchdown with 28 seconds remaining. The scoreboard now read Tennessee 28, Arkansas 24. A penalty moved the PAT try back 15 yards, and rather than risk a blocked kick or an interception, Martin took a knee to end the play. Travis Henry led all rushers with 197 yards on 32 carries. Tee Martin, after his record-breaking performance the previous game, was again human, completing 10 of 27 pass attempts for 155 yards and an interception. He also passed for one touchdown and ran for another.

Referring to Stoerner's fumble with under two minutes to play, Coach Fulmer claimed a defender forced the quarterback to trip and fumble.[5] An account of the game in Wikipedia states that Ratliff drove Arkansas offensive guard Brandon Burlsworth into Stoerner. Several pictures from different angles are inconclusive.

There was also controversy regarding the safety that occurred with three minutes remaining. According to an article by Bob Colon of the *Oklahoma City News*, Bobby

Gaston, the supervisor of officials for the SEC, acknowledged that referee Harold Mitchell erred on the call. By NCAA rule, an illegal kick results in a 15-yard penalty and loss of down from the spot of the foul. Tennessee should have had the option to take the two-point safety or to get the ball at the Arkansas 5-yard line, which would be half the distance to the goal line.[6]

Of the other remaining undefeated teams, #2 Kansas State, #3 UCLA, and #14 Tulane won their games. Previously unbeaten #8 Wisconsin lost to #15 Michigan, 27–10.

Game 10 Kentucky at #1 Tennessee

Although unranked and sporting a record of 7–3, Kentucky could present, at times, a high-powered offense. Led by quarterback Tim Couch, receiver Craig Yeast, and all-purpose back Anthony White, the Wildcats averaged 39.6 points/game. They also gave up 29 points/game.

Tennessee opened the scoring with two Jeff Hall field goals of 27 and 32 yards to take a 6–0 lead. Two minutes later, when Couch hit Lance Mickelsen for three yards and a touchdown, the Wildcats took their only lead in the game, 7–6. Shawn Bryson scored on a one-yard run and then caught a two-point conversion pass from Tee Martin to end the quarter 14–7. The second quarter was all Tennessee. A Cedrick Wilson 55-yard touchdown pass from Martin, a Bryson 58-yard touchdown run, a Hall 47-yard field goal, and a Phillip Crosby one-yard run put Tennessee ahead 38–7 at the half.

Kentucky's Derek Homer scored on a one-yard run to start the third period. The Volunteers countered with a Travis Henry two-yard touchdown run and a 33-yard run by Martin to increase the lead to 52–14. The teams traded touchdowns in the fourth period: Travis Stephens scored from the 1-yard line, and a Couch to Mickelsen three-yard touchdown pass brought the final score to Tennessee 59, Kentucky 21. Couch threw for 337 yards with one interception and two touchdowns, but the Kentucky rushing attack was non-existent, managing only 39 yards on 29 carries. Tennessee's offense was balanced, with 237 yards rushing and 229 passing.

All the other unbeaten won: Kansas State, ranked #2, beat #19 Missouri, 31–25, #3 UCLA downed archrival Southern California, 34–17, and #12 Tulane defeated Houston, 48–20.

Game 11 #1 Tennessee at Vanderbilt

Tennessee wanted a big win to maintain its #1 ranking. Kansas State at #2 was 11–0, and #3 UCLA was 10–0. Both had byes that week. Florida State at #4 (11–1) and #5 Ohio State (10–1) had completed their regular seasons. At this point, it was not certain which teams would play in the Fiesta Bowl for the national championship. The Vanderbilt Commodores were 2–9 when they hosted the Volunteers. Tennessee needed a big win.

It took eight minutes for the Volunteers to score on a Jeff Hall 22-yard field goal for an unimpressive 3–0 lead to end the first quarter. In the second period, it took another eight minutes before a Tee Martin to Peerless Price 67-yard touchdown pass started the scoring in earnest. Three minutes later, Travis Henry ran for a 12-yard touchdown, and with less than a minute remaining, Hall connected on a 42-yard field goal for a 20–0 halftime score.

Vanderbilt fumbled four times and lost two. One resulted in linebacker Chris Ramseur's 10-yard return for a touchdown to end the third quarter, 27–0. In the fourth period, Tennessee scored two more touchdowns: a Martin one-yard run with 9:34 to play, and a Travis Stephens one-yard run three minutes later. The final score read Tennessee 41, Vanderbilt 0.

In addition to causing four fumbles, the Volunteers' pass defense intercepted four passes. The Commodores were outgained, 430 yards to 174. Martin completed 13 out of 20 passes for 241 yards, no interceptions, and a touchdown, and he ran for another score. Price caught seven passes for 181 yards and one touchdown. Henry led all rushers with 136 yards on 22 carries. The Volunteers had a big win, but would it be enough? Vanderbilt began its season with a 42–0 loss to Mississippi State and ended with a 41–0 loss to Tennessee, the two teams that would play for the SEC title the following week.

Game 12 #23 Mississippi State at #1 Tennessee
SEC Championship

Mississippi State was 8–3, ranked #23, and co-champions of the SEC West at 6–2. They played for the SEC title by having beaten their co-champion, #11 Arkansas, also 6–2, 26–14.

In his book, *A Perfect Season*, coach Fulmer describes the "distraction" of the first year of the Bowl Championship Series (BCS). No one knew what to expect. Even if the Volunteers won the SEC, Kansas State and UCLA might also win, and win more impressively. Tennessee was not yet guaranteed a chance to play for the national title.

Mississippi State scored first when cornerback Robert Bean intercepted a Tee Martin pass and returned it 70 yards for a touchdown with five seconds remaining in the first quarter. Tennessee defensive back Deon Grant intercepted a Wayne Madkin pass to set up a Travis Stephens two-yard touchdown in the second period. Jeff Hall added a 31-yard field goal to give the Volunteers a 10–7 halftime lead.

After a scoreless third quarter, Mississippi State's Kevin Prentiss scored on an 83-yard punt return and Tennessee was down, 14–10, with 8:43 remaining in the game. Two and a half minutes later, Tee Martin threw to Peerless Price for a 41-yard touchdown, and only 30 seconds after that, Martin connected with Cedrick Wilson for a 26-yard score. The game ended Tennessee 24, Mississippi State 14.

Tennessee led the Bulldogs in first downs (21–9), rushing yards (151–65), passing yards (208–84), and time of possession (36:06–23:54). However, Mississippi State gained 222 return yards to 45 for the Volunteers. Even with lopsided numbers, the game was close until midway through the fourth period, and once again Tennessee had to come from behind to win. The question was now—would it be enough to maintain the #1 ranking and play for the national title? The BCS had help making their decision. In other games that week, #2 Kansas State lost to #10 Texas A&M, 36–33, in the Big 12 Championship game, and #3 UCLA lost to Miami, Florida, 45–49. Those losses moved 11–1 Florida State to #2 and 10–1 Ohio State to #3.

Game 13 Fiesta Bowl: Tennessee vs. Florida State National Championship

Florida State was ranked #2 pre-season behind Ohio State. They dropped to #11 after a 24–7 loss at North Carolina State in their second game and gradually worked their way to #4 by the end of the regular season. The Seminoles outscored their opponents, 385–138, and had defeated #14 Texas A&M, #18 Southern California, #20 Georgia Tech, #12 Virginia, and #4 Florida. Coach Fulmer, when asked to sum up the Florida State Seminoles, said they were tremendous. He especially praised wideout Peter Warrick, tailback Travis Minor, and the team's overall speed.[7]

The defenses dominated the first quarter as neither team could score. Tennessee scored two touchdowns within 25 seconds to open the second period. Shawn Bryson caught a four-yard touchdown pass from Tee Martin at 14:05, and Dwayne Goodrich intercepted a Marcus Outzen pass for a 54-yard touchdown return at the 13:40 mark. Florida State came back on a Bill McCray one-yard touchdown, but Groza Award winner Sebastian Janikowski missed the extra point. Janikowski did connect on a 34-yard field goal at 1:17 before halftime, closing the gap to 14–9.

The third quarter was scoreless. Early in the fourth quarter, Martin connected with Peerless Price on a 79-yard touchdown. Hall added a 23-yard field goal to increase the Tennessee lead to 23–9. Outzen scored on a seven-yard run with 3:42 remaining, but it was not enough for the Seminoles, and the final score stood at Tennessee 23, Florida State 16.

For the second championship game in a row (SEC and National) Tennessee led in first downs (16–13), rushing yards (114–108), passing yards (278–145), and time of possession (31:10–28:50). Consensus All America Peter Warrick was held to one reception for seven yards.

In the first year of the BCS, it is hard to find an argument against Tennessee as unanimous national champion. They were one of two un-beaten teams (#7 Tulane was 12–0 against a much weaker schedule that included no ranked teams), they were ranked #1, and they defeated #2 Florida State (23–16) in the Fiesta Bowl. Regarding the initial selection of Ohio State by Sagarin, the author objected to a changed selection years after and did not want to contend with other changed votes. However, Tennessee is the only team affected, and the Volunteers' 1998 team is rightly a member of this elite group. So what did the Sagarin System see to initially select #2 Ohio State at 11–1?

The Buckeyes were ranked #1 pre-season through the November 1 poll. They then lost to unranked Michigan State, 28–24, rebounded with a 31–16 win over #11 Michigan, and ascended the polls to #3 following losses to unbeaten (at the time) Kansas State (11–0) and UCLA (10–0) in their final games. After #2 Florida State lost to #1 Tennessee in the Fiesta Bowl and the Buckeyes beat #8 Texas A&M, 24–14 in the Sugar Bowl, Ohio State was ranked #2 in the final AP poll. Below is a comparison of the two teams.

Comparison of Tennessee and Ohio State

Team	Record	Opponent W-L	Pts. Scored/Pts. Allowed
Tennessee	13–0	82–71	431–189
Ohio State	11–1	77–66	430–149

Chapter 13. Tennessee 1998

Tennessee cornerback Dwayne Goodrich races 54 yards for a touchdown after intercepting a pass by Florida State quarterback Marcus Outzen. That touchdown helped secure the Volunteers' 23–16 win in the 1999 Fiesta Bowl and the national championship (courtesy Tennessee Athletics).

Number and Ranking of Opponents in AP Poll

Tennessee	6	#17, #2, #7, #10, #23, #2
Ohio State	5	#11, #21, #7, #11, #8

Number of Opponents Based on Power Ranking by Sorensen System

	in Top 10	in Top 20	in Top 50
Tennessee	2	3	8
Ohio State	1	4	7

Admittedly, both teams were strong candidates, but Ohio State's at-home loss (24–28) to unranked Michigan State (6–6) in game 9 should have been enough to disqualify them.

Chapter 14

Florida State 1999

The Florida State football program began in 1947. In their first year, the Seminoles played small schools and were 0–5. They continued to play small schools and over the next four years accomplished a record of 30–4, including an undefeated season in 1950. Moving up to bigger, more competitive opponents, they posted a 1–8–1 record in 1952 and were up and down over the next 24 years. Then, in 1976, Bobby Bowden took over as head coach. His team recorded their only losing season (5–6) in that year. Bowden had been coaching for six years at West Virginia before accepting the position at Florida State. Bowden's tenure at FSU was nothing short of remarkable (See Appendix B, Coaches). His teams at Florida State:

    Won the ACC title in 1992, 1993, 1994, 1996, 1997, 1999, 2000
    Shared the ACC title in 1995, 1998
    Won at least 10 games in 14 consecutive seasons
    Won 11 straight bowl games
    Were undefeated in 14 straight bowl games (13–0–1)
    Finished in Top 5 of polls from 1987 to 2000
    Had a total win-loss-tie record of 316–97–4

The Seminoles shared the National Championship in the polls in 1987, 1992, and 1994, and in 1993 again shared the title, but for the first time were the consensus National Champions. From that first shared title in 1987 to the unanimous National Championship team of 1999, FSU's record was an astounding 140–17–1 against top-caliber competition.

In 1996, and revised in 1997, rules were formulated for overtime play should a game end in a tie. This was the only major adjustment to the game between 1995 and 1999.

The 1999 Season

Expectations were high entering the 1999 season, and with good reason. The Seminoles were returning 74 players, including quarterbacks Chris Weinke and Marcus Outzen, wide receiver Peter Warrick, 15 offensive lineman, and several defensive linemen. As a team they were fast, averaging 4.5 seconds in a 40-yard dash.[1] In the pre-season AP poll, Florida State was ranked number one by a slim margin (1720–1643) over the 1998 unanimous national champion, Tennessee.[2]

Game 1 Louisiana Tech

On August 28, Florida State opened its season at home in Doak Campbell Stadium, where they had not lost in 40 games going back to 1991. The Seminoles' season began against Louisiana Tech and Tech's outstanding quarterback, Tim Rattay. A year earlier, in the 1998 season opener against defending National Champion Nebraska, Rattay had decimated the Cornhuskers' defense with 590 passing yards, 405 of those going to his favorite receiver, Troy Edwards. Rattay led the nation in passing in 1998, while he and Edwards (the 1998 Biletnikoff Award winner) combined on 140 passes for nearly 2,000 yards and 27 touchdowns. But lightning seldom strikes twice, Edwards had graduated, and the Tech offense wasn't the same. Rattay connected with John Simon in the second quarter to tie the score at 7–7. With 39 seconds remaining in the half, Warrick took a handoff, reversed field twice, then broke free on a 20-yard touchdown run to give the Seminoles a 14–7 halftime edge.

Florida State scored 17 points in the third quarter and 10 in the fourth while allowing the Louisiana Tech offense only 80 yards in the second half to win, 41–7. Despite throwing 48 times, Rattay managed only 240 yards and one touchdown, and he was intercepted twice. Florida State quarterback Chris Weinke, returning after surgery for a back injury the year before, was intercepted for the first time in 238 passes. However, the junior completed 20 of 32 passes for 242 yards and two touchdowns. Seminoles wide receiver Peter Warrick, who designed the team's t-shirt which stated "TEAM—It's not about me," had opted to return for his senior year to help the Seminoles win a national championship rather than play (and earn big money) in the NFL. Against the Bulldogs, Warrick caught nine passes for 121 yards and rushed twice for 41 yards and a touchdown. After Louisiana Tech, the Seminoles enjoyed a bye week.

Game 2 #10 Georgia Tech

Florida State played its first three games of the season at home, and game 2 against tenth-ranked Georgia Tech turned out to be a classic. The two teams combined for 53 first downs and 945 yards of offense. Weinke completed 16 of 29 passes for 262 yards and three touchdowns. Warrick caught eight passes for 142 yards and a touchdown and rushed three times for 25 yards and another score. However, the Seminoles' defense was all but powerless to stop Tech's magnificent quarterback, Joe Hamilton. The Heisman Trophy runner-up, consensus first team All America, and O'Brien Award winner completed 22 of 25 passes for 387 yards and four touchdowns and rushed for a fifth score while personally amassing 405 of Tech's 501 yards of offense.

With a minute and a half to go in the game, Georgia Tech scored, narrowing the Florida State lead to 41–35. Hamilton had been unstoppable, completing his last 14 passes. What would have been the outcome had the Yellow Jackets' on-side kick not been recovered by the Seminoles? For the second straight week, the Seminoles had faced one of the top players in the country. This time, they were fortunate to eke out a victory.

The Seminoles' schedule would have them face four of the top 10 Heisman Trophy candidates: Georgia Tech's Joe Hamilton (2nd), Michael Vick of Virginia Tech (3rd), Virginia's Thomas Jones (8th), and Louisiana Tech's Tim Rattay (10th).

Game 3 #20 North Carolina State

Surviving the Georgia Tech scare, the Seminoles made easy work of #20 North Carolina State, avenging their only regular season loss of the previous year. NC State's quarterback Jamie Barnette, who riddled the Seminoles' defense the year before for 287 yards, was held to just 129 yards on 10 of 25 passing. The game was tied, 3–3, as the first quarter ended. The Seminoles scored 15 unanswered points in the second quarter on a short touchdown run by Dan Kendra and three field goals by Sebastian Janikowski. After a bad snap from center following the touchdown, the Seminoles' holder, backup quarterback Marcus Outzen, attempted a two-point conversion pass that was intercepted by North Carolina State linebacker Clayton White. White was run down and tackled by Janikowski.

Florida State scored two touchdowns in the third period, first on a two-yard run by Travis Minor and a second when defensive end David Warren stripped the ball from Barnette and it was recovered in the end zone by defensive tackle Jamal Reynolds. North Carolina State scored eight points in the quarter on a touchdown run and successful two-point conversion. The Wolfpack were held scoreless in the final period. Janikowski converted on a fifth field goal, and an intercepted Barnette pass by sophomore defensive back Abdual Howard was returned 47 yards for a touchdown as Florida State won its third game 42–11. Chris Weinke, who threw six interceptions the year before against the Wolfpack, had two intercepted this year and did not throw a touchdown pass.

Game 4 North Carolina

Game 4, at Chapel Hill, North Carolina, found the Seminoles' offense and defense functioning smoothly. The Seminoles racked up a 28–0 lead in only 7 minutes and 57 seconds of the first quarter. Running back Travis Minor scored the first two touchdowns on runs of 14 and 5 yards. Defensive back Sean Kay intercepted Tar Heels sophomore quarterback Ron Curry and raced 25 yards for the third score. Peter Warrick's 75-yard punt return for a touchdown mercifully ended the Seminoles' first quarter scoring. Florida State added another touchdown, and the Tar Heels scored a field goal for a halftime score of 35–3. To his credit, Bobby Bowden used 52 players in that first period in an attempt to keep down the score.

Florida State intercepted Curry for the third time and scored on a one-yard run by backup quarterback Marcus Outzen in the third quarter. Weinke threw for 272 yards despite limited playing time. Florida State won, 42–10, while using 70 players in the game.

Game 5 Duke

Florida State's fifth game was played at Alltel Stadium in Jacksonville, Florida, against the Duke Blue Devils. The Seminoles scored on all eight of their first half possessions. Chris Weinke connected with Peter Warrick on three first quarter touchdown passes. In the second quarter, Sebastian Janikowski kicked 46- and 27-yard field goals, Warrick threw a 35-yard touchdown pass to Laveranues Coles, and Weinke hit fullback Dan Kendra for a seven-yard touchdown to help the Seminoles take a 44–0 halftime lead.

It was hard for State to stay focused with such a big lead. In the third period, Bobby

Bowden played the reserves and Duke scored 13 unanswered points. Bowden re-inserted his starters in the fourth quarter. Weinke threw for his fifth touchdown of the game, connecting with wide receiver Ron Dugans for an 84-yard score. Duke managed another 10 points, and the game concluded with a 51–23 Florida State win. Weinke ended the game with 19 completions on 27 attempts for 290 yards and 5 touchdowns.

After five games, Florida State remained atop the polls, averaging 43.4 points per game, and appeared to have the leading Heisman Trophy candidate in wide receiver Peter Warrick, who had averaged just under 15 yards every time he handled the ball. Warrick had caught four touchdown passes, thrown for a touchdown, rushed for two touchdowns, and returned a punt for one more. Then, suddenly, everything changed. During the week leading up to the Seminoles' game with #19 Miami of Florida, Warrick and teammate Laveranues Coles, another wide receiver, were charged with grand theft at a Dillard's department store. Coles was thrown off the team because he had a previous run-in with police. Warrick was suspended pending an investigation.

One account of the incident, co-authored by Bobby Bowden, asserts that fame and celebrity prevented Warrick from being "treated like anyone else" over "petty theft." From this account, Warrick was young, foolish, and naïve. He apparently did not hire an attorney until after he had been charged, and upon questioning said, "it wasn't like [he] killed the president." As Bowden stated, rather than vanishing out of the spotlight, Warrick agreed to some jail time so he could rejoin the team. On November 3, 1999, the *Tallahassee Democrat* published a letter from Warrick that was taken as a sincere apology.[3]

Game 6 Miami

For the Seminoles, the season continued without Warrick as #19 Miami of Florida visited. With two of the top three receivers out of the lineup, Weinke went to 11 different receivers, passing for 332 yards and two touchdowns. Miami's signal caller, Kenny Kelly, connected on 27 of 41 passes and amassed 370 yards. Tied 21–21 at halftime, the Seminoles shut out Miami in the second half and earned a 31–21 victory.

The Seminoles' offense had proven shaky at times, and the defense had yielded over 1,000 yards passing in three games (Louisiana Tech, Georgia Tech, and Miami) facing top passers. Still, they had prevailed through adversity and had now held the number one ranking for seven weeks.

Tennessee, Florida, and Michigan had fallen from the undefeated. Penn State and Nebraska, highly regarded from the outset of the season, were unscathed and ranked second and third, respectively. Relative newcomers Virginia Tech, Michigan State, and Kansas State had inched their way into the top ten with unblemished records.

Game 7 Wake Forest

In game 7 against Wake Forest, with Warrick still unable to play, Weinke again spread his passes around to 10 receivers for 354 yards and a touchdown. Sebastian Janikowski provided all the Seminoles' first half scoring on field goals of 21, 31, and 34 yards. The first half ended with the score 9–3 and had Seminoles fans worrying that 3–2 Wake Forest might pull an upset.

After the half, Weinke connected on two touchdown throws to Atrews Bell in the third period to lead, 23–3. The recovery of a Wake Forest fumble by junior linebacker

Tommy Polley led to a two-yard touchdown run by freshman quarterback Anquan Boldin. Janikowski hit his fourth field goal, a 32-yarder. Wake Forest scored a touchdown on the final play of the game with a one-yard pass as Florida State defeated the Demon Deacons, 33–10.

In other games, #2 Penn State beat #18 Ohio State, 23–10, #4 Virginia Tech clobbered #16 Syracuse, 62–0, #9 Kansas State shut out Utah State, 40–0, Nebraska enjoyed a bye week to remain undefeated, while #5 Michigan State lost to #20 Purdue, 52–28.

Game 8 Clemson

On October 23 at Clemson's Memorial Stadium, Florida State coach Bobby Bowden sought his 300th career head coaching victory. A win would take on added significance as Clemson was coached by Bowden's son, Tommy. Peter Warrick returned to the team a day after his legal issues were, somewhat, resolved with charges reduced from felony to misdemeanor.

Janikowski hit on a first quarter field goal, but Clemson scored two touchdowns in the second quarter to lead, 14–3, at the half. This was the first time all season the Seminoles entered the third quarter trailing on the scoreboard. Florida State shut out the Tigers in the second half. Two more Sebastian Janikowski field goals, a one-yard touchdown run by Travis Minor, and a Weinke to Dan Kendra two-point conversion put the Seminoles ahead, 17–14. With 1:57 left in the game, a Clemson field goal attempt fell short, and Bobby Bowden had his 300th Division 1A victory, joining only Bear Bryant, Joe Paterno, Amos Alonzo Stagg, and Pop Warner in that elite circle. In the postgame press conference, Bowden was asked if he thought Florida State was still the #1 team in the country. Bowden replied that they may be #1, but they didn't play like it against Clemson.

Clemson would finish the season at a mediocre 6–6. However, the Tigers lost to the two undefeated ranked teams, Florida State (#1) and Marshall (#10), and to #20 Georgia Tech by only a field goal apiece. They also suffered losses to #2 Virginia Tech by 20 points, and to #13 Mississippi State by 10 points in the Peach Bowl. The Tigers held their own with one of the toughest schedules in the nation in Tommy Bowden's first year.

That week, Nebraska (#3) fell from the undefeated with a 24–20 loss to #18 Texas. Virginia Tech took over the #3 slot behind the Seminoles and Penn State. Over the next two games, the Seminoles would face the third- and fifth-leading rushers in the nation, Thomas Jones of Virginia and Lamont Jordan of Maryland.

Game 9 Virginia

Game 9 for Florida State was an away game. Virginia's Thomas Jones had his usual day, rushing for 164 yards on 26 carries (he averaged 163.5 yards/game). However, the Cavaliers' passing attack was non-existent. The two quarterbacks, starter Dan Ellis (who suffered a concussion) and reserve David Rivers, combined for only 11 of 25 passes with two interceptions and a mere 76 yards. Florida State fared no better in the first half as Chris Weinke was intercepted three times. The Seminoles' lone score of the half came on a Weinke to Marvin Minnis four-yard touchdown pass in the second quarter. Virginia managed a touchdown and a field goal in the second period to lead, 10–7, at the half.

Trailing at the half for the second straight game, Florida State held the Cavaliers scoreless while scoring two touchdowns in each of the remaining quarters. After his three interceptions, Weinke recorded three touchdown passes in completing 24 of 35 passes as the Seminoles recorded another come-from-behind victory, 35–10.

The following week, while Florida State had a bye, #2 Penn State lost to Minnesota, 24–23, leaving only the Seminoles, new #2 Virginia Tech, #5 Kansas State, #8 Mississippi State, a recent addition to the top 10, #12 Marshall, undefeated.

Game 10 Maryland

In game 10, the Seminoles rolled 49–10 over a Maryland team that would end the season at 5–6. Chris Weinke tallied six touchdown passes, including three to Peter Warrick. Lamont Jordan carried 27 times for 167 yards (he averaged 148.4 yards/game) for the Terrapins, but once again an opponent couldn't make up for the lack of a passing offense, as Maryland completed 11 of 20 passes for 73 yards and had four intercepted.

Game 11 #3 Florida

The Seminoles had now won 10 straight games and topped the polls all season. Their next opponent, Coach Steve Spurrier's #3 Florida Gators, had rebounded in the polls after a 40–39 loss to Alabama in their fifth game by defeating LSU, Auburn, #10 Georgia, Vanderbilt, and South Carolina by a combined 126–47.

A Peter Warrick four-yard touchdown run put the Seminoles up, 7–0, in the first quarter. The second period scoring was limited to field goals. Janikowski made a 22-yarder and a 27-yarder, while Florida's kicker, Jeff Chandler, also connected on two, one from 50 yards and the second from 45. Florida State led at the half, 13–6.

About halfway through the third quarter, Chandler kicked a 22-yard field goal to cut the Seminoles' lead to four points, 13–9. Then Gators cornerback Bennie Alexander intercepted a Weinke pass and returned it 43 yards for a touchdown and a 16–13 Florida lead. Three minutes later, Janikowski tied the game with a 54-yard field goal. Florida State linebacker Tommy Polley blocked a Florida punt that was recovered by safety Jean Jeune at the Gators' 21-yard line. Jeff Chaney ran for a one-yard touchdown with 34 seconds remaining in the quarter to up the Seminoles' lead to 23–16.

Each team scored a touchdown in the fourth period. With 6:03 to play and the Gators driving, Seminoles safety Chris Hope intercepted a Doug Johnson pass at the Seminoles' one-yard line, leading to a Weinke to Snoop Minnis 27-yard touchdown and a 30–16 lead. With 3:33 remaining in the game, Johnson threw a three-yard touchdown pass to Brian Haugabrook, narrowing the Florida State lead to 30 to 23. After recovering a Gators on-side kick attempt, Florida State was forced to punt, giving Florida one last chance. A desperation pass by Johnson was unsuccessful, and the final score remained 30–23.

The Gators coach, 1966 Heisman Trophy winner Steve Spurrier, alternated quarterbacks Doug Johnson and Jesse Palmer every other play. Johnson ended the game 20 of 36 for 214 yards, one touchdown, and two interceptions. Palmer threw 19 times with eight completions and 166 yards. Weinke completed 24 of 36 passes for 263 yards, one touchdown, and one interception. Warrick gained 90 yards on nine pass receptions and ran for 19 yards and a touchdown.

The Gators outgained Florida State 442 yards to 346, but two interceptions, two fumbles, a blocked punt, and especially 15 penalties for 93 yards thwarted any hope of an upset. The loss was only the fourth home field loss for the Gators in 61 games under Coach Spurrier.[4]

Florida boasted the ninth-best rushing defense in the nation (91.6 yards/game) and held Florida State to 83 yards on 38 rushes. The Seminoles, with the 10th-best rushing defense (98.8 yards/game) allowed the Gators only 62 yards on 22 rushes. As the season progressed, the FSU rushing game had diminished:

	First 6 Games	*Last 5 Games*
Rushes/Game	37.5	34.4
Yards/Game	152.5	87.2
Avg. Yards/Rush	4.1	2.5

Bobby Bowden had reason to be concerned going into the national championship game with Virginia Tech in the Sugar Bowl. Florida State opponents had a better win-loss record than the Cavaliers opponents (71–60 to 62–66), but against three common opponents, Virginia Tech had won by 105–28 while the Seminoles' margin of victory was 83–45. Virginia Tech, like Florida State, had defeated four ranked teams (Virginia #24, Syracuse #16, Miami of Florida #19, and Boston College #22) by a combined 167–28.

By season's end, Virginia Tech was among the nation's top ten in most team statistics:

Virginia Tech National Team Statistics Ranking

Team Statistic	*Rank*	*Average*
Scoring Offense	1	41.4 ppg.
Rushing Offense	8	253.9 ypg.
Total Offense	9	451.8 ypg.
Scoring Defense	1	10.5 ppg.
Rushing Defense	3	75.9 ypg.
Passing Defense	7	98.1 ypg.
Total Defense	3	247.3 ypg.

Florida State ranked fifth in Scoring Offense (37.5 ppg), 10th in Scoring Defense (15.8 ppg), and 10th in Rushing Defense (98.8 ypg).

National Championship Game

Sugar Bowl #2 Virginia Tech

The game to decide the National Championship was played on January 4, 2000. Neither team had played since late November. In that game, Virginia Tech would lead in many categories, including time of possession (36:25–23: 35), rushing yards (278–30), return yards (222–155), and total net yards (503–359). Unfortunately for the Cavaliers, they were on the short end of fumbles/fumbles lost (3–3 to 2–0) and fourth down efficiency (0–4 to 1–1), plus they had a punt blocked for a touchdown.

Florida State scored first on a 64-yard touchdown pass from Chris Weinke to Peter Warrick with 3:22 remaining in the first quarter. The Seminoles blocked a Virginia Tech punt that was returned six yards for a touchdown by Jeff Chaney with 2:14 left in the quarter. Less than two minutes later, Virginia Tech's Michael Vick connected with Andre Davis on a 49-yard touchdown pass, and the first period ended: Florida State 14, Virginia Tech 7. Less than two minutes into the second period, Ron Dugans grabbed a 63-yard touchdown pass from Weinke, and two minutes later Warrick returned a punt 59 yards for another touchdown and a 28–7 lead for the Seminoles. With only 37 seconds remaining in the half, Vick scored on a three-yard run.

The Seminoles led at the half, 28–14, but Virginia Tech dominated the third quarter. Shayne Graham kicked a 23-yard field goal halfway through the period. In a span of less than four minutes, Andre Kendrick scored two touchdowns on runs of 29 and six yards. The Hokies failed on two-point conversion tries after each score, but the quarter had produced 15 unanswered points for a 29–28 Virginia Tech lead going into the fourth period.

The fourth quarter was all Florida State. The Seminoles scored two minutes into the quarter on a Weinke to Dugans 14-yard pass and a successful Weinke to Warrick two-point conversion. Sebastian Janikowski added a 32-yard field goal, and a Weinke to Warrick 43-yard touchdown pass finished the scoring to secure a 46–29 win and the National Championship.

Weinke completed 20 of 34 passes for 329 yards with one interception, four touchdowns, and one two-point conversion. Warrick, who was named the MVP and received the Miller-Digby Award, caught six passes for 163 yards, including two touchdowns and a two-point conversion, and returned a punt 59 yards for another touchdown. Virginia Tech quarterback Michael Vick completed 15 of 29 passes for 225 yards and a touchdown while rushing 23 times for 97 yards and another score.

At season's end, Chris Weinke completed 61.5 percent (232 of 377) passes for 3,103 yards and 25 touchdowns, Peter Warrick led Seminoles receivers with 71 catches for 934 yards and a total of 12 touchdowns (one passing, eight receiving, and three on kick returns), and Travis Minor rushed for a team-high 815 yards on 180 carries (4.5 yard per carry) and seven touchdowns.

Warrick was a unanimous All America on offense along with lineman Jason Whitaker and placekicker Sebastian Janikowski, who were consensus picks. Janikowski received the Lou Groza Award, and Warrick was sixth in the Heisman Trophy voting. Lineman Corey Simon was a consensus All America on the defensive team.

The All America quarterback was Joe Hamilton of Georgia Tech. Surprisingly, Chris Weinke was not voted to any All America team and was not in the top ten in the Heisman voting. The following year Weinke would take home the Heisman Trophy and the O'Brien and Unitas Awards, although again he would not be the consensus All America quarterback. Josh Heupel of Oklahoma would become the consensus All America quarterback even after losing to Weinke, 1,628–1,552 in the Heisman balloting.

Corey Moore, a defensive lineman, was a unanimous All America for Virginia Tech. Moore also picked up the Lombardi and Nagurski Awards. With the Cavaliers' dominance in so many defensive categories (see chart above) it's a wonder there weren't more Cavaliers on the All America Defense. Penn State, for example, landed three players, including two unanimously, on the defensive All America team.

Virginia Tech's Frank Beamer was named the National AFCA Coach of the Year. Beamer also received the Eddie Robinson Award as coach of the year given by the Football Writers Association of America.

With the exception of #10 Marshall of the MAC East Conference, Florida State was the only undefeated team. More importantly, they had won against top competition, defeating teams that, at the time, were ranked #10, 20, 19, 3, and 2. They played against three of the top ten nationally ranked passers, two top ten nationally ranked rushers, and four of the top ten Heisman Trophy finalists. Since the first AP poll in 1936, Florida State was, at that time, the only team to start at number one, maintain that rank throughout the season, and finish at number one.

In the case of Florida State 1999, it isn't difficult to see why they were unanimous National Champions.

Chapter 15

Miami 2001

The BCS must have thought it struck gold when its first two national champions became unanimous choices. However, in the third year, 2000, BCS and consensus champion Oklahoma (13–0) was not a unanimous choice among all selectors and had to share the title with Miami (11–1).

This may have prompted the BCS to change its computing method. Wins against better teams would now weigh more heavily than the margin of victory in the computation of a team's strength. The *New York Times* computer model and the Dunkel Index were replaced in the BCS computation because they wouldn't alter their systems.[1]

Although finishing the 2000 season as co-National Champion, Miami found itself ranked #2 in the AP pre-season poll behind #1 Florida. The poll favored the Gators (10–3 and ranked #10 in the final 2000 poll) by the slimmest of margins, 1716–1710.[2] Still, the Hurricanes had reason to be optimistic:

Last year's superb sophomore class, including QB Ken Dorsey, RB Clinton Portis, TE Jeremy Shockey, DB Phillip Buchanon, and PK Todd Sievers were returning.

LB Chris Campbell and DBs James Lewis, Ed Reed, and Markese Fitzgerald would provide senior leadership on defense.

Highly touted incoming freshmen, including RBs Willis McGahee and Frank Gore, and TE Kellen Winslow, were coming aboard.

Penn State

The Hurricanes started the season at unranked Penn State. Kicker Todd Sievers opened the scoring with a 36-yard field goal. Quarterback Ken Dorsey threw a 27-yard touchdown pass to Ethenic Sands and Sievers added a 43-yard field goal, putting Miami up by 13–0 to end the first quarter. At 13:56 of the second quarter, Sievers made a 37-yard field goal. Dorsey scored on two touchdown passes: a 26-yard toss to Najeh Davenport and a 10-yard completion to Jeremy Shockey. At the half, Miami was up, 30–0.

Coach Larry Coker played reserves in the second half. After a scoreless third quarter, Sievers hit a 23-yard field goal early in the fourth period. Penn State got on the scoreboard with a Zach Mills to Bryant Johnson 44-yard touchdown pass with 9:58 remaining. Dorsey completed 20 of 27 passes for 344 yards, three touchdowns and one interception. Tailback Clinton Portis rushed for 164 yards as the Hurricanes outgained the Nittany Lions, 602 to 323 yards. The defense posted two interceptions. Miami left with an impressive 33–7 win.

Top-ranked Florida beat Marshall, 49–14, but it wasn't enough, and Miami moved to the #1 spot. Oklahoma (2–0) continued at #3, while Texas (1–0) replaced Nebraska (2–0) at #4.

Rutgers

Miami thoroughly dominated the Scarlet Knights in a 61–0 win. Using three quarterbacks, Rutgers managed only 62 yards through the air on 9 of 22 passes and 64 yards in 40 rushes, for 126 yards of offense. Miami's Ken Dorsey connected on two touchdown passes, one to Jeremy Shockey and the other to Andre Johnson. Four rushers each scored a touchdown, Phillip Buchanon returned a punt for a touchdown, and Todd Sievers (seven of eight extra point attempts, and two of three field goals attempts) added 13 points.

In other games: #2 Florida beat Louisiana-Monroe, 55–6, #3 Oklahoma downed North Texas, 37–10, #4 Texas topped North Carolina, 44–14, and #5 Nebraska beat #17 Notre Dame, 27–10.

The carefree atmosphere that normally surrounds college football was shattered three days later on September 11. A terrorist attack on United States soil had left nearly 3,000 dead at the World Trade Center in New York City, the Pentagon in Virginia, and a failed terrorist attempt over the skies of Pennsylvania. The following week's games on September 15 were either re-scheduled or cancelled.

Pittsburgh

A minute and a half into the game, Miami's Clinton Portis scored on a 4-yard touchdown run, but the extra point was missed. Two minutes later, Pitt quarterback Rod Rutherford scored on a one-yard run, and the Panthers were up, 7–6. The Hurricane's scored twice more, Portis on a one-yard run and a Ken Dorsey to Andre Johnson 18-yard pass, to lead 20–7 after the first quarter. The second period saw a Todd Sievers 24-yard field goal to put Miami ahead 23–7 at the half.

In the third quarter, Portis scored on a one-yard run to cap a nine-play, 80-yard drive, and Sievers connected on a 26-yard field goal. Miami started the fourth period scoring with a Willie McGahee five-yard touchdown run with 13:59 to play. Pitt got its second touchdown of the game on a Rutherford to Kris Wilson 10-yard pass to end a 70-yard drive with under nine minutes remaining. Sievers made a 38-yard field goal with 1:30 left to play. Pitt ended the scoring when Rutherford ran three yards to the end zone with only 19 seconds left as Miami defeated the Panthers, 43–21.

Dorsey completed 18 of 32 pass attempts to nine different receivers for 208 yards, one touchdown, and one interception. Portis rushed 24 times for 131 yards and three touchdowns as the Hurricanes outgained the Panthers, 467 to 308 yards. Rutherford accounted for all of Pitt's touchdowns, one passing and two rushing.

The top five teams all won and held their rankings.

Troy State

Troy State, in Alabama, wasn't supposed to give the Hurricanes much competition, but at the end of the first quarter the score was tied at 7–7. Thereafter, it was all Miami as the Hurricanes scored 31 unanswered points for a 38–7 win.

Florida (#2) defeated LSU, 44–15 to take over #1, with Miami now #2. Oklahoma (#3) beat #5 Texas, 14–3, and #4 Nebraska beat Iowa State, 48–14. The loss would drop Texas to #11 and move Oregon to #5.

#14 Florida State

The 14th-ranked Seminoles (3–1) were listed at #6 pre-season but fell after a 41–9 loss at unranked North Carolina. This week, following a bye, they were at home, riding a 54-game home win streak at Doak Campbell Stadium, to face the Hurricanes.

Miami's Markese Fitzgerald recovered a blocked Florida State punt and advanced it 18 yards for a touchdown. A minute and a half later, quarterback Ken Dorsey hit Andre Johnson for a 27-yard score, and the Hurricanes were up, 14–0 to end the first quarter. Dorsey connected with Jeremy Shockey on a one-yard touchdown pass and a 21–0 lead at 11:25 of the second period. Florida State rallied with short touchdown rushes by Greg Jones and William McCray following drives of 74 and 70 yards. One PAT conversion was missed, and the half ended with Miami holding a 21–13 edge.

Dorsey and Johnson connected for their second touchdown of the game, an 18-yarder. Jonathan Vilma returned a Florida State fumble for a 36-yard touchdown, and Miami increased the lead to 35–13. The Seminoles cut the margin to 15 on a Chris Rix to Talman Gardner 57-yard touchdown pass. But before the third quarter ended, the Hurricanes scored twice more as Freddie Capshaw ended a 13-play, 84-yard drive with a seven-yard touchdown run and, a minute later, Willis McGahee scored on an eight-yard run. With seven minutes remaining, a Capshaw fumble was returned 73 yards for a score by Seminoles linebacker Michael Boulware, and the game ended Miami 49, Florida State 27.

Florida State led Miami in first downs (30–18), rushing yards (214–142), and total offense (476–391). The Seminoles also committed six turnovers to three for the Hurricanes. Clinton Portis led all rushers with 122 yards on 17 carries. Dorsey completed 14 of 27 passes for 249 yards, three touchdowns, and no interceptions. Johnson had five receptions for 111 yards and two scores. Phillip Buchanon and Ed Reed each had two interceptions for Miami.

Top-ranked Florida fell to Auburn, 23–20 and dropped to #7. Miami took over #1, while Oklahoma and Nebraska advanced to #2 and #3 respectively. Oregon remained at #5, with UCLA taking over #4 following its 35–13 win over #10 Washington.

The following week, while Miami had a bye, #5 Oregon was defeated, 49–42 by unranked Stanford, dropped to #11, and was replaced by Virginia Tech. All of the other top five5 won and retained their positions. That week, the BCS announced its first ranking based on the new criteria set up: Oklahoma #1, followed by Nebraska, UCLA, Miami, and Virginia Tech.

West Virginia

West Virginia (2–4) tied the game at 3–3 on a Brendan Rauh 26-yard field goal to end the first quarter. Todd Sievers had connected on a 32-yard field goal earlier. From there it was all Miami as the Hurricanes took advantage of six Mountaineers turnovers to score two touchdowns in each of the remaining periods for a 45–3 win.

Miami quarterback Ken Dorsey threw for 192 yards and two touchdowns, one each to Andre Johnson and Jeremy Shockey. He also had one pass intercepted. Frank Gore rushed six times for 124 yards and two touchdowns. Clinton Portis added 72 rushing yards and a touchdown. The Hurricanes' offense generated 436 yards to 265 for the Mountaineers. The defense registered six West Virginia turnovers. Ed Reed had two interceptions, while James Lewis and Maurice Sikes each had one. Reed also returned a Mountaineers fumble for a touchdown.

In other games, #3 Nebraska topped #2 Oklahoma, 20–10, #4 UCLA lost to #20 Stanford, 38–28, and #5 Virginia Tech lost to Syracuse, 22–14. The AP top five was now: Miami, Nebraska, Oklahoma, Florida, and Texas. The BCS poll now had Nebraska #1 and Oklahoma #2, in spite of its loss. Miami moved up to #3, while Michigan (5–1) was #4 and Texas (7–1) #5. Of major schools, only Miami, Nebraska, and #14 Brigham Young remained undefeated.

Temple

For the second week in a row, Miami had little trouble with an unranked opponent. The Temple Owls, 2–5, gave up a Ken Dorsey to Kevin Beard touchdown pass in the first quarter and a Clinton Portis rushing touchdown in the second period for a 14–0 Hurricanes lead at the half.

The third period saw a Dorsey to Andre Johnson touchdown pass, a Frank Gore 13-yard rushing touchdown, and a Phillip Buchanon 52-yard punt return for another score. Todd Sievers added a 37-yard field goal in the fourth quarter for a 38–0 shutout for the Hurricanes.

The top five teams in the AP poll all won and retained their rankings.

In the BCS poll, #4 Michigan lost to Michigan State, 26–24. Nebraska remained #1, followed by Miami, Oklahoma, Tennessee (6–1), and Texas (8–1).

Boston College

Todd Sievers connected on 38-yard, 24-yard, and 43-yard field goals in the second quarter for a lead 9–0 at the half. At 5:55 remaining in the third period, Eagles quarterback Brian St. Pierre engineered a 61-yard drive. He connected on a 21-yard touchdown pass to wide receiver Dedrick Dewalt on a fourth down and 10 to put Boston College down by only two points. Five seconds into the fourth period, Sievers made his fourth field goal, a 47-yarder to extend the Miami lead to five points. Miami defensive tackle Matt Walters intercepted a Boston College pass and lateralled the ball to safety Ed Reed, who ran 80 yards for a touchdown as the Hurricanes won their closest game of the year, 18–7. Ken Dorsey accounted for 222 passing yards but was intercepted four times. Clinton Portis rushed for 160 yards.

All five teams in the AP poll won and retained their rankings.

In the BCS poll, Nebraska remained at #1, with Miami #2 and Oklahoma at #3. Even though Tennessee and Texas won their games, they were replaced by 9–1 Oregon at #4 and Florida (8–1) at #5.

#14 Syracuse

Syracuse started the season with losses to #10 Georgia Tech (13–7) and #8 Tennessee (33–9). They then won eight straight games, including a 22–14 victory at #5 Virginia Tech. During those eight wins, they outscored opponents, 253–111. After the Virginia Tech game, they entered the AP poll at #18 and advanced to #14 the following week.

Syracuse's upset hopes were quickly crushed as Miami rolled up 566 yards of offense and 25 first downs to 185 yards for the Orange with only 12 first downs. Ken Dorsey threw for 224 yards and four touchdowns. Frank Gore rushed for 153 yards and Clinton Portis for 132 yards and one touchdown. Miami shut out Syracuse, 59–0.

Nebraska, Texas, and Oregon all had byes. The AP poll ranking was: Miami, Nebraska, Florida, Oklahoma, and Texas.

The BCS ranking was: Nebraska, Miami, Oklahoma, Florida, and Oregon.

#12 Washington

The year before, Washington beat the Hurricanes, 34–29. The Huskies were also responsible for ending Miami's home winning streak at 58 games back in 1994.[3] But surely, Miami wasn't thinking about any of that when they crushed Washington, 65–7.

The Hurricanes led 37–0 at the half on five touchdowns and a safety. Miami scored two touchdowns in each of the last two quarters. The Huskies got their only points on a Rich Alexis five-yard rush sandwiched between the two Miami scores in the third period. Ken Dorsey was 14 of 21 on pass attempts for 189 yards, three touchdowns, and one interception. Clinton Portis led all rushers with 105 yards and two touchdowns. The Hurricanes outgained the Huskies, 413 yards to 292.

This was a week of upsets that helped Miami to get to the BCS title game. Although they would need to defeat #14 Virginia Tech the following week, Colorado and Oklahoma State helped clear the way. Colorado defeated Nebraska (#2 AP, #1 BCS), 62–36, while down the road, Oklahoma (#4 AP, #3 BCS) lost to rival Oklahoma State, 13–16.

The AP top 5 was now: Miami, Florida, Texas, Oregon, and Tennessee. Nebraska fell to #6 and Oklahoma to #11.

The BCS ranking was now: Miami, Florida, Texas, Nebraska, and Oregon.

#14 Virginia Tech

To secure a spot in the BCS Championship Game, Miami only needed a win at 8–2 Virginia Tech. A comparison of common opponents would make a Miami win appear certain:

Opponent	Miami	Virginia Tech
Boston College	18–7 W	34–20 W
Pittsburgh	43–21 W	38–7 L

Opponent	Miami	Virginia Tech
Rutgers	61–0 W	50–0 W
Syracuse	59–0 W	22–14 L
Temple	38–0 W	35–0 W
West Virginia	45–3 W	35–0 W
	264–31	175–70

The concern was that the Hurricanes had not won at Virginia Tech since 1992.[4] Virginia Tech scored the only points in the first quarter on a 27-yard field goal by Carter Warley. But in this must-win situation, Miami rebounded. Two minutes into the second period, Ken Dorsey hit Jeremy Shockey for a 14-yard touchdown. Clinton Portis ran for a seven-yard touchdown six minutes later. Todd Sievers hit on two field goals from 34 and 43 yards out, the last with 24 seconds remaining. At the half, Miami held a 20–3 advantage.

Four minutes into the third period, the Hokies cut the Miami lead to 10 points on a one-yard touchdown run by Jarrett Ferguson. Later in the quarter, Sievers connected on a 42-yard field goal. Early in the fourth period, Sievers scored his fourth field goal, a 39-yarder, and Miami enjoyed a 16-point lead with 11:36 to play. But Virginia Tech scored on Ferguson's second one-yard touchdown run. A two-point conversion pass from Hokies quarterback Grant Noel to Terrell Parham was good, and Virginia Tech now trailed, 26–18. With 6:30 remaining, the Hokies blocked a Miami punt, and Brandon Manning returned it 22 yards for a touchdown. Down by only two points, Tech attempted a second two-point play, but the ball was dropped by the receiver, and the final score read Miami 26, Virginia Tech 24.

Miami's defense allowed only 11 first downs and intercepted Noel four times while allowing 61 passing yards and causing five turnovers. Dorsey threw for 235 yards, one touchdown, and no interceptions. Clinton Portis rushed for 124 yards. Tech's Kevin Jones gained 160 rushing yards.

In the AP top 5, #2 Florida lost to #5 Tennessee, 34–32, #3 Texas lost to #9 Colorado, 39–37 in the Big 12 Championship game, while #4 Oregon topped rival Oregon State, 17–14.

The AP ranking was: Miami, Tennessee, Oregon, Colorado, and Nebraska.

The BCS ranking was: Miami, Tennessee, Nebraska, Colorado, and Oregon.

The regular season had ended for all except for AP and BCS #2 Tennessee. The following week, the Volunteers lost to #21 LSU, 31–20 in the SEC Championship game.

The final regular season AP poll now had Miami at #1, Oregon #2, Colorado #3, Nebraska #4, and Florida #5.

The BCS ranking was: Miami #1, Nebraska #2, Colorado #3, Oregon #4, and Florida #5. As the BCS Rankings determined the teams to play for the championship, it would be Miami and Nebraska, to the chagrin of Oregon and Colorado.

#4 AP, #2 BCS Nebraska Rose Bowl National Championship Game

The National Championship game was played in the Rose Bowl. This year would be the first time the Big 10 champion would not square off against the PAC 10 winner since the 1946 game that paired #3 Alabama with #11 Southern California (Alabama won, 34–14) following the World War II-altered 1945 season. The pact between the two conferences began the following year.[5]

From the standpoint of BCS rankings, the Rose Bowl paired #1 vs. #2. But by the AP ranking, the Rose Bowl matched #1 vs. #4, while the Fiesta Bowl had #2 vs. #3, a perfect single elimination tournament culminating in a championship game between the winners. However, the football world would have to wait until 2014 before a College Football Playoff was established.

The Rose Bowl would more resemble a #1 vs. #4 as Miami scored 27 points in the second quarter to take a 34–0 lead at the half. The Hurricanes scored on a 49-yard Ken Dorsey to Andre Johnson touchdown pass following a fumble recovery in the first quarter. Early in the second period, Clinton Portis scored on a 39-yard run. Less than two minutes later, Miami's James Lewis intercepted a Nebraska pass and returned it for a 47-yard touchdown. Dorsey connected with Jeremy Shockey for a 21-yard score, and seven minutes later with Johnson on an 8-yard touchdown. The first of these two extra point attempts was missed, and Miami led by 34 points.

The only third quarter scoring was a Judd Davis 16-yard rush to cut Miami's lead to 27 points with 17:45 to play in the game. Fifteen seconds into the fourth period, a Miami punt was returned 71 yards by the Cornhuskers' DeJuan Groce to further cut the lead to 20 points. Todd Sievers ended the scoring four minutes later with a 37-yard field goal, and the game ended Miami 37, Nebraska 14.

Dorsey completed 22 of 35 passes for 362 yards, three touchdowns, and one interception. Johnson caught two touchdown throws as he and Dorsey were named co–Rose Bowl MVPs. Clinton Portis rushed 20 times for 104 yards and one touchdown. Nebraska quarterback Eric Crouch had a disappointing game following his Heisman Trophy–winning season. But a lot of that was because of the relentless Miami defense. Crouch rushed for 114 yards but was only 5 of 15 passing for 62 yards. He also was intercepted once and fumbled once, each turnover leading to Miami points.

Post Season

Miami offensive lineman Bryant McKinnie and defensive back Ed Reed were unanimous All America picks. Tight end Jeremy Shockey, offensive lineman Joaquin Gonzalez, and kicker Todd Sievers were placed on some All America teams, but were not consensus. Florida's Rex Grossman was the consensus All America quarterback, although he placed second in the Heisman Trophy voting to Nebraska's Eric Crouch. The Hurricanes' Ken Dorsey was named to no All America teams, but he was third in the Heisman voting and took home the Maxwell Award. Bryant McKinnie received the Outland Trophy.

Of individual leaders, Ed Reed led the nation with nine interceptions, and Todd Sievers had the most field goals with 21 (of 26 attempts). Sievers was also fourth nationally in scoring with 119 points (21 field goals and 56 extra points). Junior defensive back Phillip Buchanon was seventh nationally in punt returns, averaging 15 yards per return and scoring two touchdowns.

Miami was third in scoring offense (43.2 points per game) and eighth in total offense (454.8 yards per game). On defense, the Hurricanes finished first in passing defense (allowing 138 yards per game) and in scoring defense (9.4 points per game). They were also sixth in total defense (270.9 yards per game) and first in turnover margin (2.4 per game).

Why Was Miami Unanimous

Even with the disagreement between the AP and BCS as to which team should be #2 and play for the national title, Miami convincingly beat Nebraska (BCS #2). Oregon (AP #2 & BCS #4) similarly defeated Colorado (AP and BCS #3), 38–16. Although Miami was the only undefeated team, Oregon was the only top 25 team with only one loss. The Ducks would, therefore, appear to be the only other team that should be considered.

However, Oregon only finished fifth in turnover margin among team statistical leaders. The Ducks had wins over #22 Wisconsin, #14 Washington State, #17 UCLA, and #3 Colorado. They also had a 49–42 loss in October to then-unranked Stanford (9–2, #11 in final AP poll).

Miami had wins over: #14 Florida State, #14 Syracuse, #12 Washington, #14 Virginia Tech, and #4 Nebraska. Furthermore, Miami's margin of victory for the season was 33.8 points per game, compared to 12.2 for Oregon.

In spite of occasional disagreements over rankings, the BCS champion proved to be the choice of all other selectors.

Chapter 16

Southern California 2004

After the Trojans' unanimous championship in 1972, they enjoyed great success through the rest of the decade, with shared titles in 1974, 1976, 1978, and 1979. Moderate success followed under head coaches Ted Tollner (26–20–1), Larry Smith (44–25–3), John Robinson (37–21–2), and Paul Hackett (19–18).

Pete Carroll became head coach in 2001, and after a 6–6 initial season guided the Trojans to shared titles in 2002 and 2003. Southern California ended the 2003 season ranked #1 after defeating #4 Michigan in the Rose Bowl, 28–14, but shared the title with consensus champion #2 LSU and #3 Oklahoma, even though the Sooners lost to LSU, 21–14 in the Sugar Bowl. The Trojans began the 2004 season ranked #1, followed by Ohio State, Miami (FL), Michigan, and Texas. However, Southern California would not have wide receiver Mike Williams, a consensus 2003 All America and #8 in the Heisman Trophy voting. Williams had opted to apply for the NFL draft, was not picked up, and was ineligible to rejoin the Trojans.[1]

August 28, 2004 Virginia Tech

Southern California began the season hosting Virginia Tech in the 2004 Black Coaches Association Classic.[2] This would be the final year of the Classic, which began in 1997. The site of the game was different each year, with the 2004 contest held at FedEx Field, the home of the NFL Washington Redskins.

A pair of future Heisman Trophy winners combined for the first score of the game. Trojans quarterback Matt Leinart connected with running back Reggie Bush for a 35-yard touchdown with six minutes remaining in the first quarter. Virginia Tech's Brandon Pace hit a 35-yard field goal, and the score remained 7–3 after one period. The Hokies' Bryan Randall threw a 12-yard touchdown pass to Josh Hyman, and the half ended with Virginia Tech up, 10–7.

Leinart and Bush again connected on a touchdown throw, this a 53-yarder for the only third period score. Southern California was now up, 14–10. Pace hit a 42-yard field goal to narrow the margin to one point. But in the last 5:35 of the game, the Trojans scored on a third Leinart to Bush touchdown and a Ryan Killeen 41-yard field goal for a 24–13 Southern California win.

Leinart was 19 of 29 passes for 272 yards, no interceptions, and three touchdowns. Bush rushed nine times for 27 yards and caught five passes for 127 yards, including three touchdowns. The Trojans' total offense amassed 373 yards to 294 for Virginia Tech. The Hokies would finish the season ranked #10.

September 11, 2004 Colorado State

At home in the L.A. Memorial Coliseum, Southern California made short work of Colorado State in a 49–0 shutout. Sophomore running back LenDale White rushed 14 times for 123 yards and three of the Trojans' seven touchdowns. Reggie Bush carried 12 times for 84 yards and scored one touchdown. Matt Leinart completed 20 of 31 passes for 231 yards and two scores, the first to sophomore Steve Smith and the other to freshman Dwayne Jarrett. Leinart again threw no interceptions. The seventh touchdown was a fumble recovered by sophomore defensive lineman Manuel Wright and returned 20 yards for a score. Southern California outgained Colorado State, 553 yards to 281, made 32 first downs to 14 for the Rams, and forced seven turnovers.

September 18, 2004 Brigham Young

On the road at Brigham Young, the #1 Trojans missed two field goals, did not score in the first quarter, and saw the Cougars take a 3–0 lead four minutes into the second period. The remainder of the quarter was all Southern California: Matt Leinart threw a 21-yard touchdown to Reggie Bush, Bush rushed 66 yards for a touchdown, and Leinart found Dwayne Jarrett for a 15-yard score to take a 21–3 lead at the half.

The only third period score was a BYU touchdown pass from quarterback John Beck to Todd Watkins to cut the Trojans' lead to 11 points. Southern California scored 21 unanswered points in the fourth quarter to secure a 42–10 win. Leinart rushed for a one-yard touchdown, LenDale White scored on a 43-yard run to cap a 17-carry, 110-yard game, and senior fullback Lee Webb ran for a nine-yard touchdown. Bush rushed 14 times for 124 yards and one touchdown. He also had four pass receptions for 42 yards and another score. Leinart suffered his first interception of the year but passed for 236 yards and two touchdowns. Overall, the #1 Trojans outgained the Cougars, 514 yards to 221.

September 25, 2004 Stanford

Southern California's first close game came against rival Stanford at the Cardinal's home field. The Trojans struck first with a Ryan Killeen 23-yard field goal, followed by a Matt Leinart to Steve Smith two-yard touchdown pass to take a 10–0 lead with 5:40 remaining in the first quarter. Stanford then drove 79 yards in 11 plays to score on a Trent Edwards to Evan Moore three-yard pass. Edwards capped a 15-play 76-yard drive with a two-yard scoring pass to Patrick Danahy at 6:15 in the second quarter, putting the Cardinal up, 14–10. Stanford extended the lead to 11 points when Kyle Matter rushed 11 yards for a touchdown on a fake field goal.[3] Reggie Bush answered with a 17-yard touchdown run with exactly one minute remaining in the half to cut Stanford's lead to four points. But with 10 seconds on the clock, Cardinal junior running back J. R. Lemon scored on an 82-yard run, and Stanford ended the first half up, 28–17.

Near the end of the third period Leinart scored on a one-yard run to cut the Cardinal's lead back to four points. Midway through the fourth period, Southern California's

LenDale White carried it in from the 2-yard line. The Trojans shut out Stanford the final 6:30 to go home with a hard-fought 31–28 win. Leinart finished with 284 yards in 23 of 30 passes with one touchdown and one interception. Bush had 95 yards and one touchdown in 16 rushes as the Trojans out-gained the Cardinal, 383 yards to 327. Southern California would have a bye week before hosting #7 California.

The AP poll now ranked the top 5: Southern California, Oklahoma, Georgia, Miami, and Texas.

October 9, 2004 #7 California

The California Golden Bears were ranked #13 in pre-season and had moved up to #7 after defeating Air Force (56–4), New Mexico State (41–14), and Oregon State (49–7). The Golden Bears had handed Southern California their only loss in 2003, a 34–31 upset when the Trojans were ranked #3.

The first quarter started off well for the Trojans as Matt Leinart threw a five-yard touchdown pass to LenDale White and Ryan Killeen added a 31-yard field goal with 0:09 left in the period to take a 10–0 lead. California got on the board on a 39-yard field goal by Tom Schneider. Four minutes later, Killeen hit a 33-yard field goal to put the Trojans up, 13–3. With less than two minutes until halftime, Golden Bears quarterback Aaron Rodgers hit Geoff McArthur for a 20-yard touchdown to cap a nine-play, 80-yard drive and close the gap to three points. With only six seconds remaining, Killeen made his third field goal, a 42-yarder, to increase the Trojans' lead to six points at the intermission.

Leinart tossed his second touchdown pass of the game, a 16-yarder to Dwayne Jarrett, less than three minutes into the second half, for a more comfortable 23–10 lead. Late in the third quarter, California's Marshawn Lynch ended a 12-play 80-yard drive by scoring from two yards out. The fourth period was scoreless but not without excitement. Late in the game, Rodgers moved the Golden Bears to the Southern California 9-yard line and a first-and-goal. With the game on the line for both teams, the Trojans' defense sacked Rodgers once and forced three incomplete passes. Possession went back to Southern California with 1:47 to play. The final score: Southern California 23, California 17.

The statistics for the game would suggest a very different outcome:

	California	*Southern California*
Rushing yards	157	41
Passing yards	267	164
Total yards	424	205
First downs	28	12
Sacks by	4	5
Interceptions by	1	0
Time of possession	37:11	22:49

Rodgers completed his first 23 passes. That tied Tennessee's Tee Martin for the NCAA record.[4] Rodgers finished with 29 of 34 for 267 yards and a touchdown.

The 2004 University of Southern California unanimous national champion football team. Behind Heisman Trophy winners Matt Leinart (2004) and Reggie Bush (2005), the 13–0 Trojans defeated Oklahoma, 55–19, to win the title (courtesy USC Athletics).

Leinart completed 15 of 24 passes for 164 yards and two touchdowns, and had one pass intercepted. California won the remainder of their games, were ranked #4 in the last regular season poll, and lost to #23 Texas Tech, 45–31 in the Holiday Bowl to finish at #9.

October 16, 2004 #15 Arizona State

Arizona State was undefeated and had outscored its five unranked opponents, 167–64. Unranked themselves in the pre-season, the Sun Devils at 3–0 entered the polls in September and worked their way to #15.

Any hopes for a Sun Devils upset soon vanished. Southern California scored 14 points in the first quarter and 28 points in the second. Matt Leinart completed 13 of 24 passes for 224 yards and four touchdowns, and he ran for another score. Dwayne Jarrett caught five passes for 139 yards and three touchdowns, two from Leinart and a 52-yarder from Reggie Bush. Leinart had touchdown throws to Bush and LenDale White in the first period. Ryan Killeen made a 34-yard field goal in the fourth quarter to round out the Southern California scoring. Arizona State avoided a shutout with a Hakim Hill two-yard touchdown run in the second period. The final score read Southern California 45, Arizona State 7. Unlike California the previous week, the game statistics greatly favored the Trojans:

	Arizona State	Southern California
Rushing yards	24	145
Passing yards	219	301
Total yards	243	446
First downs	13	23
Interceptions by	0	2

The rankings had changed in the past two weeks: Southern California and Oklahoma remained #1 and #2, Auburn replaced Georgia at #3, while Miami remained at #4, and Florida State moved up to #5, replacing Texas.

October 23, 2004 Washington

Southern California made easy work of a Washington team that was in an off-year. The Huskies would end the season at 1–10, beating only 2–9 San Jose State. The Trojans scored 38 unanswered points, handing Washington its first shutout (38–0) since 1981. Matt Leinart threw for two touchdowns, LenDale White rushed for two scores, freshman Desmond Reed ran for one, and Ryan Killeen added a field goal. The Trojans made 28 first downs and 453 total yards to six first downs and 113 yards for the Huskies.

The AP top five rankings remained unchanged. There were still seven undefeated teams in the top 25.

October 30, 2004 Washington State

In 2003, the Washington State Cougars ended the season at 10–3, defeated #5 Texas in the Holiday Bowl, and finished at #9. Unranked in 2004, the Cougars were 3–4 when hosting the game with the Trojans.

Only a minute and a half into the game, Reggie Bush scored on a 19-yard touchdown run. A minute later, LenDale White scored on a one-yard run. Exactly halfway through the period, Bush returned a Washington State punt 57 yards for a 21–0 Trojans lead. In the second quarter, Matt Leinart hit Dwayne Jarrett for a 42-yard touchdown and White ran seven yards for his second touchdown of the game to make the score 35–0 at the half.

Leinart and Jarrett teamed up for their second touchdown completion, a five-yarder, midway through the third period. Washington State quarterback Alex Brink found Michael Bumpus for a 24-yard touchdown. After the kickoff, Trojans senior backup quarterback Matt Cassell's pass was intercepted by Cougars defensive back Pat Bennett and returned for a touchdown. Washington State attempted a two-point conversion after each score, but both failed. The fourth period was scoreless, and Southern California notched another win, 42–12. The Trojans gained 421 yards on offense to 156 for the Cougars, including only nine rushing yards in 25 carries.

The top three remained the same in the polls: #1 Southern California, #2 Oklahoma, and #3 Auburn. Miami, #4, and #5 Florida State both lost and were replaced by California and Wisconsin.

November 6, 2004 Oregon State

Oregon State hosted the Trojans amid a thick fog at Reser Stadium. Their record was 4–4, but the Beavers had won the last three games by a total of 95–47 over Washington, Washington State, and Arizona.

Oregon State took a 6–0 lead in the first quarter on two Alexis Serna field goals of 25 and 33 yards. They extended the lead to 13 points early in the second period on a Derek Anderson to Marcel Love eight-yard touchdown pass. Before the half ended, Matt Leinart threw 18 yards to junior tight end Dominique Bird for a Trojans touchdown. Oregon State led, 13–7.

Early in the third quarter, Leinart and Bird again connected, this time for a 25-yard touchdown and a one-point Trojans lead. At 12:27 of the fourth period, Reggie Bush returned a punt 65 yards for a touchdown and a more comfortable nine-point lead. Lendale White scored on a five-yard run with 7:11 to play putting Southern California up, 28–13. With little time remaining, Anderson hit Josh Hawkins on a 36-yard touchdown pass, and the game ended with a 28–20 Southern California win.

Leinart was 17 of 31 for 205 yards, two touchdowns, and one interception. The offense produced 415 total yards compared to the Beavers' 364 yards. Anderson threw for 330 yards, while the Trojans' defense held the Oregon State rushing game to 34 yards. Bush's punt return for a touchdown with the game close at 14–13 was the turning point to secure the win.

The top five remained the same although Wisconsin and California switched positions. The rankings were now: #1 Southern California, #2 Oklahoma, #3 Auburn, #4 Wisconsin, and #5 California.

November 13, 2004 Arizona

The Arizona Wildcats were another team having an off-year. They had not had a winning season since 1998, when they were 12–1 and ended the season ranked #4. Since then, the Wildcats had posted a 22–36 record. This year would end no better at 3–8.

Arizona led 3–0 after one quarter on a Nicholas Folk 48-yard field goal. Just as the second period began, Matt Leinart passed to junior fullback David Kirtman for a five-yard touchdown. LeDale White made the score 14–3 at the half when he rushed for a three-yard score.

White rushed two yards for his second touchdown early in the third period. Arizona got its last points when Richard Kovalcheck passed nine yards to Steve Fleming. The try for a two-point conversion failed, and the score remained 21–9. White rushed six yards for his third touchdown, and Leinart passed 13 yards to Dwayne Jarrett to end the third quarter with the Trojans ahead, 35–9. The Leinart to Jarrett duo struck again early in the fourth period for a 12-yard touchdown. Junior running back Herschel Dennis rushed for a one-yard score with 7:35 remaining to be played. The game ended Southern California 49, Arizona 9. Led by Leinart's 280 passing yards and White's 118 rushing yards, the Trojans' offense amassed 585 yards and 25 first downs to 255 and 14 for Arizona. The win clinched the Pac-10 title for Southern California for the third consecutive year, assuring them a spot in a major bowl game. The Trojans were now two wins away from the Orange Bowl and a shot at a national championship.

Following #4 Wisconsin's 49–19 loss to unranked Michigan State, the poll now had the top five as: 10–0 Southern California #1, 10–0 Oklahoma #2, 10–0 Auburn #3, 8–1 California #4, and 10–0 Utah #5. The Trojans had a bye week before their game with rival Notre Dame. In that bye week, all of the other top five won, and the rankings remained the same.

November 27, 2004 Notre Dame

Whereas the Irish were 6–4 and unranked coming to Southern California, they had defeated #13 Michigan (28–20), #15 Tennessee (17–13), and unranked Washington, 38–3 (the Trojans beat the Huskies, 38–0). Notre Dame could be dangerous.

The Irish struck first on a Brady Quinn to Billy Palmer one-yard touchdown pass, capping a 92-yard, 13-play drive on their first possession. Ryan Killeen kicked a 39-yard field goal, and the first quarter ended with Notre Dame up, 7–3. Early in the second period, D. J. Fitzpatrick kicked a 28-yard field goal, extending the Notre Dame lead 10–3. But for the Irish, there would be no more points. Before the first half ended, Matt Leinart and Dwayne Jarrett would combine for two touchdowns of 12 and 57 yards and a 17–10 edge.

The third quarter saw a 42-yard field goal by Killeen and a Leinart to Reggie Bush 69-yard touchdown. Leinart threw for two more scores in the fourth period: a 35-yard pass to Steve Smith and a 23-yarder to Jason Mitchell. Southern California won, 41–10. Leinart completed 24 of 34 passes for 400 yards and five touchdowns, tying a Trojans single-game record. (Vernon Adams would break the record with six touchdown passes against Oregon in 2015.[5])

December 4, 2004 UCLA

The annual cross-town rivalry game, this year hosted by the Bruins, was played at the Rose Bowl. UCLA came in unranked at 6–4.

Forty-five seconds into the game, Reggie Bush broke a 65-yard touchdown run, and Ryan Killeen added a 37-yard field goal to give Southern California a 10–0 lead at the end of the first quarter. UCLA got on the scoreboard when Craig Bragg returned a Trojans punt 95 yards for a touchdown five minutes into the second period. Four minutes later, Bush answered with a touchdown run of 81 yards. Justin Medlock kicked a 43-yard field goal for the Bruins, cutting the Trojans' lead to seven points. But nine seconds before halftime, Killeen made a 42-yard field goal, putting Southern California up, 20–10.

Eight minutes into the third quarter, Killeen again connected on a field goal, this from 34 yards away. UCLA answered with a nine-yard touchdown run by Manuel White that put the Bruins behind by only six points at 23–17. In the fourth quarter, Killeen made two more field goals of 36 and 34 yards. Ahead 29–17 with 3:49 remaining to play, the Trojans may have felt more comfortable, but 1:29 later, UCLA completed a seven-play 80-yard drive with a Drew Olson to Marcedes Lewis four-yard touchdown pass. The game for the Victory Bell ended Southern California 29, UCLA 24.

Leinart completed 24 of 34 pass attempts for 242 yards but did not have a touchdown for the first time all season. Bush carried 15 times for 204 yards, had six pass receptions for 73 yards, returned two punts for 19 yards, and two kickoffs for 39 yards, for 335 all-purpose yards. Killeen set a Southern California and PAC-10 single game record with five field goals as the Trojans were now officially in the BCS Championship game. Their opponent would be #2 Oklahoma. The Sooners had defeated Colorado (unranked at 8–4), 42–3 for the Big 12 Championship.

Fans of #3 Auburn were not happy, and they had some legitimate reasons to think the Tigers should play for the title. Auburn was 12–0 and had defeated #15 Tennessee, 38–28 for the SEC title. Auburn had worked its way to #3 after a pre-season ranking of #17. And a comparison of the two teams shows little difference:

	Oklahoma	*Auburn*
Record	12–0	12–0
Points scored-allowed	433–164	401–134
Ranked opponents	#s 5, 21, 22	#s 5, 8, 11, 15
National team leaders	#6 rushing defense #8 total offense	#1 scoring defense #5 total defense

This season was yet another argument for a college football playoff.

From the pre-season poll through the regular season, Oklahoma held the #2 ranking behind the Trojans. The Sooners were not a strong team throughout most of the 1990s. In 1999 Bob Stoops was hired as head coach and almost immediately turned the program around:

1999	7–5	
2000	13–0	Consensus national champion
2001	11–2	
2002	12–2	
2003	12–2	Shared national championship
2004	12–0	(going into the Orange Bowl)
	67–11	

Although the Sooners averaged 36 points per game, the Trojans had one of the nation's top defenses. Southern California ranked in the Top 10 of national team defense leaders:

Southern California Ranking

Rushing defense	#1	74.9 yards per game
Passing defense	#9	a rating of 101.3
Total defense	#6	279.3 yards per game
Scoring defense	#3	13 points per game
Turnover margin	#1	38 turnovers for a margin of 1.5

The Trojans also ranked #6 in scoring offense, averaging 38.2 points per game.

January 4, 2005 #2 Oklahoma

BCS Championship game in the Orange Bowl

Oklahoma started the scoring with a 5-yard touchdown pass from Jason White to Travis Wilson to take an early 7–0 lead. Before the first quarter ended, Southern California had scored twice: a Matt Leinart to Dominique Byrd 33-yard pass completion and a Lendale White six-yard run to take a 14–7 lead.

Leinart threw for two more touchdowns in the first six minutes of the second period. The first was a 54-yarder to Dwayne Jarrett, and the second a five-yard toss to Steve Smith, putting the Trojans up, 28–7. Garrett Hartley made a 29-yard field goal for the Sooners, but in the last two minutes of the first half, Southern California managed another Leinart to Smith touchdown and a 44-yard field goal by Ryan Killeen with three seconds remaining. That put the Trojans up, 38–10, at the half.

The third quarter started as the second period had ended: a Leinart to Smith touchdown pass followed by a Killeen field goal. Southern California entered the fourth quarter leading 48–10. With less than 10 minutes remaining, White scored his second rushing touchdown from eight yards out. The Trojans were now ahead, 55–10. Oklahoma got the final two scores of the game: a two-point safety and a nine-yard run by Wilson. The final score: Southern California 55, Oklahoma 19.

The Trojans gained more offensive yards, 525–372, but the Sooners ran more plays and had more time of possession. They were hurt by five turnovers to none for the Trojans. Matt Leinart completed 18 of 35 passes for five touchdowns and had no interceptions.

University of Southern California head coach Pete Carroll should be all smiles as his team dominated opponents, 496–169. Carroll did not win either major Coach of the Year award in 2004. He had won the award in 2003 from the AFCA (courtesy USC Athletics).

Lendale White led all rushers with 118 yards on 15 carries, and Dwayne Jarrett was the top receiver with five catches for 115 yards and a touchdown. Steve Smith was right behind Jarrett, gaining 113 yards on seven receptions, three going for touchdowns.

Post Season

Southern California quarterback Matt Leinart and all-purpose back Reggie Bush were consensus All Americas on offense. Defensive lineman Shaun Cody and linebacker Matt Grootegoed were consensus All Americas on the defense, while defensive lineman Mike Patterson made some All America teams. Leinart won the Heisman Trophy and the Walter Camp Award. He was also seventh nationally in passing (3,322 yards). Reggie Bush, who finished fifth in the Heisman voting, was fifth nationally in all-purpose yards (179.2 yards per game), eighth in yards per carry (6.4), and ninth in punt returns (15.7 yards per return). As a team, Southern California ranked sixth in scoring offense (38.2 points per game) and ranked in the top ten in every defensive category.

The previous two years, the BCS had failed to achieve a unanimous national champion. So why was the 2004 Southern California team different?

In addition to the Trojans, there were two remaining undefeated teams after the bowl games. Auburn, #2 at 13–0, probably had the best argument for being ignored. The Tigers' team comparison to Oklahoma is described above. Very probably the post-season ruined any chance for the Tigers. Ranked #3, they played #9 Virginia Tech in the Sugar Bowl.

Had they been able to play and handily defeat #4 California (or more thoroughly dominate #9 Virginia Tech), the possibility of being voted national champion by some selector(s) would have increased. As it was, Auburn defeated the #9 Hokies by only 16–13. The Trojans beat Virginia Tech, 24–13, at the start of the season.

The other undefeated team, the Utah Utes, did not play a ranked team until they defeated #19, 8-4 Pitt, 35-7 in the Fiesta Bowl. The Utes and Trojans had defeated three common opponents:

	Utah	Southern California
Arizona	23–6	49–9
Colorado State	63–31	49–0
Brigham Young	52–21	42–10
Points scored/allowed	138–58	140–19

Most probably it was Utah's lack of quality ranked opponents that hurt them. Southern California so dominated their opposition through most of the season, and especially the #2 Sooners, it was a fitting tribute that they were unanimous national champion in 2004.

Now the Bad News

Sports agents had been giving gifts to sophomore sensation Reggie Bush beginning in December 2004. These gifts, reportedly substantial, would nullify an athlete's amateur status. The NCAA came down hard on Southern California for its lack of oversight. One result was the school having to vacate the wins over UCLA and Oklahoma. This action moved the BCS to vacate the Trojans' national championship. Bush was also required to relinquish the Heisman Trophy he would receive in 2005.

The AP poll did not vacate the Trojan's championship, and for the purpose of this book their achievement stands.

Chapter 17

Texas 2005

Texas achieved a unanimous championship in 1963. Over the next two decades, the Longhorns continued to do well with a consensus title in 1969 and shared titles in 1968, 1970, 1977, and 1981. In 1983, Texas ended the regular season 11-0 and ranked #2 behind #1 Nebraska. In the Orange Bowl, the Cornhuskers lost, 31-30 to #5 Miami (10-1). Texas could have slid into #1 and a national championship except they lost, 10-9, in the Cotton Bowl to #7 Georgia. Since the 1983 season, the Longhorns were a modest 92-68-3 through the 1997 season. In 1998, Mack Brown took over as head coach. Brown led the Longhorns from 1998-2013. His record, especially during the middle years, was terrific:

Years	Won-Lost
1998-2000	27-11
2001-2009	101-16
2010-2013	30-21

In 2004, Texas ended the season ranked #5. Their record was 11-1, with the only defeat a 12-0 shutout to #2 Oklahoma in the fifth game. Winning the remaining six games, they then beat #13 Michigan in the Rose Bowl, 38-37. With a wealth of talent, expectations were high to start the 2005 season.

Louisiana-Lafayette

Maybe as an omen of greatness, the Longhorns wore throwback uniforms similar to those of the 1963 unanimous championship team when they hosted the Louisiana-LaFayette Cajuns.

Junior running back Selvin Young scored on a nine-yard touchdown run halfway through the first quarter, but the extra point was missed and the Longhorns were up, 6-0. The Cajuns rallied with a 40-yard drive that produced a 47-yard field goal by Sean Comiskey to cut the lead in half. After that, Texas dominated with another seven points in the first quarter, 26 points in the second, 14 in the third, and seven more points in the fourth period to win, 60-3.

Quarterback Vince Young passed for three touchdowns and ran for another score. Nate Jones caught one Vince Young touchdown and David Thomas two scoring passes. Selvin Young, Jaamal Charles, and Ramonce Taylor each rushed for a touchdown, while Kyle Phillips ran for two scores. The Longhorns' offense produced 591 yards to 238 yards for the Cajuns. Texas had 30 first downs to the visitors' 11.

Throughout the regular season, Southern California would rank #1 with Texas at #2. Six teams were ranked #3 that season: Tennessee (one week), Michigan (one week), LSU (four weeks), Virginia Tech (six weeks), Miami (Florida, two weeks), and Penn State (two weeks). The following game figured to be a struggle as Texas visited #4 Ohio State.

#4 Ohio State

In 2004, the Buckeyes were 8–4, finished fifth in the Big 10 Conference, defeated unranked Oklahoma State, 33–7 in the Alamo Bowl, and ended the season at #20. This year, Ohio State was ranked #6 pre-season, defeated Miami (Ohio), 34–14, and would ascend to #4 before facing the Longhorns.

Texas opened the scoring with a David Pino 42-yard field goal and a Vince Young to Billy Pittman five-yard touchdown pass to take a 10–0 lead. Ohio State mirrored the scoring in the second quarter with a 45-yard field goal by Josh Huston followed by a Troy Smith to Santonio Holmes 36-yard touchdown to tie the score at 10–10. Huston added two more field goals of 36 and 25 yards, the last with just over half a minute remaining in the half. With only two seconds remaining, Pino made a 37-yard field goal to end the first half at Ohio State 16, Texas 13.

The third period was a battle of more field goals. Huston hit a 44-yarder, Pino a 25-yarder, and Huston another from 26 yards for a 22–16 Buckeyes advantage at the end of three quarters. Young found Limas Sweed with a 24-yard touchdown pass, and the Longhorns retook the lead, 23–22, with 2:37 to play. Texas finished the scoring as defensive tackle Larry Dibbles sacked quarterback Troy Smith for a two-point safety with 0:19 remaining.[1] The Longhorns came away with a hard-fought, 25–22 win.

Vince Young accounted for 346 of the Longhorns' 382 offensive yards. He passed for 270 yards on 18 completions in 29 attempts, with two touchdowns and two interceptions. He also led all rushers with 76 yards in 20 carries. Texas junior defensive back Michael Griffin accounted for 10 tackles. Ohio State managed 255 yards of offense. Texas won despite three turnovers: two intercepted passes and one fumble lost (of four committed).

Rice

The previous week Ohio State had essentially shut down the Longhorns' running attack, allowing 112 yards in 38 rushes. The Rice Owls were unable to contain the run, allowing 361 yards on 47 carries, a 7.7 yards per carry average. Texas amassed 483 yards of offense and 24 first downs to 209 yards and 12 first downs for the Owls in a 51–10 win.

Jamaal Charles scored three rushing touchdowns, Henry Melton and Ramonce Taylor each rushed for a touchdown, and Frank Okam recovered a Rice fumble in the end zone for a touchdown. David Pino's 40-yard field goal completed the Texas scoring. Rice managed a field goal in the third quarter and a touchdown in the fourth period against Longhorns reserves.

Missouri

The Missouri Tigers kept the game close through the first quarter. Jamaal Charles scored for Texas on a three-yard run. Jimmy Jackson of Missouri answered with a 12-yard touchdown. Vince Young scampered 33 yards for another Longhorns touchdown, but the Tigers' Brad Smith came back with a three-yard score. After this last touchdown, the extra point was missed, and Texas was up, 14–13 at the end of one quarter. The Longhorns added 10 points in the second period. Jamaal Charles caught a 32-yard pass from Vince Young for his second touchdown, and David Pino made a 26-yard field goal as Texas increased their lead 24–13 at the half.

With a little over a minute gone in the third quarter, Young threw to Ramonce Taylor for a 27-yard touchdown. Henry Melton scored on a one-yard run, but the kick failed. After three quarters, Texas led, 37–13. Melton got his second one-yard touchdown with 10:18 remaining. Two minutes later, the Longhorns' Aaron Ross returned a Missouri punt 88 yards for a touchdown and a 51–13 lead. Missouri ended the scoring as Brad Smith scored on a 1-yard run to make the final score Texas 51, Missouri 20.

Young was 15 of 22 passing for 236 yards, two touchdowns and one interception, and again led all rushers with 108 yards on 13 carries. As a team, Texas made 585 yards of offense to 330 for the Tigers. For the second time this year, Texas fumbled the ball four times, losing one.

Oklahoma

The Texas-Oklahoma rivalry (or the Red River Rivalry) goes back to 1900. The Longhorns hold a slight edge in wins, but in 2005 they hadn't won since 1999. In each of those last 5 years, both teams had been highly ranked: Oklahoma #10, #3, #2, #1, #2 and Texas #11, #5, #3, #11, #5. Despite the rankings, the Sooners had outscored Texas, 189–54. The year 2005 had started for Oklahoma with a devastating 55–19 loss to Southern California in the January Orange Bowl. They were ranked #7 in pre-season, lost two of their first four games, and fell from the polls. The Sooners' fortunes would not improve against Texas.

A Vince Young to Ramonce Taylor 15-yard touchdown pass started the scoring. Oklahoma came back with two Garrett Hartley field goals of 52 and 26 yards to cut the lead to 7–6. Jamaal Charles ran 80 yards for touchdown to end the first quarter at 14–6. The second period saw a David Pino 37-yard field goal and a Vince Young to Billy Pittman 64-yard touchdown pass with 17 seconds remaining. The first half ended with the Longhorns up, 24–6.

A second Young to Pittman touchdown throw, this a 27-yarder, was the only third quarter score. Texas running back Selvin Young scored on a five-yard run. The Sooner's Rhett Bomar connected with Joe Jon Finley for a 15-yard touchdown, but a two-point conversion attempt failed. Senior defensive tackle Rodrique Wright returned an Oklahoma fumble 67 yards for a touchdown. The final score read Texas 45, Oklahoma 12.

Vince Young accounted for 286 yards: 241 yards passing with three touchdowns and another 45 yards rushing. The Texas defense allowed the Sooners only 171 yards of offense, 77 rushing and 94 passing.

#24 Colorado

The Colorado Buffaloes came into Darrell Royal Stadium at 4-1 and ranked #24. They had outscored four unranked opponents by 145-48, but lost 23-3 to #12 Miami (FL).

The Longhorns took a 28-0 lead after one and a half quarters. Vince Young had three touchdowns on runs of one, 16, and 9 yards. Selvin Young scored from five yards out for the other touchdown. Late in the second quarter, Mason Crosby made a 48-yard field goal to put the Buffaloes on the board. But a minute and a half later, Vince Young threw to Limas Sweed for a 35-yard touchdown, extending the Texas lead to 35-3. With one second remaining in the first half, Colorado senior quarterback Joel Klatt threw a nine-yard completion for a touchdown to senior wide receiver Evan Judge, making the halftime score Texas 35, Colorado 10.

The third period was scoreless. The Longhorns and Buffaloes exchanged touchdowns in the fourth quarter: Young again hit Sweed and Klatt connected with senior tight end Jo Klopfenstein for a final score of 42-17. Young completed 25 of 29 passes for 336 yards and two touchdowns. He also led all rushers with 58 yards and three touchdowns. As a team, Texas amassed 482 yards of offense (394 from Young) while allowing Colorado 237 yards: 45 rushing and 192 passing.

The first BCS Ranking was released and agreed with the AP top five: Southern California, Texas, Virginia Tech, Georgia, and Alabama.

#10 Texas Tech

At 6-0 and outscoring all opponents, 322-99, the Red Raiders of Texas Tech travelled to #2 Texas for a battle of top 10 teams.

After an early Longhorns lead on a David Pino 40-yard field goal, Tech quarterback Cody Hodges passed to Taurean Henderson for a three-yard score and a 7-3 advantage. Texas running back Henry Melton scored on a one-yard run, and the Longhorns re-took the lead, 10-7 at the end of one period. An Alex Trica 32-yard field goal tied the score at 10-10. After that, Texas ran off three touchdowns to end the half at 31-10. Selvin Young ran for touchdowns of 10 and seven yards, and Vince Young connected with Billy Pittman on a 16-yard score.

A little over a minute into the second half, Young and Pittman again combined, this time on a 75-yard touchdown pass. The Red Raiders responded with a Hodges to Joel Filani six-yard touchdown. Late in the third period, Vince Young ran for a 10-yard score and a Texas lead of 45-17. Chris Ogbonnaya ran for a 22-yard touchdown and a final score of Texas 52, Texas Tech 17. The Red Riders outgained the Longhorns by 468 yards to 444.

The BCS and AP rankings remained the same: Southern California, Texas, Virginia Tech, Georgia, and Alabama.

Oklahoma State

Boone Pickens Stadium, home of the Oklahoma State Cowboys, was the setting for the Longhorns' next Big 12 contest. The Cowboys were suffering through an off-year.

After a 3–0 start, they had lost their last four games by a combined 171–64 to unranked opponents. It was, therefore, a shock to Longhorns fans when the Cowboys led, 21–9 after the first quarter. Oklahoma State scored first on an Al Pena to D'Juan Woods 49-yard pass completion. Vince Young responded with a 20-yard touchdown to David Thomas, but the PAT failed. State's Julius Crosslin ran in a touchdown from the 4-yard line, and 23 seconds later Pena ran 17 yards for another score following a Longhorns' fumbled kickoff return. Texas kicker David Pino made a 45-yard field goal, and the first quarter ended with a 21–9 Oklahoma State lead. Pena again connected with Woods, who caught the ball as it deflected off teammate Luke Frazier for a 29-yard touchdown.[2] The Cowboys now led, 28–9. Pino hit a 21-yard field goal as time ran out and the half ended at 28–12.

Young took over in the third period. Fifty-seconds into the second half, Young ran 80 yards for a touchdown, with 2:23 left he ran for an 8-yard score, and with 48 seconds remaining, Young hit Neale Tweedie for a 21-yard touchdown and Ahmard Hall for a two-point conversion pass. Entering the final period, Texas finally had the lead, 34–28. The Longhorns' Ramonce Taylor scored twice in the fourth quarter on runs of 57 and 12 yards. A two-point conversion try failed, but one PAT was good. Texas, with a hard-fought, come-from-behind effort, finally prevailed, 47–28.

Vince Young had another outstanding day. He was 15 of 30 passing for 239 yards and two touchdowns. He again led all rushers with 267 yards on 21 carries and another two touchdowns. Texas compiled 606 yards of offense (506 by Young) while allowing 402 yards.

Georgia, #4 the week before, lost 14–10 to #16 Florida and dropped out of the top five. Both the BCS and AP had the same top four: Southern California, Texas, Virginia Tech, and Alabama. In the AP, Miami moved into #5, and in the BCS, UCLA was #5.

Baylor

The Baylor Bears were 4–4. The week before, they were shut out, 28–0 at #16 Texas Tech. They fared no better against the #2 Longhorns. Texas had 645 yards and 35 first downs in shutting out the Bears, 62–0. Ramonce Taylor rushed for three touchdowns and scored another on a pass from Vince Young. Jamaal Charles had two rushing touchdowns, Henry Melton and Matt Nordgren each had one rushing score. Young also had a touchdown pass to Quan Cosby.

There was another shakeup of teams in the two polls. #3 Virginia Tech lost to Miami (AP #5), 27–7 and UCLA (BCS #5) lost to unranked Arizona, 52–14. Southern California and Texas remained atop both rankings. The AP included #3 Miami, #4 Alabama, and #5 LSU. The BCS had Alabama at #3, Miami #4, and Penn State #5.

Kansas

Kansas was another Big 12 team having a so-so year. The Jayhawks were 5–4 when they played Texas in Austin. As they did the previous week against Baylor, the Longhorns overwhelmed the Jayhawks.

Texas took a 28–0 lead in the first quarter. Vince Young scored on pass completions to Limas Sweed and Quan Cosby, Jamaal Charles ran for a 10-yard touchdown, and Aaron Ross returned a Baylor punt 71 yards for a score. The Longhorns scoring continued in the second period with a Ramonce Taylor eight-yard run, a 20-yard Young to David Thomas pass completion, a Young to Peter Ullman three-yard pass, and a David Pino 31-yard field goal for a 52–0 halftime score.

Kansas did outscore Texas, 14–7, in the third quarter. The Jayhawks' Jon Cornish ran 59 yards for a touchdown and Brandon McAnderson 16 yards for another score. Ramonce Taylor scored his second rushing touchdown of the game on a 13-yard carry. Kansas narrowed the Texas lead to 59–14 after three quarters. Selvin Young scored on a 21-yard run in the fourth quarter, and the game ended Texas 66, Kansas 14. For the third week in a row, Texas gained over 600 yards offensively, accumulating 617 yards to 267 for the Jayhawks.

Both rankings agreed: Southern California #1, Texas #2, and Miami #3. The AP ranked LSU #4 and Penn State #5. The BCS reversed #s 4 and 5.

Texas A&M

The rivalry between the Longhorns and the Aggies dates back to 1894. In 2005, Texas had won the previous five years by a combined 186 points to 72. In each of those years, the Longhorns were ranked in the top 15, and from 2001–2004 in the top 10.[3] The rivalry would end after 2011, when A&M left the Big 12 to go to the Southeastern Conference.

Halfway through the first quarter, Henry Melton rushed for an eight-yard score. Ramonce Taylor added a four-yard touchdown run for a 14–0 longhorns lead. However, in the last 20 seconds of the quarter, A&M got a 32-yard Todd Pegram field goal followed by a Jorvorskie Lane to Jason Carter 35-yard touchdown pass after a Texas fumble. A two-point conversion was unsuccessful, and the Texas lead was now 14–9. The Aggies took the lead at 9:26 of the second period on a Brandon Leone 16-yard run. Again a two-point conversion was missed, but A&M led, 15–14. With a Vince Young to Ahmard Hall 13-yard touchdown, Texas re-gained the lead, 21–15, to end the first half.

Early in the third quarter, freshman quarterback Stephen McGee rushed 11 yards for an A&M touchdown. The PAT by Samson Taylor was good, and the Aggies led, 22–21. Ramonce Taylor ran for an eight-yard touchdown as Texas retook the lead, 28–22. An Aggies punt was blocked and returned 11 yards for a touchdown by senior cornerback Cedric Griffin. Behind by 34–22, McGee scored on a one-yard run to close the gap to 34–29 at the end of three quarters. That was as close as the Aggies would come to an upset. David Pino made field goals of 41 and 29 yards in the fourth period, and the final score read Texas 40, Texas A&M 29.

The Aggies outgained the Longhorns, 395 yards to 336. Both teams committed four turnovers. Vince Young was held to 162 yards total although he did throw for a touchdown. Texas was 11–0 and 8–0 to lead the Big 12 Southern Division. They would now face Big 12 Northern Division Champion Colorado for the overall title.

The AP and BCS agreed on the top five teams. Southern California and Texas were ranked 1 and 2 and needed only to win their remaining regular season game to play for the national title. Penn State's regular season had ended. LSU was to play Georgia for the

SEC title, and Virginia Tech would play Florida State for the ACC Championship. Penn State, LSU and the Hokies all were 10-1.

Colorado Big 12 Championship

The Buffaloes had gone 3-2 since losing to the Longhorns in their sixth game. In the previous two weeks, Colorado lost to Iowa State (30-16) and Nebraska (30-3). The season got no better for the Buffaloes.

Vince Young scored four touchdowns. He rushed for a two-yard touchdown and passed for three scores: one each to Limas Sweed, David Thomas, and Jamaal Charles. Charles and Henry Melton each had two rushing scores, Selvin Young had one rushing touchdown, and cornerback Brandon Foster recovered a blocked punt for a score. Colorado avoided a shutout with a Mason Crosby 25-yard field goal to start the second quarter. Texas won the Big 12 Championship, 70-3. The Longhorns gained 486 yards of offense compared to 482 yards in their first meeting with the Buffaloes. The defense allowed 191 total yards, less than the 237 yards allowed in the first game.

By the final regular season AP Poll, only #1 Southern California (12-0) and #2 Texas (12-0) were undefeated. They had held their rankings all season and would now play for the national championship in the Rose Bowl on January 4, 2006. LSU and Virginia Tech had both lost their conference championship games.

All America Selections and Awards

Texas offensive lineman Jonathan Scott and defensive back Michael Huff, both non-consensus All America in 2004, were unanimous selections this year. Vince Young and defensive lineman Rodrique Wright were consensus All Americas. Other Longhorns players named to various All America teams were linebacker Aaron Harris and offensive linemen Will Allen and Justin Blalock. Young was runner-up in the Heisman Trophy voting to Southern California's Reggie Bush. Young did take home the Maxwell, O'Brien, and Manning Awards. Aaron Ross won the Jim Thorpe Award.

#1 Southern California BCS National Championship

The Rose Bowl

Southern California was the unanimous national champion in 2004, was ranked #1 through the entire season, and was the only other undefeated team at 12-0. The Trojans were on a 34-game winning streak that began after California defeated the #3 Trojans, 34-31 on September 27, 2003. This season, they outscored opponents by a combined 600-256, including ranked teams: #24 Oregon, #14 Arizona State, #9 Notre Dame, #16 Fresno State, and #11 UCLA.

Texas had every reason to be wary of the Southern California offense. Junior quarterback Matt Leinart, who won the Heisman Trophy in 2004, had passed for 3,450 yards and 27 touchdowns with only seven interceptions during the regular season. Junior running back Reggie Bush, who took home the Heisman Trophy in 2005 (later vacated, see Chapter 16), rushed for 1,658 yards, with an 8.9 yards per carry average, scored 15 rushing touchdowns, and had 31 receptions for 383 yards and another two touchdowns during the regular season.

Texas was riding its own winning streak of 19 games, dating from October 9, 2004, when #2 Oklahoma defeated the #5 Longhorns, 12–0. Texas had scored a total of 611 points in their 12 games of 2005 while allowing only 175 points. The Longhorns had defeated three ranked teams: #4 Ohio State, #24 Colorado, and #10 Texas Tech.

Southern California knew it had to contain Vince Young. The quarterback averaged 302 yards per game, passing for 2,769 yards and 26 touchdowns while leading all Texas rushers with 850 yards and another nine touchdowns.

	Southern California	*Texas*
Record	12–0	12–0
Points scored	600	611
Points allowed	256	175
Ranked teams played	#s 9, 11, 14, 16, 24	#s 4, 10, 24

This was another championship game that lived up to the hype.

Southern California took an early lead when Lendale White rushed for a four-yard touchdown less than three minutes into the game, following a Texas fumble on a punt return. The remainder of the first quarter was scoreless. David Pino hit a 46-yard field goal at 10:38 in the second period. Six minutes later, Selvin Young scored on a 12-yard run. The PAT was missed, but Texas had the lead, 9–7. With less than three minutes left in the first half, Selvin Young again scored, this time running for a 12-yard Texas touchdown and a 16–7 lead. Southern California drove to the Texas 13-yard line, but after two sacks, the Trojans had to settle for a Mario Danelo 43-yard field goal with two seconds remaining, and the first half ended Texas 16, Southern California 10.

The Trojans retook the lead, 17–16, on White's second scoring run, this one from three yards out. The touchdown capped a seven-play, 62-yard drive. Two minutes later, Vince Young regained the lead for Texas, 23–17, on a 14-yard touchdown run. The lead changed hands again when White scored his third touchdown for the Trojans, a 12-yard run on fourth down. The third quarter ended Southern California 24, Texas 23. Early in the fourth quarter, Pino missed a field goal attempt from the Trojans' 14-yard line. Four minutes later, Reggie Bush broke free for a 26-yard touchdown to end a nine-play, 80-yard drive. That put the Trojans up, 31–23. Pino later added his second field goal, a 34-yarder, to narrow the Trojans' advantage to five points. But Southern California increased the lead to 12 when Matt Leinart hit Dwayne Jarrett for a 22-yard touchdown. As had happened so often during the season, Vince Young then took over the game.

With 4:03 remaining, Young ran 17 yards for a touchdown. The Longhorns' defense held the Trojans on a fourth down and two, giving the ball to its offense at the Texas 44-yard line. Young moved his team to the Southern California 8-yard line in one minute and 50 seconds. On fourth down and needing five yards, Young scored from eight yards out with 19 seconds remaining to give the Longhorns a 41–38 win and the national championship.

Young completed 30 of 40 passes for 267 yards and ran the ball 19 times for 200 yards (a 10.5 average) and three touchdowns. Matt Leinart was 29 of 40 for 365 passing yards and one touchdown. Southern California's Lendale White rushed 20 times for 124 yards and three touchdowns. Heisman Trophy winner Reggie Bush rushed for 82 yards with one touchdown, caught six passes for another 95 yards, and returned five punts for 101 yards.

The Trojans' offense compiled 574 yards, a Rose Bowl record at the time.[4] The Longhorns had 556 yards of offense, with Young accounting for 467 of it. Each team had 30 first downs.

Among the other top 10 ranked teams, the bowl results were:

#3 Penn State 26	#22 Florida State 23
#4 Ohio State 34	#5 Notre Dame 20
#6 Oregon 14	NR Oklahoma 17
#7 Auburn 10	#21 Wisconsin 24
#8 Georgia 35	#11 West Virginia 38
#10 LSU 40	#9 Miami (FL) 3

Based on the season, the Rose Bowl, and the results of other bowl games, it is difficult to find another team with any legitimate claim to the national championship of 2005.

Chapter 18

Alabama 2009

From a humble start, Alabama has had a long and exalted history in college football. The first season in 1892, the Tide went 2–2 against three high schools and Auburn. The following year Alabama was 0–4, including two high schools. In 1925, they celebrated their first consensus national championship. Other consensus championship seasons would follow: 1926, 1961, 1979, 1992, 2011, 2012, 2017. The Crimson Tide always appeared to be in contention. In 13 additional seasons, they have been chosen by at least one selector as national champion, but not by consensus. Those years were: 1930, 1934, 1941, 1945, 1962, 1964, 1965, 1966, 1973, 1975, 1977, 1978, and 2016. In 2009, Alabama finally became a unanimous choice.

Ranked #1 through most of 2008, the Crimson Tide ended the year at #6 after back-to-back losses against #2 Florida, 31–20 in the SEC Championship Game and 31–17 in the Sugar Bowl to #7 Utah. Still, Alabama fans had reason to be optimistic. With a strong returning class of lettermen, Alabama entered the AP pre-season poll at #5.

#7 Virginia Tech

Chick-fil-A Kickoff Game at Georgia Dome in Atlanta

Alabama kicker Leigh Tiffin made field goals of 49 and 34 yards in the first eight and a half minutes to give the Crimson Tide a 6–0 lead. Virginia Tech's Dyrell Roberts returned the second kickoff 98 yards to take the lead, 7–6. Alabama recovered a Hokies fumble, and Tiffin added a 32-yard field goal, ending the first quarter with Alabama up, 9–7. Crimson Tide quarterback Greg McElroy was intercepted, and the Hokies regained the lead, 10–9, after a 28-yard field goal by Matt Waldron. Alabama's Roy Upchurch scored on a 19-yard run, and the score again favored the Tide 16–10. The Hokies' Ryan Williams scored on a one-yard run and Virginia Tech led at the half, 17–16.

Neither team could score in the third period. Alabama scored 10 points early in the fourth quarter on a Mark Ingram six-yard touchdown and a Tiffin 20-yard field goal. Virginia Tech got its last score two minutes later on a Williams 32-yard run to close the gap, 27–24. McElroy and Ingram connected on an 18-yard touchdown pass, and Alabama won its opener, 34–24.

The Alabama defense held the Hokies to 64 yards rushing and 91 passing. Meanwhile, the Tide's offense gained 498 yards, 268 rushing and 230 passing. Ingram carried

26 times for 150 rushing yards, and Upchurch added 90 yards. McElroy was 15 for 30 passing for all 230 passing yards. The win, along with a loss by #3 Oklahoma, moved the Tide up to #4.

Florida International

The Florida International Golden Panthers were members of the Sun Belt Conference (FI would join Conference-USA in 2013). Their first game of 2009 was against #4 Alabama; they would later lose to #1 Florida, 62–3.

Leigh Tiffin kicked a 23-yard field goal six minutes into the game. Greg McElroy passed 24 yards to Mike McCoy, and Alabama led, 10–0. On the ensuing kickoff, T. Y. Hilton returned the ball 96 yards for a Florida International touchdown, and the first quarter ended 10–7. Five seconds into the second period, Tiffin made a 29-yard field goal, increasing Alabama's lead. Then Paul McCall passed to Greg Ellingson for a second Golden Panthers touchdown and a short-lived 14–13 advantage. Two minutes later, Mark Ingram scored on a two-yard run, ending the first half at 20–14.

Alabama put up 20 unanswered points in the second half. Freshman Trent Richardson scored on a nine-yard run late in the third quarter and again on a 35-yard run to open the fourth period. Terry Grant finished the scoring with a 42-yard rushing touchdown as the Tide won, 40–14. The Tide's defense held Florida International to one rushing yard and 214 total yards. Alabama had 516 yards of offense, 275 rushing and 241 passing. McElroy was 18 of 24 passing for 241 yards and one touchdown. Richardson rushed 15 times for 119 yards. Alabama remained at #4 in the weekly poll.

North Texas

The University of North Texas Mean Green, like Florida International, was a member of the Sun Belt Conference in 2009. Like FI, they would join Conference-USA in 2013 and like FI, they were at the bottom of the Sun Belt Conference standings in 2009.

In this game, Alabama would lead in most categories:

	North Texas	Alabama
Rushing yards	61	260
Passing yards	126	263
Total yards	187	523
First downs	7	28

Alabama scored 14 points in the first quarter on a Greg McElroy two-yard run and a McElroy to Marquis Maze 34-yard pass. They added 17 points in the second period on a Trent Richardson one-yard run, a McElroy to Mark Ingram pass, and a Leigh Tiffin 35-yard field goal. The PAT after the McElroy to Ingram touchdown failed. The Tide led, 30–0, at the half.

The third quarter saw two Alabama rushing touchdowns. Ingram scored on a five-yard run and Terry Grant on a one-yarder. Ten more points were scored in the fourth period as Tiffin kicked a 20-yard field goal and Grant ran for a nine-yard touchdown. The Mean Green got their lone points on a 34-yard pass from Nathan Tune to Lance Dunbar. Alabama won, 53–7.

McElroy completed 13 of 15 passes for 176 yards, two touchdowns, and no interceptions. Backup Star Jackson was 9 of 13 for 87 yards. Ingram rushed eight times for 91 yards, caught three passes for 38 yards, and had one touchdown each rushing and receiving. The win was enough to move the Tide up to #3, helped by a #3 Southern California loss to unranked Washington, 16–13.

Arkansas

The Arkansas Razorbacks lost five of six games they played against top 20 teams in 2009. Four of the five losses were by a total of 30 points. In the other, Alabama defeated the Razorbacks by 28 points. After a scoreless first quarter, Trent Richardson rushed for a 52-yard touchdown and Greg McElroy passed 50 yards to Julio Jones as Alabama took a 14–0 lead into halftime.

Arkansas got on the board with a Ryan Mallett to Greg Childs 18-yard touchdown early in the third period. The remainder of the day's scoring was by Alabama. McElroy threw to Marquis Maze for an 80-yard touchdown and 14 yards to Mark Ingram for another score, and Ingram ran in a two-yarder. The game ended Alabama 35, Arkansas 7. Richardson led all rushers with 68 yards on nine carries and caught two passes for 16 yards. Ingram chipped in 51 rushing yards, and they both scored a rushing touchdown. McElroy completed 17 of 24 passes for 291 yards and three touchdowns as the Tide outgained the Razorbacks by 425 yards to 254.

Now 4–0, Alabama remained at #3 in the AP poll.

Kentucky

The week before their game with #3 Alabama, the Kentucky Wildcats were defeated by #1 Florida, 41–7. This week, Kentucky kept the game close through one quarter. Less than a minute into the game, Mark Ingram scored on an 11-yard run. Wildcats kicker Lones Seiber made a pair of 49-yard field goals to end the first quarter 7–6. The Tide scored twice in the second period on a Greg McElroy to Colin Peek three-yard pass and a 45-yard fumble return by Courtney Upshaw to end the first half at 21–6.

Alabama added 10 points on an Ingram 32-yard run and a Leigh Tiffin 36-yard field goal. Kentucky scored on a Mike Hartline to Randall Cobb 45-yard pass. The Crimson Tide closed out the third quarter scoring with a McElroy to Darius Hanks seven-yard touchdown for a 38–13 advantage. The Wildcats made the game closer with an Alfonso Smith two-yard touchdown run in the fourth period. Ingram rushed for 140 yards and McElroy passed for 148 yards to account for 288 of the Tide's 352 total yards of offense. Alabama won its fifth game, 38–20.

Alabama retained its #3 ranking another week.

#20 Mississippi

Mississippi was ranked #8 in the AP pre-season poll. They ascended to #4 before a loss to unranked South Carolina. Alabama took a 16–0 lead into halftime on three Leigh Tiffin field goals (25, 21, and 22 yards) and a Mark Ingram 36-yard touchdown run.

Rebels kicker Joshua Shene kicked a 25-yard field goal midway through the third quarter to avoid a shutout. Tiffin added two more field goals (21 and 31 yards) to finish the scoring in a 22–3 Alabama win. The Crimson Tide outgained Mississippi, 354 yards to 197.

The Texas Longhorns had a bye week, and Alabama replaced them at #2 in the AP Poll. Florida remained at #1, beating #4 LSU, 13–3, and dropping the Tigers to #10. Virginia Tech took over the #4 spot. The following week, the first BCS standings would be announced.

#22 South Carolina

South Carolina lost a close (41–37) contest to #21 Georgia in their second game. The Gamecocks then won four straight games, including a 16–10 win hosting #4 Mississippi. After the Alabama game, South Carolina would close out the remainder of their season at 2–4. But on this day, the Tide would need to survive four turnovers, five more penalties and two fewer first downs than the Gamecocks to keep the season on track.

Alabama scored first on a Mark Barron 77-yard interception return and later on a Leigh Tiffin 25-yard field goal to lead, 10–0, after one quarter. The second quarter was an exchange of field goals in the last three minutes. South Carolina kicker Spencer Lanning made a 25-yarder with 3:14 to go. At 00:56, Tiffin connected on a 35-yarder, and Lanning booted a 31-yarder as time expired. At the half, Alabama led, 13–6.

The third period was scoreless. Mark Ingram ran for a four-yard touchdown late in the fourth quarter as the Tide won, 20–6. Greg McElroy had his worst game of the season, completing only 10 of 20 passes for 92 yards, no touchdowns, and two interceptions. Ingram ran the ball 24 times for 246 of the Tide's 264 rushing yards.

The win put Alabama at #1 in the AP poll, at least temporarily. The first BCS Standings were released, placing Florida at #1 and Alabama #2. Texas, Boise State, and Cincinnati rounded out the top five.

Tennessee

The Tennessee Volunteers were not supposed to be a problem for #1 Alabama. That prediction was very wrong. All the Alabama scoring came from the foot of Leigh Tiffin. Four field goals were all the scoring the offense could manage. Tiffin successfully kicked field goals of 38, 50, 22, and 49 yards. Had any not been made (and other events not happened), Alabama's season would have been much different.

Tiffin kicked his first, a 38-yarder, late in the first quarter after a Mark Barron interception. Tennessee's Daniel Lincoln tied the game on a 24-yard field goal early in the second period. Tiffin connected on two more, a 50-yarder halfway through the quarter and another at 1:11 before the half. The Volunteers missed a field goal and the half ended, 9–3.

Neither team could score in the third period. Terrence Cody blocked a Tennessee field goal attempt.[1] Tiffin kicked his fourth from 49 yards away with six and a half minutes left in the game, giving the Tide a 12–3 lead. Mark Ingram suffered his first career fumble, near midfield with 1:19 left on the clock.[2] The Volunteers' Jonathan Crompton passed 11 yards to Gerald Jones for a touchdown that put Tennessee only a field goal away from a huge upset. The Volunteers' on-side kick attempt worked, and they had the ball near midfield. With little time remaining, Lincoln tried a 45-yard field goal to win the game, but once again, it was blocked by Cody. The Tide had survived (barely), 12–10.

The team statistics for the game show how fortunate the Tide was to survive. McElroy was 18 of 29 passes for 120 yards, and Mark Ingram managed only 99 yards on 18 carries.

	Tennessee	*Alabama*
Rushing yards	74	136
Passing yards	265	120
Total yards	339	256
First downs	20	16

The narrow victory, combined with Florida's 29–19 win at Mississippi State gave the #1 ranking back to the Gators and dropped Alabama to #3 in the AP. The Tide remained at #2 in the BCS Standings.

#9 LSU

Starting the pre-season at #11 in the AP poll, the LSU Tigers worked their way up to #4 behind 5 straight wins that included a 20–13 victory at #14 Georgia. The following week, the Tigers lost at home to #1 Florida, 13–3. Dropping to #10 in the polls, they won two straight, ascended to #9, and would now face the #3 Crimson Tide in Alabama. After a scoreless first quarter, LSU got on the scoreboard with a Jordan Jefferson to DeAngelo Peterson 12-yard touchdown pass. Leigh Tiffin kicked a 28-yard field goal to end the first half at 7–3.

Early in the third quarter, Greg McElroy hit Darius Hanks for a 21-yard touchdown, and Alabama led, 10–7. The Tigers added eight points before the end of the third period, a safety and an eight-yard run by Stevan Ridley. A two-point conversion try failed, but LSU led after three quarters, 15–10.

The fourth period belonged to the Tide. Tiffin made a 20-yard field goal, McElroy found Julio Jones for a 73-yard touchdown, and Tiffin kicked his third field goal, a 40-yarder, for a 24–15 Alabama win. After an October slump, McElroy completed 19 of 34 passes for 276 yards and two touchdowns, but had one pass intercepted. Mark Ingram rushed 22 times for 144 yards. Despite the closeness through three quarters, Alabama managed another win and again controlled the game stats:

	LSU	Alabama
Rushing yards	95	176
Passing yards	158	276
Total yards	253	452
First downs	13	24

The Tide remained at #3 in the AP poll, behind #1 Florida and #2 Texas. They moved ahead of Texas, taking the #2 spot in the BCS Standings.

Mississippi State

The Mississippi State Bulldogs were 4–5 and had lost to three ranked opponents. The Bulldogs' fortunes would not change hosting #3 Alabama. For the second week in a row, neither team could score in the first quarter. Early in the second period, Greg McElroy completed a 45-yard touchdown to Darius Hanks, and eight minutes later, Mark Ingram scored on a 1-yard run to end the first half 14–0.

A Leigh Tiffin 39-yard field goal was all the scoring in the third period. Mississippi State averted a shutout with a Derek DePasquale 34-yard field goal with 10:35 remaining in the game. After the kickoff, McElroy and Julio Jones teamed up to score on a 48-yard pass. Mark Ingram rumbled 70 yards for a touchdown, and the game ended, Alabama 31, Mississippi State 3. McElroy continued in form, completing 13 of 18 passes for 192 yards, two touchdowns, and no interceptions. Ingram carried 19 times for 149 yards and two touchdowns. Alabama was now #2 in both the AP poll and the BCS Standings.

Chattanooga

The University of Chattanooga Mocs joined the Southern Conference in 1976. They must have wondered why #2 Alabama was on their schedule. Alabama scored 21 points in the first quarter, 14 in the second, three in the third, and seven in the fourth in a 45–0 shutout.

Mark Ingram rushed 11 times for 102 yards and two touchdowns. Roy Upchurch and Trent Richardson each had one rushing touchdown. A Greg McElroy to Julio Jones 19-yard pass was good for another score. Javier Arenas returned a punt 66 yards for a touchdown, and Leigh Tiffin kicked a 40-yard field goal. Alabama had 422 yards of offense and 26 first downs to 85 and six for the Mocs.

The AP poll and the BCS Standings remained the same and agreed: Florida #1, Alabama #2, Texas #3, and TCU #4. No less than six teams remained undefeated.

Auburn

The Auburn Tigers flirted with the top 25 after a 5–0 beginning. After that, they were 2–4, but slipped back in by defeating #24 Mississippi, 33–20. They would finish the season at 8–5 and 3–5 in the SEC. However, this was the traditional state of Alabama rivalry, the "Iron Bowl," and anything could happen. Auburn scored first on a 67-yard run by Terrell Zachery. The Tigers attempted an onside kick, recovered it, and scored on a Chris Todd to Eric Smith one-yard pass.[3] This was the unpredictable Iron Bowl, and Auburn led, 14–0, after the first quarter. Trent Richardson scored on a two-yard run early in the second period, and Greg McElroy hit Colin Peek for a 33-yard score to tie the game at 14–14 to end the first half.

Four minutes into the third quarter, Todd and Darvin Adams connected on a 72-yard touchdown to retake the lead. Late in the quarter, Leigh Tiffin kicked field goals of 27 and 31 yards, but the Tide was still down, 21–20, at the end of the third period. McElroy engineered a 15-play drive, culminating in a four-yard touchdown pass to Roy Upchurch. Alabama was unsuccessful in a two-point conversion attempt, but they held the Tigers to avert an upset and win The Iron Bowl, 26–21. Auburn outgained the Tide 332 yards to 291. McElroy was 21 of 31 passing for 218 yards and two touchdowns. Mark Ingram was held to 30 rushing yards on 16 carries.

All six undefeated teams won, and both the AP and BCS remained the same.

#1 Florida

SEC Championship

The Georgia Dome in Atlanta was the setting for the SEC Championship Game on December 5. Eastern Division Champion Florida, #1 nationally, would face Western Division Champion Alabama, the #2 nationally ranked team. This was the first time the SEC Championship game would have two undefeated teams.[4] On the line was not only the SEC Championship but an opportunity to play for the national title against Texas.

Florida was the consensus national champion in 2008, had been ranked #1 for all but one week in 2009, was perfect at 12–0, and had outscored opponents, 438–118. The Gators featured senior quarterback Tim Tebow, who had won the Heisman Trophy as a sophomore in 2007. If there was a doubt about Florida, it was that they played only one ranked team. In game 5, they had defeated #4 LSU in Tiger Stadium, 13–3.

A Leigh Tiffin 48-yard field goal put Alabama on the board first. Mark Ingram ran for a seven-yard touchdown, but the PAT was missed, and the Tide held a 9–0 lead. Florida made the score 9–3 on a Caleb Sturgis 48-yard field goal to end the first quarter. Tiffin kicked a 34-yard field goal for a 12–3 Tide lead. Tim Tebow connected with David Nelson on a 23-yard touchdown, cutting the lead to 12–10. Mark Ingram made it 19–10 on a three-yard run. Then Sturgis made a 32-yard field goal to end the first half Alabama 19, Auburn 13.

The second half saw two touchdowns by Alabama. Greg McElroy passed 17 yards to Colin Peek for the first, and Ingram ran one yard for the second. A two-point conversion failed after Ingram's touchdown, and the final score became Alabama 32, Florida 13.

That the Tide dominated can be seen in the game statistics:

	Florida	Alabama
Rushing yards	88	251
Passing yards	247	239
Total yards	335	490
First downs	13	26

Of the Gators' 335 total yards, Tebow accounted for 310—247 passing and 63 rushing. McElroy was 12 of 18 for 239 yards. Ingram carried 28 times for 113 yards.

Alabama and Texas each moved up in the polls and BCS rankings, so the championship in 33 days would again pit #s 1 and 2.

#2 Texas

BCS National Championship Game The Rose Bowl

Texas has had a proud history in college football, including two unanimous national championships, 1963 and 2005, and several consensus or shared titles. In 2008, the Longhorns played four straight mid-season games against opponents ranked among the top 11 teams. They ascended to #1 after the first game of that stretch by beating #1 Oklahoma. They got past #11 Missouri and #7 Oklahoma State before losing to #6 Texas Tech. The Longhorns ended the season at 12-1, ranked #4, and outscoring opponents, 551-244.

Going into this year's BCS Championship, the Longhorns were 13-0 and had outscored opponents, 529-196. They did not have the murderous stretch of the previous year. They faced only #20 Oklahoma and #13 Oklahoma State before the Big 12 Championship Game against #21 Nebraska. They squeaked by the Cornhuskers, 13-12 to claim the conference title.

Now playing for the national championship, Texas scored on two Hunter Lawrence field goals of 18 and 42 yards to lead, 6-0 at the end of one quarter. The second quarter was all Alabama. Less than a minute in, Mark Ingram score from two yards out. Trent Richardson made a 49-yard touchdown run and, with 29 seconds remaining, Leigh Tiffin kicked a 26-yard field goal. Marcell Dareus intercepted Longhorns' quarterback Garrett Gilbert and returned it 28 yards for a touchdown with only three seconds to go. Alabama went to the half with a 24-6 lead.

Gilbert, who had four passes intercepted in the game, hit Jordan Shipley for a 44-yard touchdown late in the third quarter to cut into the Tide's lead, 24-13. Gilbert and Shipley combined for a second touchdown, a 28-yarder, with six minutes remaining in the fourth period. A two-point conversion was successful, and the Tide's lead had shrunk to three points, 24-21. After Courtney Upshaw recovered an Alabama fumble, Ingram scored from one yard out with 2:01 remaining, making the score 31-21. With time running out, Javier Arenas picked off his second Gilbert pass. Richardson ran in a two-yard touchdown. Tiffin's PAT attempt failed, but Alabama won, 37-21.

Several Alabama players were recipients of post-season honors and All America selection. Mark Ingram won the Heisman Trophy in a close vote (1304-1276) over Stanford running back Toby Gerhart. In the long, distinguished history of Alabama football, he was the first Heisman winner.[5] Linebacker Rolando McClain took home the Butkus Award and the Lambert Trophy.

Ingram and McClain were unanimous All America selections. Offensive lineman Mike Johnson and nose guard Terrence Cody were voted on by consensus. Kicker Leigh Tiffin and return specialist Javier Arenas made some All America teams, but were not consensus.

Why Was Alabama Unanimous?

After Alabama beat Florida in the SEC Championship Game, there were five undefeated teams remaining. Bowl game results helped selectors decide:

Team/record	BCS Rank	Bowl	Opponent	Result
Alabama/13–0	1	Rose	Texas	W 37–21
Texas/13–0	2	Rose	Alabama	L 37–21
Cincinnati/12–0	3	Sugar	Florida	L 51–24
TCU/12–0	4	Fiesta	Boise St.	L 17–10
Boise St./13–0	6	Fiesta	TCU	W 17 to 10

The post-season bowl games eliminated all but two teams from the ranks of the undefeated: Alabama and Boise State. The Boise State Broncos played only one team in the top 25, #16 Oregon in their first game, until the Fiesta matchup with #3 TCU. Eight of Boise State's opponents were from the Western Athletic Conference (WAC). The WAC was not as strong as the SEC and later dropped football. The combined record of all Broncos opponents was 84–91.

Alabama defeated six ranked teams, including #1 Florida and #2 Texas. There is little reason to doubt the wisdom of all selectors in voting Alabama the unanimous national champions of 2009.

Chapter 19

Florida State 2013

There were a few rules changes for the 2013 season. Targeting a defenseless player now resulted in the ejection of the offender unless overruled by instant replay. Should the penalty stand and the player be ejected, he would sit out the first half of the next game if the ejection occurred in the second half or an overtime period. A player who lost his helmet during play no longer had to sit out a play if his team took a timeout. Finally, a team could no longer spike the ball in order to stop the clock if less than three seconds remained.

Alabama had won the two previous BCS championships, but were not unanimous among selectors either year. The Florida State Seminoles had not been voted national champion, by any selector, since they won the title unanimously in 1999. From 2000–2012, their record was 116–54. While they never had a losing season in that stretch, the Seminoles were not spectacular either, with double-digit wins only in 2000, 2003, 2010, and 2012.

After Jimbo Fisher was hired as head coach in 2010, Florida State's fortunes turned. During his first three years, the Seminoles were 31–10 compared with 30–22 the four years previous. Expectations were again high in Tallahassee as the pre-season poll placed Florida State at #11.

Pittsburgh

The Seminoles traveled to unranked Pittsburgh and fell behind, 7–0 less than five minutes into the season. Tight end Nick O'Leary tied the score on a 24-yard pass from redshirt freshman quarterback Jameis Winston with four minutes remaining in the first quarter. Florida State added three more touchdowns in the second period. The Panthers managed a field goal and the half ended, 28–10. The third quarter saw three field goals, one by Pitt and two by Seminoles kicker Roberto Aguayo. O'Leary scored his third touchdown reception in the fourth period, and the game ended, 41–13.

Winston completed 25 of 27 attempts for 356 yards and four touchdowns. He also scored on a five-yard rush in the second quarter. Winston's 92.6 percent completion percentage set a Florida State record.[1] Rashad Greene had eight receptions for 126 yards and one touchdown. Nick O'Leary scored three touchdowns on four pass receptions. Florida State amassed 533 yards of offense, averaging 8.5 yards per play. The defense allowed Pitt 297 yards and intercepted two passes.

Nevada

In their home opener, the Seminoles managed only a Roberto Aguayo field goal in the first quarter. Early in the second period, Nevada scored a touchdown, and Florida State was behind for the second week against an unranked opponent. The Seminoles then cranked out eight touchdowns and another field goal for a 62–7 win. The Florida State offense totaled 617 yards (9.8 yards per play), while the defense yielded just 214 yards.

Winston completed 15 of 18 for 214 yards, two touchdowns, and one interception. He also ran for a touchdown. In two games, "Jaboo" (Winston) had completed 40 of 45 passes for 570 yards and six touchdowns, and he had rushed for 33 yards and two more scores.

Bethune-Cookman

Florida State was #8 in the AP poll when they hosted Bethune-Cookman. The Seminoles refused to get behind in the score for a third straight week. They registered four touchdowns, a field goal, and a safety by halftime. All second half scoring came in the third period. Florida State scored three touchdowns and B-C one touchdown for a 54–6 final.

The Seminoles' offense gained 492 yards, 226 passing and 266 rushing. Jameis Winston completed 10 of 19 passes for 148 yards and two touchdowns while not playing the final 23 minutes.

Boston College

The Seminoles first real test came against Boston College. The Eagles scored a touchdown five minutes into the game. Florida State answered with a 40-yard Roberto Aguayo field goal, but Boston College engineered another touchdown to end the first quarter up, 14–3. The Eagles added another field goal early in the second period, and the Seminoles were down by 14 points. Then Jameis Winston took over. He delivered three touchdown passes of 56, 10, and 55 yards, one each to Rashad Greene, Chad Abram, and Kenny Shaw. The last score coming as time expired in the half, putting Florida State up, 24–17.

To start the third quarter, Boston College added a field goal, cutting the lead to four points. Winston completed his fourth touchdown pass of the game, a 10-yarder to Greene, and Karlos Williams scored on a one-yard run for a 38–20 Florida State lead. The Eagles scored another touchdown with two minutes remaining in the third period to cut the lead to 11 points. Less then a minute into the fourth period, Aguayo hit a 20-yard field goal, and 26 seconds later, P. J. Williams intercepted a Boston College pass for a touchdown. The Eagles came back with a 17-yard touchdown pass to end the scoring in a 48–34 Florida State win.

Winston completed 17 of 27 passes for 330 of the Seminoles' 489 total yards. He passed for four touchdowns and had one interception. Kelvin Benjamin averaged 34.3 yards per reception but scored no touchdowns. Kenny Shaw averaged 23.3 yards per reception and scored one touchdown, while Rashad Greene scored twice while averaging 22.5 yards on four receptions. The Seminoles remained at #8.

#25 Maryland

Maryland had just broken into the AP top 25 poll with impressive wins (outscoring opponents, 159–41) over less than impressive competition. FIU, Old Dominion, Connecticut, and West Virginia would end the season with a combined record of 9–38.

Generating 614 yards of offense and allowing the Terrapins only 234 yards, Florida State rolled to an easy 63–0 shutout. Jameis Winston accounted for 417 yards, completing 23 of 32 passes for 393 yards and rushing for 24 more. He threw for five touchdowns, two apiece to Kelvin Benjamin and Nick O'Leary and one to Kenny Shaw.

Florida State was now ranked #5 going into its game with #3 Clemson.

#3 Clemson

Clemson was ranked #8 in the AP pre-season poll, moved up to #4 after defeating #5 Georgia, 38–35, and then to #3 following a 52–13 win over South Carolina State. The Tigers held that ranking through wins over four unranked teams—North Carolina State, Wake Forest, Syracuse, and Boston College—by a combined 155–49.

Florida State scored on a Jameis Winston to Kelvin Benjamin 22-yard touchdown pass less than a minute and a half into the game. Roberto Aguayo added a 28-yard field goal, and Mario Edwards scored on a 38-yard fumble recovery to put the Seminoles ahead, 17–0. With less than a minute to play in the first quarter, Clemson scored on a short Tajh Boyd to Sammy Watkins pass. State scored on a 72-yard Winston to Rashad Greene touchdown pass halfway through the second quarter. Aguayo hit a 24-yard field goal with three seconds remaining for a 27–7 halftime lead.

The third period began as the first with Winston connecting on a 17-yard touchdown pass, this time to Greene, with less than a minute and a half gone. Later in the quarter, Winston rushed for a four-yard touchdown to put the Seminoles up, 41–7. Florida State scored 10 more points in the fourth period on a Devonta Freeman touchdown run and an Aguayo 20-yard field goal. Clemson scored its second touchdown when Cole Stoudt ran it in from the 2-yard line with 13 seconds remaining. The Seminoles had proven themselves with a decisive 51–14 win over a top five team.

Jameis Winston ran for a touchdown, completed 22 of 34 passes for 445 yards and three touchdowns, and threw one interception. Nick O'Leary had five pass receptions for 161 yards, and Rashad Greene had eight receptions for 146 yards and two touchdowns. The Seminoles produced 566 yards of offense, while the defense registered four sacks, two pass interceptions, and two recovered Clemson fumbles. The Tigers were held to 326 offensive yards. Florida State continued to gain respect nationally and climbed to #3 in the AP and #2 in the first BCS Ranking.

North Carolina State

If Florida State fans worried about a letdown after crushing then #3 Clemson the week before, they did not need to be concerned. In the first quarter, Jameis Winston threw three touchdown passes, one apiece to Rashad Greene, Nick O'Leary, and Kelvin Benjamin. Karlos Williams and Devonta Freeman each rushed for a touchdown as the

Seminoles took a 35–0 lead into the second period. Freeman, who would rush for 92 yards on 12 carries, added a four-yard touchdown for the only second-quarter score and a 42–0 lead at the half. The Seminoles defense held NC State to 80 total yards in the first half.[2]

North Carolina State staged a comeback in the second half, scoring a field goal and a touchdown in the third quarter and adding another touchdown in the fourth. Kermit Whitfield ran in a 33-yard Florida State touchdown to end the scoring and secure a 49–17 win.

Jameis Winston completed 16 of 26 passes for 292 yards, three touchdowns, and one interception. Now halfway through the season, Winston had thrown for 1,878 yards (1,460 yards in the last four games), 23 touchdowns, and three rushing scores. His pass completion percentage was 69.9, with an average of a touchdown every 5.6 completions. Winston had four interceptions for an average of one every 45.8 pass attempts.

Having won the BCS championship the previous two years, Alabama topped the pre-season AP poll and had maintained the #1 ranking. The Crimson Tide was now 8–0, having outscored opponents, 330–8, including wins over #6 Texas A&M and #21 Mississippi. Ranked #3 pre-season, Oregon, now 8–0, ascended to #2 after a 66–3 win over Nicholls State and had remained there. The Ducks' top wins came against #16 Washington and #12 UCLA. Along with the #3 Seminoles, Ohio State (#4), Baylor (#5), and Miami, Florida (#7), were also undefeated. Despite winning, the Seminoles dropped to #3 in the BCS, behind #1 Alabama and #2 Oregon.

#7 Miami, Florida

Florida State was set to play their second top 10 team in three weeks. Miami was unranked in pre-season but moved up quickly following a 21–16 win against #12 Florida. At 7–0, the Hurricanes had outscored opponents, 252–124. However, those opponents would complete the season with a combined season record of 31–54.

Even with Jameis Winston throwing two interceptions and only one touchdown pass, the Seminoles outgained the Hurricanes, 517–275. The teams traded touchdowns in the first quarter, Devonta Freeman scoring the first of his three touchdowns on a five-yard run. The second quarter saw a James Wilder one-yard rushing touchdown and Freeman's second score on a 48-yard pass from Winston. Miami's Allen Hurns pulled in his second touchdown reception on a 14-yard Stephen Morris pass with 22 seconds remaining in the half. Florida State was up, 21–14.

The second half was all Florida State. Wilder scored his second rushing touchdown, and Freeman rushed 12 yards for his third of the game. Roberto Aguayo converted two field goals in the fourth period for a 41–14 Seminoles win. After its game with the Seminoles, Miami would lose three of its next five games, including a 36–9 defeat to Louisville in the Citrus Bowl.

In the BCS Ranking, Alabama remained at #1. Oregon had a bye week, and Florida State replaced them at #2. The Ducks were #3 and Ohio State #4.

Wake Forest

Jameis Winston would throw for only 159 yards, but his two touchdown passes would set the record (26) for a freshman in the Atlantic Coast Conference (ACC).[3] The offense gained 296 yards: 207 passing and 89 rushing. That would be the lowest offensive output for the season. However, the defense produced a 56-yard interception return and a 23-yard fumble recovery for touchdowns. Special teams added a 97-yard Kermit Whitfield kickoff return for another score. Wake Forest kicked a shutout-saving field goal with nine minutes remaining and would finish the season at 4–8. Florida State won easily, 59–3.

In the BCS Ranking, Alabama and the Seminoles remained at #1 and #2. Ohio State and Stanford, 8–1 and 26–20 winners over #3 Oregon, moved up to #3 and #4.

Syracuse

For the second week in a row, the Seminoles won by a score of 59–3. For the second week in a row, their opponent kicked a mid-fourth quarter field goal to prevent a shutout. Jameis Winston played only the first half, but he completed 19 of 21 passes for 277 yards and two touchdowns. Syracuse dominated time of possession, 41:42 to 18:18, yet were outgained, 523–247 yards.

Florida State still held the #2 BCS Ranking behind Alabama. Ohio State remained at #3, and Baylor moved up to #4, replacing Stanford, 20–17 losers to unranked Southern California. The top four plus #15 Fresno State and #16 Northern Illinois remained undefeated.

Idaho

The Idaho Vandals would end the season at 1–11, their sole victory a 26–24 home field win over Temple. They would give up 561 points (46.8 per game). Florida State, in their last home game of the season, nearly doubled that in an 80–14 win. The 80 points scored was a Florida State school record.[4] While the offense was rolling up 645 yards, the defense registered eight sacks and four interceptions. Jameis Winston accounted for 225 passing yards and four touchdowns to bring his season total to 32.

Baylor dropped from the undefeated with a 49–17 loss to #11 Oklahoma. The top five in the AP were now: Alabama (11–0), Florida State (11–0), Ohio State (11–0), Auburn (10–1), and Missouri (10–1). It was the same order in the all-important BCS Ranking.

Florida

The Florida Gators began the season at #10. They went up and down in the second 10 until dropping from the polls after consecutive losses to #10 LSU and #14 Missouri. They then lost their next four games before facing Florida State.

A Roberto Aguayo field goal was the only scoring in the first quarter. Florida kicker Austin Hardin had missed a field goal earlier after the Gators intercepted a Jameis Winston pass. Winston connected with Kelvin Benjamin for 45- and 29-yard touchdowns in the second period to take a 17–0 lead into halftime.

The Seminoles added 10 points in the third quarter on a 40-yard Aguayo field goal and an 11-yard rushing touchdown by Devonta Freeman. Florida got on the scoreboard early in the fourth quarter when quarterback Skyler Mornhinweg threw a five-yard touchdown pass to fullback Hunter Joyer. Florida State answered with Winston throwing his third touchdown pass to Benjamin and Aguayo kicking a 28-yard field goal, his third of the game. The Seminoles beat their cross-state rivals, 37–7.

Winston's three touchdown passes gave him 35 for the year to surpass Heisman Trophy winner Chris Weinke's previous Seminoles record of 33, set in 2000.[5] Winston completed 19 of 31 passes for 327 yards, three touchdowns, and one interception. Florida State had completed the regular season at 12–0. As winners of the Atlantic Division of the ACC, the Seminoles would face #20 Duke, 10–2, for the overall ACC title.

Florida State replaced Alabama at #1 after the Tide lost their annual "Iron Bowl" game to Auburn, 34–28. Ohio State, perfect at 12–0, advanced to #2, while Auburn, Alabama, and Missouri (all 11–1) completed the top five.

#20 Duke for ACC Championship

Duke began the season at 2–2 following mid–September losses to unranked Georgia Tech and Pitt. The Blue Devils then recorded eight straight wins, including #16 Virginia Tech and #24 Miami (Florida), to win the Coastal Division of the ACC.

After a scoreless first quarter, the Seminoles put up 17 points in the second period, 21 in the third, and seven in the fourth. The Blue Devils got a shutout-saving touchdown with 1:01 remaining in the game. Duke held a slight edge in time of possession, 30:44 to 29:16, but managed only 239 yards to 569 for the Seminoles. Jameis Winston completed 19 of 32 passes for 320 yards and three touchdowns, but he was intercepted twice. Devonta Freeman rushed 17 times for 95 yards to lead a ground attack that totaled 244 yards.

Ohio State (#2) lost to #10 Michigan State, 34–24 in the Big 10 Championship game, leaving the Seminoles as the only undefeated team. In the SEC Championship game, #3 Auburn defeated #5 Missouri, 59–42, took over #2, and moved into the BCS Championship against Florida State.

#2 Auburn for BCS National Championship

Auburn's road to the national championship game was a "Cinderella Story." Unranked in pre-season, the Tigers started at 3–0 before losing, 35–21 to #6 LSU. The following week, they defeated #24 Mississippi, 30–22, and a week later Western Carolina 62 to 3. At 5–1, Auburn first entered the polls at #24 on October 13.

On the road at #7 Texas A&M, the Tigers outlasted the Aggies for a 45–41 win that vaulted them to #11. Two more decisive wins against Florida Atlantic (45–10) and Arkansas (35–17) brought a #9 ranking. A 55–23 victory over Tennessee elevated the Tigers to #7 in the polls. Defeating #25 Georgia, 43–38, took them to #4 and an "Iron Bowl" showdown with #1 Alabama. The Tigers beat the Tide, 34–28 to take the Western Division of the SEC and the #3 ranking. The following week, they faced #5 ranked Missouri, Eastern Division winners, for the SEC title. In a wild game that saw over 100 points scored, Auburn won, 59–42. The Tigers had some help that week. In a game to decide the Big 10 championship, #10 Michigan State topped #2 Ohio State, 34–24.

With the Buckeyes' loss, Auburn took over the #2 ranking and a chance to play for the national championship.

After a Roberto Aguayo 35-yard field goal, Auburn scored three unanswered touchdowns to take a 21–3 lead with five minutes remaining in the half, and it looked as if the SEC was on its way to an eighth consecutive title.[6] With under a minute and a half to go in the second quarter, Devonta Freeman rushed for a three-yard touchdown, narrowing the Auburn lead to 21–10.

With six minutes remaining in the third quarter, Aguayo made a 41-yard field goal, and going into the fourth period, the Seminoles trailed, 21–13. Early in the final quarter, Jameis Winston got his first score of the game with an 11-yard touchdown pass to Chad Abram, and the Seminoles trailed, 21–20. Auburn kicked a 22-yard field goal, extending their lead to 24–20 with 4:42 to play. On the ensuing kickoff, Kermit Whitfield ran the ball back 100 yards for a touchdown, putting Florida State up, 27–24.

Auburn moved the ball 75 yards in a little over three minutes. Tre Mason, who had scored the Tigers' first touchdown, rushed the final 37 yards to put Auburn up, 31–27 with only 1:19 remaining. Winston then took the Seminoles 80 yards to a touchdown in a seven-play, one minute and six-second drive. Kelvin Benjamin finished the scoring with a two-yard touchdown pass from Winston and a 34–31 Florida State win for the BCS Championship.

Winston finished with 20 completions in 35 pass attempts for 237 yards, two touchdowns, and 26 rushing yards, and was named Offensive Player of the Game. Seminoles defensive back P. J. Williams was named Defensive Player of the Game with seven tackles and an interception.

Post-Season

Freshman quarterback Jameis Winston ended the season completing 66.9 percent of his passes for 4,057 yards, 40 touchdowns, and the highest rating at 184.8. He also rushed for over 200 yards and four touchdowns. Winston would take home the Heisman Trophy and the Walter Camp, Davey O'Brien, and Manning Awards. He would be the consensus All America quarterback, sharing selectors with A. J. McCarron of Alabama, who gathered the Maxwell, Johnny Unitas, and Kellen Moore Awards.

Senior defensive back Lamarcus Joyner was a unanimous All America. Joyner made 69 tackles, including 45 solo, and had two interceptions. Offensive lineman Bryan Stork was a consensus All America and picked up the Dave Rimington Trophy. Wide receiver Kelvin Benjamin, offensive lineman Cameron Erving, defensive lineman Timmy Jernigan, defensive back Terrence Brooks, and kicker Roberto Aguayo all received some All America votes, but not a consensus. Aguayo received the Lou Groza and Vlade Awards for placekicking.

Florida State played against some of the best players in the country including:

> Andre Williams of Boston College was a unanimous All America running back, received both the Doak Walker Award and Jim Brown Trophy, and was fourth in the Heisman Trophy voting.
> Aaron Donald of Pitt was a unanimous All America defensive lineman who

Chapter 19. Florida State 2013

gathered the Outland and Bronco Nagurski Trophies, plus the Chuck Bednarik, Bill Willis, and Lombardi Awards.

Running back Tre Mason of Auburn received some All America votes and was sixth in the Heisman Trophy balloting.

Wide receiver Sammy Watkins of Clemson also was named to some All America teams.

The 2013 season was the last year of the BCS, whose winner was not always a unanimous national champion among selectors. The previous three years had seen a divided vote:

2010—Auburn (14–0) and TCU (13–0)
2011—Alabama (12–1), LSU (13–1), and Oklahoma State (12–1)
2012—Alabama (13–1) and Notre Dame (12–1)

This year, Florida State was the sole undefeated team, with only #3 Michigan State, #10 U of Central Florida, and #15 Louisville having a single loss. Michigan State had an early-season loss to #22 Notre Dame. Both the Spartans and Ohio State were locked into schedules against relatively weak Big Ten opponents.

Naming the Seminoles the unanimous champions of 2013 was an easy decision for all selectors.

CHAPTER 20

Ohio State 2014

Ohio State first shared a national title in 1933 and later in 1944, 1957, 1961, 1969, 1970, 1973, 1974, and 1975. In 1942, 1954, 1968, and 2002, they were named consensus champions.

Much of that success came during the tenure of Woodrow "Woody" Hayes, who coached the Buckeyes from 1951–1978 and compiled a record of 205–61–10. Success mostly continued under Earle Bruce (81–26–1), John Cooper (111–43–4), Jim Tressel (106–22), and Luke Fickell (6–7).

Urban Meyer was hired in 2012. Meyer had been head coach at Florida from 2005–2010, where his 2006 and 2008 teams were consensus national champions. In Meyer's first year, Ohio State went 12–0, but because of NCAA sanctions imposed from the Jim Tressel years, the Buckeyes could not play in the Big 10 Championship Game and could not participate in a post-season bowl game.

In 2013, the Buckeyes went through the regular season 12–0, outscoring opponents, 578–243. They were ranked #2 going into the Big 10 Championship Game with #10 Michigan State before losing to the Spartans, 34–24. The loss dropped them to #7 before an Orange Bowl date with #8 Clemson, where they again lost, 40–35.

At the 2014 training camp, senior quarterback Braxton Miller was injured and would play in only one game that season. The year before, Miller had passed for 2,094 yards, with 24 touchdowns, and rushed for 1,068 yards and another 12 touchdowns. Although he was a distant ninth in Heisman Trophy voting in 2013, claiming only 91 points out of a possible 5,157 points among the top 10 finishers, he was certainly on Heisman watch lists. A severe quarterback crisis loomed for Urban Meyer. J. T. Barrett, a mature freshman leader, got the nod to start at quarterback over Cardale Jones for the season opener in Baltimore.[1]

Navy

Navy took a 7–6 lead into halftime on a Debrandon Sanders one-yard touchdown run one minute into the second quarter. The Buckeyes' points came on Sean Nuerberger field goals of 46 and 28 yards. Midway through the quarter, with a first and goal at Navy's 8-yard line, Barrett's pass was intercepted, and an Ohio State lead would have to wait.

Early in the third period, Buckeyes defensive end Joey Bosa forced a fumble, and linebacker Darron Lee returned the ball 61 yards to put Ohio State up, 13–7. Two minutes later, Navy's Keenan Reynolds scored from one yard out, and the Midshipmen again led,

14–13. Barrett hit Devin Smith with an 80-yard touchdown pass to end the third quarter with Ohio State on top, 20–14.

A 32-yard field goal by Navy's Nick Sloan closed the margin to three points early in the fourth quarter. The Buckeyes scored twice in the final period, an Ezekiel Elliott 10-yard run and a Barrett to Michael Thomas nine-yard pass. Ohio State had won its opener, 34–17. But the Mid-Shipmen, with the misdirection-oriented triple-option offense, had rushed the ball 63 times through a porous Ohio State defense, gaining 370 yards for a 5.9 yards per carry average.

Barrett completed 12 of 15 passes for 226 yards, two touchdowns, and one interception. He also ran the ball nine times for another 50 yards to lead all Ohio State rushers. The Buckeyes gained 420 yards of offense to 390 for Navy. Ohio State was ranked #5 in the pre-season poll, but the close game with the unranked Midshipmen dropped them to #8.

Virginia Tech

Ohio State began a three-game stretch at home in Columbus. Its first opponent was another unranked team, 1–0 Virginia Tech. The Hokies wanted to force the Buckeyes' inexperienced quarterback to throw the ball. To do that, they employed a tight defense at the line of scrimmage and used their safeties as extra linebackers and to blitz the quarterback. This defense was known as "Bear Zero," the "Bear" referring to the run-stopping tight defense employed by the NFL Chicago Bears, and the "Zero" to the number of safeties covering the deep pass.[2]

Virginia Tech took the early lead on a Shai McKenzie two-yard run midway through the first quarter. The Buckeyes had a chance to score with a first down on the Hokies' 10-yard line, but Sean Nuernberger's field goal attempt was missed. On their next possession, J. T. Barrett tied the score on a two-yard run. With only 19 seconds remaining in the first period, Marshawn Williams rushed 14 yards for a Virginia Tech touchdown and a 14–7 lead. The only scoring in the second period was a 10-yard pass from the Hokies' Michael Brewer to Sam Rogers for the fullback's only touchdown of 2014. The halftime score was Virginia Tech 21, Ohio State 7.

The Buckeyes closed the deficit to seven points on a Barrett to Michael Thomas 53-yard touchdown toss late in the third quarter, and an Ezekiel Elliott 15-yard run tied the game at 21–21 with 11:40 to play. After that, the Hokies scored twice. Brewer threw his second touchdown, a 10-yarder to Bucky Hodges, and defensive back Donovan Riley intercepted a Barrett desperation pass and returned it 63 yards for a touchdown with only 46 seconds remaining. Ohio State lost, 35–21 and was 1–1 on the season. The second loss to an unranked opponent pushed the Buckeyes to #22 in the AP poll.

The Buckeyes gained only 327 yards on offense. Barrett completed 9 of 29 passes for 219 yards for one touchdown, but suffered three interceptions. He again led Ohio State rushers with 70 yards on 24 carries and one touchdown.

Kent State

Ohio State was on a mission, and Kent State, of the Mid–America Conference, was outmatched. J. T. Barrett threw six touchdown passes, and the Buckeyes outgained the

Golden Flashes, 628 yards to 126. Ohio State scored 21 points in the first quarter, 24 in the second, 14 in the third, and seven in the fourth en route to a 66–0 shutout.

The blowout win did not help their national status as the Buckeyes dropped one ranking to #23. The following week, they had a bye and re-took their #22 position in the polls.

Cincinnati

Ohio State's third consecutive home game began with a Cincinnati 83-yard, four-play drive, culminating in a Gunner Kiel to Chris Moore 60-yard touchdown. With a minute and a half gone, the Bearcats were up, 7–0.

The Buckeyes responded with 30 unanswered points over the next 16 minutes. Rod Smith ran for a three-yard touchdown, Ezekiel Elliott scored on a three-yard run, and eight seconds later, the Ohio State defense registered a safety when a Bearcats player knocked the ball out of the end zone following a Joey Bosa forced fumble.[3] J. T. Barrett threw two touchdown passes, the first a 19-yarder to Devon Smith late in the first quarter and the second another 19-yard toss, this time to Evan Spencer early in the second period.

At 30–7, the Buckeyes seemed in control, but before the first half ended, Kiel threw for two touchdowns. Following a Curtis Samuel fumble that gave the Bearcats good field position, Kiel hit Johnny Holton for a 19-yard touchdown with 5:23 remaining. After the defense held the Buckeyes, Kiel again connected with Moore for a long scoring pass, this one an 83-yarder with only 26 seconds remaining. Ohio State led at the half by only nine points, 30–21.

Sean Nuernberger hit a 25-yard field goal, but then Kiel and Moore combined for a 78-yard touchdown, and the Buckeyes' lead was cut to five at 33–28. Rising to the challenge, Ohio State scored 17 unanswered points. Before the third quarter ended, Nuernberger made a 42-yard field goal and Barrett threw to Donte Wilson for a 24-yard touchdown. The only score in the fourth period was a Barrett to Smith 34-yard pass with 10:26 to play. The game ended Ohio State 50, Cincinnati 28.

The Bearcats had struck quickly with three Kiel to Moore touchdown passes totaling 221 yards, exactly one-half of the Cincinnati offensive production. Ohio State lead in most categories: total yards 710–422, rushing yards 380–70, first downs 45–15, and time of possession 41:56–18:04. Barrett completed 26 of 36 passes for 330 yards and four touchdowns, throwing to 10 different receivers. Elliott had 182 rushing yards and one touchdown on 28 carries. The win moved the Buckeyes to #20 in the polls.

Maryland

The Maryland Terrapins left the Atlantic Coast Conference to join the Big 10 Conference in 2014. They would end the season at 4–4 in conference play and 7–6 overall.

The Buckeyes started quickly, scoring two touchdowns in the first eight and a half minutes. Rod Smith scored on one-yard run, and J. T. Barrett threw a nine-yard touchdown pass to Jalin Marshall. Brad Craddock hit a 57-yard field goal for the Terrapins, and the first quarter ended at 14–3. The first six minutes of the second period saw two more Ohio State scores. Barrett threw a 25-yard touchdown to Michael Thomas, who made a one-handed catch in the corner of the end zone, and Sean Nuernberger made a 28-yard field goal to give the Buckeyes a 24–3 lead.

Maryland's Wes Brown ran for a two-yard touchdown with 2:34 remaining in the half. The Terrapins' defense held on the next series, and Ohio State was forced to punt. Cameron Johnston, the Australian precision-punter, boomed a 69-yarder to the Maryland 7-yard line.[4] Buckeyes linebacker Darron Lee intercepted quarterback C. J. Brown, and on the next play Barrett threw a one-yard touchdown strike to Nick Vannett with under a minute to play. Ohio State led at intermission, 31–10.

The third quarter saw an exchange of touchdowns: Barrett threw 30 yards to Devin Smith, and Maryland's Brandon Ross scored on a two-yard run.

Barrett rushed for a nine-yard touchdown early in the fourth period. Less than a minute and a half later, Maryland quarterback Caleb Rowe completed a four-yard touchdown pass to Stefon Diggs, and the Ohio State lead was 45–24. The final touchdown came on a Raekwon McMillan 19-yard interception return. Besides McMillan, Eli Apple, Doran Grant, and Darron Lee all had an interception in the game.

The Buckeyes showed a balanced offense with 269 rushing yards and 264 yards passing. Barrett was 18 of 23 for 267 yards with four touchdowns (backup Cardale Jones was 1 of 1 for -3 yards). Barrett also contributed 71 yards rushing. Elliott accounted for 139 rushing yards on 24 carries. The defense held Maryland to 66 rushing yards and 310 overall. The win moved them up to #15 in the polls, where they stayed through the following bye week.

Rutgers

Like Maryland, Rutgers joined the Big 10 in 2014 from the American Athletic Conference. The AAC was made up of Big East football schools. Like Maryland, the Scarlet Knights had a difficult first year in the new conference.

It took the Buckeyes nine and a half minutes to take a 14–0 lead this week. J. T. Barrett threw a 12-yard touchdown to Nick Vannett, and Ezekiel Elliott scored on a one-yard run. Late in the first quarter, Rutgers' Desmon Peoples had a one-yard touchdown run. The second period was dominated by Ohio State as they put up 21 unanswered points. Barrett and Vannett teamed up for their second score of the game, a 26-yarder, Eli Apple scored on a four-yard fumble return, and Rod Smith scored on a run from the 3-yard line. The Buckeyes owned a comfortable 35–7 halftime lead.

Barrett scored the next two touchdowns on runs of 33 and five yards. Rutgers added a 42-yard field goal by Kyle Federico, making the score 49–10. Before the third period ended, Barrett hit Evan Spencer for an 11-yard touchdown. Peoples finished the scoring early in the fourth period with a 12-yard touchdown run. Ohio State won their fifth game, 56–17.

The Buckeyes had 585 total offensive yards to 345 for Rutgers. Barrett completed 19 of 31 passes for 261 yards and three passing touchdowns, led all rushers with 107 yards on seven carries, and scored another two touchdowns rushing. The win advanced them to #13 in the polls.

Penn State

It was extremely loud with the familiar and famous Penn State "White-out" as nearly 108,000, mostly Nittany Lions, fans packed Beaver Stadium in University Park, Pennsylvania. They were all hoping to see a good game, and they were not disappointed.

Ezekiel Elliott scored on a 10-yard run for the only score in the first quarter. Sean Nuernberger made a 49-yard field goal, and J. T. Barrett tossed a one-yard touchdown pass to Jeff Heuerman. Despite the hostile environment, Ohio State took a 17–0 lead into halftime. Barrett suffered a sprained left knee just before the half and wore a brace for the remainder of the game.

Anthony Zettel intercepted a Barrett pass and returned it 40 yards for a touchdown a minute and a half into the third period, and the quarter would end 17–7. The Nittany Lions scored twice in the fourth period. After Barrett was intercepted a second time, Christian Hackenberg passed to Saeed Blacknall for a 24-yard touchdown, cutting the Ohio State lead to three points.

The Buckeyes were forced to punt, and the Nittany Lions got possession at their own 9-yard line with three minutes on the clock. In a sustained drive, Penn state moved the ball to the Buckeyes' 14-yard line. At that point, they mismanaged the clock and the game, settling for a Sam Ficken 31-yard field goal with nine seconds remaining to send the game into overtime.

In an overtime, each team gets the ball at the opponent's 25-yard line. The teams exchanged touchdowns in the first overtime. Penn State scored on a Bill Belton one-yard run, and Ohio State answered with a five-yard run by Barrett. A penalty on Ohio State's PAT allowed the Buckeyes to start the second overtime from the Penn State 12-yard line. On third down and 2 from the 4-yard line, Barrett kept the ball and scored, pushed in the last yard by guard Pat Elflein.[5] Penn State now needed a touchdown to force a third overtime. The Nittany Lions had the ball on fourth and 5 at the Buckeyes' 20-yard line, needing a touchdown or a first down. Joey Bosa ran through running back Akeel Lynch to sack Hackenberg and end the game. Ohio State went home with a 31–24 victory.

The Buckeyes outgained Penn State, 293 yards to 240. Barrett passed 19 times with 12 completions for 74 yards, one touchdown, and two interceptions. He also rushed the ball 20 times for 94 yards even though hobbled by his knee in the second half. Elliott carried 26 times for 119 yards and a touchdown. On defense, the Buckeyes held Penn State to 16 rushing yards. Joshua Perry led the way with 18 tackles, including 12 solo.

Ohio State remained at #13 in the AP poll, while the first CFP rankings placed the Buckeyes at #16.

Illinois

The Fighting Illini were having another difficult year. The previous season, they finished at 4–8 and 1–7 in the conference. This season would end at 7–6 overall and 3–5 in the Big 10. Before the game, the Buckeyes lost the services of senior running back Rod Smith, who was dismissed from the team for failing a drug test

Until the end of the third quarter, the Illini did not get on the scoreboard as Ohio State racked up 48 unanswered points. Illinois' Donovonn Young rushed for a five-yard touchdown and Aaron Bailey passed seven yards to Matt Lacosse for the other score, both coming against Buckeyes reserves. For Ohio State, Curtis Samuel scored two rushing touchdowns and Jalin Marshall scored one. J. T. Barrett threw two touchdowns to Devin Smith, and backup quarterback Cardale Jones also had two touchdown passes, one to Donte Wilson and the other to Michael Thomas. Sean Nuernberger added two field goals. The Buckeyes' offense gained 545 yards to 243 for Illinois. Barrett had 167 passing yards on 15 of 24 attempts. Jones was 5 of 9 for 82 yards.

Even with the 55–14 win, Ohio State remained at #13 in the AP, but moved up to #14 in the CFP ranking. Of top contenders, only #1 Mississippi State and #2 Florida State remained undefeated.

#7 Michigan State

Michigan State at #7 AP and #8 CFP loomed as a challenge for the Buckeyes, but also an opportunity to gain more national respect. The Spartans, ranked #8 in pre-season, lost to #3 Oregon, 46–27 in their second game. Since then, they had won six straight games by a combined score of 292–109, including a 27–22 victory over #19 Nebraska.

This game was a much-anticipated rematch for the Buckeyes. In 2013, the loss to Michigan State had ended: (1) #2 Ohio State's chance to play for the national championship; (2) Ohio State's chance for a Big 10 Title; and (3) Ohio State's 24-game winning streak. This year, the Spartans had both a bye week to prepare and home field advantage.

After a failed 47-yard field goal attempt by Ohio State kicker Sean Nuernberger, Michigan State began the scoring on a Connor Cook to Keith Mumphrey 15-yard touchdown at 9:42 in the first quarter. Eli Apple, the Buckeyes' regular wide-field cornerback, who had suffered a hamstring injury and was watching from the sideline, was inserted into the game, as the makeshift deep coverage wasn't working out.[6] A minute and one second later, the Buckeyes had covered 71 yards, and J. T. Barrett scored on a five-yard run to tie the score. After holding the Spartans, Ohio State fumbled the punt, lost possession, and on the next series, Michigan State's Jeremy Langford burst for a 33-yard touchdown. The Spartans led, 14–7, at the end of one quarter.

Early in the second period, Barrett again scored, this time on a one-yard run. The score remained tied for about eight minutes before Langford scored his second touchdown on a one-yard run. In the final 3:19 of the first half, Barrett threw for two touchdowns. Michael Thomas hauled in a 79-yarder and Devin Smith a 44-yarder to put the Buckeyes ahead for good, 28–21, ending the first half.

The Spartans' Michael Geiger made a 40-yard field goal, closing the gap to four points. Ezekiel Elliott closed out the third period scoring with a one-yard touchdown to push the lead to 11 entering the fourth quarter. Barrett hit Dontre Wilson for a seven-yard touchdown three minutes into the final period. The Spartans' Connor Cook connected with Josiah Price on a 16-yard touchdown making the score Ohio State 42, Michigan State 31. Two minutes later, Elliott scored from 17 yards away for a commanding 49–31 lead. Langford scored his third touchdown on a one-yard run, and Ohio State had defeated the Spartans, 49–37. The stats were more equal than most other games:

Place	Ohio State	Michigan State
Rushing yards	268	178
Passing yards	300	358
Total yards	568	536
First downs	25	29

Barrett was 16 of 26 passing for 300 yards and three touchdowns. Elliott gained 154 yards on the ground in 24 carries, and Barrett added 86 in 14. The win propelled the Buckeyes to #8 in both the AP poll and CFP ranking.

#25 Minnesota

A 15-degree day with continual snowfall greeted the Buckeyes at TCF Bank Stadium in Minneapolis. Ohio State scored first on an 86-yard run by J. T. Barrett. Barrett then hit Jalin Marshall for a 57-yard touchdown, and the Buckeyes led, 14–0 at the end of the first quarter.

After a Barrett pass was intercepted and returned 56 yards, Minnesota's David Cobb scored on a five-yard run half a minute into the second period. Minnesota's defense caused a fumble at their own 2-yard line and returned it to their 20. The Golden Gophers moved the ball 80 yards and tied the game with 1:24 remaining in the first half on a Cobb 30-yard touchdown run. As time expired, Sean Nuernberger connected on a 22-yard field goal to close the half at Ohio State 17, Minnesota 14.

Halfway through the third period, Barrett hit Michael Thomas for a 30-yard touchdown. Five minutes into the final quarter, Barrett passed for another score, a 22-yarder to Evan Spencer, and the Buckeyes led, 31–14. Three minutes later, Cobb scored his third rushing touchdown from 12 yards out to bring Minnesota to within 10 points. Hoping for a successful on-side kick, the Gophers opted for a Ryan Santoso 34-yard field goal, closing the gap to seven points with 1:19 remaining. The on-side attempt failed, and the game ended with a Buckeyes win, 31–24.

Ohio State's offense gained 489 yards to 303 for the Golden Gophers. Barrett had another outstanding game, completing 15 of 25 passes for 200 yards, three touchdowns, and 1 interception. He also led all rushers with 189 yards and one touchdown on 17 carries. Ezekiel Elliott added 96 rushing yards on 18 carries.

The win moved the Buckeyes to #7 in the AP poll and to #6 in the CFP ranking, the one that mattered to get to a title shot. A Mississippi State loss had removed them from #1, but they were still in the running at #4. Alabama ascended from #5 to #1 for dethroning Mississippi State, 25–20. Oregon at 9–1 was #2, and Florida State, the only remaining undefeated (10–0) team, was #3. The Buckeyes still had a long way to go.

Indiana

In their third game, Indiana beat #18 Missouri in an away game, 31–27. After that, the Hoosiers lost six of seven games before meeting the Buckeyes. Indiana would end the season at 4–8 and 1–7 in the Big 10 East.

Ezekiel Elliott raced 65 yards for a touchdown 1:11 into the game. J. T. Barrett threw a four-yarder to Jeff Heueman for the first of his four touchdown passes. Tevin Coleman put Indiana on the board with a two-yard run, and Griffin Oakes hit a 30-yard field goal to end the first quarter scoring, 14–10 in favor of the Buckeyes.

Oakes connected on a 37-yard field goal for the only second period score that cut the lead to one point, 14–13. The Hoosiers briefly took the lead halfway through the third quarter when Coleman ran 90 yards for a touchdown and a 20–14 score. Five minutes later Jalin Marshall returned a punt 54 yards to regain the lead for the Buckeyes, 21–20. Barrett and Marshall teamed for three touchdowns in the fourth period on passes of 6, 15, and 54 yards. With 2:49 remaining, Ohio State enjoyed a 42–20 lead. Cole scored again for the Hoosiers on a 52-yard run with 1:13 to go, and the final outcome was Ohio State 42, Indiana 27.

Ohio State outgained Indiana by 527–395 yards. The defense gave up 281 rushing yards, 230 by Coleman on 27 carries. Barrett completed 25 of 35 passes for 302 yards and four touchdowns with two interceptions. He also rushed the ball for 78 yards. Ezekiel Elliott gained 107 rushing yards on 13 carries and scored a touchdown. The Buckeyes remained at #7 in the AP Poll. In the CFP ranking, the top four teams, Alabama, Oregon, Florida State, and Mississippi State, all won while TCU at #5 had a bye week and Ohio State remained at #6.

Michigan

The Ohio State–Michigan football rivalry is one of the biggest in college sports. Many times, the game has had Big 10 championship and even national championship implications. Over the first 150 years of college football, these two have played 115 times. Although Michigan leads the series, 58–51 with six ties, the past eight games, dating back to 2012, have been won by Ohio State.[7]

J. T. Barrett opened the scoring with a six-yard pass to Nick Vannett. Michigan tied the score on a Devin Gardner to Jake Butt 12-yard touchdown. Midway through the second period, the Wolverines took the lead on a Drake Johnson two-yard run. With only seven seconds remaining, Barrett ran for a 25-yard touchdown and a 14–14 halftime score.

Barrett opened the third quarter with a two-yard run for a touchdown. Johnson scored again on a four-yard run to knot the score at 21–21. Ezekiel Elliott's two-yard touchdown run with 1:08 left in the third period gave the lead back to the Buckeyes, 28–21. Elliott scored again late in the fourth quarter on a 44-yard carry. A minute later, Darron Lee recovered a Michigan fumble, returning it 33-yards for a touchdown that pushed the Ohio State lead to 42–21. Freddy Canteen scored on a three-yard pass from Gardner to end the scoring at Ohio State 42, Michigan 28. The Buckeyes' next game would be for the Big 10 title.

At the beginning of the fourth quarter, facing a second down and one, Barrett kept the ball on an option play. With the weight of a defender on him, Barrett's leg went underneath him, breaking his ankle. Braxton Miller and now J. T. Barrett, two great quarterbacks, with Heisman Trophy–caliber potential and performances, sidelined in the same season and from the same team. What were the odds? And how would the Buckeyes respond?

Barrett had thrown for 2,834 yards and 34 touchdowns. He also rushed for 938 yards and another 11 touchdowns. Barrett, a freshman, had more than adequately replaced Miller, who would have been a senior in 2014. The year before, Miller was fifth in the Heisman Trophy voting, and this year Barrett would also finish fifth. Urban Meyer, for the second time this season, had to replace a seasoned quarterback, this time with a sophomore, Cardale Jones.

In Barrett's last game, he passed for 176 yards and one touchdown and rushed for 89 yards, scoring two more. Elliott picked up 129 rushing yards and two scores. Barrett's successor, Cardale Jones, was 2 for 3 passing for seven yards.

The win moved the Buckeyes up to #6 in the AP poll and to a #5 ranking in the CFP. Alabama (11-1) remained #1 in the CFP ranking, followed by #2 Oregon (11-1), #3 TCU (10-1), #4 Florida State (12-0), and #5 Ohio State (11-1). The Buckeyes were just outside the playoffs and would need some help.

#11 Wisconsin—Big 10 Championship

Wisconsin was 10-2 overall, 7-1 in conference play, and on top of the Western Division going into the Big 10 Championship Game. Ranked #14 in pre-season, the Badgers lost, 28-24 in their season opener against #13 LSU. After three wins against non-ranked teams, they suffered a surprising 20-14 loss at 2-2 Northwestern. The Badgers rebounded with seven straight wins, including a 59-24 victory against #11 Nebraska and a 34-24 win against #22 Minnesota that clinched the Division.

The Buckeyes wasted little time claiming the Big 10 title. Two minutes in, Cardale Jones hit Devin Smith for a 39-yard touchdown. Ezekiel Elliott scampered 81 yards for touchdown nine minutes later to end the first quarter 14-0. Ohio State added 24 more points in the second period. Jones and Smith combined for their second score of the game, a 44-yard completion. Elliott ran 14 yards for his second touchdown, Sean Nuernberger provided a 23-yard field goal, and Joey Bosa returned a Wisconsin fumble four yards for a touchdown and a 38-0 halftime advantage.

A Jones to Smith 42-yard touchdown was all the scoring in the third quarter. Curtis Samuel scored twice in the fourth period on runs of 12 yards and one yard. The Buckeyes totally dominated the Badgers, 59-0. They now waited and watched to see if they would make the four-team playoff.

In the last week before playoffs and bowls, four of the top five CFP teams played in a conference championship. TCU did not, and that probably knocked the Horned Frogs out of the playoffs. Each conference championship paired top 20 teams. TCU's final was against unranked Iowa State, with a record of 2-10 (0-9 in the Big 12).

Team (CFP rank)	Opponent	AP	CFP	Conference
Alabama (1)	Missouri	14	16	SEC
Oregon (2)	Arizona	8	7	PAC-12
TCU (3)	Iowa State	—	—	
Florida State (4)	Georgia Tech	12	11	ACC
Ohio State (5)	Wisconsin	11	13	Big 10

All five teams won:

#1 Alabama	42–13
#2 Oregon	51–13
#3 TCU	55–3
#4 Florida State	37–35
#5 Ohio State	59–0

When the final CFP ranking was released on December 7, the top four were: Alabama, Oregon, Florida State, Ohio State. Alabama at #1 would play #4 Ohio State, while #2 Oregon would face #3 Florida State.

#1 Alabama—CFP Semi-Final

The Alabama Crimson Tide was 12–1. Their sole loss was to #11 Mississippi in their fifth game. They ascended to the top after beating #1 Mississippi State in game 10. Along the way, they defeated #14 LSU in overtime, #14 Missouri, #15 Auburn, and #21 Texas A&M. Over the season, they outscored opponents, 482–216. With yet another unseasoned quarterback, the Buckeyes expected to have their work cut out for them.

The neutral site game was played at the Superdome in New Orleans. Ohio State got on the board first with a Sean Nuernberger 22-yard field goal. Two minutes later, the Tide's Derrick Henry scored on a 25-yard touchdown run following a lost fumble by Ezekiel Elliott at the Buckeyes' 37-yard line to take a 7–3 lead. Nuernberger made his second field goal, a 21-yarder, and the Tide led, 7–6. Alabama scored on a Blake Sims to Amari Cooper 15-yard pass to end the first quarter 14–6. Midway through the second period, Alabama scored on a two-yard run by T. J. Yeldon. Down 21–6, it did not look promising for the Buckeyes.

From late in the second period to the end of the third, Ohio State scored 28 unanswered points to take a 34–21 lead. Elliott scored on a three-yard run, Evan Spencer passed 13 yards to Michael Thomas, Cardale Jones hit Devin Smith with a 47-yarder, and Steve Miller intercepted a Sims pass and returned it 41 yards for a touchdown. Sims made up for the interception by guiding Alabama 84 yards in seven plays, taking it into the end zone himself from the 5-yard line. The score remained 34–28 until 3:24 remaining in the game when Elliott broke an 85-yard run to increase the Buckeyes' lead to 42–28. With just under two minutes to play, Sims hit Cooper on a six-yard touchdown. The game ended Ohio State 42, Alabama 35.

On 20 carries, Elliott gained 230 of the Buckeyes' 281 rushing yards. Now-starting quarterback Jones completed 18 of 35 passes for 243 yards, one touchdown and one interception. He also rushed 17 times for 79 yards. The Buckeyes would now play Oregon in the first-ever CFP Championship Game.

#2 Oregon—CFP Final National

Championship Game

The Oregon Ducks were ranked #3 in pre-season. An October 2 upset by unranked Arizona dropped them out of the top 10 for only a week. A win at #18 UCLA brought the Ducks to #9, and over the next seven games, they ascended to #2 with victories over #17 Utah and #8 Arizona in a rematch, this time for the PAC-12 title. Oregon decisively defeated #3 Florida State, 59–20 in the other CFP semi-final, held at the Rose Bowl.

Oregon featured quarterback Marcus Mariota, winner of the Heisman Trophy and the Camp, Maxwell, O'Brien, and Unitas Awards. In 445 pass attempts, Mariota completed 304 (68 percent) for 4,454 yards, 42 touchdowns, and only four interceptions. He also rushed for 770 yards, another 15 touchdowns, and received one pass for yet one more score.

Oregon opened the scoring on a seven-yard pass from Mariota to Keanon Lowe. Ohio State tied the game on an Ezekiel Elliott 33-yard run, then took the lead on a one-yard pass from Cardale Jones to Nick Vannett to end the first quarter at 14–7. Jones ran for a one-yard touchdown, making the Buckeyes lead 21–7. Ducks kicker Aidan Schneider made a 26-yard field goal with 48 seconds remaining, and the first half ended Ohio State 21, Oregon 10.

Oregon scored twice in the third quarter, a Mariota to Byron Marshall 70-yard pass and a 23-yard Schneider field goal to make the score 21–20. From that point on, it was all Ohio State and, especially, Ezekiel Elliott. As time expired in the third period, Elliott scored on a nine-yard run. He scored two more touchdowns in the fourth period. The first was a two-yard run midway through the quarter, the second a one-yarder with 28 seconds remaining. Ohio State had won the inaugural CFP Championship, 42–28.

Elliott accounted for 246 of the Buckeyes' 296 rushing yards and four of the team's six touchdowns. Jones completed 16 of 23 passes for 242 yards, one touchdown, and one interception, while netting another 38 yards on the ground. Elliott and Jones made up 525 of the Buckeyes' 538 total yards. Mariota completed 24 of 37 passes for 333 yards, two touchdowns, and one interception. He added another 39 yards rushing. Marshall led all receivers with eight catches for 169 yards and one score. Oregon's total offense was 465 yards.

The Buckeyes received no individual awards, and only sophomore defensive end Joey Bosa was a unanimous All America. Senior defensive lineman Michael Bennett was named to some AA teams, but was not a consensus pick.

Ohio State certainly deserved being a unanimous champion. They were resilient enough to weather two quarterback crises and an early-season loss. They were probably aided by TCU playing a weak team in its last game while the other top ranking CFP teams vied for conference championships against ranked opponents.

The Horned Frogs had a close loss (61–58) against #5 Baylor, but they had wins over (at the time) #4 Oklahoma, #15 Oklahoma State, #20 West Virginia, and #7 Kansas State, and a 42–3 blowout of #9 Mississippi in the Peach Bowl. TCU had reason to be upset at being kept from the championship playoffs in the last week, especially as they had won the last regular season game handily, 55–3.

With the CFP's top three teams falling, it would have taken only one selector to pick (as of the last CFP ranking) #5 TCU over the #4 Buckeyes to have Ohio State not be unanimous.

Of the 33 out of 150 years of college football where a team was selected unanimously, only Ohio State in 2014 and Notre Dame in 1943 were not undefeated.

Chapter 21

Alabama 2015

Nick Saban, who had won a consensus national title at LSU in 2003, came to Alabama in 2007. Under Saban, Alabama football won the national championship unanimously in 2009. The Tide would win the title by consensus in 2011 and 2012 while posting a record of 72–9 from 2009–2014. In 2014, Alabama played Ohio State in the semi-final of the CFP, losing 42–35. Eight months later, Alabama was ranked third in the pre-season AP poll, with Ohio State at #1 and TCU #2. The Crimson Tide fans had reason to be optimistic going into the 2015 season.

September 5—#20 Wisconsin (in Texas)

On a fourth down and 1, Alabama's Derrick Henry scored on a 37-yard run with 5:54 remaining in the first quarter. Nine minutes later, Wisconsin scored on a six-yard pass from Joel Stave to Alex Erickson to tie the game at 7–7. Before the first half ended, the Tide regained the lead on a 17-yard touchdown pass from quarterback Jake Coker to wide receiver Bob Foster.

In the third period, Henry scored twice on runs of 56 and two yards, extending Alabama's lead to 28–7. With a minute remaining in the third period, Wisconsin's Rafael Gaglianone kicked a 43-yard field goal. Alabama's senior running back, Kenyan Drake, raced 43 yards for a touchdown halfway through the fourth period. With less than five minutes remaining, Stave threw his second touchdown pass, a three-yarder to Robert Wheelwright, and the game ended, Alabama 35, Wisconsin 17.

Alabama held the Badgers to 40 yards rushing while gaining 238 on the ground, 147 by Henry in only 13 carries. Total offense favored the Tide, 502 yards to 268. The only turnover in the game was an intercepted Wisconsin pass. Alabama played two quarterbacks: Coker completed 15 of 21 passes for 213 yards and one touchdown, and Cooper Bateman was 7 of 8 for 51 yards.

September 12—Middle Tennessee State

Following their win over Wisconsin, Alabama was ranked #2 behind Ohio State, with TCU #3, Baylor #4, and Michigan State #5. This week against Middle Tennessee State, the Tide was a favored by 30 or more points.

Following an MTS fumble, Jake Coker threw a 19-yard touchdown pass to Robert Foster for the only score in the first quarter and a 7–0 Alabama lead. Early in the second period, MTS's Cody Clark made a 20-yard field goal for a respectable 7–3 score. But Derrick Henry scored on a pair of short touchdown runs over the next seven minutes. Alabama closed out the first half scoring when an MTS punt was blocked through the end zone for a safety and a 23–3 Tide lead.

The third period saw two more Alabama touchdowns: a 14-yard pass from Cooper Bateman to Kenyan Drake, and a 28-yard run by Henry. The only fourth quarter scoring was an MTS 15-yard touchdown pass from Austin Grammer to Rod Duckworth. The final score was Alabama 37, Middle Tennessee State 10. Coker and Bateman each had a touchdown pass and an interception. Henry rushed for 96 yards and three touchdowns. Alabama's offense totaled 532 yards, while the defense yielded 275 yards, including only 91 rushing, and caused four turnovers.

September 19—#15 Mississippi

The Tide had to be wary of the Rebels as Mississippi had bested the Tide, 23–14 the year earlier for their only regular season loss. Ole Miss had defeated the University of Tennessee at Martin, 76–3, and Fresno State, 73–21, for a 2–0 start and a #15 ranking.

Alabama wide receiver ArDarius Stewart fumbled the opening kickoff, and Mississippi's Gary Wunderlich kicked a 32-yard field goal a minute into the game for the only first quarter score. Early in the second period, Alabama kicker Adam Griffith tied the score on a 20-yard field goal. Mississippi then scored two short rushing touchdowns in less than a minute. The first was set up by a Cooper Bateman intercepted pass that was returned to Alabama's 26-yard line. Six plays later, Rebels running back Jordan Wilkins scored on a one-yard run. Mississippi's second score followed a fumbled kickoff by Alabama's Kenyan Drake. Quarterback Chad Kelly took it in from four yards out, and the Rebels led, 17–3. With 1:03 remaining in the half, Jake Coker topped off a 75-yard drive by hitting Richard Mullaney on a nine-yard touchdown pass. The half ended with Mississippi up, 17–10.

The third quarter belonged to Ole Miss. Chad Kelly threw a 66-yard deflected pass for a touchdown to Quincy Adeboyejo, ending a five-play 87-yard drive with only 2:07 gone in the period. Wunderlich then connected on 34- and 45-yard field goals to give the Rebels a commanding 30–10 lead. Alabama scored with 1:33 left in the quarter when Coker ran the ball in from the 3-yard line.

Behind 30–17 starting the fourth period, Coker passed eight yards to Stewart, cutting the Ole Miss lead to six points. But Kelly threw two touchdown passes, a 73-yarder to Cody Core and a 24-yarder to Laquon Treadwell, less than two minutes apart. The second score came off an interception of a Coker pass. A two-point attempt failed after the first score, and Ole Miss led, 43–24, with ten minutes remaining.

Henry scored on a two-yard run with 6:36 left in the game. A two-point conversion failed, but the Tide kept possession with a successful on-side kick. Alabama scored two minutes later on a Coker to Mullaney pass and now trailed, 43–37 with 4:33 remaining. Forcing an Ole Miss punt, Alabama still had life with 0:31 left to play, but four incomplete passes ended the game.

Alabama had 29 first downs to Mississippi's 16, led in rushing yards, 215–92, and in total offense, 510–433. The difference was turnovers. Alabama had three passes intercepted to none for Ole Miss, and lost two of two fumbles. The Rebels fumbled once but recovered it, allowing no turnovers in the game. The loss dropped the Tide to #12 in the poll, while Mississippi leap-frogged several teams to take the #3 spot. The AP Top 11 teams were all undefeated.

September 26—Louisiana-Monroe

College football fans as well as the media had all but written off Alabama from national championship consideration. Nick Saban realized that from here on, every game was a true elimination game.[1] Alabama had lost to Mississippi the previous year (2014) and bounced back to play in the national championship semi-final.[2] The upperclassmen held a meeting to remind the team that the Ole Miss loss wasn't necessarily the end of the season. It was déjà vu!

The Louisiana-Monroe Warhawks had upset Alabama, 21–14, in 2007 on the Tide's home field. This year would be much different as the Tide shut out Louisiana-Monroe, 34–0. Jake Coker, now officially the starting quarterback, passed for 158 yards, three touchdowns, and one interception. Calvin Ridley, Mike Nysewander, and ArDarius Stewart each had a touchdown reception. Derrick Henry, seeing limited action after an illness, rushed for 52 yards and a touchdown. Kicker Adam Griffith, who had been struggling recently, connected on field goals of 40 and 35 yards.

The Alabama offense had averaged 512 yard in the first three games. However, this week it produced only 303 yards. The Tide's defense, allowing an average of 325 yards per game, held the Warhawks to 92 total yards, including nine yards rushing. They sacked the quarterback six times and intercepted two passes.

Despite the win, Alabama moved down to #13. All top 12 ranked teams remained undefeated. The top five were: Ohio State, Michigan State, Mississippi, TCU, and Baylor.

October 3 at #8 Georgia

A steady rain, and at times a heavy downpour, lasted throughout the game.

Late in the first quarter, Adam Griffith put Alabama ahead, 3–0, on a 29-yard field goal. Early in the second period, the Bulldogs' Marshall Morgan tied the score with a 27-yard field goal. But Alabama scored three touchdowns in the last half of the quarter: Derrick Henry ran one in from 30 yards out, freshman defensive back Minkah Fitzpatrick blocked a Georgia punt and ran it back for a touchdown, and freshman wide receiver Calvin Ridley hauled in a Jake Coker 45-yard touchdown. At the half, Alabama led, 24–3.

Two minutes into the third period, Alabama safety Eddie Jackson intercepted a pass and ran 50 yards for a touchdown. Three minutes later, Coker scored on a two-yard run to put the lead at 38–3. With five seconds left in the third period, Georgia's outstanding sophomore running back Nick Chubb, who had gained 1547 rushing yards as a freshman, broke free for an 83-yard touchdown. There was no scoring in the fourth quarter, and Alabama won, 38–10.

Coker completed 11 of 16 passes for 190 yards and a touchdown. Henry ran the ball 26 times for 148 yards and a touchdown. The Alabama offense totaled 379 yards and held the ball eight minutes longer than Georgia. They also fumbled the ball twice and lost both. The Tide's defense allowed Georgia 299 yards of offense. They forced four fumbles, recovering one, and intercepted three passes. As a result of that game, Alabama rose from #13 to #8, while Georgia tumbled to #19 (from #8). The top five were: Ohio State, TCU, Baylor, Michigan State, and Utah. Except for Alabama, the top 10 teams remained undefeated.

October 10—Arkansas

The Arkansas Razorbacks were ranked #18 in the pre-season but quickly fell from the polls following a 16–12 loss to Toledo. Their record was 2–3 when they traveled to Alabama, but the Tide remembered barely winning a 14–13 victory the year before. They weren't about to take the visitors lightly. Adam Griffith made a 24-yard field goal to put Alabama up, 3–0 in the first quarter. In the second period, a Jake Coker interception set up a Razorbacks touchdown on a pass from Brandon Allen to Drew Morgan with 1:29 remaining. The half ended with Arkansas ahead, 7–3.

With 1:39 remaining in the third quarter, Alabama retook the lead, 10–7, on an 81-yard pass from Coker to Calvin Ridley. An early-fourth quarter Coker to Richard Mullaney three-yard touchdown pass ended a seven-play drive and increased the Tide's lead to 17–7. Griffith connected on a 35-yard field goal, and the lead was now 13 points with 10 minutes to play. At 2:44 remaining on the clock, Derrick Henry rushed for a one-yard touchdown and a 27–7 lead. Allen threw for his second touchdown, a 54-yard strike to Dominique Reed, with a minute and a half remaining. The final score was Alabama 27, Arkansas 14.

The Alabama defense allowed the Razorbacks just 44 rushing yards, 220 total yards, and 10 first downs. The offense compiled 396 yards: 262 passing and 134 rushing. Henry carried 27 times for 95 hard-fought yards. Despite the win, Alabama dropped two rankings to #10. Ohio State remained at #1, followed by Baylor, TCU, Utah, and Clemson. All top 10 teams except Alabama remained undefeated halfway through the season.

October 17 at #9 Texas A&M

Midway through the first quarter, defensive back Minkah Fitzpatrick intercepted Aggies quarterback Kyle Allen's pass and returned the ball 33 yards for a touchdown. At 5:26 in the period, Derrick Henry ran through Texas A&M defenders for a 55-yard touchdown. The Aggies got on the board with a 54-yard field goal by Taylor Bertolet, and the quarter ended, Alabama 14, Texas A&M 3.

Nine seconds into the second period, Henry scored his second touchdown of the game on a six-yard run. Bertolet kicked a 52-yard field goal, and the Tide's advantage was 21–6. Alabama's junior defensive back, Eddie Jackson, intercepted a pass deep in his own territory and ran 93 yards for a touchdown with 6:28 remaining in the half. Three minutes later, A&M's Christian Kirk returned an Alabama punt 68 yards for a touchdown. The Tide went to the half up, 28–13.

Four minutes into the third period, Allen threw a three-yard touchdown pass to Ricky Seals-Jones that cut Alabama's lead to 28–20. Griffith kicked two field goals, a 32-yarder at 3:04 in the third quarter and a 20-yarder with 11:17 remaining in the fourth.

Bertolet made a 36-yard field goal that ended the A&M scoring. With a little over five minutes left in the game, Fitzpatrick, who opened the scoring with an interception return for a touchdown, again intercepted and this time raced 55 yards to score. Alabama won, 41–23.

The Tide defense intercepted Allen four times, three being returned for touchdowns, recorded six sacks, caused two fumbles, and allowed the Aggies only 32 rushing yards. Henry accounted for 236 of 258 total rushing yards and two touchdowns. The offense gained 396 yards as Alabama defeated its second top 10 opponent in the past three games. This win moved the Tide up to #6 in the polls. After the weekly shuffling, the top five were now: Ohio State, Baylor, Utah, TCU, and new arrival LSU. Michigan State (7–0) had dropped throughout October, going from #2 to #7 despite continuing to win.

October 24—Tennessee

The Tennessee Volunteers were ranked #25 in the pre-season poll, ascended to #23 following a 59–30 win against Bowling Green, and then fell from the polls after losing to #19 Oklahoma (the Sooners would finish the season 11–1 and ranked #4). The Volunteers were 3–3 when they played Alabama but would finish the regular season with five straight wins and defeat #12 Northwestern, 45–6, in the Outback Bowl.

Alabama moved the ball 75 yards in nine plays, with Derrick Henry scoring from 20 yards out to put the Tide up, 7–0, midway through the first quarter. Tennessee countered with its own 75-yard, 10-play drive capped by a Josh Dobbs to Josh Smith 11-yard touchdown pass. There was no scoring in the second period, and at the half the score remained 7–7.

After the opening kickoff of the third quarter, Alabama took six minutes on a 12-play, 73-yard drive that stalled on the Tennessee 2-yard line. Adam Griffith kicked a 19-yard field goal, putting the Tide ahead, 10–7. Griffith added a 28-yard field goal at 7:08 in the fourth period, extending the lead to 13–7. Tennessee answered with a four-play, 75-yard drive and a 12-yard touchdown run by running back Jalen Hurd. With 5:49 to play, Alabama found itself down by a point and the season's aspirations evaporating. Putting together a 71-yard drive, Henry scored his second touchdown of the game on a 14-yard run with 2:24 remaining. Linebacker Ryan Anderson caused Dobbs to fumble, and defensive tackle A'Shawn Robinson recovered the ball. Alabama won another hard-fought game, 19–14.

Tennessee outrushed the Tide, 132–117, while Alabama passed for 247 yards to 171 for the Volunteers. Total offense favored Alabama by 364 yards to 303. Derrick Henry gained 143 yards in 28 carries. ArDarius Stewart picked up 114 yards on six pass receptions. Both Texas A&M and Tennessee had bye weeks immediately before playing Alabama. In these two hard contests, Alabama played through fatigue. They would now have a bye week of their own before hosting #4 LSU.[3]

The win against Tennessee moved the Tide to #7. The jockeying of teams in the top five stabilized over the next two weeks with: Ohio State remaining at #1, Baylor #2, Clemson #3, LSU #4, and TCU #5.

The first CFP rankings were announced on November 3: #1 Clemson, #2 LSU, #3 Ohio State, #4 Alabama. The Crimson Tide had recovered from the Mississippi loss to be considered #4 by the CFP, the only ranking that really mattered.

November 7—#4 LSU

LSU was 7–0, and with the leading Heisman Trophy candidate in Leonard Fournette (1,352 yards, averaging 7.7 yards per carry), it was feared that the Tigers were a serious hurdle in the road to the national title.

A defensive struggle provided no scoring in the first quarter of play. Four minutes into the second period, Adam Griffith connected on a 22-yard field goal. Two minutes later, Derrick Henry punched in a two-yard touchdown, and the Tide led, 10–0.

LSU quarterback Brandon Harris hit Travin Dural for a 40-yard touchdown, and four minutes later, Tigers kicker Trent Domingue made a 39-yard field goal to tie the game. With only 14 seconds until the half, Griffiths hit a 55-yard field goal, putting Alabama back in the lead, 13–10.

On the first play of the third quarter, Alabama linebacker Dillon Lee intercepted a Harris pass deep in LSU territory. Four plays later, Henry scored from the 1-yard line, and the Alabama lead was now 10 points. Later in the third quarter, Henry scored another touchdown on a seven-yard run. Griffith added a 29-yard field goal two minutes into the fourth period, and the Tide had a comfortable 30–10 lead. Fournette scored on a one-yard run with 9:18 remaining, the extra point attempt was blocked, and the final score read Alabama 30, LSU 16.

Alabama's defense held Fournette to just 31 yards and one touchdown in 19 rushing attempts. Henry amassed 210 yards and three touchdowns in 38 rushes, and the tables had now turned in the race for the Heisman Trophy. Alabama's defense effectively shut down the LSU offense that had averaged 38.9 points per game.

	LSU	*Alabama*
Total yards	182	434
Rushing yards	54	250
Passing yards	128	184
First downs	12	28
Time of possession	20:33	39:27

The win propelled Alabama to #3 in the AP poll and #2 in the CFP ranking. The AP top five: Clemson, Ohio State, Alabama, Baylor, Oklahoma State. The CFP ranking: Clemson, Alabama, Ohio State, Notre Dame.

November 14 at #20 Mississippi State

The first quarter was scoreless, and the game looked to be another defensive struggle. At 10:44 in the second period, Alabama senior defensive back Cyrus Jones returned a Mississippi State punt 69 yards for a touchdown.

Two minutes later, a Jake Coker to Calvin Ridley 60-yard touchdown pass put the Tide up, 14–0. The Bulldogs managed three points on a Westin Graves field goal. Following the kickoff, Alabama's Derrick Henry ran 74 yards for a touchdown and a 21–3 halftime lead.

The teams exchanged field goals in the third period: Adam Griffith hit from 42 yards, and Graves made a 39-yarder for his second of the game. Midway through the fourth period, Henry rushed 65 yards for the game's final score and a 31–6 Alabama win.

Mississippi State outgained the Tide, 393 yards to 379. Most of the Bulldogs' offense came from star quarterback Dak Prescott, who had 304 yards despite being sacked nine times. Henry rushed for 204 yards on 22 rushes with two touchdowns. Alabama's rush defense continued to shine. They allowed the Bulldogs a net 89 rushing yards. There was also bad news as senior running back Kenyon Drake suffered a broken arm.

The AP Top five: Clemson, Ohio State, Alabama, Oklahoma State, Notre Dame. The CFP ranking remained the same: Clemson, Alabama, Ohio State, Notre Dame.

November 21—Charleston Southern

The Charleston Southern Buccaneers are a member of the NCAA Division 1 Football Championship Subdivision or FCS. They are in a lower division and not part of the FCP. That they were still a good team (9–1, averaging 29.4 points per game) that Alabama needed to take seriously was a point Coach Nick Saban stressed throughout the week. The game unfolded as almost everyone expected. Alabama scored 28 points in the first quarter and 21 in the second for a 49–0 halftime lead.

Derrick Henry, who scored twice in the first period on runs of 17 and two yards, sat out the second half, as did most starters. Cyrus Jones returned a punt 43 yards for a touchdown in the first quarter and another punt 72 yards for a score in the second period. Jake Coker threw for two touchdowns: a 21-yard strike to Richard Mullaney and a 30-yarder to Calvin Ridley. The Buccaneers avoided a shutout on a Kyle Copeland three-yard touchdown run early in the fourth quarter. A two-point conversion try failed, and the Tide won, 56–6.

Charleston Southern managed 85 yards rushing and 134 total yards. The Buccaneers had the edge in time of possession, 31:18 to 28:42, but managed only eight first downs.

Following a loss by CFP #3 Ohio State to CFP #9 Michigan State (17–14) the CFP ranking was: Clemson, Alabama, Oklahoma, Notre Dame.

November 28 at Auburn

The Auburn Tigers were having an off-year. They were 6–5 as they hosted Alabama for the traditional Iron Bowl. Still, the Tide couldn't take the Tigers lightly. Memories of the 2013 "Kick 6" lingered.[4] In that game, with one second on the clock and the score knotted at 28–28, Adam Griffith's 57-yard field goal attempt was short. Auburn's Chris Davis fielded the kick and returned it 109 yards for a touchdown, defeating the #1 Crimson Tide. This year would be different.

The first half was a battle of field goals. Alabama's Adam Griffith kicked one in the first quarter (26 yards) and three3 in the second quarter (40, 26, and 50 yards). Auburn's Daniel Carlson made two in the first quarter (24 and 44 yards). At the half, Alabama led, 12–6.

Ten minutes into the third period, Jake Coker hit ArDarius Stewart for a 34-yard touchdown. Auburn answered on their next possession when Jeremy Johnson connected with Jason Smith for a 77-yard score to cut the Alabama lead to 19–13. Alabama scored twice in the fourth quarter: Griffith made his fifth field goal of the game, a 47-yarder, and Derrick Henry ran for a 25-yard touchdown with 0:26 left. The Iron Bowl ended Alabama 29, Auburn 13. Henry had carried 46 times for 271 rushing yards giving him 1,797 for the season—an Alabama single-season record with at least one more game to play.

Once more, the Alabama defense was superb:

	Auburn	*Alabama*
Total yards	260	465
Rushing yards	91	286
Passing yards	169	179
First downs	12	24
Time of possession	24:37	35:23

In the CFP, #4 Notre Dame suffered its second loss of the season to #9 Stanford. The CFP ranking was now: Clemson, Alabama, Oklahoma, Iowa. Alabama would face AP & CFP #18 Florida for the SEC Championship.

December 5—SEC Championship—#18 Florida

The Florida Gators were coached by Jim McElwain, who had served as Alabama's offensive coordinator from 2008–2011 under Nick Saban. The unranked Gators won four straight games and entered the AP poll at #25 before their game with #3 Mississippi. The convincing 38–10 win propelled them to #11. They defeated Missouri and were ranked #8 before a 35–28 loss to #6 LSU. Florida then won another four straight and again ranked #8 before a devastating 27–2 loss to #14 Florida State the week before playing Alabama for the SEC Championship.

A blocked Florida punt at 9:05 in the first quarter led to a safety. Alabama's special teams blocked a field goal attempt, and the quarter ended, 2–0. The Gators' Antonio Callaway returned an Alabama punt 85 yards for a touchdown early in the second period for a 7–2 Florida lead. Adam Griffith kicked a 28-yard field goal that cut the Gators' lead to 7–5. With under three minutes until the half, Derrick Henry ran in a two-yard touchdown, and the Tide was back on top, 12–7.

Alabama opened the third quarter with a seven-minute, 65-yard drive and a 30-yard field goal by Griffith. Late in the third period, Jake Coker hit ArDarius Stewart for a 32-yard touchdown to end an 81-yard, 10-play drive that ate up almost five minutes. Florida had possession for only 1:05 of the quarter. Alabama was ahead by 15 points entering the fourth quarter. Halfway through the period, Coker found Richard Mullaney for a nine-yard touchdown to put the Tide ahead, 29–7. With just over five minutes remaining, Gators quarterback Treon Harris hit C. J. Worton for a 46-yard touchdown. Harris ran in a two-point conversion to make the final score Alabama 29, Florida 15. Alabama totally dominated the game:

	Florida	Alabama
Total yards	180	437
Rushing yards	15	233
Passing yards	165	204
First downs	7	25
Time of possession	16:31	43:29

Derrick Henry gained 189 yards in 44 rushes to strengthen his case for the Heisman Trophy. Henry compiled 1,986 yards, setting a new single-season SEC record.

The stage was now set for the CFP. Clemson (13–0) at #1 would face #4 Oklahoma (11–1), while #2 Alabama (12–1) would play #3 Michigan State (12–1) on December 31.

There were distractions before the semi-final game. On December 10, Derrick Henry picked up the Maxwell Award, the Walter Camp Award, and the Doak Walker Award at the College Football Awards presentation held at the College Football Hall of Fame in Atlanta. At that ceremony, Alabama center Ryan Kelly received the Rimington Trophy. Two days later, Henry was in New York City as one of three finalists for the Heisman Trophy. The other two were Clemson sophomore quarterback Deshaun Watson and Stanford sophomore running back Christian McCaffrey. Henry won the Trophy with a score of 1,832 to 1,539 for McCaffrey and 1,165 for Watson. He collected 378 first place votes to McCaffrey's 290 and Watson's 148.

In mid–December, Alabama's offense line was awarded the first-ever Joe Moore Award as the best offensive line in college football.

December 31 Cotton Bowl—#3 Michigan State

National Semifinal

Michigan State came in determined to stop Derrick Henry and the Alabama rushing game. To an extent they did, as Henry only gained 75 yards in 20 carries and the Alabama offense picked up just 154 yards on the ground. However, the Crimson Tide showed it had weapons other than Henry. Running back Kenyan Drake returned from the injury he sustained on November 14 to gain 60 yards on four carries. Freshman Calvin Ridley caught eight passes for 138 yards and two touchdowns as Alabama outgained Michigan State, 440 yards to 239. Jake Coker completed 20 of 25 passes for 286 yards and two touchdowns to Calvin Ridley, Cyrus Jones returned a punt 57 yards for a touchdown, Adam Griffith kicked a 47-yard field goal, and Henry did score twice on runs of one and 11 yards.

The Alabama defense sacked Spartans quarterback Connor Cook four times and intercepted two passes while allowing only 19 completions in 39 attempts for 210 yards. They also negated the Michigan State rushing game as the Spartans ran the ball 26 times for a net 29 yards. The final score read: Alabama 38, Michigan State 0.

In the other semi-final game played that day, the #1 Clemson Tigers defeated the #4 Oklahoma Sooners, 37–17, in the Orange Bowl. Like Alabama, the Tigers' rush defense allowed Oklahoma a net 67 yards on 33 rushes.

January 11—National Championship—#1 Clemson

At University of Phoenix

Clemson coach William "Dabo" Swinney played on Alabama's consensus national championship team of 1992.[5] That team went 13-0, was ranked #2, and defeated #1 Miami (FL), 34-13, in the Sugar Bowl. Alabama was an underdog going into that Sugar Bowl and, although ranked #1, Clemson was considered the underdog now. This would be a national championship game that lived up to the hype.

Halfway through the first quarter, Derrick Henry rumbled through Clemson defenders for a 50-yard touchdown. At 5:18 in the first period, Clemson quarterback Deshaun Watson connected with wide receiver Hunter Renfrow on a 31-yard touchdown pass. The same duo scored again on an 11-yard pass as time ran out in the quarter for a 14-7 Clemson lead. Henry scored from the one-yard line for the only points in the second quarter, and the half ended tied at 14-14.

Two minutes into the third period, Jake Coker hit O. J. Howard on a 53-yard touchdown pass for a 21-14 Alabama advantage. Clemson scored twice, on a Greg Huegel 37-yard field goal and a Wayne Gallman one-yard touchdown run, to take a 24-21 lead into a wild fourth quarter.

At 10:34 on the clock, Adam Griffith's 33-yard field tied the game at 24-24. Alabama tried an onside kick. The Tide noticed that Clemson tended to shift slightly to one side, anticipating a deep kick near the corner. They also noticed how this left a gap on the other side and had practiced kicking for this scenario. Freshman defensive back Marlon Humphrey caught the ball at midfield for a successful onside kick. On the second play from scrimmage, Coker hit O. J. Howard on a 51-yard touchdown for a 31-24 edge. A Huegel field goal cut the Alabama lead to four points.

Two minutes later, Huegel hit his second field goal, this time from 31 yards away, to narrow Alabama's lead to 31-27. Kenyan Drake took the Clemson kickoff 95 yards for a touchdown, and the Tide was feeling more comfortable up by 11 points with 7:31 to play. Three minutes later, Watson connected with Artavis Scott on a 15-yard touchdown pass. A two-point conversion failed, but Clemson had cut the Tide's lead to five points.

Alabama took 3:33 off the clock driving 75 yards in eight plays with Derrick Henry scoring on a one-yard run. Alabama now led, 45-33, with only 1:07 remaining. Watson engineered a six-play, 68-yard drive culminating in a 24-yard touchdown pass to Jordan Leggett. With 12 seconds remaining and the score Alabama 45, Clemson 40, the Tigers attempted an onside kick. ArDarius Stewart fielded the ball for the Tide, and a classic championship game ended.

Alabama's junior tight end, O. J. Howard, with five receptions for 208 yards and two touchdowns, was named the game's MVP on offense. The Tide's junior defensive back, Eddie Jackson, was named the defensive MVP. Jackson's second quarter interception thwarted a Clemson drive. Derrick Henry carried the ball 36 times for 158 yards and three touchdowns. He finished the season with 2,219 yards and 28 touchdowns, setting both Alabama and SEC single-season records. Clemson's Deshaun Watson completed 30 of 47 passes for 405 yards and four touchdowns, and he rushed for 73 yards. He was intercepted once. Despite losing, the Tigers' statistics were impressive:

	Clemson	Alabama
Total yards	550	473
Rushing yards	145	138
Passing yards	405	335
First downs	31	18
Time of possession	29:29	30:31

Post Season

Alabama's defense led the nation rushing defense, allowing only 74 yards per game, and were third in scoring defense (14.2 points per game). They were 17th in pass defense (184.2 yards per game).

Nick Saban picked up his fifth national championship and his second unanimous title. He would pick up two more: a non-consensus shared championship in 2016 and a consensus championship in 2017.

Alabama, despite the early loss to Mississippi, beat the top competition while other contenders fell late in the season or in the playoffs. The Tide had defeated nine teams that were ranked at the time, the most of a national championship team.[6] The newly formed CFP was now 2–0 in selecting a unanimous champion; however, the next two years would be different.

Chapter 22

Clemson 2018

The Clemson Tigers were crowned consensus national champions in 1981, a title they had to share with five other teams.[1] That was their only selection as a national champion up to the beginning of the College Football Playoff in 2014. Beginning with the 2015 season, the Tigers have been in the CFP every year.

	Season	Result
2015	Lost to Alabama in final.	
2016	Beat Alabama in final.	Consensus champion.
2017	Lost to Alabama in semifinal.	
2018	Would beat Alabama in final.	Unanimous champion.

Clemson also made the CFP Final in 2019, losing to LSU.

With so much success to build on, with many returning lettermen, and with starting the season at #2 (behind #1 Alabama) in the AP pre-season poll, expectations were high.

Furman

Clemson opened at home to face the Furman Paladins. The on-line dictionary (are there any others now?) defines a paladin as a medieval champion, not Richard Boone as an Old West champion for hire. Clemson scored 10 points in the first quarter, 17 in the second, 14 in the third, and seven in the fourth. Freshman quarterback Trevor Lawrence had three touchdown passes, Kelly Bryant threw for one and ran for one, Travis Etienne ran for one touchdown, and Greg Huegel kicked two field goals. With 1:18 remaining in the game, Furman got on the board with a 16-yard pass from Darren Grainger to Ryan DeLuca as Clemson won, 48–7.

Texas A&M

The Texas A&M Aggies would finish the season at 9–4, with two of the losses coming to #1 Alabama and #2 Clemson. On November 24, the Aggies would play a marathon seven-overtime game, beating #8 LSU, 74–72. At #21, they would win the Gator Bowl over unranked North Carolina State, 52–13. On this day, they gave the Clemson Tigers the closest game of their championship season.

The Aggies scored first on a 40-yard field goal by Dan LaCamera. Three minutes later, Clemson took the lead, 7–3, on a Kelly Bryant one-yard run. Early in the second period, Trevor Lawrence passed for a 64-yard touchdown to Tee Higgins, and the Tigers led at the half, 14–3.

In the third quarter, LaCamera kicked another 40-yard field goal, cutting Clemson's lead to eight points. Bryant passed eight yards to Diondre Overton, and the Tigers' lead was again 15 points. Still in the third period, Aggies Kellen Mond and Kendrick Rogers connected on a nine-yard touchdown. With a minute remaining, Travis Etienne scored on a one-yard run, and Clemson took a 28–13 lead into the final quarter. A minute into the fourth period, Mond threw to Quartney Davis for a 14-yard touchdown. The Clemson lead remained eight points until 46 seconds remained in the contest. Mond again found Rogers on a 24-yard touchdown. An A&M two-point conversion pass was intercepted by safety K'Von Wallace, and the Tigers' Hunter Renfrow recovered the ensuing onside kick to secure Clemson's 28–26 win.[2] Texas A&M had more first downs (25–14) and more total yards (510–413). They also had two turnovers to none for the Tigers.

Georgia Southern

Sandwiched between what would be the Tigers' two closest games were games with two teams from Georgia. The first was Georgia Southern of the Sun Belt Conference. The Eagles would end the season at 10–3, including a Camellia Bowl win over East Michigan, 23–21.

Travis Etienne and Tavien Feaster each had first half one-yard rushing touchdowns, Trevor Lawrence and Justyn Ross connected on a 57-yard score, and Greg Huegel kicked a 37-yard field goal before the Eagles' Shai Werts put points on the board early in the fourth quarter. Etienne and Adam Choice each scored a touchdown in the last six minutes of the game for a 38–7 Clemson win.

The game statistics reflect the outcome:

	Ga. Southern	*Clemson*
Rushing yards	80	309
Passing yards	60	286
Total yards	140	595
First downs	7	27
Turnovers	1	3

Georgia Tech

Tech was the other Georgia team between the Tigers' two closest contests. Ending the season at 6–6, the Yellow Jackets qualified for a minor bowl game and would play (and lose, 34–10) to 6–6 Minnesota.

The Tigers' Clelin Ferrell returned a Tech fumble one yard for a touchdown late in the first quarter. The second period began with two touchdown passes by Trevor

Lawrence, a 17-yarder to Hunter Renfrow and a 53-yarder to Justyn Ross. Clemson was up, 21–0, before the Yellow Jackets' TaQuon Marshall scored on an 11-yard run. With five seconds until halftime, Lawrence hit Travis Etienne on a three-yard touchdown to lead, 28–7.

Etienne scored on touchdown runs of 27 and three yards in the third period. Tech scored on a Nate Cottrell two-yard run. At the end of three quarters, Clemson was on top, 42–14. Georgia Tech scored on a Tobias Oliver to Clinton Lynch five-yard pass, and Lawrence threw to Tee Higgins for a 30-yard touchdown. The Tigers won, 49–21. Clemson outgained Georgia Tech, 480 yards to 203. Etienne rushed 11 times for 122 yards. The Yellow Jackets hurt themselves with eight fumbles, losing one.

The top four teams in the AP were: #1 Alabama, #2 Clemson, #3 Georgia, and #4 Ohio State.

Syracuse

The Syracuse Orange were 4–0, outscoring those opponents 198–80, or 49.5 to 20 points per game. They featured senior Eric Dungey, an above-average, but oft-injured quarterback. They also had the kicking services of freshman Andre Szmyt, who would win the Lou Groza Award in 2018.

Szmyt kicked 35- and 51-yard field goals for the Orange to take the early lead, 6–0. With less than a minute left in the first period, Travis Etienne scored on a one-yard run to put the Tigers up, 7–6. Halfway through the second period, Eric Dungey scored on a one-yard run, and Szmyt hit his third field goal with 24 seconds remaining. Syracuse went to the half ahead, 16–7.

Clemson kicker Greg Huegel made 43- and 37-yard field goals late in the third quarter, and the Tigers trailed, 16–13. Two minutes into the final period, Dungey again scored on a one-yard run to put Syracuse ahead by 10 points. Two minutes later, Etienne scored on a 26-yard touchdown run, closing the gap to three points, 23–20.

Redshirt freshman Chase Brice had replaced Trevor Lawrence after the starter was injured in the second quarter.[3] With time running out, Brice engineered a 13-play, 94-yard drive, and with only 41 seconds to play, Etienne ran in a two-yard score. The Tigers won their second close game, 27–23, and the only one where they had to come from behind with under a minute to play.

A look at the game statistics doesn't indicate a close, come-from-behind contest:

	Syracuse	*Clemson*
Rushing yards	61	293
Passing yards	250	176
Total yards	311	469
First downs	12	28
Turnovers	1	3

The game would appear to be fairly one-sided until you get to the turnovers. Clemson lost two of three fumbles. Trevor Lawrence and Dungey each had an interception.

Etienne carried 27 times for 203 yards. Tigers linebacker Kendall Joseph recorded 12 tackles, including eight solo.

Syracuse would finish the season at 10–3, ranked #17, and defeat #15 West Virginia in the Camping World Bowl. The Tigers lost some respect in the AP poll, dropping from #2 to #4. Alabama remained on top, followed by #2 Georgia, #3 Ohio State, #4 Clemson, and #5 Oklahoma.

Wake Forest

Clemson gained 698 yards on offense to 249 for the Demon Deacons. Travis Etienne rushed for 167 yards in 10 carries and scored three rushing touchdowns. Lyn-J Dixon ran for two scores and Adam Choice for one. Trevor Lawrence threw for two touchdowns and backup Chase Brice for one. Wake Forest averted a shutout with a Nick Sciba field goal in the middle of the third quarter. Clemson again won handily, 63–3.

The top four of the AP didn't change. The Tigers now had a bye week.

#16 North Carolina State

Unranked in the pre-season, the North Carolina State Wolfpack entered the poll at #19 after defeating five unranked teams by a total of 165–84. This was Clemson's first ranked opponent and first opportunity to prove they deserved a top five ranking. Again this week, Clemson scored first and built a good lead, this time 31–0, before allowing a score. To that point in the game, Travis Etienne had scored three touchdowns on short runs, Tee Higgins had a 46-yard touchdown reception from Trevor Lawrence, and Greg Huegel kicked a 28-yard field goal. Reggie Gallaspy ran for an 11-yard touchdown early in the fourth period to put NC State on the board, but down 31–7. Huegel kicked a 27-yard field goal, and Lyn-J Dixon ran for a two-yard score to end the game 41–7.

With Georgia and Ohio State losing, Clemson was back at #2, followed by Notre Dame, 8–0, and LSU, 7–1.

Florida State

It was becoming "standard operating procedure" that Clemson score early, score often, and build a big lead before opponents could get on the board against the Tigers' reserves. This game would continue that trend. This season, the Seminoles were not the powerhouse program of a few years back. Playing five ranked teams and losing to four, they would also lose to unranked Syracuse (30–7) and North Carolina State (47–28).

Into the middle of the third quarter, Clemson had scored 45 unanswered points before Florida State kicked a field goal. The Tigers scored twice more and the Seminoles once for a final score of 59–10. The Seminoles were also hit with 16 penalties for over 130 yards, fumbled four times, and were tackled for a loss on 14 plays.[4]

	Fl. State	Clemson
Rushing yards	21	120
Passing yards	268	404
Total yards	289	524
First downs	14	25
Turnovers	2	1

The top four AP ranked teams remained the same. The first CFP Ranking was out: Alabama #1, Clemson #2, Notre Dame #3, and LSU #4.

Halfway through the season:

#1 Alabama, 8–0, had outscored opponents, 433–127.
#2 Clemson, 8–0, had outscored opponents, 353–104.

The teams had 1 one common opponent, Texas A&M. The Aggies were unrated when Clemson beat them, 28–26, in an away game. A&M was rated #22 when Alabama won, 45–23, at home. Up to now, each team had played one ranked team.

Louisville

The pattern of previous games was only slightly altered. Clemson scored two touchdowns within the first three minutes, but Louisville would get a field goal later in the first quarter. From there, the Tigers' juggernaut made the score 63–3 into the last minute of the third period. Louisville scored when Hassan Hall returned a kickoff 93 yards. The PAT was missed, and the lead was now 63–9. The Tigers scored two more touchdowns and the Cardinals once for a final score of 77–16.

	Louisville	Clemson
Rushing yards	81	492
Passing yards	231	169
Total yards	312	661
First downs	16	28
Turnovers	3	2

Travis Etienne gained 153 rushing yards on only eight carries. Lyn-J Dixon had 116 yards in four carries, and Tavien Feaster rushed six times for 101 yards. Tigers rushers averaged 11.6 yards per carry, setting a new school record.[5] Backup quarterback Chase Brice passed for 110 yards and three touchdowns. Trevor Lawrence chipped in 59 yards, two scores, and one interception.

The CFP Ranking: Alabama #1, Clemson #2, Notre Dame #3, and Michigan #4, replacing LSU after the Baton Rouge Tigers lost.

Chapter 22. Clemson 2018

#17 Boston College

The BC Eagles were 7–2 when they hosted Clemson. The Tigers scored first on a 30-yard Greg Huegel field goal. Boston College's Michael Walker returned a punt 74 yards to take the lead with 2:13 left in the first quarter. Clemson retook the lead on a Trevor Lawrence to Milan Richard two-yard pass four minutes later. At the end of one quarter, Clemson led, 10–7. Huegel kicked a 23-yard field goal for a 13–7 halftime edge.

The Tigers scored a touchdown in each of the last two quarters, Lawrence ran six yards for the first, and Amari Rodgers returned a punt 58 yards for the second, making the final score 27–7. Lawrence was 29 of 40 passing for 295 yards, one touchdown, and one interception. Travis Etienne carried 11 times for 78 rushing yards. A look at the game statistics shows the Tigers' dominance, yet again.

	BC	Clemson
Rushing yards	9	129
Passing yards	104	295
Total yards	113	424
First downs	8	19

Over the first 10 games of the season, Clemson's offense had varied, responding to the defense. Some weeks it was very balanced, and other weeks skewed to one attack or the other.

Team	Rushing yards	Passing yards
Furman	266	277
Texas A&M	115	298
Ga. Southern	309	286
Georgia Tech	248	232
Syracuse	293	176
Wake Forest	471	227
NC State	91	380
Florida State	120	404
Louisville	492	169
Boston College	129	295

The top four AP and CFP team rankings did not change.

Duke

For the second week in a row, an opponent took an early lead and could then score no more. Two Collin Wareharn field goals late in the first quarter put the Blue Devils up,

6–0. Tavien Feaster ran in a two-yard touchdown early in the second period. With 1:16 until the half, Trevor Lawrence found Justyn Ross for a 19-yard score. At the half, it was Clemson 14, Duke 6.

The third quarter saw two Travis Etienne touchdown runs of 27 and 29 yards. Lawrence passed 10 yards to T. J. Chase for the final score and a 35–6 Tigers win. This week provided a balanced Clemson attack with 208 yards rushing and 251 passing. Lawrence completed 21 of 38 passes for 251 yards and two touchdowns. Etienne gained 81 yards on nine rushes. The CFP top four remained the same.

South Carolina

Through the regular season, the South Carolina Gamecocks played teams ranked, at the time, #s 3 (Georgia), 17 (Kentucky), 22 (Texas A&M), 19 (Florida), and 2 (Clemson). They would lose them all.

The Gamecocks scored first on a Jake Bentley to Deebo Samuel nine-yard touchdown pass. The Tigers responded with two touchdowns before the first quarter ended, an Adam Choice one-yard run and then a Trevor Lawrence to Tee Higgins 22-yard pass. The Tigers and Gamecocks would alternate two touchdowns apiece in the second period: Christian Wilkins' one-yard run for Clemson, a Bentley to Kiel Pollard 67-yard pass, a two-yard run by Choice, and a Bentley to Samuel 75-yard pass. At the half, Clemson was up, 28–21.

The third quarter saw two Tigers rushing touchdowns, a Travis Etienne two-yard run and Tavien Feaster 13-yarder. The Tigers led, 42–21. To start the fourth quarter, Choice scored his third rushing touchdown from 15 yards out. South Carolina answered with two touchdown passes by Bentley. The first was 32 yards to Samuel, the second a 20-yarder to Shi Smith. With 39 seconds remaining, Etienne scored from seven yards away to make the final score Clemson 56, South Carolina 35. That was the most points scored on the Tigers that season. Both offenses were in full swing:

	S. Carolina	Clemson
Rushing yards	90	351
Passing yards	510	393
Total yards	600	744
First downs	29	38

Lawrence completed 27 of 36 passes for 393 yards and one touchdown. Bentley completed 32 of 50 for 510 yards, five touchdowns, and one interception. Etienne rushed 28 times for 150 yards and two scores.

After a loss by Michigan, Georgia retook the #4 spot. The CFP ranking was: #1 Alabama (12-0), #2 Clemson (12-0), #3 Notre Dame (12-0), #4 Georgia (11-1), and #5 Oklahoma (11-1). Notre Dame's season was finished, but the other three would play for their conference championships.

Pittsburgh—ACC Championship Game

Although unranked and with a 7–5 record, the Pitt Panthers had managed to win the games they had to in order to lead the ACC Coastal Division and face Clemson, winners of the Atlantic Division, for the overall title.

Thirteen seconds into the game, Travis Etienne scored on a 75-yard run. Etienne scored again five minutes later on a three-yard run. Pitt's Alex Kessman kicked a 37-yard field goal to end the first quarter at 14–3. The Panthers' Qadree Ollison started the second period on a one-yard touchdown run. After that, it was all Clemson. Tee Higgins rushed for five- and 10-yard touchdowns to end the first half 28–10.

The third quarter was scoreless. In the fourth period, Adam Choice ran for a one-yard touchdown and Lyn-J Dixon for a four-yard score. The Tigers had won the ACC, 42–10. Clemson generated 419 yards of offense to 199 yards for Pitt. After the previous week's offensive performance with 38 first downs, the Tigers were held to 13 and Pitt 11. Lawrence passed for 118 yards and two touchdowns. Etienne rushed 12 times for 156 yards.

In other conference play, #1 Alabama beat #4 Georgia, 35–28, to win the SEC, and Oklahoma won the Big-12, defeating #9 Texas, 39–27. Oklahoma replaced Georgia at #4. Top-seeded Alabama would play Oklahoma, and #2 Clemson would face #3 Notre Dame in the CFP semifinals.

#3 Notre Dame—CFP Semifinal

Cotton Bowl

Ranked #11 in the pre-season AP poll, the Irish had steadily worked their way up to contend for the national title. With Notre Dame the only Independent in the top 25 rankings, some conference champions felt the Irish didn't deserve to play for the title. But now, at 12–0, having defeated four ranked teams #14 (Michigan), #7 (Stanford), #24 (Virginia Tech), and #12 (Syracuse), and having outscoring opponents, 405–207, Notre Dame had a chance for yet another national championship.

The Tigers and Irish exchanged field goals in the first quarter. The second and third quarters were all Clemson. Trevor Lawrence threw three touchdown passes before the half. Justyn Ross caught two scores (52 and 42 yards) and Tee Higgins the third (a 19-yarder). The first PAT failed, but Clemson led, 23–3, at the half. Travis Etienne scored on a 62-yard run late in the third period. The fourth quarter was scoreless. Clemson won, 30–3 to advance to the CFP Championship.

The other semifinal game, held in the Orange Bowl, matched #1 Alabama and #4 Oklahoma. Both teams were high-scoring: Alabama averaged 47.9 points per game and Oklahoma 49.5. The Sooners' offense generated 50 yards per game more, 577.9 to 527.6, but the Tide's defense appeared better, at least on paper. Alabama gave up an average of 14.8 points per game and 295.4 yards per game. Oklahoma's defense allowed an average of 32.4 points and 448.1 yards per game.

Alabama led, 21–0, after the first quarter and 31–10 at the half. The Sooners could get no closer than 11 points, and the game ended Alabama 45, Oklahoma 34.

#1 Alabama—CFP Championship

Levi's Stadium—Santa Clara

A quick look at the statistics for the season shows how even these two teams appeared on paper:

	Alabama	Clemson
Offense yards per game	527.6	528.0
Points per game scored	47.9	44.3
Defense yards allowed per game	295.4	291.5
Points allowed per game	14.8	12.9

Comparing the quarterbacks:

	Clemson	*Alabama*
	Trevor Lawrence	Tua Tagovailoa
Passing yards total	3,280	3,966
Passing percentage	65.2	69.0
Passing touchdowns	30	43
Interceptions	4	6
Rushing Yards Total	177	190
Rushing touchdowns	1	5

The Game

Clemson and Alabama exchanged two touchdowns apiece in the first quarter: an A. J. Terrell interception return of 44 yards for Clemson, a Tua Tagovailoa 62-yard pass to Jerry Jeudy for Alabama, a Travis Etienne 17-yard run, and a Tagovailoa one-yard pass to Hale Hentges (PAT failed). Early in the second quarter, a Joseph Bulovas 25-yard field goal gave Alabama the lead, 16–14. Clemson scored on two Travis Etienne touchdowns, a one-yard run and a five-yard pass reception from Trevor Lawrence. With 45 seconds remaining, Greg Huegel kicked a 36-yard field goal, and Clemson led at the half, 31–16.

In the third quarter, Lawrence and Justyn Ross teamed for a 74-yard score. With only 20 seconds left in the period, Lawrence threw his third touchdown of the game, this a five-yard strike to Tee Higgins. The fourth quarter was scoreless. Clemson had won the CFP Championship, 44–16.

Post Season

Defensive lineman Christian Wilkins was named a unanimous All America. Running back Travis Etienne, offensive tackle Mitch Hyatt, and defensive end Clelin Ferrell were consensus All America selections. Other Clemson players named to some All

America teams but not consensus were: defensive tackle Dexter Lawrence, linebacker Tre Lamar, and defensive back Trayvon Mullen.

Trevor Lawrence won the Archie Griffin Award. Clelin Ferrell won the Ted Hendricks Award. Travis Etienne was seventh in the Heisman Trophy voting.

Why Was Clemson Unanimous?

Even with a playoff system in place, there is no certainty that the CFP Champion will be the choice of all selectors. Opinions and formulas differ and, as in so many seasons, those differences translate into different choices. At the end of the regular season, the AP poll and the CFP agreed on the top four teams. Clemson at #2 had defeated #3 Notre Dame and then #1 Alabama. The Crimson Tide had defeated #4 Oklahoma in the other CFP semi-final game. Further, Clemson was the only undefeated team and the first program to go 15–0 since Penn in 1897.[6]

As has been seen, any of these factors, or in combination, do not guarantee a unanimous champion. Looking down the final rankings, it is difficult to see another possible contender. It should have been an easy choice, and all selectors ultimately agreed.

Chapter 23

LSU 2019

In 1908, LSU became the first school from the Deep South to be selected as a co-national champion. That year they became only the fourth school (after Michigan, Chicago, and Vanderbilt) to break the Eastern hold on a share of the national title.

In 1908, 1935, 1936, and 1962, the Tigers' share of the title was from the vote of a single selector. They were co-champions in 2011 by the choice of two selectors. LSU was also crowned national champions in 1958, 2003, and 2007 by a consensus. Finally, in 2019, on the 150th anniversary of college football, the Tigers would be a Unanimous National Champion.

In 2018, the Tigers were 10–3, beating teams ranked #s 8, 7, 2, 22, and 7, while losing to #22 Florida, #1 Alabama, and #22 Texas A&M. Of 13 games, eight were against top 25 opponents. LSU was ranked #6 in the pre-season for 2019. The team returned senior quarterback Joe Burrow, a transfer from Ohio State, where he saw little action. As a junior, Burrow had mediocre numbers, completing 58 percent of his passes for 2,894 yards and 16 touchdowns, with six interceptions. He also rushed for 399 yards and another seven touchdowns. There was also a host of returning linemen, backs, and receivers. Head Coach Ed Orgeron (see Appendix B, Awards and Coaches), in his third year, had to be confident.

Georgia Southern

Georgia Southern from the Sun Belt Conference averted a shutout with a Tyler Bass 47-yard field goal in the second quarter. LSU scored 21 points in each of the first two quarters, 10 in the third, and three in the fourth in a 55–3 win. Joe Burrow completed 23 of 27 passes for 278 yards and five touchdowns. Terrace Marshall had four receptions, with three going for touchdowns. Justin Jefferson and Ja'Marr Chase each had a touchdown reception. Lanard Fournette and Clyde Edwards-Helaire both had a rushing touchdown, and Cade York connected on both of his field goal attempts.

The game stats show the Tigers' domination:

	Georgia Southern	*LSU*
Rushing yards	74	122
Passing yards	24	350
Total yards	98	472
First downs	8	22
Turnovers	2	0

The Tigers remained at #6 in the rankings.

#9 Texas

Beginning the pre-season ranked #10, the Longhorns moved up one notch to #9 after beating Louisiana Tech, 45–14 in their opener. Texas would drop five games (three to ranked teams) and be out of the polls by regular season's end. Yet they defeated #11 Utah in the Alamo Bowl.

LSU took an early 3–0 lead on a Cade York 36-yard field goal in the first quarter. In the second period, Longhorns quarterback Sam Ehlinger passed 55 yards to Brennan Eagles to take a 7–3 advantage. The Tigers rattled off 17 points on two Joe Burrow to Justin Jefferson passes and a York 33-yard field goal, to lead, 20–7 at the half.

York kicked his third field goal of the game for the Tigers, and Ehlinger scored twice on a two-yard run and a 20-yard touchdown pass to Jake Smith. LSU led, 23–21, at the end of the third period. The fourth quarter was a wild ride. Burrow hit Terrace Marshall for a 26-yard touchdown eight seconds into the period. Three minutes later, Ehlinger passed 44 yards to Devin Duvernay for a touchdown, and the LSU lead was again two points, 30–28. The Tigers answered two minutes later on a Clyde Edwards-Helaire 12-yard touchdown run, and LSU led, 37–28. Texas kicker Cameron Dicker made a 47-yard field goal, and the Longhorns were down by only six points.

Burrow and Jefferson combined for their third touchdown of the game. The 61-yarder made the score LSU 45, Texas 31, after a successful two-point conversion with only 2:27 to play. With only 22 seconds remaining, Ehlinger passed 15 yards to Duvernay for a score. LSU had won a tough game, 45–38.

Burrow was again sensational, completing 31 of 39 passes for 471 yards and four touchdowns. It was the second-most passing yards in a game in school history.[1] He did have one interception. His counterpart, Sam Ehlinger, was 31 of 47 for 401 yards and four touchdowns. Edwards-Helaire ran for 87 of the Tigers' 104 rushing yards and scored their only touchdown on the ground. LSU outgained Texas by 573 yards to 530, while the Longhorns made more first downs, 30–28. The Tigers moved up to #4 in the polls.

Northwestern State

The Northwestern State Demons were also from the state of Louisiana and were affiliated with the Southland Conference. Their 2019 record would be 3–9, and their worst defeat a 65–14 drubbing by LSU.

Cade York scored on a 26-yard field goal midway through the first quarter. With 00:16 remaining in the opening period, Shelton Eppler passed 17 yards to Quan Shorts for a touchdown and a brief 7–3 lead for the Demons over the #4 Tigers. Clyde Edwards-Helaire scored from four yards out, Joe Burrow passed 14 yards to Terrace Marshall, and LSU again had the lead, 17–7. Eppler's 26-yard touchdown pass to David Fitzwater made it 17–14, and the Demons may have been hopeful of an upset. But from that score at 5:38 before the half, the bottom fell out of Northwestern State's chances. Edwards-Helaire scored on a three-yard run, making the score at the half 24–14. The second half was all LSU. The Tigers scored on four touchdown runs, a pass completion, and a 54-yard punt return by Trey Palmer. Burrow left the game after the third quarter, having completed 21 of 24 passes for 373 yards, with two touchdowns passing and one running, and accounting for 403 total yards.

	Northwestern St.	LSU
Rushing yards	46	123
Passing yards	232	488
Total yards	278	611
First downs	15	31

Clemson at #1, Alabama at #2, and Georgia #3 had not changed since the pre-season. LSU remained at #4.

Vanderbilt

In the Tigers' SEC season opener, the Vanderbilt Commodores scored first on a Ke'Shawn Vaughn five-yard run. LSU tied the score a little over a minute later on a Joe Burrow to Justin Jefferson four-yard pass. The Tigers scored three more touchdowns in the first period to lead, 28–7. LSU and Vanderbilt exchanged touchdowns and field goals in the second quarter to make the halftime score 38–17. After the half, the Tigers scored four touchdowns and the Commodores three for a final score of 66–38.

Burrow continued to shine with 25 completions in 34 pass attempts for 398 yards and six touchdowns. He became the first LSU quarterback to pass for over 350 yards in three consecutive games.[2] Chase had 10 receptions good for 229 yards and four touchdowns, a school record for touchdown receptions in an SEC game.[3] Edwards-Helaire picked up 106 yards and one touchdown on 14 rushing attempts. The Tigers gained 599 total yards to 374 for Vanderbilt.

The top four ranked teams remained the same. However, the following week the Tigers had a bye, and Ohio State took over #4 while the Tigers dropped to #5. That same week, Alabama and Clemson switched rankings, and the Tide was now #1.

Utah State

LSU never trailed the Aggies. Joe Burrow hit Derrick Dillon with a seven-yard touchdown early in the first quarter. Utah State kicker Dominik Eberle made field goals of 30 and 47 yards, and the first period ended at 7–6. The remainder of the Tigers' scoring involved Burrow, who ran for a score and threw for four more as LSU won handily 42–6 for its sixth win.

The Aggies managed 168 total yards (28 rushing and 140 passing) to 601 for the Tigers. Burrow was 27 of 38 through the air for 344 yards, five touchdowns, and one interception. He also ran for 42 yards and a touchdown. Justin Jefferson caught two touchdown passes, and Derrick Dillon, Ja'Marr Chase, and Thaddeus Moss each caught one.

The top five would remain the same for another week: Alabama, Clemson, Georgia, Ohio State, and LSU.

#7 Florida

The Florida Gators were ranked #8 in the AP pre-season poll. They bounced around from week to week, settling at #7 when they visited the Tigers. The Gators were 6-0 and had outscored opponents, 194–57, including a 24–13 win against #7 Auburn.

Joe Burrow started where he left off the week before, with a touchdown pass, this one nine yards to Ja'Marr Chase. Florida tied the score on a Kyle Trask to Trevon Grimes five-yarder. Burrow hit Justin Jefferson for a seven-yard touchdown early in the second quarter. The Gators tied the score again, on an Emory Jones to Lamical Perine one-yard score. Clyde Edwards-Helaire ran 39 yards to put the Tigers up, 21–14. But with only four seconds left, Trask hit Van Jefferson for a six-yard touchdown, tying the score, 21–21, at the half.

The Gators took the lead early in the third period on a Trask to Jefferson two-yard pass. Edwards-Helaire tied the game, yet again, 28–28. Tyrone Davis-Prince put LSU in front on a 33-yard run to end the third quarter. The only fourth period score was a Burrow to Chase 54-yarder to end the back-and-forth contest, LSU 42, Florida 28.

Burrow completed 21 of 24 passes for 293 yards and three touchdowns. Edwards-Helaire rushed for 134 yards on 13 attempts. Chase had seven receptions for 127 yards and two touchdowns. Jefferson scored once on 10 receptions for 123 yards. LSU outgained Florida, 511 yards to 457.

The win was enough to propel the Tigers to #2 behind #1 Alabama. Clemson dropped to #3, and Ohio State was #4. Halfway through the regular season, 11 teams remained undefeated.

Mississippi State

The Mississippi State Bulldogs were having an off-year. In the two games before facing the Tigers, the Bulldogs had lost, 56–23 at #7 Auburn and 20–10 at unranked Tennessee. Under second-year coach Joe Moorhead, they would finish at 6–7 overall and 3–5 in the SEC.

Cade York kicked a 20-yard field goal in the first quarter and 23- and 25-yarders midway through the second period as LSU took the lead, 9–0. The Bulldogs' Garrett Shrader ran for a 12-yard touchdown to make the score 9–7 with five and a half minutes until the half. The Tigers used the time well to score on two Joe Burrow passes, the first 60 yards to Racey McMath and the second an 8-yarder to Ja'Marr Chase with under a minute left. The PAT after the McMath reception failed, but LSU was up, 22–7. After the half, Burrow threw for two more touchdowns: a 37-yarder to Derrick Dillon and an 18-yarder to Justin Jefferson. The Bulldogs scored on a Shrader to Stephen Guidry 24-yard pass with under a minute remaining in the game. LSU won, 36–13.

Another game, another Joe Burrow show. The quarterback went 25 of 32 for 327 yards and four touchdowns, giving him the LSU record (29) for touchdown passes in a season.[4] Edward-Helaire led all LSU rushers with 53 yards.

Clemson (6–0) continued to fall in the polls. Alabama (6–0) remained at #1 and LSU (6–0) at #2, but Ohio State (6–0) moved to #3 with Clemson at #4.

#9 Auburn

At 6–1 and ranked #9, Auburn was in a position to advance if they could upset #2 LSU. Earlier in the season, Auburn had defeated #11 Oregon and #17 Texas A&M, but two games before, they had lost, 24–13, to #10 Florida. With top five teams Georgia and Alabama still ahead, they needed this win. LSU wanted it more.

Auburn's Anders Carlson kicked a 30-yard field goal for the only first quarter score. Joe Burrow threw to Terrace Marshall for a 20-yard touchdown early in the second period. With three minutes remaining, a Bo Nix one-yard touchdown gave the lead back to Auburn. But 33 seconds before the half, Cade York made a 20-yard field goal to tie the game, 10–10, at the half.

Carlson made a 23-yard field goal, and Clyde Edwards-Helaire ran for a six-yard touchdown. The PAT failed, but LSU had the lead back, 16–13 at the end of three quarters. Early in the fourth quarter, Burrow ran for a seven-yard touchdown. This time the PAT was good, and the LSU lead was extended to 10 points. With two and a half minutes to play, Auburn scored on a Nix to Seth Williams five-yard pass to end the game, LSU Tigers 23, Auburn Tigers 20.

Burrow was 32 of 42 with 321 passing yards, one touchdown, and one interception. Edwards-Helaire rushed 26 times for 136 yards and one touchdown. He also had seven pass receptions for 51 yards. JaMarr Chase led all receivers with eight catches for 136 yards.

Freshman cornerback Derek Stingley, Jr., recorded his fourth consecutive game with an interception. He would lead the SEC with six this season. Stingley also made 31 solo tackles on defense. The grandson of Darryl Stingley, a New England Patriots receiver who was paralyzed during a game in 1977, Derek Jr. was raised in a football-oriented home. Coached by his father, Derek Sr., he was the top prospect out of high school.

Looking at the game statistics, it would appear that LSU had won by a much greater score:

	Auburn	*LSU*
Rushing yards	130	187
Passing yards	157	321
Total yards	287	508
First downs	16	30

LSU took over #1, and Alabama fell to #2. Both teams had a bye before they played each other in the big game.

#2 Alabama

The Crimson Tide was 8–0 and had outscored opponents, 389–122. Since 2009, Alabama had two unanimous championships, three consensus championships, and one shared title. They had a strong case to be the team of the decade, and they were once again in a #1–#2 contest.

LSU had lost eight straight games to Alabama, but the Tigers led, 10–7, after the first quarter. Joe Burrow passed 33-yards to Ja'Marr Chase, and Cade York booted a 40-yard field goal before Alabama's Jaylen Waddle returned a punt 77 yards for a touchdown late in the quarter. Terrace Marshall scored on a 29-yard pass from Burrow early in the second period. The PAT failed, and Tua Tagovailoa hit Devonta Smith for a 64-yard touchdown, but Alabama's PAT also failed. LSU led, 16–13. The Tigers managed to score 17 more points before the half. York kicked a 45-yard field goal, Clyde Edwards-Helaire ran for a one-yard score, and 20 seconds later caught a 13-yard pass from Burrow. LSU went to the half up, 33–13.

The Tide scored the only points in the third period, a Tagovailoa to Najee Harris 15-yard touchdown. Harris opened the fourth quarter scoring with a one-yard run, and LSU now had a tenuous 33–27 lead. An Edwards-Helaire five-yard run extended the Tigers' lead, 39–27. Tagovailoa threw his third touchdown pass, a five-yarder to Jerry Jeudy. Edwards-Helaire scored his third rushing touchdown on a seven-yard run to put the Tigers up, 46–34. Sixteen seconds later and with 1:21 to play, Tagovailoa and Devonta Smith connected for an 85-yard score. The game ended with a 46–41 LSU victory.

Burrow was 31 of 39 for 393 yards and three touchdowns. He was also sacked five times. Tagovailoa was 21 of 40 for 418 yards, four touchdowns, and one interception. LSU had 559 yards of offense to 541 yards for the Tide. LSU was now #1, followed by #2 Ohio State, #3 Clemson, and #4 Alabama.

Mississippi

LSU led 31–7 at the half. Joe Burrow had three touchdown passes, two to JaMarr Chase (34 and 51 yards) and a 12-yarder to Justin Jefferson. Tyrion Davis-Price ran for a four-yard touchdown, and Cade York kicked a 33-yard field goal with five seconds remaining. Mississippi's score came on a five-yard run in the second quarter. After the half, the Rebels scored 30 points and the Tigers scored 27 for a 58–37 LSU win.

The game statistics were incredible. They looked as though both teams left their defense home:

	Mississippi	*LSU*
Rushing yards	402	227
Passing yards	212	489
Total yards	614	716
First downs	26	35

Burrow threw for 489 yards and five touchdowns with two intercepted. Clyde Edwards-Helaire rushed for 172 yards on 23 carries.

In the AP, LSU stayed at #1, as did #2 Ohio State, and #3 Clemson. Georgia replaced Alabama at #4. The CFP ranking was: LSU, Ohio State, Clemson, and Oklahoma. Over the next two weeks, LSU would outscore unranked opponents, 106–27, before facing #4 Georgia for the SEC Championship.

Arkansas

The Razorbacks kept it close trailing only 7–6 with 9:43 remaining in the second quarter. After that, the Tigers scored 49 points before Arkansas managed two touchdowns in the last half of the fourth period. Joe Burrow threw three touchdown passes and Clyde Edwards-Helaire scored three rushing touchdowns as LSU rolled up 612 yards to 304 for the Razorbacks in a 56–20 win.

In the CFP Rankings, Ohio State took over #1 after defeating #8 Penn State, 28–17, while LSU dropped to #2. Clemson, Georgia, and Alabama rounded out the top five.

Texas A&M

The Tigers led, 31–0, at the half and 34–0 before the Aggies put five points on the board late in the third quarter to avert a shutout. Joe Burrow threw three touchdown passes. The Tigers' offense totaled 553 yards (128 rushing and 425 passing) to 169 yards for Texas A&M.

The CFP Ranking remained the same. #1 Ohio State defeated #13 Michigan, 56–27, and would now play #8 Wisconsin for the Big 10 title.

#4 Georgia

SEC Championship Game

LSU scored 14 points in the first quarter on Joe Burrow touchdown passes to Ja'Marr Chase (23 yards) and Terrace Marshall (seven yards) before Georgia's Rodrigo Blankenship kicked a 39-yard field goal. Cade York made a 41-yard field goal to end the first half at 17–3.

In the third quarter, York added a 28-yard field goal and Burrow threw for two more touchdowns, another to Marshall (four yards) and the second to Justin Jefferson (eight yards). In the fourth period, the Bulldogs Jake Fromm passed two yards to George Pickens for a touchdown. York ended the scoring with a 50-yard field goal for a 37–10 Tigers win.

Burrow completed 28 of 38 passes for 349 yards, four touchdowns, and no interceptions.

	Georgia	*LSU*
Rushing yards	61	132
Passing yards	225	349
Total yards	286	481
First downs	20	26
Turnovers	2	0

The AP and the CFP both agreed: #1 LSU, #2 Ohio State, #3 Clemson, and #4 Oklahoma.

#4 Oklahoma—CFP Semifinal

The Sooners had lost to Kansas State on October 26, 48–41, but they were 12–1 with a high-powered offense that produced 562 points (43.2 points per game). However, the defense had allowed 24.5 points per game.

Joe Burrow threw a 19-yard touchdown pass to Justin Jefferson three minutes into the game. Oklahoma tied the score on a Kennedy Brooks three-yard run. Then the Tigers scored on four Burrow passes, a Terrace Marshall eight-yarder and three to Justin Jefferson of 35, 42, and 30 yards. Jalen Hurts scored on a two-yard run for the Sooners, and it was 35–14 with under five minutes left in the half. With the time remaining, Burrow found Thaddeus Moss on a 62-yard touchdown and Marshall for a two-yard score to end the half: LSU 49, Oklahoma 14.

The two teams traded touchdowns in the third and fourth quarters for a 63–28 Tigers win. Burrow completed 29 of 39 pass attempts for 493 yards and seven touchdowns, and he rushed for 26 yards and another score.

Once again, the game statistics reflected the dominance of LSU:

	Oklahoma	LSU
Rushing yards	97	160
Passing yards	225	532
Total yards	322	692
First downs	16	31
Turnovers	1	0

The decisive win advanced the Tigers to the CFP Championship against the 14–0 #3 Clemson Tigers, the 2018 unanimous champions. Clemson had won a tight semifinal against #2 Ohio State in the Fiesta Bowl. The Tigers came back from 16–0 in the second quarter and 23–21 in the fourth period. Over the season, the Clemson offense had put up 634 points (45.3 points per game), while a stingy defense had allowed 161 points (11.5 points per game).

#3 Clemson—CFP National Championship Final

Superdome, Louisiana

Clemson sophomore quarterback Trevor Lawrence scored on a one-yard run. Joe Burrow found Ja'Marr Chase for a 52-yard touchdown four minutes later, and the first quarter ended at 7–7. Early in the second period, Clemson added 10 points on a B. T. Potter 52-yard field goal and a 36-yard touchdown run by Tee Higgins. At that point, Burrow took over. He ran for a three-yard touchdown and passed for two more, a 14-yarder to Ja'Marr Chase and a six-yard strike to Thaddeus Moss with only 10 seconds remaining. LSU had the lead at the half, 28–17.

Four minutes into the third period, Travis Etienne scored on a three-yard run. Lawrence passed to Amari Rodgers for a two-point conversion, and Clemson now trailed by only three points, 28–25. Burrow hit Moss for a four-yard touchdown late in the third quarter and Terrace Marshall for another early in the fourth to seal the LSU win, 42–25.

Burrow ended the game with 463 passing yards and five touchdowns, and he rushed for 58 more yards and another score. In all, LSU gained 631 yards, with 521 coming from Burrow. For the season, Joe Burrow would complete 76.3 percent of his passes for 5,671 yards and 60 touchdowns, with only six interceptions out of 527 attempts. He would also rush for 368 yards and another five touchdowns.

Ja'Marr Chase had 84 pass receptions, 20 going for touchdowns, for a total of 1,780 yards. Justin Jefferson had 111 receptions for 1,540 yards with 18 touchdowns. Clyde Edwards-Helaire rushed for 1,414 yards and 16 touchdowns and had 55 pass receptions for 453 yards and one touchdown.

Joe Burrow and Ja'Marr Chase were selected unanimous All Americas, while defensive back Derek Stingley would be consensus. Safety Grant Delpit would be named to some AA teams.

Burrow won the Heisman Trophy and the Camp, Maxwell, O'Brien, Unitas, and Manning Awards. He was also the AP and *Sporting News* Player of the Year. Chase won the Biletnikoff Award and Delpit the Thorpe Award.

Why Was LSU Unanimous?

>They were the only undefeated team.
>They defeated teams ranked #s 2, 4, 6, 7, and 8 in the final ranking.
>The #2 team (Clemson) had beaten the #3 team (Ohio State).
>The #5 team (Oregon) had two losses including Auburn, a team LSU beat.
>Once again the question must be asked—if not LSU, who?

Chapter 24

Summary and Conclusions

So, finally, why were these teams unanimous National Champions? First we need to consider the different eras of college football's 150-year history. The early years from 1869–1899 are difficult to assess because of the limited number of teams, even more limited records and statistics, and the lack of uniformity in play and in rules.

With these obstacles present, the teams in the early years are not a part of this analysis.

At the other end, with the Bowl Alliance and Bowl Championship Series of the 1990s into 2013, and the College Football Playoff initiated in 2014, progressive strides have been made to crown a unanimously accepted national champion. It has not always succeeded.

The most interesting period is the "middle years," comprising the 1900s. They are interesting from the perspective of (usually) having no clear method of determining a champion. It was the developing era of polls (opinions), and analytical methods using various and varying factors plugged into a myriad of mathematical formulas to assess performance.

For the purpose of drawing conclusions as to what factor(s) are vital to becoming a unanimous champion, these "middle years" will be weighed the most. The unanimous teams during the 1990s that occurred during the Bowl Alliance (Florida State 1995) and the BCS (Tennessee 1998 and Florida State 1999) are also included. However, the nine unanimous teams from 2000–2019 will be figured in the results later.

Where to Start?

When this project was begun, an elaborate chart was constructed with the hope of answering this question. Among the categories considered were:

Was the team undefeated?
Was the team among the nation's best in offensive, defensive, and scoring categories?
Were there players who ranked nationally among the top 10 in individual categories?
Were there All Americas (or future AAs) on the team?
Were there individual award winners (or future award winners) on the team?
Was the coach honored as Coach of the Year?
Were there other major undefeated teams that year?

What was their strength of schedule?
Did they play the top contenders?
Did they have common opponents with other top contenders?
Were they helped by other contenders' losses?
What was the strength of their conference (if applicable)?
Did events outside college football affect them?
Did events outside football affect other top contenders?
Did a bowl-conference alliance help or hurt?
[the Rose, Sugar, and Cotton Bowls were once aligned with particular conferences, thus preventing certain matchups]
Did bowl discrimination policies help or hurt?
[At one time, teams with black players could not play in Southern bowl games or in certain stadiums]
Were they affected by whims of selectors?
Were they affected by indecision of selectors?
Were they affected by regional bias among selectors?

Let's first assess the importance of some of these categories. The category of "was the team undefeated?" is easily resolved. Notre Dame in 1943 (like Ohio State in 2014 and Alabama in 2015) was not undefeated, taking that category out of consideration as being essential.

Yale in 1900 and 1909, and Georgia Tech in 1917, played before certain of these categories were available: the AP Poll began in 1936, the only bowl game was the Rose Bowl, the National Coach of the Year Award through the AFCA was begun in 1935, there was inconsistent record-keeping of individual and team statistics, and there were no individual honors such as the Heisman Trophy, Maxwell Award, etc.

Some categories are clearly objective, at least where the data is available. For example, was the team among the Nation's best in offensive, defensive, and scoring categories? Of the teams considered here, those records are available beginning with Notre Dame 1943.

The full list of top 10 leaders in team statistics was available for six separate categories in 1937. By 1947, there were eight categories, and beginning in 1992 there were nine categories.[1]

The table below shows the number of categories in which a team was ranked:

Team/year	# of team / total #
Notre Dame 1943	3/6
Michigan 1948	3/8
Texas 1963	4/8
Nebraska 1971	5/8
Southern California 1972	6/8
Nebraska 1995	6/9
Tennessee 1998	3/9
Florida State 1999	3/9

Chapter 24. Summary and Conclusions

No statistical data is available for Yale (1900, 1909) and Georgia Tech (1917); otherwise, all the unanimous teams show a marked consistency in national team dominance.

The same cannot be said for individual statistical leaders. Michigan (1948) had no individual leaders in the eight categories; however the category "Interceptions" only showed the three players tied for first. Tennessee (1998) also had no national individual leaders in any of the 11 categories. All of the other six unanimous teams had at least one player among the national leaders in various categories:

Team / Year	Player (Category)
Notre Dame 1943	Creighton Miller (rushing yards, yards/rush, scoring)
Texas 1963	Hugh Crosby (kick scoring)
Texas 1963	James Hudson (interceptions)
Nebraska 1971	Johnny Rodgers (all-purpose, receiving, punt returns)
Nebraska 1971	Rick Sanger (kick scoring)
So. California 1972	Anthony Davis (all-purpose, yards/rush, scoring)
So. California 1972	Lynn Swann (punt returns)
So. California 1972	Mike Rae (kick scoring)
Nebraska 1995	Mike Fullman (punt returns)
Florida State 1999	Chris Weinke (passing)
Florida State 1999	Peter Warrick (receiving)
Florida State 1999	Sebastian Janikowski (scoring, field goals)

However, without at least one player from each of the unanimous teams, this category had to be discarded.

Another objective category thought worthy of consideration was whether the coach was honored as Coach of the Year? The two oldest such awards are considered here: the American Football Coaches Association (AFCA), which began in 1935, and the Eddie Robinson Award, given by The Football Writers Association of America since 1957. Again, early team coaches are not considered. The table below shows the voting for the 2 awards over the years given.

AFCA Award	Year	Eddie Robinson Award
Bennie Oosterbaan Michigan	1948	N/A
Darrell Royal Texas	1963	Darrell Royal Texas
John McKay So. California	1972	John McKay So. California
Phillip Fulmer	1998	Phillip Fulmer

Only four of the eight coaches eligible were named "coach of the year," therefore, this category was also eliminated. It is probably a good thing that it is not a necessity to your team being a unanimous national champion, otherwise we'd have coaches crisscrossing the nation, giving political-style campaign speeches.

Another objective consideration was whether there were other major undefeated and untied teams that year? No other top 10-ranked team had an unblemished record in three of the considered seasons: Texas (1963), Southern California (1972), and Nebraska (1995).

The other undefeated teams in the years 1900 (Yale), 1909 (Yale), 1917 (Georgia Tech), 1943 (Notre Dame), and 1948 (Michigan) have been discussed in the individual chapters. In each case, reasons are given why these teams should not be considered a threat to the unanimous vote tallied.

In 1971, Toledo, was in the Mid-America Conference, had a 12-0-0 record, and held a well-deserved ranking of #14 in the AP poll. However, the Rockets played no teams in the top 20 and were not a serious threat to the Nebraska Cornhuskers team of that year.

Likewise, the 1998 Tulane team, out of Conference-USA, was 12-0 and ended the season ranked #7 after defeating unranked Brigham Young in the Liberty Bowl, 41-27. The Green Wave was fourth nationally in total offense (507.1 yards per game) and second in scoring offense (45.4 points per game). But the defense, against a weaker schedule that included no top 20 team, allowed an average of 24.6 points per game. Tulane was not a genuine contender with Tennessee that year.

Another MAC team, Marshall, was 13-0 in 1999. Again, although the Thundering Herd were deserving of an AP ranking (#10), they played only #25 Brigham Young (8-4) and posed no threat to Florida State's unanimous selection.

Undefeated teams certainly hurt the unanimous hopes of some consensus national champion teams, but does not appear to have influenced the 11 unanimous selections during the 1900s.

Some categories are subjective or at least semi-subjective. For example, did a team play the top contender(s)? The advent of polling nationwide brought "top contenders" into better (although not perfect) focus. Although reasonably accurate though subjective, the polls remain the best yardstick available. Based on the polls, chronologically from Notre Dame (1943) to Florida State (1999), all the unanimous choices played the top contender(s). However, for the three earliest teams considered, some leaps of faith must be made.

In the early 1900s, the East had the only established football programs, and Eastern football predominated. With arguably the best teams residing there and playing each other regularly, Yale's teams of 1900 and 1909 probably played the best contenders available (Princeton, Harvard, Penn, and Army). Still, it requires a leap of faith that the top contenders were among these teams.

Although interrupted by war, in 1917, good teams were popping up around the country, but the East still dominated. How, then, did Georgia Tech become unanimous in 1917? Relying on another "leap of faith," a comparison of common opponents is, at best, a second-hand way of comparing the contenders, but is essential in understanding Georgia Tech's unanimity. Tech defeated Eastern power Penn, 41-0, while undefeated Pitt (9-0) edged the Quakers, 14-6. Georgia Tech also defeated Tulane, 48-0, after the Green Wave had lost to another undefeated team, Texas A&M (8-0), 35-0. And finally, Tech disposed of (6-2-1) Auburn, 68-7, while 8-0-1 Ohio State trudged to a 0-0 tie.

"Leaps of faith" aside, it does appear that playing the top contender(s) is an important criterion for a unanimous title. How other factors prevented these "top contenders" matchups will be discussed later in this chapter.

Were there individual award winners (or future award winners) on the team? This is another objective category. Teams near the end of the century benefited from many

Chapter 24. Summary and Conclusions

more awards being given, whereas no individual awards were available for Yale (1900 and 1909), and Georgia Tech (1917).

Two teams, Michigan (1948) and Southern California (1972), had no award-winning players. No Tennessee (1998) player won an award that year, although defensive lineman John Henderson won the Outland Award in 2000. The remaining five teams are summarized below:

Team / Year	Player / Award / Year
Notre Dame 1943	Angelo Bertelli, Heisman 1943
Notre Dame 1943	Johnny Lujack, Heisman 1947
Texas 1963	Scott Appleton, Outland 1963
Texas 1963	Tommy Nobis, Maxwell 1965
Texas 1963	Tommy Nobis, Outland 1965
Nebraska 1971	Larry Jacobson, Outland 1971
Nebraska 1971	Johnny Rodgers, Heisman 1972
Nebraska 1971	Johnny Rodgers, Camp 1972
Nebraska 1971	Rich Glover, Outland 1972
Nebraska 1971	Rich Glover, Lombardi 1972
Nebraska 1995	Tommy Frazier, Unitas 1995
Nebraska 1995	Grant Wistrom, Lombardi 1997
Nebraska 1995	Aaron Taylor, Outland 1997
Florida State 1999	Sebastian Janikowski, Groza 1998–1999
Florida State 1999	Chris Weinke, Heisman 2000
Florida State 1999	Chris Weinke, O'Brien 2000
Florida State 1999	Chris Weinke, Unitas 2000
Florida State 1999	Jamal Reynolds, Lombardi 2000

Although many individual awards went to players on this limited number of teams, because no awards were received by players from Michigan (1948) and Southern California (1972), this category cannot be deemed absolutely essential to a unanimous choice.

Another objective category question would be whether there were All America players on the team? The table below summarizes:

Team / Year	# of Consensus All Americas
Yale 1900	7
Yale 1909	6
Georgia Tech 1917	1
Notre Dame 1943	5
Michigan 1948	2
Texas 1963	1

1965 Offensive and Defensive All America Teams Began

Nebraska 1971	1-offense	2-defense
Southern California 1972	1-offense	0-defense
Nebraska 1995	1-offense	0-defense
Tennessee 1998	0-offense	1-defense
Florida State 1999	3-offense	1-defense

All of the unanimous teams had at least one All America player in the year considered, as would be expected, and therefore this category must be viewed as essential to a team being chosen unanimously.

Most of the other categories, such as "whims of selectors" and "events outside of football affecting a team," are necessarily based on speculation. They are subjective and cannot be answered with the certainty of statistics or the outcome of a poll or vote.

It appears that "whims" played a role in certain years (see Chapter 1), with the result that certain deserving teams were deprived of a unanimous vote. A certain degree of bias among selectors was evident with Parke Davis (see Chapter 3, The Early Years), who always included an Eastern team, some with dubious credentials.

In the same way, sometimes events occurred within a team, but outside of football. Florida State (1999) lost its two top receivers, Peter Warrick and Laveranues Coles, to legal issues. Although one would return and contribute much to the team's success, the Seminoles were deep enough that they were able to adapt and flourish even facing top-caliber competition.

A similar situation arose for Tennessee (1998) when their star running back, Jamal Lewis, was forced to leave the team because of legal problems. Again, the team was talented enough to succeed until the player returned.

A legal issue that occurred the year before could have kept Johnny Rodgers from playing for Nebraska in 1971. As #1 Nebraska and #2 Oklahoma were evenly talented and played what has been called the "Game of the Century," Rodgers' return of a punt for a touchdown was the difference in that game, a 35–31 Nebraska win. The Cornhuskers were talented, but could they have won that game and remained undefeated without Rodgers? Of the dream matchups involving unanimous champions and their top contenders, that game was, by far, the closest.

Notre Dame (1943) during the war years lost Emil Sitko to Great Lakes Naval Training facility. After the war, Sitko would return to Notre Dame and become a consensus All America, but against the Irish that year, he scored a touchdown to help hand Notre Dame its only loss. The Irish also lost Heisman Trophy winner Angelo Bertelli in mid-season to the Marines. Many teams would not have been able to compensate for the loss of such key players. It is difficult to know about, much less factor in, these events and assess how a deserving team may have been affected.

"Indecision of selectors" can be easily seen. When two or more teams are chosen by a selector, an inability to decide is obvious. This author is not in favor of split votes. A decision should be made. As outlined in Chapter 2, some teams were deprived of a unanimous championship honor by indecision.

A strong conference and/or top opponents have figured in many unanimous championships, for example, Nebraska 1971. The Cornhuskers belonged to the Big 8 conference, which at season's end boasted the three top teams in the polls: Nebraska,

Chapter 24. Summary and Conclusions

Oklahoma, and Colorado. The Cornhuskers had beaten Oklahoma and Colorado in the regular season. The 4th-ranked team was Alabama, and the Cornhuskers had defeated them handily, 38–6, in the Orange Bowl when the Crimson Tide was ranked 2nd. Comparing the record of the opponents for the top eight ranked teams of that year (1971) shows a sharp decline from #s 1–4 to #s 5–8:

TEAM OPPONENTS' RECORD

1. Nebraska 83–63–1
2. Oklahoma 75–59–2
3. Colorado 81–54–1
4. Alabama 86–50–2
5. Penn State 60–69–2
6. Michigan 43–74–1
7. Georgia 66–68–1
8. Arizona State 65–66–3

The Cornhuskers played against some of the best individual players (see Chapter 10) and national team statistical leaders:

#1 & #4 Rushing Offenses (Oklahoma & Alabama)
#10 Passing Offense (Utah State)
#1 & #9 Total Offense (Oklahoma & Colorado)

Against all those great players and powerful team offenses, Nebraska allowed an average of only eight points per game.

Now, how might this have had a different result?

What if the top four (#1–4) and the next four (#5–8) opponents' records were reversed? What if the Big Ten and the Independents were strong? What if, in addition, the Big 8 was weak? Could Penn State (11-1) or Michigan (11-1) have played for the national title? This conceivably could have happened if Nebraska didn't command the respect it did, because the conference had been weak and subsequently they had a weak schedule.

Sometimes luck plays a role. Over the years, other teams with a legitimate claim to the title were probably overlooked or under-considered because they played in a weaker or less respected conference. Oklahoma suffered from schedules comprised in large part of members of the relatively weak Big 8 Conference during the 1950s (see Chapter 2).

Texas in 1963 overcame a poor showing (winning six conference games by an average of 6.5 points) in the weaker Southwest Conference (34-36-2 without Texas) by defeating the top contenders decisively: #1 Oklahoma, 28-7, and #2 Navy, 28-6.

It can be said of all 11 unanimous teams that they all played top competition, as seen in the table below.

Year	Team	Opponent	Rank (if applicable)
1900	Yale	Princeton 8–3	N/A
1900	Yale	Harvard 10–1	N/A
1909	Yale	Princeton 7–2–1	N/A
1909	Yale	Harvard 8–1	N/A
1917	Georgia Tech	Penn 9–2	N/A
1917	Georgia Tech	Auburn 7–1	N/A

1943	Notre Dame	Georgia Tech	#13
1943	Notre Dame	Michigan	#2
1943	Notre Dame	Navy	#3
1943	Notre Dame	Army	#3
1943	Notre Dame	Northwestern	#8
1943	Notre Dame	Iowa Pre-Flight	#2
1948	Michigan	Purdue	#15
1948	Michigan	Northwestern	#3
1948	Michigan	Minnesota	#13
1948	Michigan	Ohio State	#18
1963	Texas	Oklahoma	#1
1963	Texas	Navy	#2 Cotton Bowl
1971	Nebraska	Colorado	#9
1971	Nebraska	Oklahoma	#2
1971	Nebraska	Alabama	#2 Orange Bowl
1972	Southern California	Arkansas	#4
1972	Southern California	Stanford	#15
1972	Southern California	Washington	#18
1972	Southern California	UCLA	#14
1972	Southern California	Notre Dame	#10
1972	Southern California	Ohio State	#3 Rose Bowl
1995	Nebraska	Kansas State	#8
1995	Nebraska	Colorado	#7
1995	Nebraska	Kansas	#10
1995	Nebraska	Florida	#2 Fiesta Bowl
1998	Tennessee	Syracuse	#17
1998	Tennessee	Florida	#2
1998	Tennessee	Georgia	#7
1998	Tennessee	Arkansas	#10
1998	Tennessee	Mississippi State	#23
1998	Tennessee	Florida State	#2 Fiesta Bowl
1999	Florida State	Georgia Tech	#10
1999	Florida State	NC State	#20
1999	Florida State	Miami, Fl	#19
1999	Florida State	Florida	#3
1999	Florida State	Virginia Tech	#2 Sugar Bowl

A strong conference (where applicable) goes along with playing the top contender(s) as being a necessary factor for a team to be a unanimous champion.

Other consensus national champions were not unanimous, at least partly because they either: (a) played a weak schedule; or (b) did not play the top contender(s).

Some examples of prestigious teams in this dilemma were presented in Chapter 2. Below is another example that combines a number of the categories being considered.

1959 Syracuse

The Syracuse team, at 11–0, was the only major undefeated team that year. As a team, they led the nation in several categories:

Team Category	Rank	Average
Total Offense	1st	451.5 ypg
Rushing Offense	1st	313.6 ypg
Scoring Offense	1st	39 ppg
Total Defense	1st	96.2 ypg
Rushing Defense	1st	19.3 ypg
Scoring Defense	6th	5.9 ppg

In early November, the Orangemen (as they were known at the time) were scheduled to play #2 Texas (8–0 and the top contender) in the post-season Cotton Bowl. But a week later, Texas lost to TCU and was replaced at #2 by Mississippi (8–1).

Circumstances had changed: (1) Syracuse was committed to the Cotton Bowl to play Texas (now ranked #4); and (2) Syracuse, with its black players (including 1961 Heisman Trophy winner Ernie Davis), could not have played Mississippi (now ranked #2) in the Sugar Bowl because of Southeastern Conference and Sugar Bowl policies preventing black players from participating.

Syracuse was unable to defend its #1 ranking against the top contender. The team was also considered to have played a weaker schedule (as seen by a comparison of opponents' weeks in Top 20 poll and overall records).

Top Contender Opponents 1959

Team	# of Opponents/Weeks in Top 20	Opponents W-L Record
LSU	5/38 weeks	47–47–5
Mississippi	3/30 weeks	48–47–4
Syracuse	4/17 weeks	49–47–2
Texas	4/32 weeks	47–50–3

Syracuse, through some bad luck, would not have a chance to be a unanimous selection. They were doomed by a perceived weak schedule, being unable to play the leading contender, and bowl discrimination policies of that era. In many other categories, they excelled:

Only undefeated team.
Led in many national team statistics.
Had All America (and future AA) players.
Had a future individual award winner.
Had the 1959 Coach of the Year, Ben Schwartzwalder

Throughout the range of this study (1900–1999), other consensus teams faced similar dilemmas.

Did Georgia Tech (1917) and Notre Dame (1943) benefit from the war years? In both seasons, some schools curtailed or cancelled their football programs. It appears that Georgia Tech did not lose many players to the war effort, and their performance throughout the season reflected this. Likewise, Notre Dame did lose some players, including Emil Sitko, who would score a touchdown against them and contribute to their only defeat. But the Irish were both deep enough and benefited from Naval training that transferred in additional talent.

Luck: The ultimate intangible.

Notre Dame (1943) may have had some luck in the polls that year. Although Great Lakes (Notre Dame's only loss) had a winning season (9–2), the Bluejackets never ascended higher than #12, and they were usually unranked, as they were in the November 22 poll before the Notre Dame contest. After that game, Great Lakes ended the season at #6 as a result of beating the #1 team. Would the Irish, with one loss, have been unanimous if Great Lakes had been more respected and ranked higher? Historical comparisons suggest that Notre Dame may not have achieved a unanimous vote. As it was, Great Lakes had lost to Purdue, the only undefeated top 10 team (although their opponents' record was an unimpressive 32–48–6). Luck often plays a major role, including the scheduling of games, often arranged years ahead.

The weekly polls bring the national college football season into focus probably as much as can be expected. Even during the latter portion of the timeframe considered (1900–1999), college football has become such a big business, with such high monetary stakes, it is difficult to imagine a team, or even a player, that is not assessed—and assessed correctly.

Summary

The purpose of this book is both to acknowledge the teams honored as unanimous champions and to determine what factors contributed to making a team a unanimous national champion from 1900–1999. Examples can be found where most of the categories considered at the beginning of this chapter played a part in some determinations over those 100 years. However, many of the categories can be eliminated as being a major contributing factor in a number of seasons.

Returning to the original list of possible categories essential to a team being named a unanimous national champion, but with those categories deemed not necessary removed, the result would be:

OBJECTIVE CATEGORIES

Was the team among the nation's best in offensive, defensive, and scoring categories?
Were there All Americas (or future AAs) on the team?

Chapter 24. Summary and Conclusions

SUBJECTIVE CATEGORIES

What was their strength of schedule?
Did they play the top contenders? (Top Contender is subjective)
Did they have common opponents with other top contenders?
What was the strength of their conference (if applicable)?
Were they helped by other contenders' losses?

There are some other subjective categories that, whereas their influence cannot be fully assessed, did not appear to affect the unanimous teams considered here. However, they most probably played a role in some consensus champions not being unanimous. These would include:

Did events outside college football affect them?
Whims of selectors?
Indecision of selectors?
Regional bias among selectors?

It appears that strength of schedule and, especially, playing top contenders are the two major categories in selecting a unanimous national champion. Having All America players was something all 11 unanimous teams possessed.

The top reasons a team was selected as a unanimous national champion 1900–1999 would appear to be:

1. The team had played the top contender(s).
2. The team had played a strong schedule.
3. The team had All America talent.
4. The team was statistically among the best nationally in offense, defense, and scoring.
5. Luck—in its multiple and varied aspects.

Some teams appeared, to this author, lucky to be selected unanimously. Considering the number of very good teams in most years, the lack of a uniform and accepted playoff system, the varying criteria used by different selectors, and a certain amount of regional bias, it's a wonder that even 11 teams were able to so impress as to be unanimous.

Once the BCS and CFP systems began, the percentage of unanimous teams rose drastically. However, not all BCS or CFP crowned champions were unanimous. Despite the pundits' best efforts to identify the top teams and arrange a championship matchup, there is still division.

As all of the BCS and CFP champions meet the criteria established, it must be reasoned that luck and the diversity of selectors' methods play a larger role than first expected. Over the years, the number of "systems" used to decide a champion have grown. Systems vary in what they deem most important in choosing a champion. In spite of best efforts at matching top contenders, the day may come when no team will meet every system's requirements.

Chapter 25

Is There a "Best Ever" Team?

Is there a "Best Ever" college football team? Intuitively, the answer is "No!" During the 150 years of college football, the polls and selectors disagreed 117 times as to which team was the best in a particular season.

There are a variety of factors that make choosing a "Best Ever" team difficult, if not impossible. These include:

DIFFERENT ERAS:
  How the game was played at that time
  The rules and restrictions at that time
  The evolution of the game from era to era

DIFFERENT TYPES OF PLAYERS:
  Two-way players
  Platoon system players
  Specialization of players
  Coaching, training, and size of players

SCHEDULE OF GAMES:
  Regional restrictions
  Opponent strength
  Conference strength (where applicable)
  National coverage of games

The 33 unanimous national champion teams considered here represent the various eras and stages in the evolution of college football. The evolution of the game is an important consideration in any attempt to choose a "Best Ever" team.

The early teams (1869–1899) are not considered because the game was evolving. It was often more like soccer or even rugby than what we today call football. The forward pass was not yet a part of the game.

For this book, the nine unanimous teams from 1900 to 1995 (including the Bowl Alliance), the seven unanimous teams of the BCS era, and the four teams selected unanimously from the CFP years will be used.

The early-20th century unanimous teams (Yale in 1900 and 1909) relied completely on the running game and with little attempt to spread out the field. Eastern schools were predominant as football originated in the East, and both enthusiasm for the game and

Chapter 25. Is There a "Best Ever" Team?

emphasis on the game were high on campuses. With decades of game experience ahead of other regions of the country, better coaching developed in the East. But that knowledge would soon be passed on as Eastern players took on coaching duties throughout the country. The game was new but catching on quickly.

These early Eastern teams, especially Yale, Harvard, Princeton, and Penn, were dominant in their time. However, they lacked the varied offenses that would come a few years later. The passing game transformed offenses. Defenses were forced to adapt as different formations were explored over the years. Platooning and liberal substitution rules ultimately led to specialization.

The formation of conferences has both helped and hindered teams seeking national recognition over the years. With a certain number of games necessarily devoted to conference play, teams are often limited in scheduling quality opponents. Games within a conference considered weak by the polls and selectors can hinder a team's national prominence.

In the early 1900s, fans and selectors were limited to which games they could attend and newspaper accounts of other games. Coverage of games was enhanced and extended by radio, by newsreels, and then by television.

The size (and athleticism) of players has increased over the history of college football. Below is a table comparing the average front line (end to end) weight for the two prominent programs, and their chief opponents, at each end of the 20th century. These two programs were chosen for comparison, but the size and athleticism of players continues to increase.

Yale had two unanimous champion teams in 1900 and 1909. In each year, their rival for championship honors was Harvard. At the other end, Nebraska also boasted two unanimous champions, 1971 and 1995. In 1971, the #1 Cornhuskers defeated #2 Oklahoma during the regular season and later topped #2 Alabama in the Orange Bowl to secure the title. Because it can be considered the "Game of the Century" and the Sooners would end the season at #2, Oklahoma is compared. In the first year of the Bowl Alliance, #1 Nebraska played #2 Florida in the 1996 Fiesta Bowl to decide the title for the 1995 season.

The players on the early Yale and Harvard teams played both ways, therefore, the offensive and defensive lines were the same.

1900

	Yale		*Harvard*	
Position	Name	Weight	Name	Weight
LE	Gould	165	Campbell	170
LT	Bloomer	190	Eaton	202
LG	Brown	202	Lee	195
C	Olcott	197	Sargent	201
RG	Sheldon	216	Barnard	188
RT	Stillman	188	Lawrence	171
RE	Coy	174	Hallowell	158
	Avg.	190.3	Avg.	183.6

1909

Position	Yale		Harvard	
	Name	Weight	Name	Weight
LE	Kilpatrick	190	Smith	169
LT	Hobbs	208	McKay	208
LG	Andrus	208	Withington	188
C	Cooney	232	Withington	190
RG	Goebel	210	Fisher	193
RT	Lilley	188	Fish	200
RE	Browne	174	Savage	184
	Avg.	201.4	Avg.	190.3

1971: Offense

Position	Nebraska		Oklahoma	
	Name	Weight	Name	Weight
LE/SE	Cox	180	Harrison	157
LT	White	238	Unruh	235
LG	Rupert	221	Emmert	218
C	Dumler	237	Brahaney	231
RG	Wortman	238	Jones	236
RT	Austin	222	Jensen	244
RE/TE	List	218	Chandler	234
	Avg.	222.0	Avg.	222.1

1971: Defense

Position	Nebraska		Oklahoma	
	Name	Weight	Name	Weight
LE	Adkins	221	Hamilton	237
LT	Jacobson	250	Selmon	221
NG	Glover	234	Moore	252
RT	Janssen	228	Day	236
RE/LB	Harper	207	Qualls	222
LB	Terrio	209	Aycock	205
LB	Branch	203	Driscoll	208
	Avg.	221.7	Avg.	225.9

1995: Offense

	Nebraska		Florida	
Position	Name	Weight	Name	Weight
LE/WR	Johnson	210	Doering	191
LT	Dishman	310	Odom	298
LG	Ott	290	Green	296
C	Graham	275	Story	277
RG	Taylor	305	Young	299
RT	Anderson	300	Collins	297
RE/TE	Gilman	240	Allen	225
	Avg.	275.7	Avg.	269.0

1995: Defense

	Nebraska		Florida	
Position	Name	Weight	Name	Weight
DE/OLB	Tomich	250	Church	264
DT	C. Peter	300	Barnard	290
DT	J. Peter	285	Chester	267
DE/OLB	Wistrom	240	Campbell	281
SLB	Foreman	220	Daniels	231
MLB	Colman	245	Bates	223
WLB	Farley	200	Hanks	221
	Avg.	248.6	Avg.	253.9

Common sense concedes that Yale's 1900 line (average weight 190.3 lbs.) could not compete against Nebraska's 1995 lines (average weight 275.7 lbs. and 248.6 lbs.). Nor could those early teams have coped with the varied and spread offenses of decades later.

Yet those early Yale teams dominated against arguably the best teams in the nation as regional parity had not yet been achieved. Should either be excluded from a consideration of the "Best Ever"?

In an article in the *Omaha World-Herald* on January 1, 2006, sportswriter Tom Shatel denied the idea of a "Best Ever" team, using much the same arguments as stated above. Shatel suggested comparing seasons or accomplishments to determine the greatest. His article compared the Nebraska teams (1971 and 1995) with the 2005 Southern California team, prior to the Trojans' loss to Texas in the Rose Bowl.

Referring to those two Nebraska squads' accomplishments, he suggested that the 1971 team had to deal with the added pressure of repeating, as they were consensus champions (among five) in 1970. He also favored the 1971 team as having defeated a tougher schedule, but he regarded the 1995 team as having more completely dominated their opponents.

Whereas his idea of a team with a "greatest season" or "greatest accomplishment" is an interesting alternative to trying to deduce a "Best Ever" team, that approach faces the same obstacles, namely comparing different eras. Shatel agreed that comparing athleticism and speed from one era to another won't work.[1]

Shatel opened his article by declaring that there is no greatest team ever, but there can always be the debate about it. Whereas that is certainly true, it has not stopped other "experts" from attempting to answer the question.

It seems everyone has an opinion, but below are four Top 10 lists from true experts. In 2002, Jeff Sagarin ranked the 27 best teams from 1956 to 2001.[2]

Top 10 of Sagarin's 2002 Ranking

1. Nebraska 1995
2. Nebraska 1971
3. Mississippi 1959
4. Oklahoma 1971
5. Ohio State 1973
6. Washington 1991
7. Oklahoma 1973
8. Oklahoma 1974
9. Southern California 1972
10. Nebraska 1972

It is interesting to note the predominance of teams from the 1970s. Three of the top five and seven of the top 10 were from that decade, and all within the time span of 1971–1974. The 1960s and 1980s were not represented.

The teams ranked #s 1, 2, and 9 were unanimous national champions. Of the others:

#6 was the consensus choice between two teams
#8 was consensus among three teams
#3 was not the consensus between two teams
#5 and #7 were not the consensus among five teams
#4 and #10 were not chosen by any selector

In 2006, ESPN ranked their 10 best teams of all time.[3]

The 2006 ESPN Top College Football Teams of All Time

1. Nebraska 1971
2. Southern California 1972
3. Nebraska 1995
4. Army 1945
5. Miami 2001
6. Michigan 1947
7. Notre Dame 1947
8. Oklahoma 1956
9. Oklahoma 1974
10. Alabama 1971

Chapter 25. Is There a "Best Ever" Team?   245

ESPN's #s 1, 2, 3, and 9 are among Sagarin's top choices. Of the others:

#5 was unanimous
#s 4, 6, and 7 was consensus between two teams
#8 was consensus among four teams
#10 was not chosen by any selector

In 2010, Bleacher Report polled its members for the top teams of all time.[4]

The 2010 Bleacher Report Top College Football Teams of All Time

1. Nebraska 1995
2. Southern California 1972
3. Army 1945
4. Miami, FL 2001
5. Notre Dame 1924
6. Oklahoma 1956
7. Texas 2005
8. Ohio State 1968
9. Alabama 1979
10. Michigan 1902

The teams ranked #s 1 and 2 were chosen by both Sagarin and ESPN. Of the others:

#s 3, 4, and 6 were also chosen by ESPN
#7 was selected by Sagarin (in 2019)
#s 5, 9, and 10 were consensus between two teams
#8 was consensus among 3 teams

In 2019, in celebration of 150 years of college football, *USA Today* (January 30, 2019) urged Sagarin to compile the Top 150 teams of all time.

Sagarin's 2019 Top 10 (of his 150 All Time Best Teams)

1. Army 1945
2. Notre Dame 1943
3. California 1920
4. Army 1944
5. Nebraska 1995
6. Texas 2005
7. Nebraska 1971
8. Michigan 1943
9. Ohio State 1944
10. Oklahoma 1971

It is interesting to note the difference in Sagarin's choices in 2002 and 2019. One reason could be that the 2001 poll only selected teams between 1956–2001. His 2019 poll covers all 150 years and includes seven teams outside the scope of his 2001 selections.

It is also interesting that five of his top 10 teams played during the war years of 1941–1945. During those years, many college teams were decimated because of the war. Some pro players were on the rosters of service teams, but none of the best-ever lists include any of these service teams.

California 1920 and Army 1945 were consensus champions, and Ohio State 1944 was co-champion only for the split vote of the National Championship Foundation, but Michigan in 1943 and Oklahoma 1971 were not even co-champions, as Notre Dame (1943) and Nebraska (1971) were unanimous.

The Sagarin System is one of the best, and I don't question his choices. I just find them interesting.

These four ranking systems chose a total of 25 teams for their top 10:

1. Nebraska 1995 was ranked in the top 10 by all four.
2. Nebraska 1971 and Army 1945 were in the top 10 of three rankings.
3. Miami 2001, Southern California 1972, and the Oklahoma teams of 1956, 1971, and 1974 were on two top 10 lists.
4. The other 17 teams were selected by only one of the four rankings and shows the variety of opinion and the diversity of the measuring tools used.

As much as fans are enthralled with the idea of a "best ever" team, in the end, there's really only debate.

Appendix A: Walter Camp

Walter Camp was born on April 17, 1859. He played for Yale from 1876–1882 and coached at Stanford in 1892 and again from 1894–1895, compiling a record of 11-3-3. While a student, Camp represented Yale at the Intercollegiate Convention in 1878 and thereafter attended every convention, rules committee meeting, or legislative function of college football for the next 47 years.

Walter Camp is credited with, among other innovations: the scrimmage line, possession of the ball as opposed to back-and-forth play, downs (or plays), and yardage needed within a certain number of plays to retain possession. He also reduced the number of players from 15 to 11, designated seven players on the offensive line of scrimmage, and a backfield consisting of a quarterback, two halfbacks, and a fullback. Camp's numerical points system was adopted in 1883; a touchdown was worth two points, a "goal" after a touchdown four points, a field goal was five points, and a safety was one point. By 1884, this had been modified: a touchdown was four points, while a goal after touchdown and a safety were both two points.

The "evolution age" of football, from 1906–1912, saw the game evolve in numerous ways, primarily designed to curb the violence, injuries, and deaths that had plagued the game for so long and threatened to have it banned. As expected, Walter Camp was at the fore of these changes.

Camp also began the selection of top players to All America teams beginning in 1889 and ending in 1924. Early on, Camp favored the prominent Eastern teams. From 1889–1905, 168 of 187 All America selections came from the "Big Four": Yale (59), Harvard (44), Princeton (39), and Penn (26). Eight schools produced the remaining 19 selections. This partisanship can be explained, if not fully excused, because of how much sooner Eastern schools embraced the game. Over time that changed drastically (see table below). Camp had limited opportunities to see good teams from other sections, though eventually his selections broadened to embrace the whole country. In 1924, Walter Camp's All America team was comprised of players from 11 schools: Army, California, Columbia, Dartmouth, Illinois, Lafayette, Michigan, Nebraska, Notre Dame, Penn, and Rutgers.

As football spread west, the prominence of Eastern schools lessened. This is shown by the decrease in consensus All America selections from Eastern schools in the following table.

Decline in Percentage of Consensus All America Players from the Ivy League and Eastern Schools

	% Big Four Schools*	% All Ivy Schools**	% Ivy & Regions+	% Other Eastern Geographic Consensus Areas#	Number AAs•
1889–94	100	100	100	0	11
1895	91	100	100	0	11
1896–97	100	100	100	0	11
1898	73	73	87	13	15
1899	92	92	100	0	13
1900	73	87	100	0	15
1901	56	78	94	6	18
1902	77	92	100	0	13
1903	60	80	87	13	15
1904	60	67	80	20	15
1905	69	75	88	12	16
1906	69	88	94	6	16
1907	69	69	94	6	16
1908	53	71	88	12	17
1909	73	82	82	18	11
1910	64	73	73	27	11
1911	73	73	100	0	11
1912	64	82	91	9	11
1913	40	47	67	33	15
1914	37	58	68	32	19
1915	17	33	61	39	18
1916	25	31	69	31	16
1917	0	0	36	73	11
1918	13	13	62	38	16
1919	14	21	50	50	14
1920	28	28	56	44	18
1921	18	27	55	45	11
1922	27	36	64	36	11
1923	27	45	64	36	11
1924	11	28	44	56	18
1925	14	36	50	50	14
1926	6	13	38	62	16
1927	31	31	46	54	13
1928	7	7	40	60	15
1929	7	7	29	71	14

	% Big Four Schools*	% All Ivy Schools**	% Ivy & Regions+	% Other Eastern Geographic Consensus Areas#	Number AAs•
1930	13	13	19	81	16
1931	7	7	21	79	14
1932	0	0	25	75	16
1933	8	8	15	85	13
1934	0	0	13	87	16
1935	7	7	7	93	15
1936	7	7	27	73	15

* The big four schools that dominated the early years of college football: Harvard, Penn, Princeton, Yale.

** The Big Four schools plus the other schools which form the Ivy League: Brown, Columbia, Cornell, Dartmouth.

+ Eastern Schools: Schools in the New England states plus Maryland, New Jersey, New York, Pennsylvania.

Geographic areas other than the East.

• Number of consensus AA players listed for that year.

Walter Camp died in his sleep sometime during the night of March 13–14, 1925, while attending the American Intercollegiate Football Rules Committee meeting in New York City to establish the rules for the 1925 season.

Walter Camp dedicated his whole life to the development and betterment of American College Football. It is no wonder he is considered the Father of American College Football.

Appendix B: Awards and Coaches

Prominent Trophies and Awards Presented Yearly in College Football

Not all were awarded in all years

Heisman Trophy
To the Outstanding Player in college football
Awarded by the Downtown Athletic Club of New York
Began in 1935

AFCA
To the Coach of the Year
Awarded by the American Football Coaches Association
Began in 1935

Maxwell Award
To the Best Player in College Football
Awarded by the Maxwell Football Club of Philadelphia
Began in 1937

Outland Trophy
To the Outstanding Interior Lineman
Awarded by the Football Writers Association of America
Began in 1946

Eddie Robinson Award
To the Coach of the Year in College Football
Awarded by the Football Writers Association of America
Began in 1957

Walter Camp Player of the Year Award
To the Best Player in College Football
Awarded by the Walter Camp Football Foundation
Began in 1967

Vince Lombardi Award
To the Top Lineman in College Football
Awarded by the Rotary Club of Houston
Began in 1970

Davey O'Brien Award
To the Best Quarterback in College Football
Awarded by the Davey O'Brien Foundation of Fort Worth
Began in 1977 [1977–1980 was Davey O'Brien Memorial Trophy and was not limited to quarterbacks but was limited to players in the Southwest]

Butkus Award
To the Top Linebacker in College Football
Awarded by the Downtown Athletic Club of Orlando
Began in 1985

Jim Thorpe Award
To the Best Defensive Back in College Football
Awarded by the Jim Thorpe Association
Began in 1986

Paul "Bear" Bryant Coach of the Year Award
To the Coach of the Year in College Football

Appendix B: Awards and Coaches

Awarded by the American Heart Association, Houston Chapter
Began in 1986

Johnny Unitas Golden Arm Award
To the Top Senior Quarterback in College Football
Awarded by the Frank Camp Chapter of the Johnny Unitas Golden Arm Association
Began in 1987

Doak Walker Award
To the Top Running Back in College Football
Awarded by the SMU Athletic Forum
Began in 1990

William Campbell Trophy
To Player Who Best Exemplifies Academics, Community Service, and Athletics (The Academic Heisman)
Awarded by the National Football Foundation
Began in 1990

Lou Groza award
To the Top Kicker in College Football
Awarded by the Greater Augusta Sports Council
Began in 1992

Bronco Nagurski Award
To the Top Defensive Player in College Football
Awarded by the FWAA / Charlotte Touchdown Club
Began in 1993

Fred Biletnikoff Award
Top Pass Receiver in College Football
Awarded by the Tallahassee Quarterback Club
Began in 1994

Chuck Bednarik Trophy
To the Top Defensive Player in College Football
Awarded by the Maxwell Football Club
Began in 1995

Broyles Award
To Top Assistant Coach in College Football
Awarded by the Broyles Foundation (selection by former head coaches)
Began in 1996

John Mackey Award
To the Top Tight End in College Football
Awarded by the Nassau County Sports Commission
Began in 2000

Ray Guy Award
To the Top Punter in College Football
Awarded by the Greater Augusta Sports Council
Began in 2000

Rimington Award
To the Top Center in College Football
Awarded by the Boomer Esiason Foundation (for Cystic Fibrosis Research)
Began in 2000

Ted Hendricks Award
To the Top Defensive End in College Football
Awarded by Ted Hendricks Foundation
Began in 2002

Manning Award
To the Best Quarterback in College Football
Awarded by the Sugar Bowl Committee
Began in 2004

Wuerffel Trophy
To Player Who Exemplifies Community Service with Athletics and Academics
Awarded by the Chick-fil-A Foundation
Began in 2005

Underdog Award
To the Best Mid-Major Player
Awarded by NationalChamps.net
Began in 2007

Coaches

The coaches of the unanimous National Championship teams, as well as coaches of certain prominent and important consensus teams, were at least as vital to the teams' success as the players.

Malcolm McBride only coached Yale's 1900 unanimous team. McBride, a back at Yale, was a consensus All America in 1898 and a unanimous All America in 1899. He was recruited to coach the Elis in 1900 by Francis Gordon Brown, the Yale captain that year. Although listed as coach, McBride probably shared the duties with Walter Camp and Brown, as was then the custom at Yale. He also had two unanimous All America Yale alums, Frank Hinkey (1891–1894) and Frank Butterworth (1893–1894) as assistants. Whereas no coach ever rivaled his record of 12 wins with 0 losses and a unanimous national title, McBride's coaching career was too short to consider here.

The coaches of all the other unanimous champion teams are recorded here: Howard Jones (Yale 1909), John Heisman (Georgia Tech 1917), Frank Leahy (Notre Dame 1943), Bennie Oosterbaan (Michigan 1948), Darrell Royal (Texas 1963), Bob Devaney (Nebraska 1971) John McKay (Southern California 1972), Tom Osborne (Nebraska 1995), Phillip Fulmer (Tennessee 1998), Bobby Bowden (Florida State 1999), Larry Coker (Miami 2001), Pete Carroll (Southern California 2004), Mack Brown (Texas 2005), Nick Saban (Alabama 2009 and 2015), Jimbo Fisher (Florida State 2013), Urban Meyer (Ohio State 2014), Dabo Swinney (Clemson 2018), and Ed Orgeron (LSU 2019).

Other prominent coaches are considered here primarily because their teams were consensus champions, usually by the vote a single pollster: Fielding "Hurry Up" Yost (Michigan 1901–1902), Knute Rockne (Notre Dame 1924), Earl Blaik (Army 1944–1945), Charles "Bud" Wilkinson (Oklahoma 1955), Lou Holtz (Notre Dame 1988), and Paul "Bear" Bryant (Alabama 1992). Herbert "Fritz" Crisler (Michigan 1938–1947) is also included as he built the Wolverines program to a consensus title (10–0 in 1947) a year before Oosterbaan took over. For each of these coaches, the following categories are considered:

1. Total record as a head coach
2. All America players coached
3. Award winners and Heisman contenders coached

A disclaimer is in order at this point. All football fans have their favorite team and coach. Not all successful coaches are listed. Choices were made based on the scope of this book.

Regarding the naming of All America players, it should be noted that sources with a particular bias sometimes remember players as having been All Americas when hard evidence for that honor cannot be found.

For this book, the All America players listed are from the following sources:

ESPN College Football Encyclopedia: The Complete History of the Game, Michael MacCambridge, ed., ESPN Books, 2005.

50 Years of College Football: A Modern History of America's Most Colorful Sport, Bob Boyles and Paul Guido, Skyhorse Publishing, 2007.

Official 2002 NCAA Football Records, Scott Deitch, ed., NCAA Publications, 2002.

Intercollegiate Football: A Complete Pictorial History and Statistical Review from 1869 to 1934, Christy Walsh, ed., Doubleday, Doran & Co., 1934.

Football Media Guides of various schools.

Coaches of Unanimous National Championship Teams

Howard Jones Collegiate Head Coaching Record

1908	Syracuse	6–3–1
1909+	Yale	10–0–0
1910	Ohio State	6–1–3
1913	Yale	5–2–3
1916	Iowa	4–3–0
1917	Iowa	3–5–0
1918	Iowa	6–2–1
1919	Iowa	5–2–0
1920	Iowa	5–2–0
1921*	Iowa	7–0–0
1922*	Iowa	7–0–0
1923	Iowa	5–3–0
1924	Duke	4–5–0
1925	S. California	11–2–0
1926	S. California	8–2–0
1927	S. California	8–1–1
1928*	S. California	9–0–1
1929*	S. California	10–2–0
1930	S. California	8–2–0
1931**	S. California	10–1–0
1932**	S. California	10–0–0
1933*	S. California	10–1–1
1934	S. California	4–6–1
1935	S. California	5–7–0
1936	S. California	4–2–3
1937	S. California	4–4–2
1938	S. California	9–2–0
1939*	S. California	8–0–2
1940	S. California	3–4–2
		194–64–21

* shared national title
** consensus national champion
\+ unanimous national champion

Appendix B: Awards and Coaches

Howard Jones–Coached All Americas

Frank Horr*	Syracuse	1908	tackle
Stephen Philbin*	Yale	1909	back
Ed Coy*	Yale	1909	back
John Kilpatrick*	Yale	1909	end
Henry Hobbs*	Yale	1909	tackle
Hamlin Andus*	Yale	1909	guard
Carroll Cooney*	Yale	1909	center
Nelson Talbott*	Yale	1913	tackle
Lester Belding*	Iowa	1919	end
Aubrey Devine*	Iowa	1921	back
Gordon Locke*	Iowa	1922	back
Bruce Taylor	S. California	1925	guard
Ralph Baker*	S. California	1926	back
Morley Drury*	S. California	1927	back
Jesse Hibbs*	S. California	1927	tackle
Don Williams	S. California	1928	back
Jesse Hibbs	S. California	1928	tackle
Francis Tappaan	S. California	1929	end
Erny Pinckert*	S. California	1930	back
Orv Mohler	S. California	1930	back
Garrett Arbelbide	S. California	1930	end
Gus Shaver*	S. California	1931	back
John Baker*	S. California	1931	guard
Erny Pinckert	S. California	1931	back
Stan Williamson	S. California	1913	center
Ernie Smith**	S. California	1932	tackle
Aaron Rosenberg	S. California	1932	guard
Cotton Warburton**	S. California	1933	back
Aaron Rosenberg*	S. California	1933	guard
Larry Stevens	S. California	1933	guard
Harry Smith	S. California	1938	guard
Harry Smith**	S. California	1939	guard

consensus

**unanimous*

John Heisman Collegiate Head Coaching Record

1892	Oberlin	7-0-0
1893	Buchtel (Akron)	5-2-0
1894	Buchtel (Akron)	1-0-0
1894	Oberlin	4-3-1
1895	Auburn	2-1-0
1896	Auburn	3-1-0
1897	Auburn	2-0-1
1898	Auburn	2-1-0
1899	Auburn	3-1-1
1900	Clemson	6-0-0
1901	Clemson	3-1-1
1902	Clemson	6-1-0
1903	Clemson	4-1-1
1904	Georgia Tech	8-1-1
1905	Georgia Tech	6-0-1
1906	Georgia Tech	5-3-1
1907	Georgia Tech	4-4-0
1908	Georgia Tech	6-3-0
1909	Georgia Tech	7-2-0
1910	Georgia Tech	5-3-0
1911	Georgia Tech	6-2-1
1912	Georgia Tech	5-3-1
1913	Georgia Tech	7-2-0
1914	Georgia Tech	6-2-0
1915	Georgia Tech	7-0-1
1916	Georgia Tech	8-0-1
1917*	Georgia Tech	9-0-0
1918	Georgia Tech	6-1-0
1919	Georgia Tech	7-3-0
1920	Penn	6-4-0
1921	Penn	4-3-2
1922	Penn	6-3-0
1923	Wash. & Jefferson	7-1-1
1924	Rice	4-4-0
1925	Rice	4-4-1
1926	Rice	4-4-1
1927	Rice	2-6-1
		187-70-18

* *unanimous national champion*

John Heisman–Coached All Americas

Everett Strupper**	Geo. Tech	1917	back
Walker Carpenter	Geo. Tech	1917	tackle
Bill Fincher**	Geo. Tech	1918	end
Joe Guyon**	Geo. Tech	1918	tackle
Ashel Day**	Geo. Tech	1918	center
John Thurman*	Penn	1922	tackle

Unanimous
**Consensus*

Frank Leahy Collegiate Head Coaching Record

1939	Boston College	9–2–0
1940	Boston College	11–0–0
1941	Notre Dame	8–0–1
1942	Notre Dame	7–2–2
1943+	Notre Dame	9–1–0
1946**	Notre Dame	8–0–1
1947*	Notre Dame	9–0–0
1948	Notre Dame	9–0–1
1949**	Notre Dame	10–0–0
1950	Notre Dame	4–4–1
1951	Notre Dame	7–2–1
1952	Notre Dame	7–2–1
1953**	Notre Dame	9–0–1
		107–13–9

shared national title
**consensus national champion*
+ unanimous national champion

Frank Leahy–Coached All Americas

Gene Goodreault**	Boston College	1940	end
Charles O'Rourke	Boston College	1940	back
Chet Gladchuk	Boston College	1940	center
Bob Dove**	Notre Dame	1941	end
Bernie Crimmins	Notre Dame	1941	guard
Bob Dove**	Notre Dame	1942	end
Angelo Bertelli	Notre Dame	1942	back
Angelo Bertelli**	Notre Dame	1943	back
Creighton Miller**	Notre Dame	1943	back
John Yonakor**	Notre Dame	1943	end

Appendix B: Awards and Coaches

Jim White**	Notre Dame	1943	tackle
Pat Filley**	Notre Dame	1943	guard
Johnny Lujack*	Notre Dame	1946	back
George Connor**	Notre Dame	1946	tackle
John Mastrangelo	Notre Dame	1946	guard
Geo. Strohmeyer	Notre Dame	1946	center
Johnny Lujack*	Notre Dame	1947	back
George Connor**	Notre Dame	1947	tackle
Bill Fischer**	Notre Dame	1947	guard
Leon Hart	Notre Dame	1947	end
Ziggy Czarobski	Notre Dame	1947	tackle
Emil Sitko**	Notre Dame	1948	back
Leon Hart**	Notre Dame	1948	end
Jim Fischer**	Notre Dame	1948	guard
Marty Wendell	Notre Dame	1948	guard
Emil Sitko*	Notre Dame	1949	back
Bob Williams**	Notre Dame	1949	back
Leon Hart*	Notre Dame	1949	end
Jim Martin	Notre Dame	1949	tackle
Jerry Groom**	Notre Dame	1950	center
Bob Williams	Notre Dame	1950	back
Bob Toneff	Notre Dame	1951	tackle
John Lattner*	Notre Dame	1952	back
John Lattner*	Notre Dame	1953	back
Art Hunter**	Notre Dame	1953	tackle

Unanimous
**Consensus*

Frank Leahy–Coached Award Winners and Heisman Trophy Contenders

1941	QB Angelo Bertelli was 2nd in Heisman voting
1942	QB Angelo Bertelli was 6th in Heisman voting
1943	QB Angelo Bertelli won the Heisman Trophy
1943	HB Creighton Miller was 4th in Heisman voting
1943	T Jim White was 9th in Heisman voting
1946	QB Johnny Lujack was 3rd in Heisman voting
1946	T George Connor won the Outland Award
1947	QB Johnny Lujack won the Heisman Trophy
1948	HB Emil Sitko was 7th in Heisman voting

Appendix B: Awards and Coaches

1948	G Bill Fischer won the Outland Award
1949	E Leon Hart won the Heisman Trophy. Won the Maxwell Award
1949	QB Bob Williams was 5th in Heisman voting
1949	HB Emil Sitko was 8th in Heisman voting
1950	QB Bob Williams was 6th in Heisman voting
1952	HB John Lattner was 5th in Heisman voting. Won the Maxwell Award
1953	HB John Lattner won the Heisman Trophy. Won the Maxwell Award

Frank Leahy was the AFCA Coach of the Year in 1941.

Benny Oosterbaan Collegiate Coaching Record

1948*	Michigan	9-0-0
1949	Michigan	6-2-1
1950	Michigan	6-3-1
1951	Michigan	4-5-0
1952	Michigan	5-4-0
1953	Michigan	6-3-0
1954	Michigan	6-3-0
1955	Michigan	7-2-0
1956	Michigan	7-2-0
1957	Michigan	5-3-1
1958	Michigan	2-6-1
		63-33-4

* unanimous national champion

Benny Oosterbaan-Coached All Americas

Dick Rifenburg**	Michigan	1948	end
Leo Nomellini**	Michigan	1948	tackle
Pete Elliott	Michigan	1948	back
Alvin Wistert**	Michigan	1949	tackle
Allen Wahl	Michigan	1949	tackle
Allen Wahl	Michigan	1950	tackle
Lowell Perry	Michigan	1952	back
Art Walker	Michigan	1954	tackle
Ron Kramer**	Michigan	1955	end
Ron Kramer*	Michigan	1956	end
Jim Pace	Michigan	1957	back

* unanimous

** consensus

Benny Oosterbaan–Coached Award Winners and Heisman Trophy Contenders

1955	E Ron Kramer was 8th in Heisman voting
1956	E Ron Kramer was 6th in Heisman voting

Benny Oosterbaan was AFCA Coach of the Year in 1948.

Darrell Royal Collegiate Head Coaching Record

1954	Mississippi State	6–4–0
1955	Mississippi State	6–4–0
1956	Washington	5–5–0
1957	Texas	6–4–1
1958	Texas	7–3–0
1959	Texas	9–2–0
1960	Texas	7–3–1
1961	Texas	10–1–0
1962	Texas	9–1–1
1963+	Texas	11–0–0
1964	Texas	10–1–0
1965	Texas	6–4–0
1966	Texas	7–4–0
1967	Texas	6–4–0
1968*	Texas	9–1–1
1969**	Texas	11–0–0
1970*	Texas	10–1–0
1971	Texas	8–3–0
1972	Texas	10–1–0
1973	Texas	8–3–0
1974	Texas	8–4–0
1975	Texas	10–2–0
1976	Texas	5–5–1
		184–60–5

shared national title
** *consensus national champion*
+ *unanimous national champion*

Appendix B: Awards and Coaches

Darrell Royal–Coached All Americas

Hal Easterwood	MSU	1954	center
Art Cavis	MSU	1955	tackle
Scott Suber	MSU	1955	guard
Maurice Doke	Texas	1959	guard
Jimmy Saxton*	Texas	1961	back
Don Talbert	Texas	1961	tackle
Johnny Treadwell*	Texas	1962	guard
Scott Appleton*	Texas	1963	tackle
Tommy Ford	Texas	1963	back
Tommy Nobis	Texas	1964	guard
Tommy Nobis*	Texas	1965+	linebacker
Corby Robertson	Texas	1967	linebacker
Chris Gilbert**	Texas	1968	offensive back
Lloyd Wainscott	Texas	1968	defensive tackle
Bob McKay**	Texas	1969	offensive tackle
Steve Worster	Texas	1969	offensive back
Charles Speyrer	Texas	1969	offensive end
Bobby Wuensch	Texas	1969	offensive guard
Glen Halsell	Texas	1969	linebacker
Steve Worster**	Texas	1970	offensive back
Bobby Wuensch**	Texas	1970	offensive tackle
Bill Atessis**	Texas	1970	defensive end
Jerry Sisemore*	Texas	1971	offensive tackle
Jerry Sisemore**	Texas	1972	offensive tackle
Roosevelt Leaks**	Texas	1973	offensive back
Bill Wyman*	Texas	1973	center
Bob Simmons	Texas	1974	offensive tackle
Doug English	Texas	1974	defensive lineman
Bob Simmons**	Texas	1975	offensive tackle
Marty Atkins	Texas	1975	quarterback
Earl Campbell	Texas	1975	offensive back

Unanimous

**Consensus*

+ *First year voted offensive and defensive All Americas*

Darrell Royal–Coached Award Winners and Heisman Trophy Contenders

1961	QB Jimmy Saxton was 3rd in Heisman voting
1963	DT Scott Appleton was 5th in Heisman voting. Won Maxwell Award
1965	LB Tommy Nobis was 7th in Heisman voting. Won Maxwell Award
1968	RB Chris Gilbert was 8th in Heisman voting
1970	RB Steve Worster was 4th in Heisman voting
1973	RB Roosevelt Leaks was 3rd in Heisman voting

In 1977, one year after Royal left Texas, senior RB Earl Campbell won the Heisman Trophy.

Darrell Royal was the AFCA and Eddie Robinson Coach of the Year in 1963.

Royal was AFCA Coach of the Year again in 1970 (tie).

Royal was the Eddie Robinson Coach of the Year in 1961.

Bob Devaney Collegiate Head Coaching Record

1957	Wyoming	4-3-3
1958	Wyoming	8-3-0
1959	Wyoming	9-1-0
1960	Wyoming	8-2-0
1961	Wyoming	6-1-2
1962	Nebraska	9-2-0
1963	Nebraska	10-1-0
1964	Nebraska	9-2-0
1965	Nebraska	10-1-0
1966	Nebraska	9-2-0
1967	Nebraska	6-4-0
1968	Nebraska	6-4-0
1969	Nebraska	9-2-0
1970**	Nebraska	11-0-1
1971+	Nebraska	13-0-0
1972	Nebraska	9-2-1
		136-30-7

* shared national title
** consensus national champion
+ unanimous national champion

Bob Devaney–Coached All Americas

Bob Brown*	Nebraska	1963	guard
Larry Kramer*	Nebraska	1964	tackle
Freeman White**	Nebraska	1965+	offensive end
Walt Barnes**	Nebraska	1965	defensive tackle
Tony Jeter	Nebraska	1965+	defensive lineman
LaVerne Allers**	Nebraska	1966	offensive guard
Wayne Meylan**	Nebraska	1966	middle guard
Wayne Meylan**	Nebraska	1967	middle guard
Joe Armstrong	Nebraska	1968	offensive guard
Bob Newton**	Nebraska	1970	offensive tackle
Jerry Murtaugh	Nebraska	1970	linebacker
Johnny Rodgers**	Nebraska	1971	offensive end
Willie Harper**	Nebraska	1971	defensive end
Larry Jacobson**	Nebraska	1971	defensive tackle
Rich Glover	Nebraska	1971	defensive tackle
Johnny Rodgers*	Nebraska	1972	wide receiver
Daryl White	Nebraska	1972	offensive tackle
Rich Glover*	Nebraska	1972	middle guard
Willie Harper**	Nebraska	1972	defensive end

Unanimous
**Consensus*
+ *First year voted offensive and defensive All Americas*

Bob Devaney–Coached Award Winners and Heisman Trophy Contenders

1967	MG Wayne Meylan was 9th in Heisman voting
1971	QB Jerry Tagge was 7th in Heisman voting
1971	DT Larry Jacobson won the Outland Trophy
1972	WR Johnny Rodgers won the Heisman Trophy. Won the Camp Award
1972	MG Rich Glover was 3rd in Heisman voting. Won the Outland Trophy. Won the Lombardi Award.

Bob Devaney was the Eddie Robinson Coach of the Year in 1971.

John McKay Collegiate Head Coaching Record

1960	S. California	4–6–0
1961	S. California	4–5–1

1962**	S. California	11-0-0
1963	S. California	7-3-0
1964	S. California	7-3-0
1965	S. California	7-2-1
1966	S. California	7-4-0
1967**	S. California	10-1-0
1968	S. California	9-1-1
1969	S. California	10-0-1
1970	S. California	6-4-1
1971	S. California	6-4-1
1972+	S. California	12-0-0
1973	S. California	9-2-1
1974*	S. California	10-1-1
1975	S. California	8-4-0
		127-40-8

* shared national title
** consensus national champion
+ unanimous national champion

John McKay–Coached All Americas

Hal Bedsole**	S. California	1962	end
Damon Blame	S. California	1962	guard
Damon Blame	S. California	1963	guard
Mike Garrett	S. California	1964	back
Bill Fisk	S. California	1964	guard
Mike Garrett*	S. California	1965+	back
Ron Yary**	S. California	1966	offensive tackle
Nate Shaw**	S. California	1966	defensive back
O. J. Simpson*	S. California	1967	offensive back
Tim Rossovich**	S. California	1967	defensive end
Adrian Young**	S. California	1967	linebacker
O. J. Simpson*	S. California	1968	offensive back
Mike Battle	S. California	1968	defensive back
Sid Smith	S. California	1969	offensive tackle
Jim Gunn**	S. California	1969	defensive end
Al Cowlings	S. California	1969	defensive tackle
Charlie Weaver**	S. California	1970	defensive end
John Vella	S. California	1971	offensive tackle
Charles Young*	S. California	1972	tight end

Sam Cunningham	S. California	1972	offensive back
Pete Adams	S. California	1972	offensive tackle
John Grant	S. California	1972	defensive lineman
Richard Wood	S. California	1972	linebacker
Lynn Swann**	S. California	1973	wide receiver
Booker Brown**	S. California	1973	offensive tackle
Richard Wood**	S. California	1973	linebacker
Artimus Parker**	S. California	1973	defensive back
Anthony Davis*	S. California	1974	offensive back
Richard Wood**	S. California	1974	linebacker
Charles Phillips	S. California	1974	defensive back
Ricky Bell*	S. California	1975	offensive back
Marvin Powell	S. California	1975	offensive lineman

* Unanimous
** Consensus
+ First year voted offensive and defensive All Americas

John McKay–Coached Award Winners and Heisman Trophy Contenders

1965	TB Mike Garrett won the Heisman Trophy
1967	TB O. J. Simpson was 2nd in Heisman voting. Won Camp Award
1967	OT Ron Yary won the Outland Trophy
1968	TB O. J. Simpson won the Heisman Trophy. Won Maxwell Award. Won Camp Award
1974	TB Anthony Davis was 2nd in Heisman voting
1975	TB Ricky Bell was 3rd in Heisman voting

John McKay was the AFCA and Eddie Robinson Coach of the Year in 1972. John McKay was the Eddie Robinson Coach of the Year in 1961.

Tom Osborne Collegiate Head Coaching Record

1973	Nebraska	9–2–1
1974	Nebraska	9–3–0
1975	Nebraska	10–2–0
1976	Nebraska	9–3–1
1977	Nebraska	9–3–0
1978	Nebraska	9–3–0
1979	Nebraska	10–2–0

Appendix B: Awards and Coaches

1980*	Nebraska	10-2-0
1981*	Nebraska	9-3-0
1982*	Nebraska	12-1-0
1983*	Nebraska	12-1-0
1984*	Nebraska	10-2-0
1985	Nebraska	9-3-0
1986	Nebraska	10-2-0
1987	Nebraska	10-2-0
1988	Nebraska	11-2-0
1989	Nebraska	10-2-0
1990	Nebraska	9-3-0
1991	Nebraska	9-2-1
1992	Nebraska	9-3-0
1993*	Nebraska	11-1-0
1994**	Nebraska	13-0-0
1995+	Nebraska	12-0-0
1996	Nebraska	11-2-0
1997*	Nebraska	13-0-0
		255-49-3

* shared national title
** consensus national champion
\+ unanimous national champion

Tom Osborne-Coached All Americas

Daryl White	Nebraska	1973	offensive tackle
John Dutton*	Nebraska	1973	defensive lineman
Marvin Crenshaw**	Nebraska	1974	offensive tackle
David Humm	Nebraska	1974	quarterback
Rik Bonness	Nebraska	1974	center
Rik Bonness*	Nebraska	1975	center
Wonder Monds	Nebraska	1975	defensive back
David Butterfield**	Nebraska	1976	defensive back
Mike Fultz	Nebraska	1976	defensive lineman
Tom Davis	Nebraska	1977	center
Kelvin Clark**	Nebraska	1978	offensive tackle
Junior Miller*	Nebraska	1979	tight end
Jarvis Redwine**	Nebraska	1980	offensive back
Randy Schleusener**	Nebraska	1980	offensive lineman
Derrie Nelson	Nebraska	1980	defensive lineman

David Rimington*	Nebraska	1981	center
Jimmy Williams	Nebraska	1981	defensive lineman
Mike Rozier**	Nebraska	1982	offensive back
David Rimington*	Nebraska	1982	center
Mike Rozier*	Nebraska	1983	offensive back
Irving Fryar*	Nebraska	1983	wide receiver
Dean Steinkuhler**	Nebraska	1983	offensive lineman
Mark Traynowicz*	Nebraska	1984	center
Bret Clark	Nebraska	1984	defensive back
Bill Lewis	Nebraska	1985	center
Jim Skow	Nebraska	1985	defensive lineman
Danny Noonan*	Nebraska	1986	defensive lineman
John McCormick	Nebraska	1987	offensive lineman
Broderick Thomas	Nebraska	1987	defensive lineman
Jake Young**	Nebraska	1988	center
Broderick Thomas**	Nebraska	1988	defensive lineman
Jake Young**	Nebraska	1989	center
Doug Glaser	Nebraska	1989	offensive lineman
Kenny Walker	Nebraska	1990	defensive lineman
Will Shields*	Nebraska	1992	offensive lineman
Travis Hill	Nebraska	1992	defensive lineman
Trev Alberts*	Nebraska	1993	linebacker
Zach Wiegert*	Nebraska	1994	offensive lineman
Brenden Stai**	Nebraska	1994	offensive lineman
Ed Stewart**	Nebraska	1994	linebacker
Tommie Frazier**	Nebraska	1995	quarterback
Aaron Graham	Nebraska	1995	offensive lineman
Jared Tomich	Nebraska	1995	defensive lineman
Aaron Taylor**	Nebraska	1996	center
Grant Wistrom**	Nebraska	1996	defensive lineman
Jared Tomich	Nebraska	1996	defensive lineman
Aaron Taylor*	Nebraska	1997	offensive lineman
Grant Wistrom**	Nebraska	1997	defensive lineman
Jason Peter**	Nebraska	1997	defensive lineman

Unanimous
**Consensus*

Tom Osborne–Coached Award Winners and Heisman Trophy Contenders

1974	QB David Humm was 5th in Heisman voting
1980	RB Jarvis Redwine was 8th in Heisman voting
1981	C David Rimington won the Outland Trophy
1982	C David Rimington was 5th in Heisman voting. Won the Outland Trophy. Won the Lombardi Trophy
1982	RB Mike Rozier was 10th in Heisman voting
1983	RB Mike Rozier won the Heisman Trophy. Won the Maxwell Award. Won the Camp Award
1983	OG Dean Steinkuhler won the Outland Trophy. Won the Lombardi Award
1983	QB Turner Gill was 4th in Heisman voting
1992	G Will Shields won the Outland Trophy
1993	LB Trev Alberts won the Butkus Award
1994	RB Lawrence Phillips was 8th in Heisman voting
1994	OT Zach Wiegert was 10th in Heisman voting. Won Outland Trophy
1995	QB Tommie Frazier was 2nd in Heisman voting. Won Unitas Award
1997	OG Aaron Taylor won the Outland Trophy
1997	DE Grant Wistrom won the Lombardi Award

Tom Osborne was the AFCA Coach of the Year in 1994.

Phillip Fulmer Collegiate Head Coaching Record

1992	Tennessee	4–0–0
1993	Tennessee	10–2–0
1994	Tennessee	8–4–0
1995	Tennessee	11–1–0
1996	Tennessee	10–2–0
1997	Tennessee	11–2–0
1998*	Tennessee	13–0–0
1999	Tennessee	9–3–0
2000	Tennessee	8–4–0
2001	Tennessee	11–2–0
2002	Tennessee	8–5–0
2003	Tennessee	10–3–0
2004	Tennessee	10–3–0

2005	Tennessee	5–6–0
2006	Tennessee	9–4–0
2007	Tennessee	10–4–0
2008	Tennessee	5–7–0
		152–52–1

unanimous national champion

Phillip Fulmer–Coached All Americas

John Becksvoort	Tennessee	1993	kicker
Peyton Manning**	Tennessee	1997	quarterback
Leonard Little	Tennessee	1997	linebacker
Al Wilson**	Tennessee	1998	linebacker
Cosey Coleman**	Tennessee	1999	offensive lineman
Deon Grant**	Tennessee	1999	defensive back
Raynoch Thompson	Tennessee	1999	linebacker
John Henderson**	Tennessee	2000	defensive lineman
Travis Stephens	Tennessee	2001	offensive back
John Henderson**	Tennessee	2001	defensive lineman
Dustin Colquitt**	Tennessee	2003	punter
Michael Munoz**	Tennessee	2004	offensive lineman
Jesse Mahelona	Tennessee	2004	defensive lineman
Kevin Burnett	Tennessee	2004	linebacker
Arron Sears**	Tennessee	2006	offensive lineman
Robert Meachem**	Tennessee	2006	wide receiver
Daniel Lincoln	Tennessee	2007	kicker
Eric Berry*	Tennessee	2008	defensive back

* Unanimous
** Consensus

Phillip Fulmer–Coached Award Winners and Heisman Trophy Contenders

1993	QB Heath Shuler was 2nd in Heisman voting
1995	QB Peyton Manning was 6th in Heisman voting
1996	QB Peyton Manning was 8th in Heisman voting
1997	QB Peyton Manning was 2nd in Heisman voting
2000	DL John Henderson won the Outland Award

Phillip Fulmer was AFCA and Eddie Robinson Coach of the Year in 1998.

Bobby Bowden Collegiate Head Coaching Record

1956–1958	South Georgia State (no records available)	
1970	West Virginia	8-3-0
1971	West Virginia	7-4-0
1972	West Virginia	8-4-0
1973	West Virginia	6-5-0
1974	West Virginia	4-7-0
1975	West Virginia	9-3-0
1976	Florida State	5-6-0
1977	Florida State	10-2-0
1978	Florida State	8-3-0
1979	Florida State	11-1-0
1980*	Florida State	10-2-0
1981	Florida State	6-5-0
1982	Florida State	9-3-0
1983	Florida State	7-5-0
1984	Florida State	7-3-2
1985	Florida State	9-3-0
1986	Florida State	7-4-1
1987**	Florida State	11-1-0
1988	Florida State	11-1-0
1989	Florida State	10-2-0
1990	Florida State	10-2-0
1991	Florida State	11-2-0
1992*	Florida State	11-1-0
1993**	Florida State	12-1-0
1994*	Florida State	10-1-1
1995	Florida State	10-2-0
1996*	Florida State	11-1-0
1997	Florida State	11-1-0
1998	Florida State	12-2-0
1999+	Florida State	12-0-0
2000	Florida State	11-2-0
2001	Florida State	8-4-0
2002	Florida State	9-5-0
2003	Florida State	10-3-0
2004	Florida State	9-3-0
2005	Florida State	8-5-0
2006	Florida State	7-6-0

2007	Florida State		7–6–0
2008	Florida State		9–4–0
2009	Florida State		7–6–0
			358–124–4

* shared national title
** consensus national champion
+ unanimous national champion

Bobby Bowden–Coached All Americas

Jim Braxton	W. Virginia	1970	offensive end
Danny Buggs	W. Virginia	1973	wide receiver
Ron Simmons**	Florida St.	1979	middle guard
Ron Simmons**	Florida St.	1980	middle guard
Rohn Stark	Florida St.	1980	punter
Rohn Stark	Florida St.	1981	punter
Greg Allen**	Florida St.	1983	offensive back
Greg Allen	Florida St.	1984	offensive back
Jamie Dukes**	Florida St.	1985	offensive lineman
Deion Sanders*	Florida St.	1987	defensive back
Paul McGowan	Florida St.	1987	linebacker
Pat Tomberlin	Florida St.	1988	offensive lineman
Deion Sanders*	Florida St.	1988	defensive back
Michael Tanks	Florida St.	1989	center
Leroy Butler**	Florida St.	1989	defensive back
Odell Haggins	Florida St.	1989	defensive lineman
Lawrence Dawsey	Florida St.	1990	wide receiver
Casey Weldon	Florida St.	1991	quarterback
Amp Lee	Florida St.	1991	offensive back
Marvin Jones**	Florida St.	1991	defensive lineman
Terrell Buckley*	Florida St.	1991	defensive back
Marvin Jones*	Florida St.	1992	linebacker
Charlie Ward*	Florida St.	1993	quarterback
Derrick Brooks*	Florida St.	1993	linebacker
Corey Sawyer**	Florida St.	1993	defensive back
Derrick Alexander	Florida St.	1993	defensive lineman
Clay Shiver	Florida St.	1994	center
Derrick Brooks**	Florida St.	1994	linebacker
Clifton Abraham**	Florida St.	1994	defensive back
Derrick Alexander	Florida St.	1994	defensive lineman

Clay Shiver	Florida St.	1995	center
Warrick Dunn	Florida St.	1996	quarterback
Peter Boulware**	Florida St.	1996	defensive lineman
Reinard Wilson**	Florida St.	1996	defensive lineman
Kevin Long	Florida St.	1997	center
Andre Wadsworth**	Florida St.	1997	defensive lineman
Sam Cowart**	Florida St.	1997	linebacker
Peter Warrick**	Florida St.	1998	wide receiver
Sebastian Janikowski**	Florida St.	1998	place kicker
Jason Whitaker	Florida St.	1998	offensive lineman
Corey Simon	Florida St.	1998	defensive lineman
Peter Warrick*	Florida St.	1999	wide receiver
Sebastian Janikowski**	Florida St.	1999	place kicker
Jason Whitaker**	Florida St.	1999	offensive lineman
Corey Simon**	Florida St.	1999	defensive lineman
Marvin Minnis**	Florida St.	2000	wide receiver
Chris Weinke	Florida St.	2000	quarterback
Tarlos Thomas	Florida St.	2000	offensive lineman
Jamal Reynolds*	Florida St.	2000	defensive lineman
Tay Cody	Florida St.	2000	defensive back
Brett Williams	Florida St.	2002	offensive lineman
Alex Barron**	Florida St.	2003	offensive lineman
Alex Barron*	Florida St.	2004	offensive lineman

Unanimous
**Consensus*

Bobby Bowden–Coached Award Winners and Heisman Trophy Contenders

1979	MG Ron Simmons was 9th in Heisman voting
1984	RB Greg Allen was 8th in Heisman voting
1987	LB Paul McGowan won the Butkus Award
1988	DB Deion Sanders was 8th in Heisman voting. Won Thorpe Award
1991	QB Casey Weldon was 2nd in Heisman voting. Won Unitas Award
1991	DB Terrell Buckley was 8th in Heisman voting. Won Thorpe Award
1992	LB Marvin Jones was 4th in Heisman voting. Won Lombardi Award. Won Butkus Award.

Appendix B: Awards and Coaches

1992	QB Charlie Ward was 6th in Heisman voting
1993	QB Charlie Ward won Heisman Trophy. Won Maxwell Award. Won Camp Award. Won O'Brien Award. Won Unitas Award.
1995	RB Warrick Dunn was 9th in Heisman voting
1996	RB Warrick Dunn was 5th in Heisman voting
1998	PK Sebastian Janikowski won the Groza Award
1999	WR Peter Warrick was 6th in Heisman voting
1999	PK Sebastian Janikowski won the Groza Award
2000	QB Chris Weinke won the Heisman Trophy. Won O'Brien Award. Won Unitas Award
2000	DL Jamal Reynolds won the Lombardi Award

For all his success Bobby Bowden was never named "coach of the year."

Larry Coker Collegiate Head Coaching Record

2001*	Miami	12–0
2002	Miami	12–1
2003	Miami	11–2
2004	Miami	9–3
2005	Miami	9–3
2006	Miami	7–6
2011	U of Texas San Antonio	4–6
2012	U of Texas San Antonio	8–4
2013	U of Texas San Antonio	7–5
2014	U of Texas San Antonio	4–8
2015	U of Texas San Antonio	3–9
		86–47

* *unanimous national champion*

Larry Coker–Coached All Americas

Bryant McKinnie*	Miami	2001	offensive line
Joaquin Gonzalez	Miami	2001	offensive line
Jeremy Shockey	Miami	2001	tight end
Ed Reed*	Miami	2001	defensive back
Phillip Buchanon	Miami	2001	defensive back
Todd Sievers	Miami	2001	place kicker

Ken Dorsey	Miami	2002	quarterback
Willis McGahee**	Miami	2002	running back
Brett Romberg**	Miami	2002	center
Jerome McDougle	Miami	2002	defensive line
Kellen Winslow*	Miami	2003	tight end
Jonathan Vilma	Miami	2003	linebacker
Sean Taylor*	Miami	2003	defensive back
Antrel Rolle*	Miami	2004	defensive back
Eric Winston	Miami	2005	offensive line
Brandon Meriweather	Miami	2005	defensive back
Kelly Jennings	Miami	2005	defensive back

Unanimous
Consensus

Larry Coker-Coached Award Winners and Heisman Trophy Contenders

2001	QB Ken Dorsey was 3rd in Heisman voting. Won Maxwell Award.
2001	OL Bryant McKinnie was 8th in Heisman voting. Won the Outland Trophy
2002	RB Willis McGahee was 4th in Heisman voting
2002	QB Ken Dorsey was 5th in Heisman voting
2002	C Brett Romberg won the Rimington Award
2003	TE Kellen Winslow won the Mackey Award

Pete Carroll Collegiate Head Coaching Record

2001	Southern California	6-6
2002*	Southern California	11-2
2003*	Southern California	12-1
2004+	Southern California	13-0
2005	Southern California	12-1
2006	Southern California	11-2
2007	Southern California	11-2
2008	Southern California	12-1
2009	Southern California	9-4
		97-19

shared national title
**consensus national champion*
+ *unanimous national champion*

Pete Carroll–Coached All Americas

Name	School	Year	Position
Troy Polamalu	Southern California	2001	defensive back
Carson Palmer**	Southern California	2002	quarterback
Troy Polamalu**	Southern California	2002	defensive back
Matt Leinart	Southern California	2003	quarterback
Jacob Rogers**	Southern California	2003	offensive line
Mike Williams**	Southern California	2003	wide receiver
Tom Malone	Southern California	2003	punter
Kenechi Udeze**	Southern California	2003	defensive line
Matt Leinart**	Southern California	2004	quarterback
Reggie Bush**	Southern California	2004	running back
Mike Patterson	Southern California	2004	defensive line
Matt Grootegoed**	Southern California	2004	linebacker
Lofa Tatupu	Southern California	2004	linebacker
Reggie Bush*	Southern California	2005	running back
Matt Leinart	Southern California	2005	quarterback
Taitusi Lutui**	Southern California	2005	offensive line
Sam Baker	Southern California	2005	offensive line
Dwayne Jarrett*	Southern California	2005	wide receiver
Darnell Bing	Southern California	2005	defensive back
Ryan Kalil	Southern California	2006	center
Sam Baker**	Southern California	2006	offensive line
Dwayne Jarrett**	Southern California	2006	wide receiver
Steve Smith	Southern California	2006	wide receiver
Sedrick Ellis	Southern California	2006	defensive line
Sam Baker	Southern California	2007	offensive line
Fred Davis	Southern California	2007	tight end
Sedrick Ellis*	Southern California	2007	defensive line
Keith Rivers	Southern California	2007	linebacker
Taylor Mays	Southern California	2007	defensive back
Rey Maualuga*	Southern California	2008	linebacker
Brian Cushing	Southern California	2008	linebacker
Taylor Mays**	Southern California	2008	defensive back
Charles Brown	Southern California	2009	offensive line
Taylor Mays	Southern California	2009	defensive back

* *Unanimous*
** *Consensus*

Pete Carroll–Coached Award Winners and Heisman Trophy Contenders

2002	QB Carson Palmer won the Heisman Trophy. Won Unitas Award.
2003	QB Matt Leinart was 6th in Heisman voting
2003	WR Mike Williams was 8th in Heisman voting
2004	QB Matt Leinart won the Heisman Trophy. Won the Camp Award.
2004	RB Reggie Bush was 5th in Heisman voting
2005	QB Matt Leinart was 3rd in Heisman voting. Won the Unitas Award.
2005	RB Reggie Bush won the Heisman Trophy. Won Walker Award.
2006	WR Dwayne Jarrett was 9th in Heisman voting
2007	TE Fred Davis won the Mackey Award.
2008	LB Rey Maualuga was 9th in Heisman voting. Won the Bednarik Award

Pete Carroll was AFCA Coach of the Year in 2003.

Mack Brown Collegiate Head Coaching Record

1983	Appalachian State	6–5–0
1985	Tulane	1–10–0
1986	Tulane	4–7–0
1987	Tulane	6–6–0
1988	North Carolina	1–10–0
1989	North Carolina	1–10–0
1990	North Carolina	6–4–1
1991	North Carolina	7–4–0
1992	North Carolina	9–3–0
1993	North Carolina	10–3–0
1994	North Carolina	8–4–0
1995	North Carolina	7–5–0
1996	North Carolina	10–2–0
1997	North Carolina	11–1–0
1998	Texas	9–3–0
1999	Texas	9–5–0
2000	Texas	9–3–0
2001	Texas	11–2–0
2002	Texas	11–2–0
2003	Texas	10–3–0
2004	Texas	11–1–0
2005*	Texas	13–0–0
2006	Texas	10–3–0
2007	Texas	10–3–0

2008	Texas	12-1-0
2009	Texas	13-1-0
2010	Texas	5-7-0
2011	Texas	8-5-0
2012	Texas	9-4-0
2013	Texas	8-5-0
2019	North Carolina	7-6-0
		252-128-1

unanimous national champion

Mack Brown–Coached All Americas

Marc Zeno	Tulane	1987	wide receiver
Bracey Walker	North Carolina	1993	defensive back
Marcus Jones**	North Carolina	1995	defensive line
Dre' Bly**	North Carolina	1996	defensive back
Greg Ellis**	North Carolina	1997	defensive line
Brian Simmons**	North Carolina	1997	linebacker
Dre' Bly**	North Carolina	1997	defensive back
Ben Adams	Texas	1998	offensive line
Jay Humphrey	Texas	1998	offensive line
Ricky Williams*	Texas	1998	running back
Roger Roesler	Texas	1999	offensive line
Kwame Cavil	Texas	1999	wide receiver
Casey Hampton	Texas	1999	defensive line
Leonard Davis**	Texas	2000	offensive line
Casey Hampton**	Texas	2000	defensive line
Chris Stockton	Texas	2000	placekicker
Mike Williams**	Texas	2001	offensive line
Cory Redding	Texas	2001	defensive line
D.D. Lewis	Texas	2001	linebacker
Quentin Jammer*	Texas	2001	defensive back
Nathan Vasher	Texas	2001	defensive back
Derrick Dockery**	Texas	2002	offensive line
Cory Redding	Texas	2002	defensive line
Rod Babers	Texas	2002	defensive back
Tillman Holloway	Texas	2003	offensive line
Roy Williams	Texas	2003	wide receiver
Marcus Tubbs	Texas	2003	defensive line
Derrick Johnson**	Texas	2003	linebacker

Appendix B: Awards and Coaches

Nathan Vasher	Texas	2003	defensive back
Jonathan Scott	Texas	2004	offensive line
Cedric Benson	Texas	2004	running back
Rodrique Wright	Texas	2004	defensive line
Derrick Johnson*	Texas	2004	linebacker
Michael Huff	Texas	2004	defensive back
Will Allen	Texas	2005	offensive line
Justin Blalock	Texas	2005	offensive line
Jonathan Scott*	Texas	2005	offensive line
Vince Young**	Texas	2005	quarterback
Rodrique Wright**	Texas	2005	defensive line
Aaron Harris	Texas	2005	linebacker
Michael Huff*	Texas	2005	defensive back
Justin Blalock*	Texas	2006	offensive line
Tim Crowder	Texas	2006	defensive line
Aaron Ross	Texas	2006	defensive back
Michael Griffin	Texas	2006	defensive back
Tony Hills	Texas	2007	offensive line
Frank Okam	Texas	2007	defensive line
Colt McCoy**	Texas	2008	quarterback
Jordan Shipley	Texas	2008	wide receiver
Brian Orakpo*	Texas	2008	defensive line
Sergio Kindle	Texas	2008	linebacker
Chris Hall	Texas	2009	center
Adam Ulatoski	Texas	2009	offensive line
Colt McCoy*	Texas	2009	quarterback
Jordan Shipley**	Texas	2009	wide receiver
Sergio Kindle	Texas	2009	defensive line
Earl Thomas**	Texas	2009	defensive back
Hunter Lawrence	Texas	2009	placekicker
Sam Acho	Texas	2010	defensive line
Alex Okafor	Texas	2011	defensive line
Kenny Vaccaro	Texas	2012	defensive back
Jackson Jeffcoat**	Texas	2013	defensive line
Anthony Fera**	Texas	2013	placekicker

* Unanimous
** Consensus

Mack Brown–Coached Award Winners and Heisman Trophy Contenders

1998	RB Ricky Williams won the Heisman Trophy. Won the Doak Walker Award. Won the Maxwell Award. Won the Camp Award.
2004	LB Derrick Johnson won the Nagurski Trophy. Won the Butkus Award.
2004	RB Cedric Benson was 6th in Heisman voting
2005	QB Vince Young was 2nd in Heisman voting. Won the Manning Award. Won the O'Brien Award. Won the Maxwell Award.
2005	DB Aaron Ross won the Jim Thorpe Award
2006	DB Michael Huff won the Jim Thorpe Award
2008	DL Brian Orakpo won the Nagurski Trophy. Won the Lombardi Award. Won the Hendricks Award.
2008	QB Colt McCoy was 2nd in Heisman voting. Won the Camp Award.
2009	QB Colt McCoy was 3rd in Heisman voting. Won the Unitas Award. Won the O'Brien Award. Won the Manning Award. Won the Maxwell Award. Won the Camp Award.
2013	DL Jackson Jeffcoat won the Hendricks Award

Nick Saban Collegiate Head Coaching Record

1990	Toledo	9–2–0
1995	Michigan State	6–5–1
1996	Michigan State	6–6–0
1997	Michigan State	7–5–0
1998	Michigan State	6–6–0
1999	Michigan State	9–2–0
2000	LSU	8–4–0
2001	LSU	10–3–0
2002	LSU	8–5–0
2003*	LSU	13–1–0
2004	LSU	9–3–0
2007	Alabama	7–6–0
2008	Alabama	12–2–0
2009+	Alabama	14–0–0
2010	Alabama	10–3–0

Appendix B: Awards and Coaches

2011*	Alabama	12–1–0
2012**	Alabama	13–1–0
2013	Alabama	11–2–0
2014	Alabama	12–2–0
2015+	Alabama	14–1–0
2016*	Alabama	14–1–0
2017*	Alabama	13–1–0
2018	Alabama	14–1–0
2019	Alabama	11–2–0
		248–65–1

* shared national title
** consensus national champion
\+ unanimous national champion
Note: NCAA reduced 2007 season to 2-6-0

Nick Saban–Coached All Americas

Flozell Adams	Michigan State	1997	offensive line
Robaire Smith	Michigan State	1998	defensive line
Julian Peterson	Michigan State	1999	linebacker
Josh Reed**	LSU	2001	wide receiver
Bradie James	LSU	2002	linebacker
Stephen Peterman	LSU	2003	offensive line
Chad Lavalais**	LSU	2003	defensive line
Corey Webster	LSU	2003	defensive back
Ben Wilkerson**	LSU	2004	offensive line
Marcus Spears**	LSU	2004	defensive line
Corey Webster	LSU	2004	defensive back
Antoine Caldwell	Alabama	2008	center
Terrence Cody**	Alabama	2008	nose guard
Rashad Johnson	Alabama	2008	safety
Andre Smith	Alabama	2008	offensive line
Terrence Cody**	Alabama	2009	nose guard
Mark Ingram*	Alabama	2009	offensive back
Mike Johnson**	Alabama	2009	offensive line
Rolando McClain*	Alabama	2009	linebacker
Leigh Tiffin	Alabama	2009	kicker
Javier Arenas	Alabama	2009	return specialist
Mark Barron	Alabama	2010	safety
Barrett Jones**	Alabama	2011	offensive line

Trent Richardson**	Alabama	2011	offensive back
Courtney Upshaw**	Alabama	2011	linebacker
Dont'a Hightower	Alabama	2011	linebacker
Dre Kirkpatrick	Alabama	2011	cornerback
DeQuan Menzie	Alabama	2011	cornerback
Mark Barron*	Alabama	2011	safety
Chance Warmack*	Alabama	2012	offensive line
Barrett Jones**	Alabama	2012	offensive line
C. J. Mosley**	Alabama	2012	linebacker
Dee Milliner*	Alabama	2012	cornerback
Cyrus Kouandjio**	Alabama	2013	offensive line
A. J. McCarron	Alabama	2013	quarterback
C. J. Mosley**	Alabama	2013	linebacker
Ha Clinton-Dix	Alabama	2013	safety
Arie Kouandjio	Alabama	2014	offensive line
Amari Cooper*	Alabama	2014	wide receiver
Trey DePriest	Alabama	2014	linebacker
Landon Collins**	Alabama	2014	safety
J. K. Scott	Alabama	2014	punter
Ryan Kelly**	Alabama	2015	offensive line
Derrick Henry*	Alabama	2015	offensive back
A'Shawn Robinson**	Alabama	2015	defensive line
Reggie Ragland**	Alabama	2015	linebacker
Cam Robinson**	Alabama	2016	offensive line
Jonathan Allen*	Alabama	2016	defensive line
Reuben Foster*	Alabama	2016	linebacker
Minkah Fitzpatrick**	Alabama	2016	defensive back
Marlon Humphrey	Alabama	2016	defensive back
Rashaan Evans	Alabama	2017	linebacker
Minkah Fitzpatrick**	Alabama	2017	defensive back
Ross Pierschbacher	Alabama	2018	offensive line
Jonah Williams*	Alabama	2018	offensive line
Tua Tagovailoa	Alabama	2018	quarterback
Jerry Jeudy	Alabama	2018	wide receiver
Quinnen Williams*	Alabama	2018	defensive line
Deionte Thompson	Alabama	2018	defensive back
Jaylen Waddle**	Alabama	2019	wide receiver
Jerry Jeudy	Alabama	2019	wide receiver
Trevon Diggs	Alabama	2019	defensive back

DeVonta Smith	Alabama	2019	defensive back
Jedrick Wills	Alabama	2019	offensive line
Xavier McKinney	Alabama	2019	safety
Raekwon Davis	Alabama	2019	defensive line
Alex Leatherwood	Alabama	2019	offensive line

Unanimous

**Consensus*

Nick Saban–Coached Award Winners and Heisman Trophy Contenders

2001	WR Josh Reed won Biletnikoff Award
2004	C Ben Wilkerson won Rimington Award
2008	OL Andre Smith won the Outland Trophy. Won Jim Parker Trophy
2009	RB Mark Ingram won Heisman Trophy. Won *Sporting News* Player of the Year
2009	LB Rolando McClain won Butkus Award. Won Jack Lambert Trophy
2011	RB Trent Richardson was 3rd in Heisman voting. Won Doak Walker Award
2011	OL Barrett Jones won Outland Trophy. Won Jim Parker Trophy
2012	OL Barrett Jones won Rimington Trophy
2013	QB A. J. McCarron was 2nd in Heisman voting. Won Maxwell Award. Won Johnny Unitas Award. Won Kellen Moore Award.
2013	LB C. J. Mosley won Butkus Award
2014	WR Amari Cooper was 3rd in Heisman voting. Won Biletnikoff Award. Won Paul Warfield Trophy.
2015	RB Derrick Henry won the Heisman Trophy. Won Maxwell Award. Won Walter Camp Award. Won Doak Walker Award.
2015	OL Ryan Kelly won Rimington Trophy.
2016	DL Jonathan Allen was 7th in Heisman voting. Won the Chuck Bednarik Award. Won Bronko Nagurski Trophy. Won Lombardi Award. Won Ted Hendricks Award.
2016	LB Reuben Foster won Butkus Award
2016	OL Cam Richardson won Outland Trophy
2017	DB Minkah Fitzpatrick won Jim Thorpe Award. Won Bednarik Award.
2018	QB Tua Tagovailoa was 2nd in Heisman voting. Won Maxwell Award. Won Camp Award. Won *Sporting News* Player of the Year.
2018	WR Jerry Jeudy won Biletnikoff Award
2018	DL Quinnen Williams was 8th in Heisman voting. Won Outland Trophy. Won Bill Willis Trophy.
2019	QB Tua Tagovailoa was 10th in Heisman voting.

Nick Saban was Eddie Robinson Coach of the Year in 2003 (LSU).
Nick Saban was Eddie Robinson Coach of the Year in 2008 (Alabama).

Jimbo Fisher Collegiate Head Coaching Record

2010	Florida State	10–4
2011	Florida State	9–4
2012	Florida State	12–2
2013*	Florida State	14–0
2014	Florida State	13–1
2015	Florida State	10–3
2016	Florida State	10–3
2017	Florida State	7–6
2018	Texas A&M	9–4
2019	Texas A&M	6–5
		100–32

* unanimous national champion

Jimbo Fisher–Coached All Americas

Rodney Hudson*	Florida State	2010	offensive line
Shawn Powell**	Florida State	2011	punter
Bjorn Werner*	Florida State	2012	defensive line
Dustin Hopkins	Florida State	2012	place kicker
Jameis Winston**	Florida State	2013	quarterback
Bryan Stork**	Florida State	2013	offensive line
Cameron Erving	Florida State	2013	offensive line
Kevin Benjamin	Florida State	2013	wide receiver
Timmy Jernigan	Florida State	2013	defensive line
Terrence Brooks	Florida State	2013	defensive back
Lamarcus Joyner*	Florida State	2013	defensive back
Roberto Aguayo	Florida State	2013	place kicker
Tre' Jackson*	Florida State	2014	offensive line
Cameron Erving	Florida State	2014	offensive line
Nick O'Leary**	Florida State	2014	tight end
Eddie Goldman	Florida State	2014	defensive line
Jalen Ramsey**	Florida State	2014	defensive back
Roberto Aguayo**	Florida State	2014	place kicker
Dalvin Cook	Florida State	2015	running back
Roderick Johnson	Florida State	2015	offensive line
Jalen Ramsey**	Florida State	2015	defensive back
Roberto Aguayo	Florida State	2015	place kicker
Dalvin Cook*	Florida State	2016	running back

Appendix B: Awards and Coaches

Roderick Johnson	Florida State	2016	offensive line
Demarcus Walker**	Florida State	2016	defensive line
Tarvarus McFadden	Florida State	2016	defensive back
Derwin James	Florida State	2017	defensive back
Jace Sternberger**	Texas A&M	2018	tight end
Braden Mann*	Texas A&M	2018	punter
Braden Mann	Texas A&M	2019	punter

* Unanimous
** Consensus

Jimbo Fisher–Coached Award Winners and Heisman Trophy Contenders

2013	QB Jameis Winston won the Heisman Trophy. Won the O'Brien Award.
2013	C Bryan Stork won the Rimington Award
2013	K Roberto Aguayo won the Groza Award
2014	TE Nick O'Leary won the Mackey Award
2014	QB Jameis Winston was 6th in Heisman voting
2015	RB Dalvin Cook was 7th in Heisman voting
2016	RB Dalvin Cook was tied for 10th in Heisman voting
2018	P Braden Mann won the Guy Award

Urban Meyer Collegiate Head Coaching Record

2001	Bowling Green	8–3
2002	Bowling Green	9–3
2003	Utah	10–2
2004	Utah	12–0
2005	Florida	9–3
2006*	Florida	13–1
2007	Florida	9–4
2008*	Florida	13–1
2009	Florida	13–1
2010	Florida	8–5
2012	Ohio State	12–0
2013	Ohio State	12–2
2014**	Ohio State	14–1
2015	Ohio State	12–1
2016	Ohio State	11–2

2017	Ohio State	12–2
2018	Ohio State	10–1+
		187–32

* *consensus champion*
** *unanimous national champion*
\+ *Meyer on administrative leave for three games. OSU record 13–1 in 2018*

Urban Meyer–Coached All Americas

Alex Smith	Utah	2004	quarterback
Chris Kemoeatu	Utah	2004	offensive line
Chad Jackson	Florida	2005	wide receiver
Reggie Nelson**	Florida	2006	defensive back
Brandon Siler	Florida	2006	linebacker
Ryan Smith	Florida	2006	defensive back
Percy Harvin	Florida	2007	wide receiver
Brandon James	Florida	2007	kick returner
Brandon Spikes	Florida	2007	linebacker
Tim Tebow*	Florida	2007	quarterback
Percy Harvin	Florida	2008	wide receiver
Brandon James	Florida	2008	kick returner
Brandon Spikes**	Florida	2008	linebacker
Tim Tebow	Florida	2008	quarterback
Phil Trautwein	Florida	2008	offensive line
Joe Haden*	Florida	2009	defensive back
Aaron Hernandez**	Florida	2009	tight end
Maurkice Pouncey**	Florida	2009	center
Mike Pouncey	Florida	2009	offensive line
Brandon Spikes**	Florida	2009	linebacker
Tim Tebow	Florida	2009	quarterback
Ahmad Black	Florida	2010	defensive back
Chas Henry**	Florida	2010	punter
Janoris Jenkins	Florida	2010	defensive back
Jonathan Hankins	Ohio State	2012	defensive line
Bradley Roby	Ohio State	2012	defensive back
Ryan Shazier	Ohio State	2013	linebacker
Jack Mewhort	Ohio State	2013	offensive line
Joey Bosa*	Ohio State	2014	defensive line
Michael Bennett	Ohio State	2014	defensive line
Taylor Decker**	Ohio State	2015	offensive line

Appendix B: Awards and Coaches

Adolphus Washington	Ohio State	2015	defensive line
Joey Bosa**	Ohio State	2015	defensive line
Vonn Bell	Ohio State	2015	defensive back
Pat Elflein*	Ohio State	2016	center
Billy Price	Ohio State	2016	offensive line
Curtis Samuel	Ohio State	2016	running back
Malik Hooker*	Ohio State	2016	defensive back
Billy Price*	Ohio State	2017	center
Nick Bosa	Ohio State	2017	defensive line
Denzel Ward**	Ohio State	2017	defensive back
Michael Jordan	Ohio State	2018	offensive line
Dre'Mont Jones	Ohio State	2018	defensive line

* Unanimous

** Consensus

Urban Meyer–Coached Award Winners and Heisman Trophy Contenders

2004	QB Alex Smith was 4th in Heisman voting
2006	DB Reggie Nelson won the Tatum Award
2007	QB Tim Tebow won the Heisman Trophy. Won Maxwell Award.
2008	QB Tim Tebow was 3rd in Heisman voting. Won Maxwell Award. Won Manning Award.
2009	QB Tim Tebow was 5th in Heisman voting
2009	C Maurkice Pouncey won the Rimington Trophy
2009	TE Aaron Hernandez won the Mackey Award
2010	P Chas Henry won the Ray Guy Award
2017	C Billy Price won the Rimington Trophy

Urban Meyer was Eddie Robinson Coach of the Year in 2004.

William "Dabo" Swinney Collegiate Head Coaching Record

2008	Clemson	4–3 (interim)
2009	Clemson	9–5
2010	Clemson	6–7
2011	Clemson	10–4
2012	Clemson	11–2
2013	Clemson	11–2
2014	Clemson	10–3
2015	Clemson	14–1
2016*	Clemson	14–1

2017	Clemson	12–2
2018**	Clemson	15–0
2019	Clemson	14–1
		130–31

* consensus national champion
** unanimous national champion

Dabo Swinney–Coached All Americas

C. J. Spiller*	Clemson	2009	offensive back
Thomas Austin	Clemson	2009	offensive guard
DeAndre McDaniel	Clemson	2009	safety
Da'Quan Bowers*	Clemson	2010	defensive end
DeAndre McDaniel	Clemson	2010	safety
Dwayne Allen	Clemson	2011	tight end
Andre Branch	Clemson	2011	defensive end
Sammy Watkins	Clemson	2011	wide receiver
Tajh Boyd	Clemson	2012	quarterback
Dalton Freeman	Clemson	2012	center
DeAndre Hopkins	Clemson	2012	wide receiver
Sammy Watkins	Clemson	2012	wide receiver
Vic Beasley**	Clemson	2013	defensive end
Sammy Watkins**	Clemson	2013	wide receiver
Vic Beasley**	Clemson	2014	defensive end
Grady Jarrett	Clemson	2014	defensive tackle
Deshaun Watson**	Clemson	2015	quarterback
Jordan Leggett	Clemson	2015	tight end
Shaq Lawson**	Clemson	2015	defensive end
Mackensie Alexander	Clemson	2015	defensive back
Jayron Kearse	Clemson	2015	defensive back
Greg Huegel	Clemson	2015	place kicker
Deshaun Watson**	Clemson	2016	quarterback
Jordan Leggett	Clemson	2016	tight end
Mike Williams	Clemson	2016	wide receiver
Carlos Watkins	Clemson	2016	defensive tackle
Christian Wilkins**	Clemson	2016	defensive end
Ben Boulware**	Clemson	2016	linebacker
Cordrea Tankersley	Clemson	2016	defensive back
Tyrone Crowder	Clemson	2017	offensive guard
Mitch Hyatt**	Clemson	2017	offensive tackle

Dexter Lawrence	Clemson	2017	defensive tackle
Austin Bryant	Clemson	2017	defensive end
Clelin Ferrell**	Clemson	2017	defensive end
Christian Wilkins**	Clemson	2017	defensive lineman
Dorian O'Daniel	Clemson	2017	linebacker
Ray-Ray McCloud	Clemson	2017	punt returner
Travis Etienne**	Clemson	2018	offensive back
Mitch Hyatt**	Clemson	2018	offensive tackle
Christian Wilkins*	Clemson	2018	defensive lineman
Dexter Lawrence	Clemson	2018	defensive tackle
Clelin Ferrell**	Clemson	2018	defensive end
Tre Lamar	Clemson	2018	linebacker
Trayvon Mullen	Clemson	2018	defensive back
Travis Etienne	Clemson	2019	offensive back
John Simpson	Clemson	2019	offensive line
Isaiah Simmons*	Clemson	2019	linebacker

* Unanimous
** Consensus

Dabo Swinney–Coached Award Winners and Heisman Trophy Contenders

2010	DE Da'Quan Bowers won Nagurski Award. Won Hendricks Award
2011	TE Dwayne Allen won John Mackey Award
2015	QB Deshaun Watson was 3rd in Heisman voting. Won Griffin Award. Won Manning Award. Won O'Brien Award
2016	LB Ben Boulware won Lambert Award
2016	QB Deshaun Watson was 3rd in Heisman voting. Won Unitas Award. Won Manning Award. Won O'Brien Award. Won Bowden Award.
2017	DL Christian Wilkins won Bill Willis Trophy
2018	QB Trevor Lawrence won Archie Griffin Award
2018	RB Travis Etienne was 7th in Heisman voting
2018	DL Clelin Ferrell won Hendricks Award
2019	QB Trevor Lawrence was 7th in Heisman voting
2019	RB Travis Etienne was 9th in Heisman voting
2019	LB Isaiah Simmons won Butkus Award

Dabo Swinney was AFCA Coach of the Year in 2015.

Appendix B: Awards and Coaches

Ed Orgeron Collegiate Head Coaching Record

2005	Mississippi	3–8
2006	Mississippi	4–8
2007	Mississippi	3–9
2013	Southern California	6–2 (interim coach)
2016	LSU	6–2 (interim coach)
2017	LSU	9–4
2018	LSU	10–3
2019*	LSU	15–0
		56–36

unanimous national champion

Ed Orgeron–Coached All Americas

Patrick Willis	Mississippi	2005	linebacker
Patrick Willis**	Mississippi	2006	linebacker
Leonard Williams	Southern California	2013	defensive line
Derrius Guice	LSU	2016	offensive back
Ethan Pocic	LSU	2016	offensive line
Jamal Adams	LSU	2016	defensive back
Tre'Davious White **	LSU	2016	defensive back
Devin White**	LSU	2018	linebacker
Greedy Williams**	LSU	2018	defensive back
Grant Delpit*	LSU	2018	defensive back
Joe Burrow*	LSU	2019	quarterback
Ja'Marr Chase*	LSU	2019	wide receiver
Grant Delpit**	LSU	2019	defensive back

* Unanimous
** Consensus

Ed Orgeron–Coached Award Winners and Heisman Contenders

2016	RB Tre'Davious White won the Walter Camp Award
2018	DB Greedy Williams won the Walter Camp Award
2019	QB Joe Burrow won Heisman Trophy. Won Camp Award. Won Maxwell Award. Won O'Brien Award. Won Unitas Award. Won Manning Award. AP and *Sporting News* Player of the Year.
2019	DB Grant Delpit won the Thorpe Award
2019	WR Ja'Marr Chase won the Biletnikoff Award

Ed Orgeron was the AFCA and Eddie Robinson Coach of the Year in 2019.

Appendix B: Awards and Coaches

Other Prominent Coaches

Fielding "Hurry Up" Yost Coaching Record

1897	Ohio Wesleyan	7–1–1
1898	Nebraska	7–4–0
1899	Kansas	10–0–0
1900	Stanford	7–2–1
1900	San Jose State	3–3–1
1901**	Michigan	11–0–0
1902**	Michigan	11–0–0
1903*	Michigan	11–0–1
1904*	Michigan	10–0–0
1905	Michigan	12–1–0
1906	Michigan	4–1–0
1907	Michigan	5–1–0
1908	Michigan	5–2–1
1909	Michigan	6–1–0
1910*	Michigan	3–0–3
1911	Michigan	5–1–2
1912	Michigan	5–2–0
1913	Michigan	6–1–0
1914	Michigan	6–3–0
1915	Michigan	4–3–1
1916	Michigan	7–2–0
1917	Michigan	8–2–0
1918*	Michigan	5–0–0
1919	Michigan	3–4–0
1920	Michigan	5–2–0
1921	Michigan	5–1–1
1922	Michigan	6–0–1
1923*	Michigan	8–0–0
1925	Michigan	7–1–0
1926	Michigan	7–1–0
		199–39–13

* shared national title
** consensus national champion

"Hurry Up" Yost–Coached All Americas

Neil Snow**	Michigan	1901	end
Willie Heston*	Michigan	1903	back
Willie Heston**	Michigan	1904	back
Adolph Schulz**	Michigan	1907	center
Albert Benbrook**	Michigan	1909	guard
Stanfield Wells**	Michigan	1910	end
Albert Benbrook**	Michigan	1910	guard
Jim Craig*	Michigan	1913	back
Miller Pontius**	Michigan	1913	tackle
John Maulbetsch*	Michigan	1914	back
Frank Culver	Michigan	1917	guard
Frank Steketee	Michigan	1918	back
Henry Vick	Michigan	1921	center
Henry Kipke**	Michigan	1922	back
Jack Blott*	Michigan	1923	center
Edliff Slaughter	Michigan	1924	guard
Benny Friedman**	Michigan	1925	back
Benny Oosterbaan**	Michigan	1925	end
Harry Hawkins	Michigan	1925	guard
Robert Brown	Michigan	1925	center
Benny Friedman**	Michigan	1926	back
Benny Oosterbaan**	Michigan	1926	end

* Unanimous
** Consensus

Knute Rockne Head Collegiate Coaching Record

1918	Notre Dame	3-1-2
1919*	Notre Dame	9-0-0
1920*	Notre Dame	9-0-0
1921	Notre Dame	10-1-0
1922	Notre Dame	8-1-1
1923	Notre Dame	9-1-0
1924**	Notre Dame	10-0-0
1925	Notre Dame	7-2-1
1926	Notre Dame	9-1-0
1927*	Notre Dame	7-1-1
1928	Notre Dame	5-4-0
1929**	Notre Dame	9-0-0

1930**	Notre Dame	10–0–0
		105–12–5

shared national title
**consensus national champion*

Knute Rockne–Coached All Americas

George Gipp*	Notre Dame	1920	back
Roger Kiley	Notre Dame	1920	end
Eddie Anderson**	Notre Dame	1921	end
Harry Stuhldreher**	Notre Dame	1924	back
Jim Crowley**	Notre Dame	1924	back
Elmer Layden**	Notre Dame	1924	back
Bud Boeringer**	Notre Dame	1926	center
John Smith**	Notre Dame	1927	guard
Chris Flanagan	Notre Dame	1927	back
Fred Miller	Notre Dame	1928	tackle
Frank Carideo*	Notre Dame	1929	back
Jack Cannon**	Notre Dame	1929	guard
Frank Carideo*	Notre Dame	1930	back
Marchy Schwartz**	Notre Dame	1930	back
Martry Brill	Notre Dame	1930	back
Bert Metzger	Notre Dame	1930	guard

Unanimous
**Consensus*

Earl "Red" Blaik Collegiate Head Coaching Record

1934	Dartmouth	6–3–0
1935	Dartmouth	8–2–0
1936	Dartmouth	7–1–1
1937	Dartmouth	7–0–2
1938	Dartmouth	7–2–0
1939	Dartmouth	5–3–1
1940	Dartmouth	5–4–0
1941	Army	5–3–1
1942	Army	6–3–0
1943	Army	7–2–1
1944**	Army	9–0–0
1945**	Army	9–0–0

1946*	Army	9–0–1
1947	Army	5–2–2
1948	Army	8–0–1
1949	Army	9–0–0
1950	Army	8–1–0
1951	Army	2–7–0
1952	Army	4–4–1
1953	Army	7–1–1
1954	Army	7–2–0
1955	Army	6–3–0
1956	Army	5–3–1
1957	Army	7–2–0
1958	Army	8–0–1
		166–48–14

* shared national title

** consensus national champion

Earl "Red" Blaik–Coached All Americas

Bob MacLeod**	Dartmouth	1938	back
Robin Olds	Army	1942	tackle
Frank Merritt	Army	1943	tackle
Glenn Davis**	Army	1944	back
Doc Blanchard**	Army	1944	back
Doug Kenna	Army	1944	back
Barney Poole	Army	1944	end
John Green	Army	1944	guard
Joe Stanowicz	Army	1944	guard
Glenn Davis*	Army	1945	back
Doc Blanchard*	Army	1945	back
Tex Coulter**	Army	1945	tackle
John Green**	Army	1945	guard
Arnold Tucker	Army	1945	back
Tom McWilliams	Army	1945	back
Hank Foldberg	Army	1945	end
Dick Pitzer	Army	1945	end
Albert Nemetz	Army	1945	tackle
Art Gerometta	Army	1945	guard
Herschel Fuson	Army	1945	center
Glenn Davis*	Army	1946	back
Doc Blanchard*	Army	1946	back

Appendix B: Awards and Coaches

Hank Foldberg**	Army	1946	end
Joe Steffy*	Army	1947	guard
Bobby Stuart	Army	1948	back
Joe Henry	Army	1948	guard
Arnold Galiffa**	Army	1949	back
Dan Foldberg	Army	1949	end
Dan Foldberg*	Army	1950	end
Charles Shira	Army	1950	tackle
J.D. Kimmel	Army	1950	tackle
Tommy Bell	Army	1954	back
Don Holleder	Army	1954	end
Ralph Chesnaukas	Army	1954	guard
Bob Anderson**	Army	1957	back
Pete Dawkins*	Army	1958	back
Bob Anderson	Army	1958	back
Bob Novogratz	Army	1958	guard

Unanimous
Consensus

Earl "Red" Blaik–Coached Award Winners and Heisman Trophy Contenders

1938	HB Bob MacLeod was 4th in Heisman voting
1944	HB Glenn Davis was 2nd in Heisman voting. Won Maxwell Award
1944	FB Doc Blanchard was 3rd in Heisman voting
1944	QB Doug Kenna was 8th in Heisman voting
1945	FB Doc Blanchard won the Heisman Trophy. Won Maxwell Award
1945	HB Glenn Davis was 2nd in Heisman voting
1946	HB Glenn Davis won the Heisman Trophy
1946	FB Doc Blanchard was 4th in Heisman voting
1946	QB Arnie Tucker was 5th in Heisman voting
1947	G Joe Steffy won the Outland Trophy
1949	QB Arnold Galiffa was 4th in Heisman voting
1950	E Dan Foldberg was 8th in Heisman voting
1954	QB Pete Vann was 9th in Heisman voting
1957	HB Bob Anderson was 7th in Heisman voting
1958	HB Pete Dawkins won the Heisman Trophy. Won Maxwell Award

Earl "Red" Blaik was AFCA Coach of the Year in 1946.

Charles "Bud" Wilkinson Collegiate Head Coaching Record

1947	Oklahoma	7–2–1
1948	Oklahoma	10–1–0
1949*	Oklahoma	11–0–0
1950*	Oklahoma	10–1–0
1951	Oklahoma	8–2–0
1952	Oklahoma	8–1–1
1953*	Oklahoma	9–1–1
1954	Oklahoma	10–0–0
1955**	Oklahoma	11–0–0
1956**	Oklahoma	10–0–0
1957*	Oklahoma	10–1–0
1958	Oklahoma	10–1–0
1959	Oklahoma	7–3–0
1960	Oklahoma	3–6–1
1961	Oklahoma	5–5–0
1962	Oklahoma	8–3–0
1963	Oklahoma	8–2–0
		145–29–4

* shared national title
** consensus national champion

Charles "Bud" Wilkinson–Coached All Americas

Buddy Burris**	Oklahoma	1948	guard
Darrell Royal	Oklahoma	1949	back
George Thomas	Oklahoma	1949	back
Jim Owens	Oklahoma	1949	end
Wade Walker	Oklahoma	1949	tackle
Stan West	Oklahoma	1949	guard
Leon Heath**	Oklahoma	1950	back
Jim Weatherall**	Oklahoma	1950	tackle
Jim Weatherall**	Oklahoma	1951	tackle
Billy Vessels**	Oklahoma	1952	back
Buck McPhail	Oklahoma	1952	back
Tom Catlin	Oklahoma	1952	center
J. D. Roberts**	Oklahoma	1953	guard
Max Boydston**	Oklahoma	1954	end
Kurt Burris**	Oklahoma	1954	center/linebacker
Bo Bolinger**	Oklahoma	1955	guard

Tommy McDonald	Oklahoma	1955	back
Tommy McDonald**	Oklahoma	1956	back
Jerry Tubbs*	Oklahoma	1956	center
Ed Gray	Oklahoma	1956	tackle
Clendon Thomas**	Oklahoma	1957	back
Bill Krisher**	Oklahoma	1957	guard
Bob Harrison**	Oklahoma	1958	center
Leon Cross	Oklahoma	1962	guard
Jim Grisham**	Oklahoma	1963	back

* Unanimous

** Consensus

"Bud" Wilkinson–Coached Award Winners and Heisman Trophy Contenders

1948	QB Jack Mitchell was 8th in Heisman voting
1950	FB Leon Heath was 7th in Heisman voting
1951	T Jim Weatherall won the Outland Trophy
1952	HB Billy Vessels won the Heisman Trophy
1952	C Tom Catlin was 10th in Heisman voting
1953	G J. D. Roberts won the Outland Trophy
1953	G J. D. Roberts was 8th in Heisman voting
1954	LB Kurt Burris was 2nd in Heisman voting
1955	G Bo Bolinger was 9th in Heisman voting
1956	HB Tommy McDonald won the Maxwell Trophy Was 3rd in Heisman voting
1956	C Jerry Tubbs was 4th in Heisman voting
1957	HB Clendon Thomas was 9th in Heisman voting
1958	C Bob Harrison was 7th in Heisman voting

Charles "Bud" Wilkinson was AFCA Coach of the Year in 1949.

Lou Holtz Collegiate Head Coaching Record

1969	William & Mary	3–7–0
1970	William & Mary	5–7–0
1971	William & Mary	5–6–0
1972	North Carolina State	8–3–1
1973	North Carolina State	9–3–0
1974	North Carolina State	9–2–1
1975	North Carolina State	7–4–1

Appendix B: Awards and Coaches

1977*	Arkansas	11–1–0
1978	Arkansas	9–2–1
1979	Arkansas	10–2–0
1980	Arkansas	7–5–0
1981	Arkansas	8–4–0
1982	Arkansas	9–2–1
1983	Arkansas	6–5–0
1984	Minnesota	4–7–0
1985	Minnesota	7–5–0
1986	Notre Dame	5–6–0
1987	Notre Dame	8–4–0
1988**	Notre Dame	12–0–0
1989*	Notre Dame	12–1–0
1990	Notre Dame	9–3–0
1991	Notre Dame	10–3–0
1992	Notre Dame	10–1–1
1993*	Notre Dame	11–1–0
1994	Notre Dame	6–5–1
1995	Notre Dame	9–3–0
1996	Notre Dame	8–3–0
1999	South Carolina	0–11–0
2000	South Carolina	8–4–0
2001	South Carolina	9–3–0
2002	South Carolina	5–7–0
2003	South Carolina	5–7–0
2004	South Carolina	6–5–0
		249–132–7

shared national title
**consensus national champion*

Lou Holtz–Coached All Americas

Bill Yoest**	N. Carolina St.	1973	guard
Don Buckey	N. Carolina St.	1975	end
Leotis Harris**	Arkansas	1977	guard
Steve Little**	Arkansas	1977	placekicker
Jim Walker	Arkansas	1978	defensive lineman
Dan Hampton	Arkansas	1978	defensive lineman
Greg Kolenda*	Arkansas	1979	offensive tackle
Bruce Lahay	Arkansas	1981	placekicker
Billy Ray Smith*	Arkansas	1981	defensive lineman

Steve Korte*	Arkansas	1982	offensive lineman
Billy Ray Smith*	Arkansas	1982	defensive lineman
Ron Faurot	Arkansas	1983	defensive lineman
Tim Brown	Notre Dame	1986	wide receiver
Tim Brown*	Notre Dame	1987	wide receiver
Andy Heck	Notre Dame	1988	offensive lineman
Frank Stams**	Notre Dame	1988	defensive lineman
Michael Stonebreaker**	Notre Dame	1988	linebacker
Raghib Ismail	Notre Dame	1989	kick returner
Chris Zorich**	Notre Dame	1989	defensive lineman
Todd Lyght*	Notre Dame	1989	defensive back
Raghib Ismail*	Notre Dame	1990	wide receiver
Chris Zorich*	Notre Dame	1990	defensive lineman
Michael Stonebreaker*	Notre Dame	1990	linebacker
Todd Lyght**	Notre Dame	1990	defensive back
Mirko Jurkovic**	Notre Dame	1991	offensive lineman
Derek Brown	Notre Dame	1991	tight end
Aaron Taylor**	Notre Dame	1992	offensive lineman
Aaron Taylor*	Notre Dame	1993	offensive lineman
Jeff Burris**	Notre Dame	1993	defensive back
Bryant Young	Notre Dame	1993	defensive lineman
Robert Taylor	Notre Dame	1993	defensive back
Robert Taylor**	Notre Dame	1994	defensive back
Sheldon Brown	S. Carolina	2000	defensive back

* *Unanimous*
** *Consensus*

Lou Holtz–Coached Award Winners and Heisman Trophy Contenders

1987	WR Tim Brown won the Heisman Trophy. Won Camp Award
1989	QB Tony Rice was 4th in Heisman voting. Won Unitas Award
1989	WR Raghib Ismail was tied for 10th in Heisman voting
1990	WR Raghib Ismail was 2nd in Heisman voting. Won Camp Award
1990	NT Chris Zorich won Lombardi Award
1992	RB Reggie Brooks was 5th in Heisman voting
1993	OT Aaron Taylor won the Lombardi Award

Lou Holtz was the Eddie Robinson Coach of the Year in 1977 (Arkansas).
Lou Holtz was the Eddie Robinson Coach of the Year in 1988 (Notre Dame).

Paul "Bear" Bryant
Collegiate Head Coaching Record

1945	Maryland	6-2-1
1946	Kentucky	7-3-0
1947	Kentucky	8-3-0
1948	Kentucky	5-3-2
1949	Kentucky	9-3-0
1950*	Kentucky	11-1-0
1951	Kentucky	8-4-0
1952	Kentucky	5-4-2
1953	Kentucky	7-2-1
1954	Texas A&M	1-9-0
1955	Texas A&M	7-2-1
1956	Texas A&M	9-0-1
1957	Texas A&M	8-3-0
1958	Alabama	5-4-1
1959	Alabama	7-2-2
1960	Alabama	8-1-2
1961**	Alabama	11-0-0
1962*	Alabama	10-1-0
1963	Alabama	9-2-0
1964*	Alabama	10-1-0
1965*	Alabama	9-1-1
1966*	Alabama	11-0-0
1967	Alabama	8-2-1
1968	Alabama	8-3-0
1969	Alabama	6-5-0
1970	Alabama	6-5-1
1971	Alabama	11-1-0
1972	Alabama	10-2-0
1973*	Alabama	11-1-0
1974	Alabama	11-1-0
1975*	Alabama	11-1-0
1976	Alabama	9-3-0
1977*	Alabama	11-1-0
1978*	Alabama	11-1-0
1979**	Alabama	12-0-0
1980	Alabama	10-2-0
1981	Alabama	9-2-1

1982	Alabama	8–4–0
		323–85–17

* shared national title
** consensus national champion

Bear Bryant–Coached All Americas

Bob Gain	Kentucky	1949	guard
Babe Parilli**	Kentucky	1950	back
Bob Gain**	Kentucky	1950	guard
Babe Parilli**	Kentucky	1951	back
Doug Moseley	Kentucky	1951	center
Steve Meilinger	Kentucky	1952	end
Steve Meilinger	Kentucky	1953	end
Ray Correll	Kentucky	1953	guard
Jack Pardee	Texas A&M	1956	back
Charles Krueger	Texas A&M	1956	tackle
John David Crow*	Texas A&M	1957	back
Charles Krueger	Texas A&M	1957	tackle
Billy Neighbors*	Alabama	1961	tackle
Lee Roy Jordan*	Alabama	1962	center
Wayne Freeman	Alabama	1964	guard
Paul Crane**	Alabama	1965	center
Ray Perkins**	Alabama	1966	offensive end
Cecil Dowdy*	Alabama	1966	offensive tackle
Bobby Jones	Alabama	1966	defensive back
Dennis Homan**	Alabama	1967	offensive end
Bobby Jones	Alabama	1967	defensive back
Mike Hall	Alabama	1968	linebacker
Johnny Musso**	Alabama	1971	offensive back
John Hannah	Alabama	1971	offensive tackle
John Hannah*	Alabama	1972	offensive guard
John Mitchell	Alabama	1972	linebacker
Buddy Brown**	Alabama	1973	offensive guard
Woodrow Lowe	Alabama	1973	linebacker
Sylvester Croom	Alabama	1974	center
Leroy Cook**	Alabama	1974	defensive lineman
Woodrow Lowe**	Alabama	1974	linebacker
Leroy Cook*	Alabama	1975	defensive end
Woodrow Lowe	Alabama	1975	linebacker

Ozzie Newsome**	Alabama	1977	wide receiver
Marty Lyons**	Alabama	1978	linebacker
Jim Bunch**	Alabama	1979	offensive tackle
E. J. Junior*	Alabama	1980	defensive lineman
Tommy Wilcox**	Alabama	1981	defensive back
Mike Pitts**	Alabama	1982	defensive lineman
Jeremiah Castile	Alabama	1982	defensive back

Unanimous
**Consensus*

Bear Bryant–Coached Award Winners and Heisman Trophy Contenders

1950	B Babe Parilli was 4th in Heisman voting
1950	G Bob Gain won the Outland Trophy
1951	B Babe Parilli was 3rd in Heisman voting
1957	B John David Crow won the Heisman Trophy
1961	QB Pat Trammel was 5th in Heisman voting
1962	C Lee Roy Jordan was 4th in Heisman voting
1971	RB Johnny Musso was 4th in Heisman voting
1972	QB Terry Davis was 5th in Heisman voting
1979	QB Steadman Shealy was 10th in Heisman voting

Paul "Bear" Bryant was AFCA Coach of the Year in 1961.
Paul "Bear" Bryant was AFCA Coach of the Year in 1971.
Paul "Bear" Bryant was AFCA Coach of the Year in 1973.

Appendix C:
Francis Gordon Brown Letters

One of many congratulatory letters (reproduced exactly) that F. Gordon Brown received upon his election as Yale football captain for 1900.

Mr. Francis G. Brown
@ Yale College
New Haven, CONN.

My Dear "Skim":

Warmest congratulations on your election as captain of the foot ball team. Of course, we all knew it was sure to come but it is none the less gratifying on that account. I feel certain that victory will come to us next year.

I am delighted also to see that you are not going to do any rowing. The captaincy of the foot ball eleven is a most important office; in fact, now the most important in the University, and it will need your undivided attention.

Again congratulating you most warmly, I remain,

                         Yours very truly

                         [signed] Julian W. Curtiss

[A handwritten P.S.] Count on me for anything and everything that I can do

Curtiss was writing from the A. G. Spalding & Bros. Company in New York. He was, no doubt, a Yale alum, but there is no record that he ever played on the Yale football team.

Excerpts from a Gordon Brown form letter (reproduced exactly) to Yale alumni, assessing the team:

                                    October 16, 1900.

Dear Sir:-

The past two weeks have been spent in trying to further the development of the different men for the various positions and in this we have been assisted by Chamberlain, Ely, Butterworth, Corbin, Stillman, Hickok and Armstrong.*.... Olcott 200 at center has improved and seems to adapt himself to the position in good shape.... Sheldon 203 turned his ankle and has been unable to play.... In the Dartmouth game he at times showed up well and with coaching should develop into a strong player. Richardson 200 and Hamlin 195 have both been doing well at guard with Hamlin a little ahead. Holt 205 at center is a good steady player, not brilliant, but a splendid understudy for Olcott. The tackle position has been troubloing [troubling] us a little, partly from lack of playing ability. [George] Stillman is improving.... Bloomer 185 the freshman hurt his knee.... Kunzig 178 has not shown up as was expected so we moved Hamlin from guard to tackle.... Coy 170 and Gould 165 have been playing the ends with Ward 150… Gould and Ward are both promising as are also Hoppin and Ferguson. Swan, a light tackle, we are going to try at end and also Rafferty.

Back of the line Wear 140 is playing a stronger game than Fincke, runs the team with more judgment and can run back punts better…. Sharpe 180, Hale 185 and Cook have been playing backs and are working pretty well together…. Hale at full back while not as fast as the others is nevertheless speedy enough. His great strength lies in his aggressiveness and assistance to his backs. Hyde 165, Miller 168, and Chadwick 158, the second set of backs are playing everyday and showing occasional streaks of brilliancy, especially Chadwick…. Taken as a whole the team are today strong at center with good possibilities at right guard and left tackle with only mediocre ends. The backs are slow and do not use their head and eyes in following interferences and are slow to take advantage of an opening.

The remainder of the letter appeals for coaching assistance.

Brown's assessment is interesting. He portrays the team as having potential, but also with a lot of problems. Brown stated that quarterback Fincke was being outplayed at the position by James Wear and that "the tackle position has been troubling us a little, partly from lack of playing ability." By season's end Fincke and both tackles, Stillman and Bloomer, as well as "second set" halfback George Chadwick, were named All America.

YALE'S 1900 ALL AMERICAS:
   Quarterback: Bill Fincke
   Halfback: George Chadwick
   Fullback: Perry Hale
   Tackle: George Stillman
   Tackle: Jim Bloomer
   Center: Herman Olcott
   Guard: F. Gordon Brown, Captain

   Burr C. Chamberlin, Yale All America tackle 1897 and 1898
   Morris U. Ely, Yale football player 1898
   Frank S. Butterworth, Yale All America fullback 1893 and 1894
   W. H. Corbin, Yale football player 1887–1888
   Phillip T. Stillman, Yale All America center 1894
   William O. Hickok, III, Yale All America guard 1893 and 1894
   Richard Armstrong, Yale football player 1893–1894

Form letter (reproduced exactly) from Brown to Yale alumni following the game with Columbia:

Oct. 30, 1900.

Dar Sir:-

The game Saturday was a very great disappointment to us all for we had expected the team to roll up a much larger score. They played a poor game in the first half and were in fact outplayed by Columbia. They seemed to be amazed that anyone could gain through them and played with no sanp [snap], dash or unity. The runner was generally alone with no assistance at all. In the second half they played better ball and helped the runner better but were very slow in starting and reaching the holes. Our kicking game was poor and handling of punts only fair. The only explanation to all this is that the men are very overconfident and need a great deal of attention and hard playing for they have been coached and drilled in all these points continually. Our ends are below the standard and need attention at once. Words seem to have no effect upon the men so we decided on a general shift to make the men realize that the team is not settled by any means. The next two weeks are critical ones to the success of this team and what they need more than anything is to have an old player behind each man driving him into every play and making him responsible for its success. We have the material here to turn out a good team but unless they receive attention at once they will go from bad to worse: of that there is not the slightest doubt. Butterworth* is to be here this week and will drive the team while on the offensive they need new voices and different expressions to arouse them.

Please make a special effort to get down here at once if only for a day for we must have this attention which you older men can give to the team.

Yours very sincerely,

Note that Brown does not mention the unexpected (and conniving) field conditions that the team had to play in. He also did not mention that adequate footwear for the conditions were not available until the second half of the game.

* Frank S. Butterworth, Yale All America fullback 1893 and 1894.

Appendix D: Service Teams of 1943

Team	State	Record
Abilene AAB	Texas	1–2–0
Alameda Coast Guard	California	4–2–1
Bainbridge NTS	Maryland	7–0–0
Bunker Hill NAS	Indiana	6–0–0
Camp Davis	North Carolina	8–2–0
Camp Edwards	Massachusetts	4–5–0
Camp Grant	Illinois	2–6–2
Camp Kearns	Utah	5–2–0
Camp Lee	Virginia	5–5–0
Camp Lejeune	North Carolina	6–2–1
Charleston Coast Guard	South Carolina	6–3–0
Cherry Point Marines	North Carolina	4–2–0
Curtis Bay Coast Guard	Maryland	4–5–0
Daniel Field Air Base	Georgia	2–7–0
Del Monte Pre-Flight	California	7–1–0
Fort Crook	Nebraska	2–4–0
Fort Jackson	South Carolina	0–4–0
Fort Knox	Kentucky	4–2–0
Fort Sheridan	Illinois	4–3–0
Ft. Frances E. Warren	Wyoming	4–3–0
Georgia Pre-Flight	Georgia	5–1–0
Great Lakes NTS	Illinois	10–2–0
Greensboro AAB	North Carolina	4–0–0
Jackson Barracks	Louisiana	2–4–0
Keesler Field	Mississippi	3–1–0
Kirtland Field	New Mexico	1–2–0
Lakehurst NAS	New Jersey	2–4–0
Lubbock AAB	Texas	5–1–0
March Field	California	9–1–0

Appendix D: Service Teams of 1943

Team	State	Record
N. Carolina Pre-Flight	North Carolina	2–4–1
Oklahoma NAS	Oklahoma	4–3–0
Ottumwa NAS	Iowa	5–1–0
Patterson Field	Ohio	2–3–1
Pleasanton Navy	California	1–4–0
Pomona Ordnance Base	California	2–6–0
Randolph Field	Texas	9–1–0*
Reno AAB	Nevada	2–1–1
Richmond AAB	Virginia	4–5–1
St. Mary's Pre-Flight	California	4–4–1
Sampson NTS	New York	7–2–0
San Diego NTS	California	7–2–0
Spokane AB	Washington	2–2–0
Will Rogers Field	Oklahoma	2–1–1
Wright Field	Ohio	1–0–1

*Randolph Field played Texas to a 7-7 tie in the Cotton Bowl

Chapter Notes

Chapter 1

1. Michael MacCambridge, *ESPN College Football Encyclopedia* (New York: ESPN Books, 2005), 1128.
2. MacCambridge, *ESPN College Football Encyclopedia*, 1128.
3. The *New Mexican*, November 21, 1961, http://www.secsportsfan.com/support-files/april_2010_college_football_historian.pdf.
4. Christopher Walsh, *Who's #1?* (Lanham, MD: Taylor Trade, 2007), 14.
5. *Official 2002 NCAA Football Records*, Indianapolis: National Collegiate Athletic Association, 2002, 69.
6. "An Interview with Harry Devold," http://yourlinx.tripod.com/Sports/interviews/D/hdevold.html.
7. Walsh, *Who's #1?*, 18–19.
8. *Ibid.*, 21.
9. "Congrove Computer Rankings 130," College Football Poll.com, http://www.collegefootballpoll.com/rankings/.

Chapter 2

1. Allison Danzig, *Oh, How They Played the Game: The Early Days of Football and the Heroes Who Made It Great* (New York: Macmillan, 1971), 134.
2. *Ibid.*, 255.

Chapter 3

1. Ronald Smith, ed., *Big Time Football at Harvard* (Chicago: University of Illinois Press, 1994), 81.

Chapter 4

1. Michael MacCambridge, ed., *ESPN College Football Encyclopedia* (New York: ESPN Books, 2005), 1144.
2. Harold Claassen, *The Ronald Encyclopedia of Football* (New York: Ronald Press, 1960) 666; Christy Walsh, *Intercollegiate Football 1869 to 1934* (New York: Doubleday, Doran, 1934), 176.
3. Alexander M. Weyand, *Football Immortals* (New York: Macmillan, 1962), 4; Christy Walsh, *Intercollegiate Football 1869 to 1934*, 175.
4. Tim Cohane, *The Yale Football Story* (New York: G. P. Putnam's Sons, 1951), 114.
5. Francis Gordon Brown Papers, from Yale Archives.
6. Sally Jenkins, *The Real All Americans* (New York: Broadway Books, 2007), 253.
7. Donald Grant "Heff" Herring, *Forty Years of Football* (New York: Carlyle House, 1940), 24.
8. Cohane, *The Yale Football Story*, 107.
9. twainquotes.com.
10. Morris Bealle, *The History of Football at Harvard* (Washington, DC: Columbia, 1948), 136.
11. *Ibid.*, 136.
12. Cohane, *The Yale Football Story*, 117–8.
13. *Ibid.*, 118.
14. Bealle, *The History of Football at Harvard*, 137.
15. *Outing Magazine* 37, no. 4: 479–489, https://babel.hathitrust.org/cgi/ssd?id=iau.31858055627149;page=ssd;view=plaintext;seq=491;num=481.
16. Francis Gordon Brown Papers, Yale Archives.

Chapter 5

1. Allison Danzig, *Oh, How They Played the Game: The Early Days of Football and the Heroes Who Made It Great* (New York: Macmillan, 1971), 177.
2. Christy Walsh, ed., *Intercollegiate Football: A Complete Pictorial and Statistical Review From 1869–1934* (New York: Doubleday, Doran, 1934), 130.
3. Arthur L. Evans, *Fifty Years of Football at Syracuse University, 1889–1939* (Norwood, MA: Syracuse Football History Committee, 1939), 71.
4. Tim Cohane, *The Yale Football Story* (New York: G. P. Putnam's Sons, 1951), 176.
5. Danzig, *Oh, How They Played the Game*, 205.
6. Alexander M. Weyand, *Football Immortals* (New York: Macmillan, 1962), 214.
7. Danzig, *Oh, How They Played the Game*, 223.
8. *Ibid.*, 206.
9. Morris Bealle, *The History of Football at*

Harvard, 1874–1948 (Washington, DC: Columbia, 1948), 191.
10. Danzig, *Oh, How They Played the Game*, 208.
11. William N. Wallace, *Yale's Ironmen: A Story of Football & Lives In the Decade of The Depression & Beyond* (New York: iUniverse, 2005), 127.

Chapter 6

1. Edwin Pope, *Football's Greatest Coaches* (Atlanta: Tupper and Love, 1955), 116.
2. *Ibid.*, 122.
3. *Ibid.*, 117.
4. *Ibid.*, 120.
5. Bill Libby, *Champions of College Football* (New York: Hawthorn, 1975), 40.
6. Adventure Quest, *The Heisman: Sixty Years of Tradition and Excellence* (Bronxville, NY: Adventure Quest, 1995), 14.
7. *Ibid.*
8. *Ibid.*, 16.
9. Georgia Tech Sports Information Office, *Georgia Tech Football Media Guide 2003*, Atlanta, 345.
10. *College Football Historical Society* Vol. 1 No. 111 (February, 1988), 1–5, https://digital.la84.org/digital/collection/p17103coll10/id/7866/rec/2.
11. Al Thomy, *The Ramblin' Wreck: A Story of Georgia Tech Football* (Huntsville, AL: Strode, 1973), 58.
12. *Ibid.*, 60.

Chapter 7

1. Harold Claassen, *Ronald Encyclopedia of Football* (New York: Ronald Press, 1960), 21.
2. Stan Grosshandler, "TVs First Game," *College Football Historical Society Newsletter* 6, no. 4: 4–5.
3. Jack Connor, *Leahy's Lads: The Story of the Famous Notre Dame Teams of the 1940s* (South Bend, IN: Diamond, 1997), 54.
4. *Ibid.*, 58–61.
5. Clary, *Navy Football: Gridiron Legends and Fighting Heroes*. (Annapolis: Naval Institute Press, 1997), 100.
6. Walter Okeson, ed., *The Official NCAA 1943 Football Guide* (New York: A. S. Barnes, 1943), 29.
7. Connor, *Leahy's Lads*, 53.
8. *Ibid.*, 63.
9. *Ibid.*
10. *Ibid.*, 65–66.
11. *Chicago Daily Tribune*, September 19, 1943.

Chapter 8

1. Stan Grosshandler, "Notre Dame 1947—the best ever?" *College Football Historical Society Newsletter* 3, no. 1 (November, 1989), 1–3, https://digital.la84.org/digital/collection/p17103coll10/id/7931/rec/25.
2. Joseph LeCastro, "A Vote For Michigan," *College Football Historical Society Newsletter* 9, no. 4 (August, 1996), 18, https://digital.la84.org/digital/collection/p17103coll10/id/8163/rec/27.
3. Cohen, Deutsch and Neft, *University of Michigan Football Scrapbook* (Indianapolis: Bobbs-Merrill, 1978), 24.
4. *Ibid.*, 125.

Chapter 9

1. Bill Van Fleet, in *The Official NCAA Collegiate Football Guide 1963*, 49.
2. Kern Tips, *Football Texas Style: An Illustrated History of the Southwest Conference* (Garden City, NJ: Doubleday, 1964), 207.
3. "National Championship Memories: Duke Carlisle," University of Texas Athletics, https://texassports.com/news/2013/8/29/FB_0829134208.aspx.
4. Mervin Hyman, "Football's Week," *Sports Illustrated*, November 25, 1963, 83.
5. Jenkins, Dan, "Two Yards and the Clock," *Sports Illustrated*, Vol. 19 No. 25 December 16, 1963, 59.
6. Dan Jenkins, "Two Yards and the Clock," *Sports Illustrated*, December 16, 1963, 59.
7. Jack Clary, *An American Classic: Army vs. Navy: The First 100 Games* (Syracuse, NY: Signature, 2000), 207–208.
8. Michael MacCambridge, ed., *ESPN College Football Encyclopedia*, 21.
9. Chris Wimmer, "The Times and Turmoil of the 1964 Cotton Bowl," *Brenham (TX) Banner-Press*, October 26, 1917, http://www.brenhambanner360.com/brenham360/the-times-and-turmoil-of-the-cotton-bowl/article_5d0862ee-97df-5370-b163-ca6562b2695c.html.
10. "National Championship Memories: Tommy Ford," University of Texas Athletics, https://texassports.com/news/2013/8/27/FB_0827133531.aspx

Chapter 10

1. Michael Corcoran, *The Game of the Century* (Lincoln: University of Nebraska Press, 2004), 45–46.
2. Johnny Rodgers, *An Era of Greatness* (Omaha: Champion Publishing, 2006), 47.
3. Michael Corcoran, *The Game of the Century*, 46.
4. *Ibid.*, 74.
5. Johnny Rodgers, *An Era of Greatness*, 238.
6. Michael Corcoran, *The Game of the Century*, 137–138.
7. *Ibid.*, 136.
8. *Ibid.*, 56.
9. *Ibid.*, 148.
10. *Ibid.*, 128.

Chapter 11

1. Bill Block, *Trojans 1972: An Immortal Team of Mortal Men* (Bloomington, IN: Xlibris, 2009), 23.
2. Bob Boyles and Paul Guido, *50 Years of College Football* (New York: Skyhorse, 2007), 284.
3. *Ibid.*, 285.
4. Block, *Trojans 1972*, 27.
5. *Los Angeles Times*, December 3, 1972, https://www.newspapers.com/newspage/386102122/.

Chapter 12

1. Tim Layden, "Thrown for a Loss," *Sports Illustrated*, September 18, 1995), 40.
2. Josh Peter, "Lawrence Phillips' Letters Reveal Another Side of Troubled Player," *USA Today Sports*, January 17, 2016, https://www.usatoday.com/story/sports/nfl/2016/01/16/lawrence-phillips-suicide-prison-letters-nebraska/78898264/.
3. Tim Layden, "Coming Into Focus," *Sports Illustrated*, November 20, 1995, 52.

Chapter 13

1. Phillip Fulmer with Jeff Hagood, *A Perfect Season* (Nashville: Rutledge Hill, 1999), 48.
2. Harry Moskos, ed., *The Road to No. 1: The Tennessee Vols' Glorious Journey to the 1998 National Championship* (Memphis: Knoxville News-Sentinel, 1999), 16.
3. "Undefeated and Unmatched: Remembering the 1998 National Champions, University of Tennessee Athletics," University of Tennessee Sports, https://utsports.com/news/2018/8/14/football-1998-season-story-needs-title.aspx.
4. Moskos, *The Road to No. 1*, 34.
5. *Ibid.*, 64.
6. Bob Colon, "Here's Why Refs Dropped Ball in Tennessee-Arkansas Game," *Oklahoma City News*, November 21, 1998, 19.
7. Fulmer and Hagood, *A Perfect Season*, 148–151.

Chapter 14

1. Charley Barnes and Bobby Bowden, *The Bowden Dynasty* (Racine, WI: BroadStreet, 2017), 342.
2. Bob Boyles and Paul Guido, *50 Years of College Football* (New York: Skyhorse, 2007), 620.
3. Barnes and Bowden, *The Bowden Dynasty*, 371.
4. Florida State Football Media Guide 2000, 136.

Chapter 15

1. Bob Boyles and Paul Guido, *50 Years of College Football* (New York: Skyhorse, 2007), 647.
2. *Ibid.*, 648.
3. *Ibid.*, 654.
4. *Ibid.*, 656.
5. Joe Hendrickson, *Tournament of Roses: The First 100 Years* (Los Angeles: Knapp Press, 1988), 96.

Chapter 16

1. Bob Boyles and Paul Guido, *50 Years of College Football* (New York: Skyhorse, 2007), 696.
2. "USC To Open 2004 Season Against Virginia Tech in BCA Classic," PAC-12.com, https://pac-12.com/article/2003/12/23/usc-open-2004-season-against-virginia-tech-bca-classic.
3. Boyles and Guido, *50 Years of College Football*, 699.
4. *Ibid.*, 700.
5. USC 2019 Football Media Guide, 188.

Chapter 17

1. Bob Boyles and Paul Guido, *50 Years of College Football* (New York: Skyhorse, 2007), 713.
2. *Ibid.*, 718.
3. *Ibid.*, 721.
4. *Ibid.*, 725.

Chapter 18

1. Brian Kelly, *Alabama Crimson Tide Championship Seasons* (Middletown, DE: Let's Go Publish, 2019), 253.
2. *Ibid.*
3. *Ibid.*, 255.
4. *Ibid.*, 257.
5. *Ibid.*, 252.

Chapter 19

1. Florida State University, *Fear the Spear: Florida State's Return to the Top* (Atlanta: Whitman, 2014), 6.
2. *Ibid.*, 55.
3. *Ibid.*, 70.
4. *Ibid.*, 86.
5. *Ibid.*, 94.
6. *Ibid.*, 114.

Chapter 20

1. Bill Rabinowitz, *The Chase* (Chicago: Triumph, 2015), 71.
2. *Ibid.*, 76.
3. *Ibid.*, 91.
4. *Ibid.*, 100.
5. *Ibid.*, 115.
6. *Ibid.*, 132.
7. All-Time UM-OSU Results 1897–2019, https://bentley.umich.edu/athdept/football/umosu/results.htm.

Chapter 21

1. Christopher Walsh, *Bama Dynasty* (Chicago: Triumph Books, 2018), 33.
2. Christopher Walsh, *Sweet 16* (Chicago: Triumph Books, 2016), 46.
3. *Ibid.*, 74.
4. Mark Mayfield, *Back On Top!* (New York: Sports Publishing, 2016), 76.
5. Walsh, *Bama Dynasty*, 35.
6. *Ibid.*, 35.

Chapter 22

1. *Clemson 2019 Online Football Media Guide*, 2, https://data.clemsontigers.com/pdf/football/2019-20/MediaGuide.pdf.
2. *Ibid.*, 78.
3. *Ibid.*, 79.
4. *Ibid.*
5. *Ibid.*
6. *Ibid.*, 2.

Chapter 23

1. Brett Blackledge, *One Team, One Heartbeat* (Chicago: Triumph, 2020), 37.
2. *Ibid.*, 50.
3. *Ibid.*, 52.
4. *Ibid.*, 67.

Chapter 24

1. Michael MacCambridge, ed., *ESPN College Football Encyclopedia* (New York: ESPN Books, 2005), 1383.

Chapter 25

1. Johnny Rodgers, *An Era of Greatness* (Omaha, NE: Champion, 2006), 63.
2. Jeff Sagarin, "Sagarin Ratings," *USA Today*, January 3, 2003.
3. "Best College Football Teams of All Time," ESPN.com, https://www.espn.com/page2/s/list/colfootball/teams/best.html.
4. "The 10 Best College Football Teams of All Time," Bleacher Report, https://bleacherreport.com/articles/526803-the-10-best-college-football-teams-of-all-time.

Bibliography

Books

Adventure Quest. *The Heisman: Sixty Years of Tradition and Excellence*. Bronxville: Adventure Quest, 1995.

Barnes, Charlie, and Bobby Bowden. *The Bowden Dynasty*. Racine, WI: BroadStreet, 2017.

Batie, Steve, ed. *Business As Usual: Nebraska Cornhuskers 1995 National Football Championship*. Rapid City, SD: Lincoln Journal Star, 1996.

Beach, Jim, and Daniel Moore. *Army vs Notre Dame: The Big Game 1913–1947*. New York: Random House, 1948.

Bealle, Morris. *The History of Football at Harvard 1874–1948*. Washington, D.C.: Columbia Publishing, 1948.

Bergin, Thomas. *The Game: The Harvard-Yale Football Rivalry, 1875–1983*. New Haven: Yale University Press, 1984.

Blackledge, Brett. *One Team, One Heartbeat: LSU's Remarkable Road to the National Championship*. Chicago: Triumph Books, 2020.

Block, Bill. *Trojans 1972: An Immortal Team of Mortal Men*. Xlibris Corporation, 2009.

Bowden, Bobby, with Steve Ellis and Wayne McGahee III. *Tales from the Florida State Seminoles Sideline*. New York: Sports Publishing, 2004.

Boyles, Bob, and Paul Guido. *50 Years of College Football*. New York: Skyhorse Publishing, 2007.

Brady, John T. *The Heisman: A Symbol of Excellence*. New York: Atheneum, 1984.

Brandt, Nat. *When Oberlin Was King of the Gridiron: The Heisman Years*. Kent, OH: Kent State University Press, 2001.

Bynum, Mike, ed. *Many Autumns Ago: The Frank Leahy Era at Boston College and Notre Dame*. Chicago: October Football, 1988.

Cavanaugh, Jack. *Mr. Inside and Mr. Outside: World War II, Army's Undefeated Teams, and College Football's Greatest Backfield Duo*. Chicago: Triumph Books, 2014.

Claassen, Harold. *Ronald Encyclopedia of Football*. New York: Ronald Press, 1960.

Clary, Jack. *An American Classic: Army vs. Navy: The First 100 Games*. Syracuse, NY: Signature Publications, 2000.

_____. *College Football's Great Dynasties: USC*. Hong Kong: Smithmark, 1991.

_____. *Navy Football: Gridiron Legends and Fighting Heroes*. Annapolis: Naval Institute Press, 1997.

Cohane, Tim. *The Yale Football Story*. New York: G. P. Putnam's Sons, 1951.

Cohen, Richard, Jordan Deutsch, and David Neft. *The University of Michigan Football Scrapbook*. Indianapolis: Bobbs-Merrill, 1978.

Connor, Jack. *Leahy's Lads: The Story of the Famous Notre Dame Football Teams of the 1940s*. South Bend: Diamond Communications, 1997.

Corcoran, Michael. *The Game of the Century: Nebraska vs. Oklahoma in College Football's Ultimate Battle*. Lincoln: University of Nebraska Press, 2004.

Cromartie, Bill. *The Big One*. Nashville: Rutledge Hill, 1979.

Daley, Arthur. *Knute Rockne: Football Wizard of Notre Dame*. New York: P. J. Kenedy, 1960.

Danzig, Allison. *Oh, How They Played the Game: The Early days of Football and the Heroes Who Made It Great*. New York: Macmillan, 1971.

Deitch, Scott, ed. *Official 2002 NCAA Football Records*. Indianapolis: National Collegiate Athletic Association, 2002.

Dent, Jim. *The Undefeated: The Oklahoma Sooners and the Greatest Winning Streak in College Football*. New York: Thomas Dunne Books, 2001.

DiMarco, Anthony. *The Big Bowl Football Guide*. New York: G. P. Putnam's Sons, 1976.

Doster, Rob, ed. *Game Day Nebraska Football*. Chicago: Triumph Books, 2006.

Evans, Arthur L. *Fifty Years of Football at Syracuse University 1889–1939*. Norwood, MA: Syracuse University Football History Committee, 1939.

Florida State University. *Fear the Spear: Florida State's Return to the Top*. Atlanta: Whitman Publishing, 2014.

Freedman, Lew. *The Rise of the Seminoles: FSU Football Under Bobby Bowden*. New York: Sports Publishing, 2015.

Fulmer, Phillip, with Jeff Hagood. *A Perfect Season*. Nashville: Rutledge Hill, 1999.

Goldstein, Richard. *Ivy League Autumns*. New York: St. Martin's, 1996.

Greunke, Lowell R. *Football Rankings*. Jefferson, NC: McFarland, 1984.

Heffelfinger, W. W. "Pudge". *This Was Football*. New York: A. S. Barnes, 1954.

Hendrickson, Joe. *Tournament of Roses: The First 100 Years.* Los Angeles: Knapp Press, 1988.

Herring, Donald Grant "Heff." *Forty Years of Football.* New York: Carlyle House, 1940.

Israel, David. *The Cornhuskers: Nebraska Football.* Chicago: Henry Regnery, 1975.

Jenkins, Sally. *The Real All Americans.* New York: Broadway Books, 2007.

Katz, Fred, ed. *The Glory of Notre Dame.* Hong Kong: Bartholomew House, 1971.

Kelly, Brian. *Alabama Crimson Tide Championship Seasons.* Middleton, DE: Let's Go Publish, 2019.

Libby, Bill. *Champions of College Football.* New York: Hawthorn Books, 1975.

MacCambridge, Michael, ed. *ESPN College Football Encyclopedia.* New York: ESPN Books, 2005.

Mayfield, Mark. *Back on Top: The Alabama Crimson Tide's 2015-16 Championship Football Season.* New York: Sports Publishing, 2016.

McCallum, John. *Big Eight Football.* New York: Charles Scribner's Sons, 1979.

_____. *Ivy League Football Since 1872.* New York: Stein and Day, 1977.

_____. *Southeastern Conference Football.* New York: Charles Scribner's Sons, 1980.

Moskos, Harry, ed. *The Road to NO. 1: The Tennessee Vols' Glorious Journey to the 1998 National Championship.* Memphis: The Knoxville News-Sentinel, 1999.

Mule, Marty. *Sugar Bowl: The First Fifty Years.* Birmingham: Oxmoor House, 1983.

Murtaugh, Jerry. *If These Walls Could Talk: Nebraska Cornhuskers.* Chicago: Triumph Books, 2015.

Newcombe, Jack, ed. *The Fireside Book of Football.* New York: Simon & Schuster, 1964.

Pope, Edwin. *Football's Greatest Coaches.* Atlanta: Tupper and Love, 1955.

Reid, Robert. *A Memorable Season in College Football: A Look Back at 1959.* Bloomington, IN: AuthorHouse, 2005.

Rodgers, Johnny. *An Era of Greatness.* Omaha: Champion Publishing, 2006.

Schembechler, Bo, with Dan Ewald. *Tradition: Bo Scehmbechler's Michigan Memories.* Ann Arbor: Clock Tower Press, 2003.

Schoor, Gene. *100 Years of Notre Dame Football.* New York: William Morrow, 1987.

_____. *A Treasury of Notre Dame Football.* New York: Funk & Wagnalls, 1962.

Shoemaker, Robert. *Famous Football Players.* New York: Thomas Y. Crowell, 1953.

Smith, Ronald, ed. *Big-Time Football at Harvard 1905.* Chicago: University of Illinois Press, 1994.

Thomy, Al. *The Ramblin' Wreck: A Story of Georgia Tech Football.* Huntsville, AL: Strode Publishers, 1973.

Tips, Kern. *Football—Texas Style: An Illustrated History of the Southwest Conference.* Garden City: Doubleday, 1964.

Wallace, William N. *Yale's Ironmen: A Story of Football & Lives in the Decade of The Depression & Beyond.* New York: iUniverse, 2005.

Walsh, Christopher. *Bama Dynasty: The Crimson Tide's Road to College Football Immortality.* Chicago: Triumph Books, 2018.

Walsh, Christopher. *Who's # 1?* Lanham, MD: Taylor, 2007.

_____. *Crimson Storm Surge: Alabama Football Then and Now.* Lanham, MD: Taylor, 2005.

Walsh, Christy, ed. *Intercollegiate Football: A Complete Pictorial and Statistical Review From 1869-1934.* New York: Doubleday, Doran, 1934.

Watterson, John Sayle. *College Football: History-Spectacle-Controversy.* Baltimore: Johns Hopkins University Press, 2000.

Weeks, Jim. *The Sooners: A Story of Oklahoma Football.* Huntsville, AL: Strode Publishers, 1974.

Weyand, Alexander. *Football Immortals.* New York: Macmillan, 1962.

Magazines

Alabama Football Media Guide
Army Football Media Guide
College Football Historical Society Newsletter
Georgia Tech Football Media Guide
Illustrated Football Annual—multiple years
LSU Football Media Guide
Michigan Football Media Guide
Nebraska Football Media Guide
Notre Dame Football Media Guide
Official NCAA Football Guide—multiple years
Oklahoma Football Media Guide
Outing Magazine
Southern California Media Guide
Sports Illustrated
Texas Football Media Guide

Other

The Banner-Press (MO)
Chicago Daily Tribune
Daily Illini
Francis Gordon Brown Papers from Yale Archives
Lewiston Morning Tribune
New Mexican
New York Times Archives
Oklahoma City News
Omaha World-Herald Archives
Outing Magazine
Pittsburgh Post-Gazette
USA Today Sports

Online Sources

BleacherReport.com
Bowling Green State University Football Media Guide
Clemson University Football Media Guide
collegefootball.org/famer

Bibliography

collegefootballpoll.com/rankings
ESPN.com
Louisiana State University website
National Review Online
Ohio State University website
Soren Sorensen Men's College Football—History
Texas A&M website
texassports.com
twainquotes.com
University of Alabama Football Media Guide
University of Michigan website
University of Nebraska website
University of Southern California website
University of Texas website
University of Tennessee Athletics site
yourlinx.tripod.com/Sports/interviews/D/hdevold

Index

Abilene AAB 304
Abraham, Clifton 270
Abram, Chad 181, 186
ACC (Atlantic Coast Conference) 134, 168, 183, 185, 217
Acho, Sam 277
Adams, Ben 276
Adams, Darvin 177
Adams, Flozell 279
Adams, George 27
Adams, Jamal 288
Adams, Pete 103, 111, 264
Adams, Tony 93
Adams, Vernon 157
Adeboyejo, Quincy 200
Adkins, John 242
AFCA (American Football Coaches Association) 88, 92, 99, 142, 231, 250
Agase, Alex 66
Aguayo, Roberto 180, 181, 182, 183, 184, 185, 186, 282, 283
Air Force Academy 19-20, 38, 153
Akin, Chris 129
Alameda Coast Guard 304
The Alamo Bowl 163, 221
Alberts, Trev 266
Alderson, Bob 11
The Alderson System 11
Alexander, Bennie 139
Alexander, Derrick 270
Alexander, Mackensie 286
Alexander, Shaun 127
Alexis, Rich 147
Allen, Brandon 202, 203
Allen, Dwayne 286, 287
Allen, Greg 270
Allen, Jonathan 280, 281
Allen, Kyle 202
Allen, Tremayne 243
Allen, Will 168, 277
Allers, LaVerne 262
Allis, Harry 75, 76
American Athletic Conference (AAC) 190, 196
American Football Coaches Association (AFCA) 35, 62, 230
American Intercollegiate Football Rules Committee 249
Ames, Knowleton "Snake" 27
Amherst College 9, 14, 24, 33, 42

Anderson, Bob 293
Anderson, Carl 61
Anderson, Derek 156
Anderson, Donny 88
Anderson, Eddie 291
Anderson, Eric 243
Anderson, "Hunk" 55
Anderson, Jim 100
Anderson, Paul 64
Anderson, Ryan 203
Andros, Dee 103
Andrus, Hamlin 42, 44, 242, 254
Anthony, Reidel 120-1
Apple, Eli 191, 193
Appleton, Scott 81, 83, 87, 88, 233, 260
Arbelbide, Garrett 254
The Archie Griffin Award 219
Arenas, Javier 176, 178, 179, 279
Arizona State University 6, 38, 49, 91, 99, 114-5, 116, 155, 168, 235
Armsley, T. 49
Armstrong, Joe 262
Armstrong, Richard 302
Army (U.S. Military Academy) 7, 14, 15, 16-7, 19, 28, 34-5, 37, 39, 40, 41-2, 43, 56, 61, 65, 66, 67, 69, 73, 74, 75, 76, 77, 78, 85-6, 232, 236, 244, 245, 246, 247
Associated Press (AP) 10
Atessis, Bill 260
Atkins, Marty 260
Atlanta Journal-Constitution 11
Austin, Al 242
Austin, Thomas 286
Aycock, Steve 98, 242

Babers, Rod 276
Bachman, Charlie 63
Bailey, Aaron 192
Bailey, Champ 127
Bainbridge NTS 304
Bakeer, John 254
Baker, Ralph 254
Baker, Sam 274
Baker, Ross 11
Ball State 127
Bandhauer, Todd 118
Banks, Tony 114
Barnard, David 243
Barnes, Bruce 107

Barnes, Walt 262
Barnette, Jamie 136
Barrett, J.T. 188, 189, 190-1, 192, 193, 194, 195, 196
Barron, Alex 271
Barron, Mark 174, 279, 280
Barry, Thomas 55
Bartkowski, Steve 105
Bass, Tyler 220
Bateman, Cooper 199, 200
Bates, James 243
Bates College 33
Battle, Mike 263
Battle, Terry 115
Baul, Reggie 113, 118
Baylor University 38, 58, 83, 88, 89, 128, 166, 183, 184, 198, 199, 201, 202, 203
BCS (Bowl Championship Series) 128, 143, 145, 146, 147, 148 149, 150, 158, 161, 165, 166, 167, 174, 176, 177, 178, 180, 182, 183, 184, 185, 186, 187, 239
Beamer, Frank 142
Bean, Robert 131
"Bear Zero" Defense 189
Beard, Kevin 146
Beasley, Vic 286
Beck, John 152
Becksvoort, John 268
Bedsole, Hal 263
Belding, Lester 254
Bell, Atrews 137
Bell, Bert 50
Bell, John 47
Bell, Ricky 264
Bell, Si 49
Bell, Tommy 293
Bell, Vonn 285
Bellard, Emory 97
Beloit College 36
Belton, Bill 192
Benbrook, Albert 44, 290
Benien, Jim 100
Benjamin, Kelvin 181, 182, 184, 185, 186
Benjamin, Kevin 282
Bennett, Michael 198, 284
Bennett, Pat 156
Benning, Damon 114, 115, 116
Benson, Cedric 277
Bentley, Jake 216

Index

Berringer, Brook 120
Berry, Eric 268
Berryman, Clyde 11, 22
The Berryman System 11, 18, 22
Bertelli, Angelo 57, 59, 61, 66, 68, 233, 234, 256
Bertolet, Taylor 202, 203
Bethune-Cookman University 181
Bevo, University of Texas mascot 84
The Big East Conference 191
Big 8 Conference 18, 235
Big 9 (Western Conference) 72
Big Ten (Western Conference) 70, 71, 106, 108, 148, 163, 185, 188, 190, 192, 193, 194, 195, 196, 226, 235
Big 12 131, 148, 158, 165, 166, 167, 168, 178, 196, 217
Bill Willis Trophy 187
Billingsley, Richard 11
The Billingsley Report 11, 14, 40, 90
Bing, Darnell 274
Bird, Dominique 156
Bironas, Robert 125
Black, Ahmad 284
Black, Jeremiah 27
Black Coaches Association Classic 151
Blacknall, Saeed 192
The Blackshirts 93, 94
Blahak, Joe 97
Blaik, Earl 16-7, 57, 252, 291-3
Blalock, Justin 168, 277
Blame, Damon 263
Blanchard, Felix "Doc" 16-7, 61, 292, 293
Blankenship, Rodrigo 226
Bleacher Report Top FB Teams Poll 245
Bledsoe, John 110
Bloomer, Jim 302
Bloomer, Ralph 33, 34, 36, 241
Blott, Jack 290
Bly, Dré 276
Boand, William 9
Boand System (Azzi Ratem System) 9-10, 18
Boeringer, Bud 291
Boise State University 174, 179
Boldin, Anquan 138
Bolinger, Bo 294, 295
Bomar, Rhett 164
Bonness, Rik 265
Booker, Michael 120
Boone, Richard 210
Boryla, Mike 104-5
Bosa, Joey 188, 190, 192, 196, 198, 284, 285
Bosa, Nick 285
Boston College 38, 58, 140, 146, 147, 181, 182, 215
Boston Globe 27
Boston University 37
Boulware, Ben 286, 287
Boulware, Michael 145

Boulware, Peter 271
Bowden, Bobby 134, 136, 137, 138, 140, 252, 269-72
Bowden, Tommy 138
Bowdoin College 33
Bowers, Da'Quan 286, 287
Bowl Alliance 23, 120, 229, 241
Bowl Championship Series (BCS) 23, 131, 229
Bowl Coalition 23
Bowling Green University 203
Boyd, Taijh 182, 286
Boydston, Max 294
Bragg, Craig 158
Brahaney, Tom 98, 111, 242
Branch, Andre 286
Branch, Cliff 94, 100
Branch, Jim 242
Braxton, Jim 270
Bray, Eddie 66
Brennan, Terry 55
Brewer, Michael 189
Brice, Chase 212, 213, 214
Brigham Young University 7, 38, 146, 152, 161, 232
Brill, Marty 291
Brink, Alex 156
Brittenum, Jon 82
Brominski, Step 122
Bronco Nagurski Award 141, 187, 251
Brooks, Derrick 270
Brooks, Kennedy 227
Brooks, Reggie 297
Brooks, Terrence 186, 282
Brown, Bob 262
Brown, Booker 264
Brown, Buddy 299
Brown, Charles 274
Brown, C.J. 191
Brown, Derek 297
Brown, Francis Gordon 32-7, 252, 241, 301-3
Brown, Kris 113, 114, 116, 117, 118, 119, 120
Brown, Lance 115
Brown, Mack 162, 252, 275-8
Brown, Robert 290
Brown, Sheldon 297
Brown, Tim 297
Brown, Wes 191
Brown University 26, 34, 35, 37, 40, 42, 43, 45-6, 66
Browne, Gilbert 42, 242
Brownson, Van 95, 100
Broyles Award 251
Bruce, Earl 188
Bryant, Austin 287
Bryant, Kelly 210, 211
Bryant, Paul "Bear" 20, 99, 100, 138, 252
Bryson, Shawn 124, 125, 128, 129, 132
Buchanon, Phillip 143, 144, 145, 146, 149, 272
Buckey, Don 296
Buckley, Terrell 270
Buggs, Danny 270

Bullock, Keith 123
Bulovas, Joseph 218
Bumpus, Michael 156
Bunch, Jim 300
Burk, Dick 62
Burlsworth, Brandon 129
Burnett, Kevin 268
Burris, Buddy 294
Burris, Jeff 297
Burris, Kurt 294, 295
Burrow, Joe 220, 221, 222, 223, 224, 225, 226, 227, 288
Bush, Reggie 151, 152, 153, 155, 156, 157, 158, 160, 161, 168, 169, 170, 274
Butler, Bill 101
Butler, Leroy 270
Butt, Jake 195
Butterfield, David 265
Butterworth, Frank 28, 252, 302, 303
Butts, Randy 92
Byrd, Dominique 159

Caldwell, Antoine 279
Callahan, Tim 28
Callaway, Antonio 206
The Camellia Bowl 211
Camp, Walter 25-6, 28, 32-3, 34, 36-7, 40, 47, 48, 53, 248, 252
Camp Davis 304
Camp Edwards 304
Camp Grant 62, 63, 304
Camp Kearns 304
Camp Lee 304
Camp Lejeune 304
Camp Lewis 63
Campbell, Chris 143
Campbell, Earl 260
Campbell, Mark 243
Camping World Bowl 213
Cannon, Jack 291
Canteen, Freddy 195
Cappelletti, John 110
Capshaw, Freddie 145
Carideo, Frank 291
Carlisle, Emmett Augustus "Duke" 80, 81-2, 83-4, 86, 87
Carlisle Indian School 14, 34, 50, 52
Carlson, Anders 224
Carlson, Daniel 205
Carpenter, Walker 49, 53, 256
Carr, Lloyd 71
Carroll, John 97, 101
Carroll, Pete 151, 252, 273-5
Carter, Allen 103
Carter, Jason 167
Cash, Walter "Monte" 27
Cassell, Matt 156
Castile, Jeremiah 300
Catlin, Tom 294, 295
Cavil, Kwame 276
Cavis, Art 260
Centre College (KY) 63
CFP (College Football Playoffs) 192
Chadwick, George 33, 36, 302

Index

Chamberlain, Burr 28, 302
Chandler, Albert 97, 242
Chandler, Jeff 139
Chandnois, Lyn 72
Chaney, Jeff 139, 141
Channing, Roscoe 27
Chappuis, Bob 71, 72
Charles, Jaamal 162, 163, 164, 167, 168
Charleston Coast Guard 304
Charleston Southern University 205
Chase, Ja'Marr 220, 223, 224, 225, 226, 227, 228, 288
Chase, T.J. 216, 222,
Cherry Point Marines 304
Chesnaukas, Ralph 293
Chester, Ed 243
Chicago Tribune 72
Chick-fil-A Kickoff Game 171
Childs, Clinton 114-5, 118
Childs, Greg 173
Choice, Adam 211, 213, 216, 217
Christiansen, Jack 105
Chubb, Nick 201
Chuck Bednarik Trophy 187, 251
Chung, Elroy 99
Church, Johnnie 243
The Citadel 38, 76
The Citrus Bowl 183
Clark, Bret 266
Clark, Cody 200
Clark, Kelvin 265
Clemens, Samuel (Mark Twain) 34
Clements, Tom 108
Clemson University 7, 38, 75, 76, 77, 78, 114, 138, 182, 188, 202, 203, 204, 205, 206, 207, 208, 222, 223, 225, 226, 227, 228
Clinton-Dix, Ha Ha 280
Coach of the Year 68, 88, 92, 99, 111, 142, 230, 231
Cobb, David 194
Cobb, Randall 173
Cody, Shaun 160
Cody, Tay 271
Cody, Terrence 175, 179, 279
Coker, Jake 199, 200, 201, 202, 204, 205, 206, 207, 208
Coker, Larry 143, 252, 272-3
Coleman, Cosey 268
Coleman, Tevin 195
Coles, Laveranues 136, 137, 234
Colgate University 7, 37, 42, 43, 61
College Football Playoff (CFP) 23, 149, 193, 195, 196, 197, 198, 199, 203, 204, 205, 206, 207, 209, 210, 214, 216, 217, 218, 219, 225, 226, 227-8, 239
College Football Research Center 11
College of William & Mary 38, 58, 75
Colley, Wes 11
The Colley Matrix 11
Collier's 15

Collins, Greg 105
Collins, Landon 280
Collins, Mo 243
Colman, Doug 243
Colon, Bob 129
Colorado State University 37, 117, 152, 161
Colquitt, Dustin 268
Columbia University 25, 30, 33, 34, 37, 45-6, 61, 247
Comisky, Sean 162
Concord, Alton 49
Conference-USA 172, 232
Congrove Computer Rankings 11
Connecticut University 182
Connor, George 257
Connor, Jack 59
Conway, Blair 110
Cook, Connor 193, 207
Cook, Dalvin 282, 283
Cook, Ernie 92
Cook, Leroy 299
Cooney, Carroll 42, 44, 242, 254
Cooper, Amari 197, 280, 281
Cooper, Collins 124-5
Cooper, John 188
Cooper High School 97
Cope, Myron 86
Copeland, Jeremaine 128, 129
Copeland, Kyle 205
Corbett, John 27
Corbin, W.H. 302
Core, Cody 200
Cornell University 10, 16, 27, 34, 37, 45-6, 60
Cornish, Jon 167
Correll, Ray 299
Cosby, Quan 166, 167
Cotton Bowl 73, 79. 85, 86, 87, 88, 162, 207, 217, 230, 236, 237, 305
Cottrell, Nate 212
Couch, Tim 130
Coulter, Tex 292
Cowan, Hector 27
Cowart, Sam 271
Cowlings, Al 263
Cox, Woody 95, 242
Coy, Edward "Ted" 28, 40, 41-3, 44, 241, 254
Coy, Sherman 33, 36, 42
Craddock, Brad 191
Craig, Jim 290
Crane, Paul 299
Cranston, John 27
Creaney, Mike 108
Crenshaw, Marvin 265
Crimmins, Bernie 256
Crisler, Herbert "Fritz" 59, 70, 72, 252
Crompton, Jonathan 175
Crosby, Hugh 231
Crosby, Mason 165, 168
Crosby, Phillip 128, 130
Crosby, Tony 80, 81, 82, 83, 84, 88
Cross, Leon 295
Crosslin, Julius 166
Crosswhite, Leon 96, 97
Crouch, Eric 149

Crow, John David 299, 300
Crowder, Tim 277
Crowder, Tyrone 286
Crowley, Jim 16, 53, 56, 69, 291
Cruze, Jay 105
Culver, Frank 290
Cumberland College 49
Cunningham, Sam "Bam" 103, 105, 106, 108, 109, 110, 111, 264
Curry, Ron 136
Curtis Bay Coast Guard 304
Curtiss, Julian W. 301
Cushing, Brian 274
Cutchin, Phil 81
Czarobski, Ziggy 257

Daley, Bill 59, 66
Daly, Charles 34-5,
Damkroger, Maury 94, 100
Danahy, Patrick 152
Danelo, Joe 106
Danelo, Mario 169
Daniel Field Air Base 304
Daniels, Dexter 243
Daniels, H.L. 88
Dareus, Marcell 178
Dartmouth University 28, 33, 37, 45-6, 247
Dashiell, Paul 47
Davenportt, Najeh 143
Davey O'Brien Award 121, 122, 135, 141, 168, 186, 198, 228, 233, 250
Davidson College 51-2, 53
Davie, Bob 56
Davis, Andre 141
Davis, Anthony 103, 104, 105, 106, 107, 108, 109, 110, 111, 231, 264
Davis, Bill 101
Davis, Chad 116
Davis, Charlie 94, 100
Davis, Chris 205
Davis, Ernie 237
Davis, Fred 274
Davis, Glenn 16-7, 61, 292, 293
Davis, Judd 149
Davis, Leonard 276
Davis, Parke 9, 14-5, 16, 24, 39, 40, 234
Davis, Quartney 211
Davis, Raekwon 281
Davis, Terry 100, 300
Davis, Tom 265
Davis, Troy 118
Davis-Prince, Tyrone 223, 225
Dawkins, Pete 293
Dawsey, Lawrence 270
Day, Ashel 53, 256
Day, Lionell 242
Dean, Dudley 27
Decker, Taylor 284
Del-Monte Pre-Flight 64, 65, 67-68, 304
Delpit, Grant 228, 288
DeLuca, Ryan 210
Dennis, Herschel 157
Depasquale, Derek 176
DePriest, Trey 280

318 Index

DeSaulles, John 28
Devaney, Bob 90, 91, 98, 99, 112, 252, 261–2
Devine, Aubrey 254
Devine, Dan 56–7
DeVold, Harry 10
DeVold System 10
Devore, Hugh 55
Dewalt, Dedrick 146
Dibble, Benjamin 36
Dibbles, Larry 163
Dick Butkus Award 179, 250
Dicker, Cameron 221
Dickinson, Frank 9
Dickinson System 9
Dietzel, Paul 19
Diggs, Stefon 191
Diggs, Trevon 280
Dillon, Derrick 222, 223
Diminick, Gary 108
Dishman, Chris 243
Dixon, Gary 91, 100
Dixon, Joe 80, 83
Dixon, Lyn-J 213, 214, 217
Doak Walker Award 186, 207, 251
Doane College 90
Dobbs, Josh 203
Dockery, Derrick 276
Doering, Chris 243
Doerr, Tommy 82
Doke, Maurice 260
Dominque, Trent 204
Donald, Aaron 186–7
Donnelly, Pat 88
Donnelly, Sport 27
Dorais, Gus 16, 39, 56, 69
Dorough, James 66
Dorsey, Ken 143, 144, 145, 146, 147, 148, 149, 273
Doyle, J. 49
Dove, Bob 256
Dowdy, Cecil 299
Dowling, Ham 49
Downtown Athletic Club of NYC 47
Drake, Kenyan 199, 200, 205, 207, 208
Drexel Tech 16
Driscoll, Mark 242
Driscoll, Paddy 63
Drury, Morley 254
Duck, John 9
Duckworth, Rod 200
Dugans, Ron 137, 141
Duke University 37, 41, 60, 63, 64, 65, 66, 67, 103, 114, 136–7, 185–6, 215–6
Dukes, Jamie 270
Dumler, Doug 242
Dunbar, Lance 173
Dungey, Eric 212
Dunkel, Dick, Jr. 9
Dunkel, Dick, Sr. 9
The Dunkel Index 9, 70, 143
Dunn, Warrick 271
Dural, Travin 204
Dutton, John 265
Duvernay, Devin 221

Eagles, Brennan 221
Early, Fred 61
East Michigan University 211
Eastern Independents Conference 63
Easterwood, Hal 260
Eberle, Dominik 222
Eberle, Capt. E.W. 63
Eck, Steve 11
The Eck Ratings System 11
Eddie Robinson Award 88, 92, 99, 142, 231, 250
Eddleman, Dwight 74
Edmiston, Bart 120
Edwards, Bill 43
Edwards, Mario 182
Edwards, Trent 152
Edwards, Troy 135
Edwards-Helaire, Clyde 220, 221, 222, 223, 224, 225, 226, 228
Ehlinger, Sam 221
Eielson, Dizzy 63
Eisenhower, Pres. Dwight D. 79
Elflein, Pat 192, 285
Elkins, Lawrence 83, 88
Ellingson, Greg 172
Elliott, Chalmers "Bump" 70, 72, 77
Elliott, Ezekiel 189, 190, 191, 192, 193, 194, 195, 197, 198
Elliott, Larry 88
Elliott, Pete 74, 77 258
Elliott, Steve 94
Ellis, Dan 138
Ellis, Greg 276
Ellis, Sedrick 274
Ellis, Shaun 125
Ellis, William Webb 30
Ely, Marcus 302
Embery, Tellie 126
Emmert, Darryl 242
English, Doug 260
Epley, Boyd 90
Eppler, Shelton 221
Erben, Bob 74
Erickson, Alex 199
Erving, Cameron 186, 282
ESPN Top 10 FB Teams of All Time 244, 245
Etienne, Travis 210, 211, 212, 213, 214, 215, 216, 217, 218, 227, 287
Evans, Rashaan 280
Evans, Ray 61
Evolution Age 247

Fairbanks, Chuck 98
Faragher, James 55
Farley, Terrell 113, 115, 116, 117, 243
Faunce, Everett 74
Faurot, Don 62
Faurot, Ron 297
Faust, Gerry 56
FCS (Football Championship Subdivision) 205
Feaster, Tavien 211, 214, 216
Federico, Kyle 191
Fellowship of Christian Athletes (FCA) 102

Fera, Anthony 277
Ferguson, James 105
Ferguson, Jarrett 148
Ferguson, Joe 103
Ferragamo, Vince 105
Ferrell, Clelin 211, 218, 287
Fesler, Wes 76
Fickell, Luke 188
Ficken, Sam 192
The Fiesta Bowl 120, 130, 132, 149, 161, 179, 227, 236, 240
Filani, Joel 165
Filley, Pat 66, 257
Fincher, Bill 49, 52, 256
Fincke, Bill (W.M.) 33, 35–6, 53, 302
Fincke, Rex 35
Fink, Mike 100
Finlayson, John 125
Finley, Joe Jon 164
Finn, Barney 85
Fischer, Bill 257
Fischer, Jim 257
Fish, Hamilton 42, 44, 242
Fisher, Jimbo 180, 252, 282–3
Fisher, Robert 42, 242
Fisk, Bill 263
Fitzgerald, Markese 143, 145
Fitzpatrick, Denny 105
Fitzpatrick, D.J. 157
Fitzpatrick, Minkah 201, 202, 203, 280, 281
Fitzwater, David 221
FIU (Florida International University) 172, 182
Flanagan, Chris 291
Fleming, Gene 88
Fleming, Steve 157
Florida Atlantic University 185
Florida State University 7, 21–22, 38, 84, 113, 114, 115, 116, 117, 118, 120, 130, 131, 132, 134–42, 145, 150, 155, 156, 168, 170, 180–7, 193, 194, 195, 196, 197, 198, 206, 213–4, 215, 229, 230, 231, 232, 233, 234, 236
Flowers, Buck 51
Flying Wedge 31, 47
Foldberg, Dan 293
Foldberg, Hank 292
Folk, Nicholas 157
Folwell, Bob 51
Football News 10
Football Research 18
Football Review Supplement 10
Football Thesaurus 9
Football Writers Association of America 10, 19, 231
Forbes, Robert 29
Ford, Tommy 80, 81, 82, 83, 84, 86, 88, 260
Fordham University 28, 57
Foreman, Jay 243
Fort Crook 304
Fort Jackson 304
Fort Knox 304
Fort Riley 62, 63
Fort Sheridan 304

Fort Francis E. Warren 304
Ft. Worth Star-Telegram 79
Foster, Bob 199
Foster, Brandon 168
Foster, Reuben 280, 281
Foundation for the Analysis of Competitions and Tournaments (FACT) 10–11
The Four Horsemen 16, 51, 53, 69, 70, 72
Fournette, Leonard 204, 220
Fouts, Dan 92, 106
Franklin & Marshall 16
Frazier, Luke 166
Frazier, Tommy 113, 114–5, 116, 117, 118, 119, 120–1, 233, 266
Fred Biletnikoff Award 121, 135, 228, 251
Freeman, Dalton 286
Freeman, Devonta 182, 183, 184, 185, 186
Freeman, Wayne 299
Fresno State University 168, 184, 200
Friedman, Benny 290
Fromm, Jake 226
Fryar, Irving 266
Fulcher, Rick 111
Fullman, Mike 117, 119, 121, 231
Fulmer, Phillip 122, 123, 126, 128, 129, 131, 132, 231, 252, 267–8
Fulz, Mike 265
Furman University 38, 49, 50, 52, 58, 63, 64, 210, 215
Fuson, Herschel 292

Gaglianone, Rafael 199
Gain, Bob 299, 300
Galiffa, Arnold 293
Gallaspy, Reggie 213
Gallego, Rhett 128
Gallman, Wayne 208
"The Game 42
"Game(s) of the Century" 240
Gannon, Billy 82
Gardner, Chris 114
Gardner, Devin 195
Gardner, Talman 145
Garrett, Mike 263
Garrison, Walt 81
Gaston, Bobby 129–30
The Gator Bowl 76, 111, 210
Geiger, Michael 193
George, Eddie 119, 121
George, William 27
George Washington University 37, 49, 58
Georgetown University 16
Georgia Pre-Flight 304
Georgia Southern University 211, 215, 220
Georgia Tech University 7, 18, 37, 47–54, 57, 59, 60, 65, 66, 67, 73, 74, 75, 86, 117, 132, 135, 137, 138, 141, 147, 185, 196, 211–2, 230, 231, 232, 233, 235, 236, 238
Gerhartt, Toby 178
Gerometta, Art 292

Gilbert, Chris 260
Gilbert, Garrett 178
Gill, Charles 29
Gill, Turner 267
Gilman, Mark 116, 243
Gipp, George 56, 59, 291
Gladchuk, Chet 256
Glaser, Doug 266
Glass, Leland 100
Glenn, Terry 121
Glover, Rich 94, 98, 101, 233, 242, 262
Goebel, William 32, 242
Gogolak, Pete 43
Goldman, Eddie 282
Gonzalez, Joaquin 149, 272
Goodreault, Gene 256
Goodrich, Dwayne 132
Gore, Frank 143, 146, 147
Gould, Alan 10
Gould, Charlie 33, 240, 302
Gradishar, Randy 109
Graham, Aaron 243, 266
Graham, Otto 61–2
Graham, Shayne 141
Grainger, Darren 210
Grammer, Austin 200
Grant, Deon 129, 131, 268
Grant, Doran 191
Grant, John 111, 264
Grant, Terry 172, 173
Grantland Rice Trophy 10
Graves, Westin 204, 205
Gray, Ed 295
Great Lakes NTS 62–4, 65, 67, 69, 234, 238, 304
"Greatest Generation" 57
Green, Ahman 113, 114–5, 116, 118, 120
Green, Hix 81
Green, Jacquez 243
Green, John 292
Green, Mark 92
Greene, Rashad 180, 181, 182
Greensboro AAB 304
Gregory, George 13
Grenier, Geoff 113
Griffin, Adam 200, 201, 202, 203, 204, 205, 206, 207, 208
Griffin, Archie 109, 110
Griffin, Cedric 167
Griffin, Michael 163, 277
Grimes, Trevon 223
Grinnell College 36
Grisham, Jim 88, 295
Groce, DeJuan 149
Groom, Jerry 257
Grootegoed, Matt 160, 274
Grossman, Rex 149
Guepe, Art 62
Guice, Derrius 288
Guidry, Stephen 223
Guill, Shorty 49
Gunn, Jim 263
Guyon, Joe 49, 50, 51–2, 53, 256

Hackenberg, Christian 192
Hackett, Paul 151

Hadden, H.G. 55
Haden, Joe 284
Haden, Pat 103, 105
Hadley, Arthur 37
Haggins, Odell 270
Halas, George 63
Hale, Perry 33, 302
Hall, Ahmard 166, 167
Hall, Chris 277
Hall, Edward 39
Hall, Hassan 214
Hall, Jeff 122, 124–5, 127, 128, 129, 130, 131
Hall, Mike 299
Hall, Parker 67
Hallowell, Frank 27
Hallowell, Jack 35
Halsell, Glen 260
Hamilton, Joe 135, 141
Hamilton, Raymond 242
Hammond, John 81
Hampton, Casey 276
Hampton, Dan 296
Hankins, Jonathan 284
Hanks, Ben 243
Hanks, Darius 173, 175, 176
Hannah, John 99, 299
Harbaugh, Jim 71
Hardin, Austin 184
Hardin, Luther 117
Hardin, Wayne 87
Hardin-Simmons College 38, 58
Hare, Greg 109
Hargett, George 84
Harlan, Judy 49, 50, 52, 53
Harmon, Mark 107
Harmon, Tom 107
Harper, Jess 16, 55
Harper, Willie 94, 101, 242, 262
Harris, Aaron 168, 277
Harris, Brandon 204
Harris, Leotis 296
Harris, Najee 225
Harris, Phillip 80, 81, 83, 86–7
Harris, Treon 206
Harrison, Bob 295
Harrison, Jon 97, 98, 242
Hart, Leon 57, 257
Hartley, Garrett 159, 164
Hartline, Mike 173
Hartwell, John 27, 29
Harvard University 7, 14, 25–9, 30, 34–6, 37, 39, 40, 42, 45–6, 58, 232, 235, 241, 242, 247
Harvin, Percy 34, 48, 284
Hatfield, Ken 88
Haugabrook, Brian 139
Haughton, Percy 43
Hawkins, Harry 290
Hawkins, Josh 156
Hayes, Bob 104
Hayes, Woodrow "Woody" 109, 188
Heath, Leon 294, 295
Heck, Andy 297
Heffelfinger, William "Pudge" 27, 29
Heilman, Bill 94

Index

Heisman, John 47–54, 252, 255–6
Heisman Trophy 47, 57, 61, 68, 71, 86, 87, 88, 90, 101, 107, 110, 111, 114, 118, 119, 120, 121, 122, 123, 135, 137, 139, 141, 142, 149, 151, 160, 161, 168, 169, 170, 177, 178, 179, 185, 186, 187, 188, 195, 196, 198, 204, 207, 219, 228, 230, 233, 237, 250
Helms, Paul H. 10
Helms Athletic Foundation 10
Henderson, John 233
Henderson, Raynoch 268
Henderson, Taurean 165
Henry, Chas 284, 285
Henry, Derrick 197, 199, 200, 201, 202, 203, 204, 205, 206, 207, 208, 280, 281
Henry, Joe 293
Henry, Travis 126–7, 128, 129, 130, 131
Henson, Harold "Champ" 109
Hentges, Hale 218
Hering, Frank E. 55
Hernandez, Aaron 284, 285
Hessler, John 117
Heston, Willie 13–4, 290
Heuerman, Jeff 192, 195
Heupel, Josh 141
Heywood, Ralph 65
Hibbs, Jesse 254
Hickok, William O. 302
Hicks, John 109
Higgins, Tee 211, 212, 213, 216, 217, 218, 227
Higgins, William 49
Hightower, Dont'a 280
Hill, Albert 49, 50, 51–2, 53
Hill, Hakim 155
Hill, Travis 266
Hilliard, Ike 120
Hills, Tony 277
Hilton, T.Y. 172
Hines, Hap 127
Hinkey, Frank 27–8, 33, 252
Hirsch, Elroy "Crazylegs" 59, 66
Hobbs, Henry 42, 44, 242, 254
Hodges, Bucky 189
Hodges, Cody 165
Hoke, Brady 71
Holbein, Brendan 116
The Holiday Bowl 155, 156
Holleder, Don 293
Holloway, Tillman 276
Holmes, Santonio 163
Holton, Johnny 190
Holtz, Lou 22, 56, 252, 295–7
Holy Cross College 38, 41, 43
Homan, Dennis 299
Homer, Derek 130
Hope, Chris 139
Hopkins, DeAndre 286
Hopkins, Dustin 282
Horr, Frank 254
Houlgate, Deke 9
Houlgate System 9
Howard, Abdual 136

Howard, O.J. 208
Howe, Arthur 29
Hudson, James 80, 82, 88, 231
Hudson, Rodney 282
Huegel, Greg 208, 210, 211, 212, 213, 215, 218, 286
Huff, Michael 168, 277
Humm, David 265
Humphrey, Jay 276
Humphrey, Marlon 208, 280
Hunter, Art 257
Hurd, Jalen 203
Hurns, Allen 183
Hurts, Jalen 227
Huston, Josh 163
Hyatt, Mitch 218, 286, 287
Hyman, Josh 151

IAAUS (Intercollegiate Athletic Association of the U.S.) 39
ICAA (Intercollegiate Athletic Association) 39
Illustrated Football 9
Illustrated Football Annual 10
Ingram, Jim 88
Ingram, Mark 171–2, 173, 174, 175, 176, 177, 178, 179, 279, 281
Intercollegiate Convention 1878 247
Intercollegiate Football Association 30
International News Service 10
Iowa Pre-Flight 62, 64, 65, 67, 69, 236
Iowa State University 37, 62, 94, 95, 96, 106, 117, 118, 119, 145, 168, 196
Iron Bowl 177, 185, 205
Irwin, Heath 117
Ismail, Raghib 297
IVY League 45–6, 72

Jackson, Chad 284
Jackson, Eddie 201, 202, 208
Jackson, Jimmy 164
Jackson, Quincy 127
Jackson, Sheldon 116
Jackson, Star 173
Jackson, Terry 124
Jackson, Tre 282
Jackson, Vershan 117, 119
Jackson Barracks 304
Jacobsen, Larry 94, 101, 233, 242, 262
James, Bradie 279
James, Brandon 284
James, Derwin 283
Jammer, Quentin 276
Janeway, House 27
Janikowski, Sebastian 132, 136, 137, 138, 139, 141, 231, 233, 271
Janssen, Bill 242
Jarman, George 88
Jarrett, Dwayne 152, 153, 155, 156, 157, 159, 160, 169, 274
Jarrett, Grady 286
Jeffcoat, Jackson 277
Jefferson, Jordan 175

Jefferson, Justin 220, 221, 222, 223, 225, 226, 227, 228
Jefferson, Van 223
Jenkins, Dan 97
Jenkins, Janoris 284
Jennings, Kelly 273
Jensen, Robert 242
Jernigan, Timmy 186, 282
Jeter, Tony 262
Jeudy, Jerry 218, 280, 281, 225
Jeune, Jean 139
Jim Brown Trophy 186
Jim Thorpe Award 168, 228, 250
The Joe Moore Ward 207
John Mackey Award 251
Johnny Unitas Award 122, 141, 186, 198, 228, 233, 251
Johnson, Andre 144, 145, 146, 149
Johnson, Bryant 143
Johnson, Charles 49
Johnson, Clester 115, 117, 243
Johnson, Derrick 276
Johnson, Doug 124, 139
Johnson, Drake 195
Johnson, Jason 117
Johnson, Jeremy 206
Johnson, Kermit 107
Johnson, Kevin 122–3
Johnson, Mike 179, 279
Johnson, Rashad 279
Johnson, Roderick 282, 283
Johnson, Steve 129
Johnston, Cameron 191
Jolly, Lee 128
Jones, Barrett 279, 280, 281
Jones, Bobby 299
Jones, Cardale 188, 191, 193, 196, 197, 198
Jones, Cyrus 204, 205, 207
Jones, Dre'mont 285
Jones, Emory 223
Jones, Gerald 175
Jones, Greg 145
Jones, Howard 28, 41, 252, 253–4
Jones, Jimmy 102
Jones, Julio 173, 175, 176
Jones, Ken 242
Jones, Kevin 148
Jones, Marcus 276
Jones, Marvin 270
Jones, Nate 162
Jones, Rag 63
Jones, T.A.D. 29, 40–1
Jones, Thomas 135, 138
Jones, Tone 113
Jordan, Lamont 138, 139
Jordan, Lee Roy 299, 300
Jordon, Michael 285
Joseph, Kendall 213
Joyer, Hunter 185
Joyner, Lamarcus 186, 282
Judge, Evan 165
Junior, E. J. 300
Jurkovic, Mirko 297
Jurwik, Steve 63

Kalil, Ryan 274
Kansas State University 38, 94,

95, 96, 100, 101, 116–7, 119, 128, 129, 131, 132, 137, 138, 139, 198, 226, 236
Kavanagh, Brian 117
Kay, Sean 136
Kearse, Jayron 286
Keith, Randy 109
The Kellen Moore Award 186
Keller, Jim 84, 88
Kelley, Jerry 82
Kelly, Bob 57–8, 61, 62, 64
Kelly, Brian 56
Kelly, Chad 200
Kelly, Ed 57
Kelly, Kenny 137
Kelly, Ryan 207, 280, 281
Kemoeatu, Chris 284
Kendra, Dan 136, 138
Kendrick, Andre 141
Kenna, Doug 292, 293
Kennedy, Jacqueline 85
Kennedy, Pres. John F. 79, 84, 85, 86
Kent State University 95, 189–90
Kessman, Alex 217
"Kick 6" (2013) 205
Kidd, James 117
Kiel, Gunner 190
Kiley, Roger 291
Killeen, Ryan 151, 153, 155, 157, 158, 159
Kilpatrick, John Reed 42, 44, 242, 254
Kimmel, J.D. 293
Kindle, Sergio 277
King, George 52
Kinney, Jeff 90, 91–2, 93, 94, 95, 97, 98, 100
Kipke, Henry 70, 290
Kirk, Christian 202
Kirkland Field 304
Kirkpatrick, Dre 280
Kirtman, David 157
Klatt, Joel 165
Klopfenstein, Jo 165
Knox, Bill 29
Knute Rockne Memorial Trophy 68
Koceski, Leo 73–4
Kolenda, Greg 296
Korte, Steve 297
Kosch, Bill 92, 97
Kouandijo, Arie 280
Kouandijo, Cyrus 280
Kovalcheck, Richard 157
Koy, Ernie, Jr. 80, 81, 83
Koy, Ernie, Sr. 81
Kramer, Larry 262
Kramer, Ron 258, 259
Krisher, Bill 295
Kristynik, Marv 81
Krueger, Bernard 75
Krueger, Charles 299
Kuffel, Ray 57
Kuharik, Joe 56
Kulbitski, Vic 57

LaCamera, Dan 210
Lach, Steve 63–4
Lacosse, Matt 192
Lafayette College 7, 9, 13–4, 24, 34, 37, 38, 247
Lahay, Bruce 296
Lake, Everett 27
Lakehurst NAS 304
Lamar, Tre 219, 287
Lambert Trophy, Jack 179
Lammons, Pete 82
Lane, Jorvorskie 167
Langford, Jeremy 193
Lanning, Spencer 174
Latourette, Todd 129
Lattner, John 57, 257
Lavalais, Chad 279
Lawrence, Dexter 219, 287
Lawrence, Hunter 178, 277
Lawrence, Trevor 210. 211–2, 213, 214, 215, 216, 218, 219, 227, 287
Lawson, Jim 16
Lawson, Shaq 286
Layden, Elmer 16, 53, 55, 56, 69, 291
Leahy, Frank 55, 56, 59, 252, 256–8
Leaks, Roosevelt 260
Leatherwood, Alex 281
Lee, Amp 270
Lee, Darron 188, 191, 195
Lee, Dillon 204
Leggett, Jordan 208, 286
Lehigh College 28
Leinart, Matt 151, 152, 153, 155, 157, 159, 160, 168–70, 274
Lemon, J.R. 152
Lentz, Chuck 73
Leone, Brandon 167
Lewis, Bill 266
Lewis, D.D. 276
Lewis, Jamal 122–3, 125, 234
Lewis, James 143, 146, 149
Lewis, Marcedes 158
Liberty Bowl 232
Lilley, Theodore 42, 242
Lincoln, Daniel 174, 268
List, Jerry 94, 99, 242
Litkenhous, Edward 10
Litkenhous System 9, 10
Little, Leonard 268
Little, Lou 68
Little, Steve 296
Locke, Gordon 254
Lockett, Kevin 117
London Football Association 24
Long, Kevin 271
Longman, Frank C. 55
Los Angeles Times 108
Lothridge, Billy 86
Lou Groza Award 132, 141, 186, 212, 233, 251
Louisiana State University (LSU) 7, 17, 19–20, 28, 38, 79, 80, 91, 99, 105, 106, 114, 115, 126, 139, 145, 148, 151, 163, 166, 167, 168, 170, 174, 175–6, 177, 184, 185, 187, 196,
197, 199, 203, 204, 206, 210, 213, 214, 220–8, 237
Louisiana Tech 128, 134, 137, 221
Love, Marcel 156
Lowe, Keanon 198
Lowe, Woodrow 299
Lowery, Leo 80
Lubbock AAB 304
Lucas, Anthony 129
Lujack, Johnny 57, 59, 61, 62, 64, 71, 233, 257
Lutui, Taitusi 274
Lyght, Todd 297
Lynch, Akeel 192
Lynch, Clinton 212
Lynch, Marshawn 153
Lyons, Marty 300

MAC (Mid-Atlantic Conference) 142
MacArthur Bowl 10
MacCraken, Chancellor Henry M. 39,
MacLeod, Bob 292, 293
Madkin, Wayne 131
Mahelona, Jesse 268
Makovicka, Jeff 115, 118, 119
Mallett, Ryan 173
Malone, Tom 274
Mann, Braden 283
Manning, Brandon 148
Manning, Peyton 122, 123, 268
Manning Award 168, 186, 228, 251
March Field 64, 65, 67, 68, 304
Mare Island Navy Yard (Marines) 53, 63
Mariota, Marcus 198
Marks, John L. 55
Marquette University 38, 62, 63, 139, 142
Marshall, Byron 198
Marshall, Jalin 191, 193, 194, 195
Marshall, TaQuon 212
Marshall, Terrace 220, 221, 224, 226, 227
Marshall University 138, 143, 232
Martin, Abe 83
Martin, Fred 88
Martin, Jim 257
Martin, Tee 122, 123, 124–5, 126, 127, 129, 130–1, 132, 153
Marx, Greg 108
Mason, Dave 93, 94, 97, 99
Mason, Tre 186, 187
Massey, Ken 11
The Massey College Football Ratings 11
Mastrangelo, John 257
Matter, Kyle 152
Matthews, Herman 10
Matthews Grid Rankings 10
Mattis, George 34
Maualuga, Rey 274
Maulbetsch, John 290
Maxon, George 61, 66
Maxwell Award 68, 86, 87, 104, 110, 1121, 122, 149, 168, 186, 198, 207, 230, 233, 250

Mays, Taylor 274
Maze, Marquis 172, 173
McAllister, James 107
McAnderson, Brandon 167
McArthur, Geoff 153
McBride, Malcolm 32, 33, 37, 252
McCaffrey, Christian 207
McCall, Paul 172
McCarron, A.J. 186, 280, 281
McCarthy, Sen. Joe 71
McCarty, Bernie 51, 53
McClain, Rolando 179, 279, 281
McCloud, Ray-Ray 287
McClung, Thomas 27, 29
McCord, John 119
McCormick, John 266
McCormick, Vance 28
McCoy, Colt 277
McCoy, Mike 172
McCray, Bill 132, 145
McDaniel, DeAndre 286
McDonald, Tommy 295
McDougle, Jerome 273
McElroy, Greg 171–2, 173, 174, 175, 176, 177, 178
McElroy, Hugh 92
McElwain, Jim 206
McFadden, Tarvarus 283
McGahee, Willis 143, 144, 145, 273
McGee, Stephen 167
McGill University 30
McGlew, Henry 55
McGovern, John 44
McGowan, Paul 270
McGriff, Travis 125
McGugin, Dan 49
McIntosh, Kyle 122
McKay, Bob (Texas) 260
McKay, J.K. 105
McKay, John 102, 103, 105, 109, 111, 231, 252, 262–4
McKay, Robert G. (Harvard) 42, 242
McKeer, Ed 55
McKenzie, Shai 189
McKinley, Jason 125
McKinney, Bobby 100
McKinney, Xavier 281
McKinnie, Bryant 149, 272
McMath, Racey 223
McMillan, Raekwon 191
McNabb, Donovan 122–3
McNeill, Ed 74
McNeill, Rod 103, 107
McPhail, Buck 294
McReynolds, Walt 82
McWeeney, James 55
McWilliams, Tom 292
Meachem, Robert 268
Medlock, Justin 158
Medo, Frank 116
Meilinger, Steve 299
Mello, Jim 59, 61
Melton, Henry 163, 164, 165, 166, 167, 168
Menzie, DeQuan 280
Meriweather, Brandon 273

Merritt, Frank 292
Metzger, Bert 291
Mewhort, Jack 284
Meyer, Urban 188, 252, 283–5
Meylan, Wayne 262
Michael, J.E. "Big Mike" 24
Michigan State University 7, 18, 38, 58, 70, 72–3, 77, 84, 85, 87, 104, 106, 109, 114, 128, 132, 137, 138, 146, 157, 185, 187, 188, 193–4, 199, 201, 202, 203, 205, 207
Mickelsen, Lance 130
Mid-America Conference 189, 232
Middle Tennessee State University 199–200,
Mildren, Jack 96, 97, 98, 100
Miller, Braxton 188, 195, 196
Miller, Creighton 59, 60, 61, 64, 66, 23, 256
Miller, Don 53, 56, 59, 69
Miller, Fred 291
Miller, Harry 59
Miller, Junior 265
Miller, Matt 116–7
Miller, Pontius 290
Miller, Steve 197
Miller, Wally 59
Miller-Digby Award 141
Milliner, Dee 280
Mills, Zach 143
Minarik, Hank 72
Minnis, Marvin 138, 271
Minnis, Snoop 139
Minor, Travis 132, 136, 138, 141
Minot, Wayland 44
Mississippi State University 38, 58, 85, 86, 87, 131, 138, 139, 175, 176, 193, 194, 195, 197, 204, 223, 236
Mitchell, Harold 130
Mitchell, Jack 295
Mitchell, Jason 157
Mitchell, John 299
Moeller, Gary O. 71
Mohler, Orv 254
Mond, Kellen 211
Monds, Wonder 265
Montana State University 38
Moore, Bobby 92, 100, 242
Moore, Chris 190
Moore, Corey 141
Moore, Derland 111
Moore, Evan 152
Moore, Jerald 119
Moorhead, Joe 223
Morgan, Drew 202
Morgan, Marshall 201
Morley, Bill 33
Mornhinweg, Skylar 185
Morris, Stephen 183
Morrison, Dennis 95, 100
Morrison, J.L. 55
Moseley, C.J. 280, 281
Moseley, Doug 299
Moss, Thaddeus 222, 227
"Mouse Trap" Play (Yale) 43
Muhammad, Mushin 114

Mullaney, Richard 200, 202, 205, 206
Mullen, Trayvon 219, 287
Mumphrey, Keith 193
Munn, Clarence "Biggie" 73
Munoz, Michael 268
Murphy, Fred 29
Murtaugh, Jerry 90, 262
Musso, Johnny 99, 100, 299, 300
Myslinski, Casamir 66, 68

The National Championship Foundation 11, 17, 246
National Football Foundation 10
Navy (US Naval Academy) 7, 17, 28, 34, 37, 60–1, 63, 64, 65, 67, 70, 72, 75, 76, 77, 84, 85, 88, 89, 188–9, 235, 236
NCAA 161
Neighbors, Billy 299
Nelson, David 177
Nelson, Derrie 265
Nelson, Lindsay 85
Nelson, Reggie 284, 285
Nemetz, Albert 292
Nevers, Ernie 16
Newel, Ashbell 27
Newell, Marshall 27
New Mexico State University 38, 58, 153
The New York Times Computer Ranking System 11, 143
New York University 28, 39
Newsome, Ozzie 300
Newton, Bob 90, 262
Nicholls State University 183
Nix, Bo 224
No Repeat Rule 77
Nobis, Tommy 82, 233, 260
Noel, Grant 148
Nomellini, Leo 74, 258
Noonan, Danny 266
Nordgren, Matt 166
Norris, Graston 118
North Carolina Pre-Flight 16, 60, 305
North Carolina State University 37, 95, 132, 135, 182–3, 210, 213, 215, 236
North Texas State University 38, 58, 144, 172–3
Northern Illinois University 118, 184
Northern Iowa College 36
Northwestern State University 221–2
Northwestern University 20, 37, 56, 61–2, 63, 64, 65, 67, 70, 73–4, 75, 76, 77, 78, 118, 120, 121, 196, 203, 236
Novogratz, Bob 293
Nuerberger, Sean 188, 189, 190, 191, 192, 193, 194, 196, 197
Nysewander, Mike 201

Oakes, Griffin 195
Oberlin College 255
O'Daniel, Dorian 287

Index

O'Day, Patrick 55
Odell, Bob 66, 68
Odom, Jason 243
Ogbonnaya, Chris 165
Ogle, Tom 125
Ohio State University 5, 7, 9, 14, 16–7, 20, 28, 37, 41, 54, 62, 63, 70, 71, 76, 85, 86, 91, 95, 103, 104, 106, 107, 109–10, 117, 118, 119, 120, 121, 122, 128, 130, 131, 132–3, 138, 151, 163, 169, 170, 183, 184, 185, 187, 188–98, 199, 201, 202, 203, 204, 205, 212, 213, 220, 222, 223, 225, 226, 227, 228, 230, 232, 236, 244, 245, 246
Ohio Wesleyan University 10, 13
Okam, Frank 163, 277
Oklahoma City News 129
Oklahoma NAS 305
Oklahoma State University 38, 81, 88, 93, 94, 96, 99, 100, 104, 109, 113, 147, 163, 165–6, 178, 187, 198, 204, 205
Olcott, Beau 33, 241
Olcott, Herman 29, 302
Old Dominion University 182
Olds, Bill 92, 93
Olds, Robin 292
O'Leary, Nick 180, 182, 282, 283
Oliver, Tobias 212
Ollison, Qadree 217
Olson, Drew 158
Oosterbaan, Benny 70, 72, 75, 231, 252, 258–9, 290
Orakpo, Brian 277
Orange Bowl 87, 91, 98, 99–100, 122, 157, 159, 162, 164, 188, 207, 217, 235, 236, 240
Oregon State University 38, 58, 70, 103–4, 107, 128, 148, 153, 156
Orgeron, Ed 220, 52, 288
O'Rourke, Charles 256
Ortman, Chuck 73–4, 75, 76
Orvis, Herb 94
Osborne, Tom 90, 112, 114, 115, 252, 264–7
Ott, Steve 243
Ottmar, Dave 104
Ottumwa NAS 305
The Outback Bowl 203
Outland Trophy 88, 98, 101, 149, 187, 233, 250
Outzen, Marcus 132, 134, 136
Overton, Diondre 211
Owen, Bennie 96
Owens, Jim 294

PAC 8 (later PAC 10) 106, 108
PAC 10 (later PAC 12) 20, 105, 148, 157, 158
PAC-12 (Pacific Athletic Conference) 196, 198
Pace, Brandon 151
Pace, Jim 258
Pace, Orlando 121
Pacific Coast Conference 41
Palmer, Billy 157
Palmer, Carson 274, 275

Palmer, Jess 124–5, 139
Palmer, Trey 221
Pardee, Jack 299
Parham, Terrell 148
Parilli, Babe 299, 300
Parker, Artimus 264
Parseghian, Ara 56–7, 91
Paterno, Joe 138
Patterson, Mike 160, 274
Patterson, Paul 74
Patterson Field 305
Paul "Bear" Bryant Award 250, 299–300
The Peach Bowl 138, 198
Peek, Colin 173, 177
Pegram, Todd 167
Pena, Al 166
Penick, Eric 108
Penn State University 7, 16, 37, 46, 60, 75, 84, 93, 94, 95, 99, 103, 104, 107, 110, 113, 114, 137, 138, 139, 142, 143, 163, 166, 167, 168, 170, 192, 226, 235
Peoples, Desmon 191
Perine, Lamical 223
Perkins, Ray 299
Perko, John 57
Perry, Joshua 192
Perry, Lowell 258
Peter, Christian 243
Peter, Jason 243, 266
Peterman, Stephen 279
Peterson, Deangelo 175
Peterson, Julian 279
Peterson, Tom 72–3, 74–5, 76
Pflugner, Ryan 127
Philbin, Stephen 42, 44, 254
Phillip, Harold 82, 83
Phillips, Charles 264
Phillips, Kyle 162
Phillips, Lawrence 113, 114, 118, 119, 120–1, 267
Phillips, Pup 49, 52
Pickens, George 226
Pierce, Capt. Palmer E. 39
Pierschbacher, Ross 280
Pinckert, Erny 254
Pino, David 163, 164, 165, 166, 167, 169
Pittman, Billy 163, 164, 165
Pitts, Mike 300
Pitzer, Dick 292
Place, Victor M. 55
Pleasanton Navy 305
Plummer, Jake 115
Pocic, Ethan 288
Poe, Edgar Allan 27
"Point-a-Minute" Teams 13, 70
Point Value System 11
Polamalu, Troy 274
Poling, Richard 10
The Poling System 9
Pollard, Kiel 216
Polley, Tommy 138, 139
Pomona Ordnance Base 305
Pontius, Mike 290
Poole, Barney 292
Poole, Keith 115

Pope, Edwin 47–8
Portis, Clinton 143, 144, 146, 147, 148, 149
Potter, B.T. 227
Pouncey, Maurkice 284, 285
Pouncey, Mike 284
Powell, Marvin 264
Powell, Ralph 9
Powell, Shawn 282
Powers, Francis 72
Prentiss, Kevin 131
Prescott, Dak 205
Price, Billy 285
Price, Josiah 193
Price, Peerless 122–3, 124, 125, 127, 128, 129, 130, 131, 132
Princeton University 7, 9, 14, 24–9, 30, 34, 37, 39, 40, 42, 43, 45–6, 47, 49, 70, 232, 235, 241
Proctor, Dewey 63–4, 67
Prokop, Eddie 66
Proposition 48 113
Pruitt, Greg 96, 97, 98, 100, 111
Purdue University 7, 37, 63, 64, 65, 66, 67, 70, 72, 73, 77, 95, 107, 117, 138, 236, 238

Quality Point Rating System 11, 22
Qualls, Albert 242
Quarterback Kick (On-Side Kick) 40
Quinn, Brady 157

Rae, Mike 102, 103, 104, 105, 106, 107, 109, 110, 111, 231
Ragland, Reggie 280
Ramseur, Chris 131
Ramsey, Jalen 282
Randall, Bryan 151
Randolph Field 17, 305
Ratliff, Billy 129
Rattay, Tim 135
Rauh, Brendan 145
Ray Guy Award 251
Reagan, Travis 84
Red River Rivalry 164
Redding, Cory 276
Redwine, Jarvis 265
Reed, Desmond 155
Reed, Dominique 202
Reed, Ed 143, 145, 146, 149, 272
Reed, Josh 279, 281
Regimbaud, Scott 125
Regnier, Adrien 44
Reid, Bill 104
Renfrow, Hunter 208, 211, 212
Reno AAB 305
Reynolds, Jamal 136, 233, 271
Reynolds, Keenan 188
Rhodes, Bill 29
Rhodes, W.C. 33
Rice, Grantland 15
Rice, Tony 297
Rice University 38, 79, 82, 88, 163
Richard, Milan 215
Richardson, Andre 113
Richardson, Cam 281

Richardson, Trent 172, 173, 176, 177, 178, 280, 281
Richmond AAB 305
Ridley, Calvin 201, 202, 204, 205, 207
Ridley, Stevan 175
Rifenburg, Dick 72, 73, 75, 76, 258
Riley, Donovan 189
Rimington, David 266
The Rimington Award 186, 207, 251
Riter, Mike 11
Rivers, David 138
Rivers, Keith 274
Rix, Chris 145
Roberts, Dyrell 171
Roberts, J.D. 294, 295
Robertson, Corby 260
Robeson, Paul 63
Robinson, A'Shawn 203, 280
Robinson, Cam 280
Robinson, John 151
Roby, Bradley 284
Rockne, Knute 9, 16, 39, 48, 55, 56, 63, 69, 252, 290–1
Rodgers, Aaron 153
Rodgers, Amari 215, 227
Rodgers, Johnny "The Rocket" 90, 91, 92, 93, 94, 95, 96, 97, 98, 100, 101, 231, 233, 234, 262
Rodgers, Pepper 107
Rodriquez, Rich 71
Roesler, Roger 276
Rogers, Jacob 274
Rogers, J.R. 49
Rogers, Kendrick 211
Rogers, Paul 90
Rogers, Sam 189
Rolle, Antrel 273
Romberg, Brett 273
Roosevelt, President Theodore 39, 47, 62
Rose Bowl 14, 16, 18, 20–1, 41, 63, 65, 70, 72, 76, 77, 78, 87, 104, 105, 106, 107, 109–10, 148–9, 151, 158, 162, 168–70, 178, 179, 198, 230, 236, 243
Rosenberg, Aaron 254
Roskie, Ken 63
Ross, Aaron 164, 167, 277
Ross, Brandon 191
Ross, Justyn 211, 212, 216, 217, 218
Rossovich, Tim 263
Rothman, David 11
Rowe, Caleb 191
Royal, Darrell 79, 82, 88, 231, 252, 259–61, 294
Rozier, Mike 266
The Rugby School (U.K.) 30
Running, Mitch 117
Rupert, Richard 242
Russell, Matt 118
Rutgers University 24–6, 30, 37, 63, 72, 144, 148, 191, 247
Rutherford, Rob 144
Rykovich, Julie 57, 61

Saban, Nick 114, 199, 201, 205, 206, 209, 252, 278–81
Sagarin, Jeff 11
The Sagarin Ratings 11, 18, 21, 122, 132, 243, 245, 246
St. Louis University 63
St. Mary's Pre-Flight 305
St. Pierre, Brian 146
Salmon, Louis 55
Sampson NTS 305
Samuel, Curtis 190, 193, 196
Samuel, Deebo 216
San Diego NTS 305
Sanders, Debrandon 188
Sanders, Deion 270
Sands, Ethenic 143
Sanford, Foster 33
Sanger, Rich 92, 95, 98, 100, 101, 231
San Jose State University 13, 38, 58, 155
Santoso, Ryan 194
Sauer, George 75, 81
Savage, Edward 42, 242
Savoy, Phil 117
Sawyer, Corey 270
Saxton, Jimmy 260
Schembechler, Glenn Edward "Bo" 70
Schleusener, Randy 265
Schneider, Aidan 198
Schneider, Tom 153
Schnellenberger, Howard 119
Schulz, Adolph 290
Schuster, Brian 116
Schwartz, Marchy 291
Schwartz, Perry 62
Schwartzwalder, Ben 238
Sciba, Nick 213
Scott, Artavis 208
Scott, J.K. 280
Scott, Jonathan 168, 277
Scripts Howard News Service 10
Seals-Jones, Ricky 202
Sears, Aaron 268
Seattle Times Rankings (Anderson/Hester) 11
SEC (Southeastern Conference) 99, 106, 120, 131, 132, 148, 158, 177, 179, 185, 196, 206, 207, 208, 217, 222, 223, 224, 225, 226
Seiber, Lones 173
Sellers, Nick 115
Selmon, Lucious 96, 97, 242
Serna, Alexis 156
Service Teams 1943 304–5
Sharpe, Al 33, 302
Shatel, Tom 243, 244
Shaver, Gus 254
Shaver, Theodore 49
Shaw, Kenny 181, 182
Shaw, Nate 263
Shazier, Ryan 284
Shealy, Steadman 300
Sheldon, Dick 33, 241
Shene, Joshua 174
Shield, Larry 88
Shields, Will 266

Shipkey, Ted 16
Shipley, Jordan 178, 277
Shira, Charles 293
Shiver, Clay 270
Shockey, Jeremy 143, 144, 145, 146, 148, 149, 272
Shorts, Quan 221
Shrader, Garrett 223
Shuler, Heath 268
Sievers, Todd 143, 144, 145, 146, 148, 149, 272
Sikes, Maurice 146
Siler, Brandon 284
Simmons, Bob 260
Simmons, Brian 276
Simmons, Isaiah 287
Simmons, Ron 270
Simon, Corey 141, 271
Simon, John 135
Simpson, John 287
Simpson, O.J. 263
Simpson College 36
Sims, Blake 197
Sims, James 113, 114, 115
Sisemore, Jerry 260
Sitko, Emil 63–4, 67, 234, 238, 257
Sixkiller, Sonny 105
Skow, Jim 266
Slaughter, Edliff 290
Sloan, Nick 189
Smith, Alex 284, 285
Smith, Alfonso 173
Smith, Andre 279, 281
Smith, Billy Ray 296
Smith, Brad 164
Smith, Devin 189, 190, 191, 193, 196, 197
Smith, DeVonta 281, 224
Smith, Emmanuel 129
Smith, Eric 177
Smith, Ernie 254
Smith, Harry 254
Smith, Jake 221
Smith, Jason 206
Smith, John 291
Smith, Josh 203
Smith, Larry 151
Smith, Lawrence 42
Smith, Robaire 279
Smith, Rod 190, 192
Smith, Ryan 284
Smith, Shi 216
Smith, Sid 263
Smith, Steve 152, 157, 159, 160, 274
Smith, Troy 163
Smith, Wally 49, 242
Snow, Neil 13, 290
Snyder, Bill 116
Sorensen Power Ranking System 14–5, 16, 17, 18, 19, 20–1, 46, 54, 87, 88, 133
South Bend High School 56
South Carolina State 182
Southeastern Conference (SEC) 99, 106, 120, 131, 132, 167, 168, 171, 177, 179, 237
Southern Conference 75, 176

Index 325

Southern Methodist University (SMU) 8, 38, 73, 75, 77, 78, 82, 85, 86, 88, 96
Southern Mississippi University 118
The Southland Conference 221
Southwest Conference (SWC) 82, 88, 235
Sovio, Henry 99
Spann, Henry 52
Sparks, Stan 82
Spears, Marcus 279
Spencer, Evan 190, 191, 194, 197
Speyrer, Charles "Cotton" 260
Spikes, Brandon 284
Spiller, C.J. 286
Spokane AB 305
Sporting News 11, 228
Sports Illustrated 81, 97, 119
Springfield College 41, 43, 46
Spurrier, Steve 124, 139, 140
Stagg, Amos Alonzo 29, 47, 48, 68, 138
Stai, Brenden 266
Stams, Frank 297
Stanford University 8, 13-4, 16, 20-21, 28, 37, 58, 70, 76, 91, 104-5, 106, 107, 109, 128, 145, 146, 150, 152-3, 184, 206, 207, 217, 236, 247
Stanowicz, Joe 292
Stark, Rohn 270
Staubach, Roger "The Dodger" 86-7, 88
Stave, Joel 199
Steber, John 66
"Steel Age" 47
Steffy, Joe 293
Steinkuhler, Dean 266
Steketee, Frank 290
Stephens, Travis 126-7, 128, 129, 130, 131, 268
Sternberger, Jace 283
Stevens, Larry 254
Stewart, ArDarius 200, 201, 203, 206, 208
Stewart, Ed 266
Stewart, George 27
Stichweh, Rollie 85
Stillman, George 33, 241, 302
Stillman, Phillip T. 302
Stingley, Derek, Jr. 224, 228
Stockton, Chris 276
Stockton, Tom 81, 83
Stoerner, Clint 129
"Stone Age" 47
Stonebreaker, Michael 297
Stoops, Bob 159
Stork, Bryan 186, 282, 283
Story, Deac 243
Stoudt, Cole 182
Strohmeyer, George 257
Strupper, Everett 49, 50, 51-2, 53, 256
Stuart, Bobby 293
Stuhldreher, Harry 16, 53, 56, 69, 291
Sturgis, Caleb 177

Suber, Scott 260
Sugar Bowl 20, 21-2, 78. 80, 87, 99, 140, 161, 162, 171, 179, 208, 230, 237
Sultan, Gen. Dan 42
Sun Belt Conference 172, 211, 220
Swann, Lynn 103, 104, 109, 110, 111, 231, 264
Sweed, Limas 163, 165, 167, 168
Sweeley, Ev 13
Sweeney, Jim 106
Swinney, Dabo 208, 252, 285-7
Synergy Stick 125
Syracuse University 8, 28, 34, 37, 40, 41, 43, 58, 122-3, 138, 140, 146, 147, 148, 150, 182, 184, 212-3, 215, 217, 236, 237-8
Szmyt, Andre 212

Tackles Back Offense 36
Tagge, Jerry 90, 92, 93, 94, 95, 97, 98, 99, 100, 101, 262
Tagovailoa, Tua 218, 224, 225, 280, 281
Talbert, Charlie 80
Talbert, Don 260
Talbott, Nelson 254
Taliaferro, George 76
Tallahassee Democrat 137
Tankersley, Cordrea 286
Tanks, Michael 270
Tappaan, Francis 254
targeting rule 180
Tatum, Jim 62
Tatupu, Lofa 274
Taylor, Aaron (Nebraska) 243, 233, 266
Taylor, Aaron (Notre Dame) 297
Taylor, Bruce 254
Taylor, Ramonce 162, 163, 164, 166, 167
Taylor, Robert 297
Taylor, Samson 167
Taylor, Sean 273
Taylor, Travis 124
Tebow, Tim 177, 178, 284, 285
Ted Hendricks Award 219, 251
Temple University 61, 146, 148, 184
Teninga, Wally 73-4, 75
Terrell, A.J. 218
Terrio, Bob 94, 242
Texas A&M University 8, 38, 46, 52, 53, 84, 88, 92, 94, 113, 114, 115, 116, 117, 131, 132, 167-8, 183, 185, 197, 202-3, 210-11, 214, 215, 216, 220, 223, 226, 232
Texas Christian University (TCU) 8, 38, 46, 83-4, 176, 179, 187, 196, 197, 198, 199, 201, 202, 203, 237
Texas Tech University 38, 80-1, 88, 114, 155, 165, 166, 169, 178
Texas Western University 38, 58
Thomas, Broderick 266
Thomas, Clendon 295
Thomas, Dan 82, 88

Thomas, David 162, 166, 167, 168
Thomas, Earl 277
Thomas, George 294
Thomas, Michael 189, 191, 193, 194, 197
Thomas, Tarlos 271
Thompson, David 113
Thompson, Deionte 280
Thompson, Raynoch 124, 126, 268
Thorpe, Jim 50
Thurman, John 256
Thweatt, William 49
Tiffin, Leigh 171, 172, 173, 174, 175, 176, 177, 178, 179, 279
Tims, Shawn 116
Todd, Chris 177
Todd, Dick 62
Tollner, Ted 151
Tomberlin, Pat 270
Tomich, Jared 243, 266
Toneff, Bob 257
Touchdown Club of New York Award 68
Townsend, Mike 109
Townsend, Willie 108
Trammel, Pat 300
Trask, Kyle 223
Trautwine, Phil 284
Traynowicz, Mark 266
Treadwell, Johnny 79, 260
Treadwell, Laquon 200
Tressel, Jim 188
Trica, Alex 165
Trinity College 33
Trout, Nate 122-3
Troy State 144
Trull, Don 83, 88
Tubbs, Jerry 295
Tubbs, Marcus 276
Tucker, Arnold 292, 293
Tufts University 33
Tulane University 21, 38, 52, 128, 130, 132, 232
Tulsa University 38, 79, 115
Tune, Nathan 173
Turman, Matt 115, 116
Twain, Mark (Samuel Clemens) 34
Tweedie, Neale 166

Udeze, Kenechi 274
Ulatoski, Adam 277
Ullman, Peter 167
Ulrich, Ray 49
Underdog Award 251
United Press (UP, UPI) 10
University of Alabama 5, 6, 17, 20-2, 37, 58, 70, 81, 84, 85, 87, 92, 94, 95, 98, 99-101, 103, 104, 105, 106, 107, 109, 110, 127, 139, 149, 165, 166, 171-9, 183, 184, 185, 187, 194, 195, 196, 197, 199-209, 210, 212, 2113, 214, 216, 217, 218, 219, 220, 222, 223, 224-5, 226, 230, 235, 236, 241, 244, 245
University of Alabama at Birmingham 128

Index

University of Arizona 38, 115, 156, 157, 161, 166, 196, 197, 198
University of Arkansas 7, 20, 38, 46, 70, 82, 88, 103, 120, 128–9, 131, 173, 185, 202, 225–6, 236
University of Auburn 7, 19, 20, 37, 52, 54, 58, 76, 84, 85, 86, 87, 93, 94, 95, 99, 104, 105, 109, 110, 111, 115, 125–6, 139, 145, 155, 156, 157, 158, 161, 170, 171, 176–7, 184, 185–6, 187, 197, 205–6, 222, 223–4, 228, 232, 235
University of California 7, 14, 16, 26, 28, 37, 68, 74, 75, 76, 77, 78, 103, 105, 107, 109, 153, 156, 157, 161, 168, 245, 246, 247
University of California at Los Angeles (UCLA) 8, 18, 38, 68, 102, 103, 106, 128, 129, 131, 132, 145, 146, 150, 158, 161, 166, 168, 183, 197, 236
University of Central Florida 115, 187
University of Chattanooga 176
University of Chicago 7, 14, 37, 54, 63, 220
University of Cincinnati 37, 174, 179, 190
University of Colorado 7, 18, 37, 46, 93, 94–5, 96, 99, 100, 101, 103, 104, 111, 115, 116, 117–8, 119, 147, 148, 150, 158, 165, 167, 168, 169, 235, 236
University of Dayton 38
University of Denver 37, 53
University of Detroit 7, 38, 58
University of Florida 7, 21, 38, 58, 85, 113, 114, 115, 116, 117, 118, 119, 120–1, 124–5, 132, 137, 139–40, 143, 144, 145, 146, 147, 148, 166, 171, 172, 173, 174, 175, 176, 177–8, 179, 183, 184–5, 188, 206–7, 216, 220, 222–3, 224, 236, 241, 243
University of Georgia 7, 37, 47, 49, 77, 78, 93, 94, 95, 99, 126–7, 139, 153, 155, 162, 165, 166, 167, 170, 174, 175, 182, 185, 201, 212, 213, 216, 217, 222, 223, 224, 225, 226, 235, 236
University of Hawaii 98
University of Houston 38, 114, 125, 130
University of Idaho 38, 58, 184
University of Illinois 7, 9, 37, 60, 62, 63, 67, 74–5, 84, 85, 86, 87, 104, 109, 192–3, 247
University of Indiana 37, 63, 75–6, 77, 194–5
University of Iowa 7, 18, 19–20, 36, 37, 41, 62, 63, 75, 76, 205, 206
University of Kansas 13, 37, 93, 94, 95, 96, 117, 118–9, 166–7, 236
University of Kentucky 7, 37, 58, 114, 130, 173, 216
University of Louisiana-Lafayette 162
University of Louisiana-Monroe 117, 144, 201

University of Louisville 183, 187, 214, 215
University of Maryland 7, 18, 37, 138, 139, 182, 190–1
University of Massachusetts 42
University of Miami (FL) 7, 21–2, 23, 38, 95, 131, 137, 140, 143–50, 151, 153, 155, 156, 162, 163, 165, 166, 167, 170, 183, 185, 208, 236, 244, 245, 246
University of Miami (OH) 163
University of Michigan 5, 7, 13–5, 18, 22, 26, 28, 37, 41, 44, 46, 55, 56, 59, 62, 64, 65, 66, 67, 70–8, 79, 85, 86, 93, 94, 95, 99, 104, 106, 107, 109, 120, 130, 132, 137, 146, 151, 157, 162, 163, 195–6, 214, 216, 217, 220, 226, 230, 231, 232, 233, 235, 236, 244, 245, 246, 247
University of Minnesota 7, 10, 28, 36, 37, 44, 59, 62, 74, 92, 118, 139, 194, 196, 211, 236
University of Mississippi 7, 38, 58, 67, 84, 85, 87, 93, 116, 174, 176, 183, 185, 197, 198, 200, 201, 203, 206, 209, 225, 237, 244
University of Missouri 7, 28, 37, 62, 73, 76, 93, 94, 96, 100, 105, 108, 116, 119, 130, 164, 178, 184, 185, 194, 196, 197, 206
University of Nebraska 5, 7, 13, 37, 71, 84, 86, 87, 90–101, 103, 105, 106, 111, 112–121, 122, 135, 137, 138, 144, 145, 146, 147, 149, 150, 162, 168, 178, 193, 196, 230, 231, 232, 233, 234, 235, 236, 241, 243, 244, 245, 246, 247
University of Nevada 14, 180
University of New Mexico 38
University of North Carolina 28, 37, 47, 49, 66, 67, 73, 75, 77, 78, 115, 136, 144, 145
University of Notre Dame 5, 7, 9, 14, 15–6, 18, 22–3, 28, 37, 39. 46, 51, 53, 55–69, 70, 71, 72, 73, 75, 76, 77, 78, 80, 89, 91, 93, 102, 105, 107–8, 117, 144, 157, 168, 170, 187, 198, 204, 205, 206, 213, 214, 216, 217, 219, 230, 231, 232, 233, 234, 236, 238, 244, 245, 246, 247
University of Oklahoma 5, 7, 13, 17–8, 19, 38, 75, 77, 78, 80, 81, 84, 85, 86, 88, 89, 90, 93, 94, 95, 96–101, 103, 105, 106, 107, 109, 110, 116, 117, 119–20, 143, 144, 145, 146, 147, 151, 153, 155, 156, 157, 158, 159, 161, 162, 164, 169, 170, 178, 184, 198, 203, 205, 206, 207, 213, 216, 217, 219, 225, 226, 234, 235, 236, 241, 244, 245, 246
University of Omaha 90
University of Oregon 38, 58, 73, 77, 78, 91, 94, 100, 106, 107, 145, 147, 148, 150, 157, 168, 170, 183, 184, 193, 194, 195, 196, 197–8, 223, 228
University of Pennsylvania 7, 16,

25–9, 34, 36, 37, 42, 45–6, 50–1, 54, 61, 65, 66, 68, 74, 75, 219, 232, 235, 241, 247
University of Pittsburgh 5, 7, 37, 46, 53–4, 59, 63, 84, 85, 86, 87, 95, 96, 106, 144, 147, 161, 180, 185, 217, 232
University of Richmond 37
University of South Carolina 38, 63, 119, 127–8, 139, 174, 216
University of Southern California 5, 7, 17, 20, 28, 37, 41, 65, 68, 70, 72, 76, 77, 78, 81, 93, 96, 99, 102–111, 115, 116, 117, 130, 132, 149, 151–61, 162, 163, 164, 165, 166, 167, 168–9, 173, 184, 230, 231, 232, 233, 234, 236, 243, 244, 245, 246
University of Tennessee 8, 18, 37, 49, 58, 63, 75, 93, 99, 104, 105, 115, 117, 118, 119, 120, 121, 122–33, 134, 137, 146, 147, 148, 157, 158, 163, 174–5, 185, 203, 223, 229, 230, 231, 232, 233, 234, 236
University of Tennessee at Martin 200
University of Texas 8, 38, 63, 79–89, 91, 93, 96, 105, 107, 110, 119, 138, 144, 145, 146, 147, 148, 151, 153, 155, 156, 162–70, 174, 176, 177, 178, 179, 217, 221, 230, 231, 232, 233, 235, 236, 237, 243, 245, 305
University of the Pacific 38, 68, 115
University of Toledo 93, 94, 95, 99, 202, 232
University of Utah 37, 157, 161, 171, 198, 202, 203, 221
University of Virginia 28, 37, 49, 118, 132, 135, 138, 140
University of Washington 8, 37, 65, 68, 76, 87, 105, 106, 107, 145, 147, 150, 155, 156, 157, 173, 183, 236, 244
University of Wichita 38, 58
University of Wisconsin 8, 9, 14, 20, 24, 36, 37, 54, 59, 60, 62, 67, 75, 85, 117, 128, 130, 150, 156, 157, 170, 196, 199, 226
University of Wyoming 38, 58
Unruh, Dean 242
Upchurch, Roy 171, 172, 176, 177
Upper Iowa College 36
Upshaw, Courtney 173, 178, 280
Ursinus College 16
USA Today 245; CNN Poll 10; ESPN Poll 10
Utah State University 37, 58, 92, 94, 100, 138, 222, 235

Vaccaro, Kenny 277
Van Brocklin, Norm 73
Van de Graaf, William 9
Vanderbilt University 7, 10, 37, 49, 52, 58, 93, 120, 130–1, 139, 220, 222
Van Fleet, Bill 79

Vann, Pete 293
Vannett, Nick 191, 195, 198
Van Pelt, Brad 104
Van Summern, Bob 75
Vasher, Nathan 276
Vaughn, Ke'Shawn 222
Veazey, Burney 125
Vedral, Jon 113, 114, 116, 117, 119
Veland, Tony 119
Vella, John 263
Verna, Tony 85
Vessels, Billy 294, 295
Vick, Henry 290
Vick, Michael 135, 141
Villanova University 38, 61
Vilma, Jonathan 145, 273
Vince Lombardi Award 98, 121, 141, 187, 233, 250
Virginia Tech (formerly VPI) 37, 58, 107, 128, 135, 137, 138, 139, 140-1, 142, 145, 146, 147-8, 150, 151, 161, 163, 165, 166, 168, 171-2, 174, 185, 189, 217, 236
Vlade Award 186
VMI (Virginia Military Institute) 37
Von Kersburg, Harry 34

WAC (Western Athletic Conference) 179
Waddle, Jaylen 224, 280
Wade, Tommy 81, 83
Wadsworth, Andre 271
Wahl, Allen 258
Wainscott, Lloyd 260
Wake Forest University 37, 49, 52, 137-8, 182, 183-4, 213, 215
Waldron, Matt 171
Walker, Art 258
Walker, Bracey 276
Walker, Demarcus 283
Walker, Jim 296
Walker, Kenny 266
Walker, Michael 215
Walker, Wade 294
Wallace, K'Von 211
Wallace, William 46
Wallis, A. Hamilton 28
Walter Camp Award 68, 121, 160, 186, 198, 207, 228, 233, 250
Walters, Matt 146
Warburton, Cotton 254
Ward, Charlie 270
Ward, Denzel 285
Wareharn, Collin 215
Warley, Carter 148
Warmack, Chance 280
Warmath, Murray 92
Warner, Glenn "Pop" 14, 16, 34, 47, 48, 50, 138
Warren, Buist 63
Warren, David 136
Warren, Ralph 27
Warrick, Peter 132, 134, 135, 136, 137, 138, 139, 141, 231, 234, 271
Washington, Adolphus 285
Washington State University 38, 58, 106, 107, 115-6, 150, 156

Washington & Jefferson University 8, 37
Washington & Lee University 52
Watkins, Todd 152
Watkins, Sammy 182, 187, 286
Watley, Tyrone 115
Watson, Carlos 286
Watson, Deshaun 207, 208, 286
Waynesburg College 57
Wear, James 34, 302
Weatherall, Jim 294, 295
Weaver, Charlie 263
Webb, Lee 152
Webster, Corey 279
Wedge Formations 31
Weekes, Harold 33
Weeks, Boss 13-4
Weinke, Chris 134, 135, 137, 138, 139, 141, 185, 231, 233, 271
Weis, Charlie 56
Weisenberger, Jack 72
Welchel, Dan 49
Weldon, Casey 270
Wells, Stanfield 290
Wendell, Marty 257
Werner, Bjorn 282
Werts, Shai 211
Wesleyan University 33, 39, 41, 43
West, Stan 294
West Texas State University 38, 58
West Virginia University 13, 37, 46, 145, 148, 170, 182, 198, 213
Western Carolina University 185
Western Conference (Big Ten) 63, 70
Western Michigan University 63
Western Reserve University 64
Wheelwright, Robert 199
Whitaker, Jason 141, 271
White, Anthony 130
White, Clayton 136
White, Daryl 242, 262, 265
White, Devin 288
White, Ed 57
White, Freeman 262
White, Jason 159
White, Jim 61, 66, 257
White, LenDale 152, 153, 155, 156, 157, 159, 160, 169, 170
White, Mac 82
White, Manuel 158
White, Tre'Davious 288
Whitfield, Kermit 183, 184, 186
Whitmire, Don 65
Whitney, Casper 9, 33
Wicks, Bob 93, 100
Wieman, Elton 70
Wiegert, Zach 266
Wilcox, Tommy 300
Wilkerson, Ben 279, 281
Wilkins, Christian 216, 218, 286, 287
Wilkins, Jordan 200
Wilkinson, Charles "Bud" 18, 62, 80, 252, 294-5
Will Rogers Field 305

William Campbell Award 110, 251
Williams, Andre 186
Williams, Bob 257
Williams, Brett 271
Williams, Don 254
Williams, Ed 118
Williams, Greedy 288
Williams, Harry 48
Williams, Jamel 119, 120
Williams, Jimmy 266
Williams, Jonah 280
Williams, Karlos 181, 182
Williams, Leonard 288
Williams, Mark 119
Williams, Marshawn 189
Williams, Mike (Clemson) 286
Williams, Mike (Texas) 276
Williams, Mike (USC) 151, 274
Williams, P.J. 181, 186
Williams, Quinnen 280, 281
Williams, Ryan 171
Williams, Ricky 276
Williams, Roy 276
Williams, Seth 224
Williams College 28
Williamson, Paul 10
Williamson, Stan 254
Williamson System 9, 10
Willingham, Tyrone 56
Willis, Patrick 288
Wills, Jedrick 281
Wilson, Al 123, 124, 125, 126, 129, 268
Wilson, Cedrick 125, 127, 128, 130, 131
Wilson, Donte 190, 193
Wilson, Kris 144
Wilson, Reinard 271
Wilson, Travis 159
Winslow, Kellen 143, 273
Winston, Eric 273
Winston, Jameis "Jaboo" 180, 181, 182, 183, 184, 185, 186, 282, 283
Winter, Wallace 27, 29
Wishbone Offense 96, 106
Wistert, Albert 76, 258
Wistert, Alvin 76
Wistert, Francis 76
Wistrom, Grant 243, 233, 266
Withington, Lothrop 42, 242
Withington, Paul 42, 242
Wolfe, Dr. Peter 11
Wood, Richard 103, 104, 107, 111, 264
Woodruff, George 48
Woods, D'Juan 166
Worster, Steve 260
Wortman, Keith 242
Worton, C.J. 206
Wright, Manuel 49, 152
Wright, Rodrique 164, 168, 277
Wright Field 305
Wuensch, Bobby 260
Wuerffel, Danny 120-1
Wuerffel Award 251
Wunderlich, Gary 200
Wylie, Joe 96, 97
Wyman, Bill 260

Yale "Tackles-Back" Offense 36
Yale University 8, 14–5, 25–9, 30–7, 39–46, 61, 230, 231, 232, 233, 235, 240, 241, 242, 243, 247
Yary, Ron 263
Yeast, Craig 130
Teldon, T.J. 197
Yerges, Howard 72
Yoest, Bill 296
Yonaker, John 61, 256

York, Cade 220, 221, 223, 224, 225, 226
Yost, Fielding (Hurry Up) 13–4, 48, 49, 70, 252, 289–90
Young, Adrian 263
Young, Bryant 297
Young, Charles 103, 105, 111, 263
Young, Donnie 243
Young, Donovonn 192
Young, Jake 266

Young, Selvin 162, 164, 165, 167, 168, 169
Young, Vince 162, 163, 164, 165, 166, 167, 168, 169, 277

Zachery, Terrell 177
Zeno, Marc 276
Zettel, Anthony 192
Zorich, Chris 297
Zow, Andrew 127
Zupke, Robert 48

www.ingramcontent.com/pod-product-compliance
Ingram Content Group UK Ltd.
Pitfield, Milton Keynes, MK11 3LW, UK
UKHW050543150426
5217IPUK00026B/2049